The Penguin
GOOD AUSTRALIAN WINE GUIDE
1995–96

Huon Hooke & Mark Shield

Penguin Books

McPhee Gribble Publishers
Penguin Books Australia Ltd
487 Maroondah Highway PO Box 257
Ringwood, Victoria 3134, Australia
Penguin Books Ltd
Harmonsworth, Middlesex, England
Viking Penguin, A Division of Penguin Books USA Inc
357 Hudson Street, New York, New York 10014, USA
Penguin Books Canada Limited
10 Alcorn Avenue, Toronto, Ontario, Canada M4V 3B2
Penguin Books (NZ) Ltd
182–190 Wairau Road, Auckland 10, New Zealand

First published by Penguin Books Australia 1995

10 9 8 7 6 5 4 3 2 1

Copyright © Penguin Books Australia Ltd 1995
Copyright © 🅐 1995

All rights reserved. Without limiting the rights under
copyright reserved above, no part of this publication may be
reproduced, stored in or introduced into a retrieval system,
or transmitted, in any form or by any means (electrical,
mechanical, photocopying, recording or otherwise) without the
prior permission of both the copyright owner and the
above publisher of this book.

Produced by McPhee Gribble
487 Maroondah Highway, Ringwood, Victoria 3134, Australia
A division of Penguin Books Australia Ltd

Typeset in 10/11 Berner by Midland Typesetters, Maryborough
Printed in Australia by Australian Print Group

ISBN 0140 25107 3
ISSB 1038-6467

Contents

Acknowledgements	vi
Introduction	1
The Rating System	5
Best Wines	10
Standard Drinks Made Easy	14
Eating in the Great Outdoors	17
Red Wines	19
White Wines	181
Sparkling Wines	333
Fortified Wines	355
Wine Casks	388
Food/Wine Combinations – Reds	390
Food/Wine Combinations – Whites	397
Index of Common Names	405
Wine Terms	407
Tasting Terms	412
Directory of Wineries	415

Acknowledgements

Jim Humphrys and Linda White, BRL Hardy
Sarah Gough, Brown Brothers
Dennis Pender and Nick Guy, de Bortoli
Michael Price, Negociants Australia
Arch Baker, Henschke
Boardwalk Cafe, Sydney Opera House
Sheryl Henriks, Lindemans
Judy Farrow, Richmond Hill Cellars
Hugh Cuthbertson, Mildara Blass
Marshal Waters, Coriole
Andrew Watts, Yarra Valley Wine Shippers
Australian Wine Club

Introduction

The big news from the vintage of 1995 was a dire shortage of grapes in almost all the important wine regions. The national crop was about 25 per cent under what was expected, and this happened at a time when an increase was needed to supply still-growing export demand. The few areas that escaped the dearth were mostly premium southern and cooler regions: Yarra Valley and Mornington Peninsula, parts of Tasmania, the Adelaide Hills and, happily, Coonawarra.

The causes were several. In the Barossa there was frost, but in most areas, except some of the most southerly, drought wreaked havoc with vine growth and grape yields. But the less obvious factor at work was poor bud fruitfulness in the vines. This is a high-fallutin expression which means that the nascent 1995 bunches, which are always formed two springs before they are harvested (in this case during the universally wet spring of 1993), did not form properly. Further yield losses resulted.

The good news is that quality is very good right across Australia, and exceptional in some areas, especially for reds which benefited from drought-induced concentration.

Around the same time as the pickers were hunting through the vines for bunches, winemakers and drinkers alike were hit with a double whammy. Not only was Mother Nature taxing us in the form of a grape shortage, which was predicted to push wine prices up between 10 and 15 per cent, bad news also arrived from the direction of the taxman. The Wine and Grape Industry Commission of Inquiry, which arose out of the 1993 Dawkins Budget's sales tax debacle, came to a climax. The draft report tabled in March saw a split panel recommending tax measures that varied from the unpleasant to the draconian.

The chairman, Bill Scales, wanted a 32 per cent sales tax (it's currently 26 per cent, having gone up 2 per cent on 1 July) plus a $4-a-litre of absolute alcohol volumetric tax. The two together equate to a 50 per cent sales tax!

The other two inquiry members, Petaluma winemaker Brian Croser and Monash University economist John Freebairn, agreed that a $4-a-litre volumetric tax was needed but argued that sales tax be dropped to 10 per cent. Their plan would disadvantage the cask-wine makers and benefit the premium-quality producers. What the federal government will conclude from all this is unknown at the time of going to press, but one thing seems certain: taxes will continue to rise. And so will wine prices. Hardest hit will be casks: a $10 cask would rise to $12.70 under Scales's plan.

Whether Australia shoots itself in the foot is a moot point, and the risk of pricing itself out of the world market is a distinct possibility. All this is happening at a time when export growth is finally starting to level out, and domestic wine sales are stagnant or generally declining.

It is worth remembering that the greatest wine nation on earth, France, taxes its wine at the rate of 18.6 per cent, as a general value-added tax on all consumer items, plus a 5-cents-a-litre excise. Nothing more.

Only two things in life are certain: taxes and death. And we sadly record that a great wineman departed this life on 18 February 1995. David Wynn, founder of Wynns Coonawarra Estate and Mountadam, the saviour of Coonawarra, the man who popularised the wine cask, the creator of the once-famous Wynvale flagon, died soon after his 80th birthday. David Wynn not only contributed enormously to wine (and the arts), but he was a fine and gentle man who was loved by many. His son Adam continues to run Mountadam with his customary flair.

Amalgamations slowed somewhat in the past 12 months. Perhaps the industry's unaccustomed state of prosperity is the reason. Mildara Blass, however, continued its acquisitive march, raking up both Andrew Garrett and Garrett Family Wines in McLaren Vale. As well, Mildara took over the fortified portfolio of Yalumba. These scalps were added to the 1993 acquisitions of Tisdall and Yarra Ridge (majority shareholding). By the end of the 1994–95 financial year Mildara had added Tolley Pedare and the remainder of Yarra Ridge, as well as Ingoldby, to its pile.

High-profile Andrew Garrett winemaker Warren Randall quit to devote himself to his Manning Park and Tinlins ventures. Petaluma Wines combined with Mitchelton in a sort of Jonah-swallowing-the-whale trick. Grant Burge took over Basedows, which was left adrift after the Peter Lehmann float. And just about everybody expanded their vineyards. Despite the feverish planting, it became clear that the industry would not meet its target of $1 billion a year in export sales by the year 2000. It was simply not possible to plant vines quickly enough without massive capital investment – which was not forthcoming.

This year we have gone to extra trouble to ensure that our retail prices are not only accurate but represent the full undiscounted retail price you're likely to pay in a pub or liquor store. In doing this we have applied the same formula to each wholesale price, ie. the same percentage mark-up to every wine.

This means some of our prices may seem unreasonably high. But at least we won't have cranky retailers upset because we're undermining their excessive pricing regimes.

Especially with wines from big companies, prices vary enormously. It is possible to find some of their wines at, say, a low of $6 and a high of $10. And the retailer is not necessarily cutting his profit to the bones: it's just that the big companies offer big discounts for large quantities. If Cut-throat Joe buys a semitrailer load he gets a much better price than if he only takes a couple of cases. Hence few liquor stores bother to stock the big-discount items unless they can get a quantity buy and do a competitive price.

That said, it seems quantity discounts will be severely restricted this year, thanks to the lack of product. But, if you see a ⓢ symbol after the RRP for an entry in this guide, it means the price could be a great deal cheaper than the one we quote.

Vintage charts have been axed this year. The authors take the view that vintage charts are far too generalised to be of real value to you, the consumer. Not only does a figure out of seven or ten attempt to roll red and white wines into one, but all vineyards in an entire region. Even nextdoor neighbours can have differences in weather and vintage success. In averaging everybody's figures it is possible to arrive at a number that is meaningless. We would prefer to say nothing than to oversimplify a complex subject.

It's obvious that people are watching how much they drink these days. Per-capita alcohol consumption continues its gentle decline, and 'drink less but drink better' has become a catchcry. So this year we have a section explaining the important Standard Drinks Labelling initiative.

Finally, a major preoccupation of the wine business today is geographical indications. To comply with the Australia–European Commission agreement on wine labelling, each region's winemakers and grapegrowers must decide on official names and boundaries. Many regions have already done so but several, such as Coonawarra, are having difficulty agreeing. Do they draw a line which includes all current plantings, or do they limit the area which may be called Coonawarra? If so, where do they draw the line? With such a famous name, those growers left on the wrong side of the fence will be far from happy. Should we have a greater and lesser Coonawarra? Do we append lesser or newer sub-regions to Coonawarra, as the French did with Puligny–Montrachet, Chassagne–Montrachet, etc? It is a vexed problem and one which will impact on the consumer. If, as some stalwarts want, Coonawarra becomes a very small, exclusive region which includes only the original area along the main road, what ramifications will that have for prices? Coonawarra could become the Pauillac of the south.

The Rating System

The rating system used in this guide is designed to give you an immediate assessment of a wine's attributes, as they will affect your purchasing decision. The symbols provide at-a-glance information, and the written descriptions go into greater depth. Other wine guides are full of numbers, but this one places importance on the written word.

The authors assess quality and value, provide an estimate of cellaring potential and optimum drinking age, and give notes on source, grape variety, organic cultivation where applicable, decanting, and alcohol content. We list previous outstanding vintages where we think they're relevant.

We assess quality using a cut-down show judging system, marking out of a possible ten. Wine show judges score out of 20 points – three for nose, seven for colour, ten for palate – but any wine scoring less than ten is obviously faulty, so our five-glass range (with half-glass increments) indicates only the top ten points. When equated to the show system, two and a half to three glasses is roughly equivalent to a bronze medal, and five glasses, our highest award, equals a high gold medal or trophy-standard wine.

Value is arrived at primarily by balancing absolute quality against price. But we do take some account of those intangible attributes that make a wine more desirable, such as rarity, great reputation, glamour, outstanding cellarability, etc. We take such things into account because they are part of the value equation for most consumers.

If a wine scores more for quality than for value, it does not mean the wine is overpriced. As explained below, any wine scoring three stars for value is fairly priced. Hence, a wine scoring five glasses and five stars is extraordinary value for money. Very few wines manage this feat. And of course good and bad value for money can be found at $50 just as it can at $5.

If there are more stars than glasses, you are looking at unusually good value. We urge readers not to become star-struck: a three-glass three-star wine is still a good drink.

Where we had any doubt about the soundness of a wine, a second bottle was always sampled.

QUALITY

🍷🍷🍷🍷🍷 The acme of style, a fabulous, faultless wine that Australia should be proud of.

🍷🍷🍷🍷🍷⁄ A marvellous wine that is so close to the top it almost doesn't matter.

🍷🍷🍷🍷 An exciting wine that has plenty of style and dash. You should be proud to serve this.

🍷🍷🍷½ Solid quality with a modicum of style, very good drinking.

🍷🍷🍷 Decent, drinkable wine that is a cut above everyday quaffing. You can happily serve this to family and friends.

🍷🍷½ Sound, respectable wines, but the earth won't move.

🍷🍷 Just okay, but in quality terms, starting to look a little wobbly.

(Lower scores have not been included.)

VALUE

★★★★★ You should feel guilty for paying so little, this is great value for money.

★★★★½ Don't tell too many people because the wine will start selling and the maker will put the price up.

★★★★ If you complain about paying this much for a wine, you've got a death adder in your pocket.

★★★½ Still excellent value but the maker is also making money.

★★★ Fair is fair, this is a win-win exchange for buyer and maker.

★★½ They are starting to see you coming but it's not a total rip-off.

★★ This wine will appeal to label drinkers and those who want to impress the bank manager.

★½ You know what they say about fools and their money ...

★ Makes the used-car industry look saintly.

GRAPES

Grape varieties are listed in dominant order; percentages are cited when available.

CELLAR

Any wine can of course be drunk immediately, but for maximum pleasure we recommend an optimum drinking time, assuming correct cellaring conditions. We have been deliberately conservative, believing it is better to drink a wine when it is a little too young than to risk waiting until it is too old.

An upright bottle 🍾 indicates that the wine is ready for drinking now: it may also be possible to cellar it (for the period shown). Where the bottle is lying on its side ⊸ the wine is not ready for drinking now and should be cellared for the period shown.

🍾 Drink now, there will be no improvement achieved by cellaring.

🍾 3 Drink now or during the next three years.

⊸ 3–7 Cellar for three years at least before drinking; can be cellared for up to seven years.

8 THE RATING SYSTEM

🍾 **10+** Cellar for ten years or more – will be at its best in ten years from this book's publication date.

ALCOHOL BY VOLUME

Australian labelling laws require that alcohol content be shown on all wine labels. It is expressed as a percentage of alcohol by volume, eg. 12.0% A/V means that 12 per cent of the wine is pure alcohol.

RECOMMENDED RETAIL PRICE

Prices were arrived at either by calculating from the trade wholesale using a standard full bottleshop mark-up, or by using a maker-nominated recommended retail price. In essence, however, there is no such thing as RRP because retailers use different margins and there are different state taxes. The prices in this book are indicative of those in Sydney and Melbourne, but they will still vary from shop to shop and city to city. They should only be used as a guide. Cellar-door prices have been quoted when the wines are not available in the retail trade.

⊛ *ORGANIC*

The wine has passed the tests required to label it as 'organically grown and made'.

🍶 *DECANT*

The wine will be improved by decanting.

ⓢ *SPECIAL*

The wine is likely to be 'on special', so it will be possible to pay less than the recommended retail. Shop around.

Best Wines

Close to publication time, we get quite a few calls that go like this: 'Hi, how ya going? How's the book going? Got any results yet?'

It's flattering and frustrating, but such fishing invariably meets with a curt reply because the conclusions of our year's work are confidential and remain that way until publication. Our reason for such secrecy is not show business, but rather to ensure that the winners are still available in the shops when the guide is launched.

We want readers to be able to taste the fruits of our labour, to agree or disagree with our judgements. A major criterion for inclusion is availability, rather than price.

The best wines this year are, to our minds, very fine ones. But, as usual, a word of caution: don't get stars in your eyes. A three-star wine in this book is a good drink and something we would be happy to drink and serve to guests.

And the winners are ... (This part of the Guide is becoming more like Hollywood every year.)

BEST RED WINE

Henschke Abbott's Prayer 1993

Sophisticated and complex, a cool-climate style with substance and evidence of highly skilled winemaking.

PENGUIN WINE OF THE YEAR

BEST WHITE WINE/CHARDONNAY

Hardys Eileen Hardy Chardonnay 1994

Absolutely fabulous! This is not an obvious style, but the more you taste the more is revealed. It is complex, artfully made and full of potential.

BEST SPARKLING WINE

Hanging Rock Macedon (Mark III)

No beg pardons here, this is a wine that is not afraid of setting a style. It's good to find some individualism and flavour.

BEST FORTIFIED WINE

Campbells Isabella Tokay

Isabella is quite a temptress, offering seductive kisses and loads of class. Age is the key to this wonderful fortified.

PICKS OF THE BUNCH

BEST RIESLING

Paulett's Polish Hill River Riesling 1995

Get it while it's fresh – this wine is full of varietal and regional character and lots of charm. It is drinking beautifully now.

BEST SAUVIGNON BLANC

Brokenwood Cricket Pitch Sauvignon Blanc Semillon 1995

This wine shows all the positives and avoids the negatives associated with sauvignon blanc. It drinks like a charm and offers flavour satisfaction.

BEST WINES

BEST SEMILLON

De Bortoli Noble One Botrytis Semillon 1992

What better use for semillon – this is a world-class wine with rich botrytis flavours and major character.

BEST WHITE BLEND

Mitchelton III Marsanne Viognier Roussanne 1994

This is a modern generic style that combines varieties to enhance flavour and satisfaction. Could this be a wine of the future? Let's hope so.

BEST SHIRAZ

Mount Langi Ghiran Shiraz 1993

Let the good times roll: this is a full-flavoured wine that continues a well-developed cellar style offering all the best of the variety.

BEST PINOT NOIR

Diamond Valley Estate Pinot Noir 1993

Very complex and well crafted, this shows that extra dimension the variety can achieve.

BEST CABERNET SAUVIGNON

Leconfield Cabernet Sauvignon 1993

A very fine wine that has great structure and style. It shows the region and the variety in a very positive light and should age well.

BEST RED BLEND

Leasingham Bin 56 Cabernet Malbec 1993

This is a scrumptious flavour-bomb of a wine that is balanced by well-handled oak. Get it while you can!

BARGAINS

BEST BARGAIN RED

Penfolds Koonunga Hill Shiraz Cabernet 1993

Quality fruit and winemaking here gives generous flavour at a more than generous price. ($10.35 ⓢ)

BEST BARGAIN WHITE

Deen De Bortoli Vat 2 Sauvignon Blanc 1994

A very polished style that drinks like a wine of twice the price. ($9.00)

BEST BARGAIN SPARKLING

Tulloch Hunter Cuvée Brut 1991

This has some development and a lot of flavour, and at this price it's hard to beat. ($13.30 ⓢ)

BEST BARGAIN FORTIFIED

Hardys Tall Ships Tawny Port

The arrival of the tall ships is long gone but the port gets better and better; a very affordable style. ($9.40 ⓢ)

Standard Drinks Made Easy

Wine labels aren't getting any simpler, and sometimes it seems they're calculated to baffle rather than make things easy for the consumer. Standard Drinks Labelling is a new addition in recent times. In small print on back labels, a lot of wines now declare 'Approx. 7.5 std drinks', or something similar. The first wines carrying this information came out in 1994, and by the end of 1995 most Australian wines will have it.

What it means is that if you want to keep a tab on how much alcohol you're absorbing and how safe it is for your health, you can use the labelling to work out a safe level of drinking. Problem is, you need to know a bit more than the label tells you if you're to make useful sense of it.

A standard drink is enshrined in legislation as the equivalent of 10 grams of alcohol. The health authorities have deemed that for sensible, healthy alcohol consumption, men should limit themselves to four standard drinks a day, and women two. Of course, you might choose to drink more and, depending on the amount, you mightn't do yourself any harm. Bingeing is the most destructive way to drink, and health authorities like to remind us that the now well-known health-giving effects of moderate drinking are quickly reversed by drinking to excess.

According to its back label, a 750ml bottle of 1993 Lindemans Nyrang Hermitage contains 7.7 standard drinks. The alcohol content of the wine is 13.0% by volume. Using the chart on page 16, you can see the people at Lindies have done their sums correctly.

So, 7.7 standard drinks, eh? Just how does that help the punter, sitting down with his/her spouse at a restaurant table? The scenario could be this: between them they can, if they're listening to health authorities, have six standard drinks – four for him, two for her. He takes a bit more than half the bottle; she takes a bit more than a quarter – and they leave a bit for the cook. It's not hard to divvy up the bottle as long as you do the pouring yourself. When the waiter's pouring, it's odds-on you'll lose track of what's gone into whose glass.

Why only half the quantity for women? It's not just a matter of men usually being bigger, although that is important, it's simple biology. Men's livers are capable of metabolising more alcohol than women's in a given time. Unfair but true. Of course, two large people could safely put away more than a small couple, because body mass is a factor in alcohol metabolism.

The wine industry has introduced Standard Drinks Labelling voluntarily. No government has forced it. Beer drinkers will note that breweries have gone down a different path: they tell you how many grams of alcohol are in each can, which is probably a little less meaningful to the average Joe or Josephine. (A 375ml can of beer with 4.2% alcohol contains about 12 grams of alcohol: a little more than one standard drink.)

The wine industry sees its step as a responsible move, an extension of the 1988 initiative which saw many producers adding the words 'Enjoy wine in moderation' to their labels. Both types of message are positive information, as opposed to the draconian warnings all wine bottles must carry in the USA:

> Government warning: (1) According to the Surgeon General, women should not drink alcoholic beverages during pregnancy because of the risk of birth defects. (2) Consumption of alcoholic beverages impairs your ability to drive a car or operate machinery, and may cause health problems.

Our winemakers see this as a needlessly scary and negative message, and they're keen to short-circuit anything like that happening here. Hence the responsible, voluntary changes.

If it all sounds like someone's trying to take the fun out of dinner, we'd have to agree. We believe the abusers of wine are a small minority and they'll continue to abuse it, no matter what's written on labels. But at least the industry is taking responsible, and positive, steps.

NUMBER OF STANDARD DRINKS PER 750ml BOTTLE

(Halve these figures for 375ml bottles)

% Alcohol/Volume	Standard drinks
10.0	5.9
10.5	6.2
11.0	6.5
11.5	6.8
12.0	7.1
12.5	7.4
13.0	7.7
13.5	8.0
14.0	8.3
14.5	8.6
18.0	10.6
18.5	11.0
19.0	11.2
19.5	11.5
20.0	11.8

FORMULA FOR CALCULATING STANDARD DRINKS

Volume of container in litres (eg. 0.75)
multiplied by % alcohol by volume
multiplied by 0.789
equals number of standard drinks.

Eating in the Great Outdoors

Why does wine seem to taste different when you're eating and drinking outdoors? There is no scientific reason, but perhaps it's the range of smells, the extra light and the altered mood.

Maybe the other factor is the food. Even at the grandest picnic, the food is different from that in restaurants or at a dinner party. Food for the outdoors has to be capable of travelling. At the great Australian barbecue, the food is usually very different. Strange things happen at an Australian barbecue.

Why is it always the male who dons the silly apron and takes out the long-handled tongs? He never cooks during the week, and he believes that black is beautiful. Anything pink inside is suspicious – it has to be grey.

The fare usually consists of humble bangers, chump chops, and minute steak (which gets cooked for ten minutes) combined with limp iceberg lettuce, dried white dinner rolls and oceans of tomato sauce.

This is not the time or place to pull the plug on a fine bottle of red and slosh it into a peanut-butter jar or beer glass. That's why reviewers tend to recommend rather humble wines for the great outdoors. Bag in box, cleanskins, cheap commercial brands – why bother? Beer is a better bet.

It doesn't have to be this way. A barbecue meal can be cooked with sensitivity and the food doesn't have to be mundane. Seafood shaslicks, fish parcels wrapped in foil with dill and white wine, marinated kidneys cooked until just pink, exotic rather than sawdust sausages – with kettle-style cookers the possibilities are vast. And when these are exercised, finer wine is required.

Here are a few suggestions for getting the best out of your wine while out of doors:

- Never leave the bottles in the sun – light has a deleterious effect on wine. (The same applies to beer.)

- Use the right glasses, the ISO (International Standards Organisation) tasting glass is ideal and isn't expensive. It's not like you're risking the ancestral crystal.
- If the weather is hot, it's a good idea to chill the red slightly and keep it in a cool place.
- If possible, take plenty of glasses so you can have a fresh one for each wine, this beats the grease build-up on the glass. And chill the glasses if possible.

The great outdoors doesn't exclude you from enjoying quality wines. They just need a little more care to get the best out of them. Perhaps the best advice of all is to nobble the clown in the silly apron, and send him down the road for another packet of firelighters.

Red Wines

All Saints Cabernet Sauvignon Merlot

New livery and new owners (Brown Brothers of Milawa), who have lavished money and respect on this historic cellar. It is a very fine development that's well worth a visit. Maker Neil Jericho.

CURRENT RELEASE 1992 The colour is a mid-garnet and the nose is minty with eucalyptus aromas. The medium-bodied palate has sweet berry characters that give way to astringent black tea-like tannins on a grippy finish. Would go well with spicy bratwurst sausages.

QUALITY ▧▧▧▧
VALUE ★★★½
GRAPES cabernet sauvignon, merlot
REGION Rutherglen, Vic.
CELLAR 🍾 3
ALC./VOL. 13.0%
RRP $12.00

All Saints Shiraz

Now proudly owned by Brown Brothers, All Saints has been restored and is ready to rock and roll. If this release is any indication, it will be heavy-metal reds. Maker Neil Jericho.

CURRENT RELEASE 1992 A typical north-eastern blockbuster with mammoth alcohol and slabs of tannin. The nose has hints of port but the main aroma is ripe dark plums. The palate is juicy with dark cherry and ripe plum flavours followed by assertive tannins on a dry and pugnacious finish. Great stuff with a rare ox steak.

QUALITY ▧▧▧▧
VALUE ★★★★
GRAPES shiraz
REGION Rutherglen, Vic.
CELLAR 🍾 2–6
ALC./VOL. 14.0%
RRP $12.50

Allandale Cabernet Sauvignon

QUALITY ▧▧▧
VALUE ★★½
GRAPES cabernet sauvignon
REGION Hunter Valley, NSW
CELLAR 🍶 1
ALC./VOL. 12.0%
RRP $13.50

Allandale was established in 1977 and it produces around 15,000 cases. Maker Bill Sneddon.

CURRENT RELEASE 1993 Is this a product of the climatic conditions of that year? The colour is pale ruby and the nose has a vegetal smell. The palate is light with leafy flavours and modest fruit. The finish is dominated by acid. A luncheon style, it's good for the backyard barbecue.

Allandale Matthew Shiraz

QUALITY ▧▧▧▧
VALUE ★★★½
GRAPES shiraz
REGION Hunter Valley, NSW
CELLAR 🍶 4
ALC./VOL. 12.0%
RRP $14.50

Just who is Matthew? There's no mention of him on the back label.

Previous outstanding vintages: '89, '91

CURRENT RELEASE 1993 The nose is very sappy and vegetal with hints of blackberry. The medium-bodied palate confirms the blackberry notion with sweet fruit flavours matched by medium-strong tannins on a dry finish. Great with mushroom risotto.

Andreas Park Foundation Shiraz

QUALITY ▧▧▧▧
VALUE ★★★½
GRAPES shiraz
REGION Mudgee, NSW
CELLAR 🍶 5
ALC./VOL. 12.5%
RRP $15.00 (cellar door)

This new five-hectare vineyard at Mudgee sells most if its grapes to Rosemount, but manager Sally Langdon scored a top gold medal with her own wine at the Mudgee wine show.

CURRENT RELEASE 1993 This is a lean, cool-climate style with captivating aromas of spicy shiraz and oak, exhibiting ripeness and complexity. The palate offers sweet berry/plummy flavours, crisp acid and elegance. Very promising indeed. Drink it with a pepper steak.

Andrew Garrett Bold Style Shiraz

Mildara Blass paid a bold $20 million for the Andrew Garrett vineyards and winery. It adds 140,000 cases to their production. Maker Warren Randall (now retired).
Previous outstanding vintages: '90, '91

CURRENT RELEASE 1992 Softening nicely since the last review, this wine has a generous amount of fruit. The colour is dense and the nose has plenty of plum and spice aromas. The palate is mouthfilling, with a supple texture on a main flavour of dark plum alongside a raft of spice. American oak dominates the finish and gives a vanillan lift. A good casserole style.

QUALITY 🍷🍷🍷🍷🍷
VALUE ★★★★½
GRAPES shiraz
REGION McLaren Vale, SA
CELLAR 🍾 6
ALC./VOL. 13.0%
RRP $12.70 ⓢ

CURRENT RELEASE 1994 Lots of flavour and richness but not quite as bold as before. The nose has some stewed aromas and spice; the palate is full and fruity with rich plum flavours matched by soft tannins on a dry finish. It drinks well now with a rabbit stew.

QUALITY 🍷🍷🍷🍷🍷
VALUE ★★★★½
GRAPES shiraz
REGION McLaren Vale, SA
CELLAR 🍾 4
ALC./VOL. 13.5%
RRP $12.95 ⓢ

Andrew Garrett Cabernet Merlot

This is the fighting brand from the Andrew Garrett stable. It is made to drink now.

CURRENT RELEASE 1993 Well balanced and easy to drink. The nose is leafy with some chocolate undertones. The palate has sweet berry characters matched by well-tuned oak. The structure is admirable and it's great with lamb and rosemary sausages.

QUALITY 🍷🍷🍷🍷
VALUE ★★★★
GRAPES cabernet, merlot
REGION not stated
CELLAR 🍾 3
ALC./VOL. 12.5%
RRP $15.50 ⓢ

Andrew Garrett Cabernet Sauvignon

QUALITY 🍷🍷🍷🍷🍷
VALUE ★★★★½
GRAPES cabernet sauvignon
REGION Mornington Peninsula, Vic.
CELLAR ← 2–6
ALC./VOL. 13.5%
RRP $13.00

What will happen to this label is known only in the mind (and boardroom) of honcho Ray King, who steers Mildara Blass.

CURRENT RELEASE 1993 There are similarities to a young Bordeaux in this wine: the colour is an intense ruby and the nose has cigarbox and leaf aromas. The middleweight palate is complex, with blackberry flavours balanced by firm oak on a dry, grippy finish. A wine that goes well with smoked duck.

Angoves Sarnia Farm Cabernet Sauvignon

QUALITY 🍷🍷🍷🍷🍷
VALUE ★★★★½
GRAPES cabernet sauvignon
REGION Padthaway, SA
CELLAR 🍷 4
ALC./VOL. 14.0%
RRP $15.00

This is a new label from a sleeping giant. Sarnia Farm is the name of one of Angove's original vineyards in the Adelaide Hills. The label is dedicated to regional and varietal wines from premium growing areas. Maker Frank Newman.

CURRENT RELEASE 1993 A very impressive wine that has some high-society Italian qualities. The colour is a deep ruby and the nose has strong berry aromas plus hints of pencil-shavings. The medium-full body has rich redcurrant flavours with underlying Italianesque tartness. The finish is dry to the point of being chalky. It drinks well with char-grilled kangaroo.

Arrowfield Cabernet Merlot

QUALITY 🍷🍷🍷🍷
VALUE ★★★½
GRAPES cabernet sauvignon, merlot
REGION Upper Hunter Valley, NSW
CELLAR 🍷 3
ALC./VOL. 14.0%
RRP $12.50

This vineyard is located on an impressive (and expensive) horse stud. You can put the Lear down on the strip, check out the horse flesh, then stroll up to the winery and buy a case for the trip home while wondering how the poor folk are doing.

CURRENT RELEASE 1993 This is a very convincing style with an emphatic nose of cherries, berries and dusty spice. The palate is a middleweight with some sweet fruit followed by well-matched oak. It drinks well now with a lamb casserole.

Arrowfield Shiraz Cabernet

Shiraz and cabernet form a typical Australian blend, and in the Upper Hunter these varieties combine well to make a wine that is usually bigger than the sum of its parts. Maker Simon Gilbert.

CURRENT RELEASE 1993 The colour is a dark brick-red and the nose has some earthy components with a hint of berries. The palate is a middleweight with sweet cherry flavoured fruit followed by dusty oak on a dry finish. An easy-to-drink style that goes well with a hearty casserole.

QUALITY ▼▼▼▼
VALUE ★★★½
GRAPES shiraz, cabernet sauvignon
REGION Upper Hunter Valley, NSW
CELLAR 🍾 3
ALC./VOL. 12.5%
RRP $12.50

Ashton Hills Cabernet Merlot

Given the climate near Mount Lofty in the Adelaide Hills, the reds from the district should, and do, show great elegance. Maker Steve George.

CURRENT RELEASE 1991 Shows a combination of cool climate and bottle development. The colour is still youthful and the nose has a ripe cherry character plus hints of leaf. The medium-bodied palate has attractive dark cherry flavours enhanced by the other varieties in the blend. The oak on the finish is discreet and well tailored. It drinks well with venison sausages.

QUALITY ▼▼▼▼▼
VALUE ★★★★
GRAPES cabernet sauvignon 60%, cabernet franc 17%, merlot 23%
REGION Adelaide Hills, SA
CELLAR 🍾 6
ALC./VOL. 13.5%
RRP $16.00

Ashton Hills Pinot Noir

The Adelaide Hills district is the great white hope (perhaps that should be 'red hope') for this variety. It produces some excellent wines.

CURRENT RELEASE 1994 The colour is a mid-ruby and the nose is meaty with some strawberry aromas. The palate is quite complex with cherry and strawberry flavours and a touch of astringent stalk character. The finish is well balanced and dry. It drinks well with a rabbit and mushroom stew.

QUALITY ▼▼▼▼
VALUE ★★★½
GRAPES pinot noir
REGION Adelaide Hills, SA
CELLAR 🍾 4
ALC./VOL. 13.5%
RRP $20.00

Augustine Cabernet Merlot

QUALITY 🍷🍷🍷🍷
VALUE ★★★½
GRAPES cabernet sauvignon, merlot
REGION Mudgee, NSW
CELLAR 🍾 3
ALC./VOL. 12.9%
RRP $12.00

This is one of the first vineyards planted in the Mudgee district of mid-western New South Wales. It is now part of the Rothbury group.
CURRENT RELEASE 1993 The colour is a bright ruby and the nose has hints of confectionery plus perfumed cigar box. The middleweight palate offers sweet berry characters with blackberry flavours supported by discreet oak on a gentle finish. It goes well with turkey.

Bailey's 1920s Block Shiraz

QUALITY 🍷🍷🍷🍷
VALUE ★★★
GRAPES shiraz
REGION Glenrowan, Vic.
CELLAR ➞ 5–15
ALC./VOL. 13.5%
RRP $23.00 🍾

When the Rothbury group bought Bailey's, there were moves afoot to rip out the block of shiraz vines that made this wine. But it lives to assault us another day!
Previous outstanding vintages: '91
CURRENT RELEASE 1993 The nose of this nigh-impenetrable wine is gumleaf/mint and earthiness; the palate is well stacked, as they say in the classics. It's a solid, tannic, extracted wine which finishes a little bitter at this stage, but then it's a juvenile which needs time to grow up. Cellar, then drink with a T-bone steak.

Balgownie Estate Cabernet Sauvignon

QUALITY 🍷🍷🍷🍷🍷
VALUE ★★★★
GRAPES cabernet sauvignon
REGION Bendigo, Vic.
CELLAR ➞ 3–10+
ALC./VOL. 13.5%
RRP $19.00 🍾

These wines are as big as ever, but the winemaking has been refined and they're no longer prone to rough edges. Maker Lindsay Ross says on the label: 'a long period of careful cellaring is recommended'. He's not kidding.
Previous outstanding vintages: '76, '80, '86, '88, '90
CURRENT RELEASE 1992 This is a tannic monster, but it has the flavour to match. Deep berry fruit with vanilla and chocolate nuances, discreet oak, and a lift of gumleaf/mint. It says goodbye with a phenomenal tannin grip, but there's no hint of bitterness. Cellar, then drink with rare beef.

Balgownie Estate Hermitage

Founded by Bendigo renaissance man Stuart Anderson in the '60s, this winery is now owned by Mildara Blass and the winemaker is Anderson acolyte, Lindsay Ross.
Previous outstanding vintages: '76, '80, '86, '90
CURRENT RELEASE 1993 The vivid purple-red colour is echoed by a solid inky, spicy, plummy nose with some earthiness and central Victorian mint. A seriously fruit-dominant concentrated red with rich, powerful yet smooth flavour and high extract. The sweet plum/vanilla flavours linger well and it will repay keeping. Try a mild Indian curry.

QUALITY ★★★★
VALUE ★★★★
GRAPES shiraz
REGION Bendigo, Vic.
CELLAR 10+
ALC./VOL. 14.0%
RRP $17.00 Ⓢ

Bannockburn Cabernet Sauvignon Merlot

This vineyard takes its name from the nearby town of the same name. It was established by Stuart Hooper in 1974. Maker Garry Farr.
Previous outstanding vintages: '84, '87, '88
CURRENT RELEASE 1991 Like all Gary Farr's wines, this is full of character, even slightly wild. The nose has smoky, currant/cassis and gamey nuances, and the palate is seriously full-bodied and tannic, yet smooth, ripe and fruit-sweet. The merlot imparts a faint greenness to the mid-palate. A wine of true individuality. Try it with marinated venison.

QUALITY ★★★★
VALUE ★★★★
GRAPES cabernet sauvignon, merlot
REGION Geelong, Vic.
CELLAR 2–8+
ALC./VOL. 12.5%
RRP $18.50

Bannockburn Pinot Noir

QUALITY ▼▼▼▽
VALUE ★★★
GRAPES pinot noir
REGION Geelong, Vic.
CELLAR 🍷 3+
ALC./VOL. 13.5%
RRP $30.60

This is a wine with quite a reputation these days, as much has been written about winemaker Gary Farr's many vintage stints in Burgundy where he's learnt about the fickle pinot grape.

Previous outstanding vintages: '86, '88, '90, '91, '92

CURRENT RELEASE 1993 Gary Farr believes in using the grape stalks and this vintage pushes stalkiness to the limit, resulting in a pervading green vegetal character. It's missing the ripe, sweet mid-palate and all-round charm we look for in pinot, but there's tannin and structure and we'd like to watch how it develops.

Bannockburn Shiraz

QUALITY ▼▼▼▽
VALUE ★★★
GRAPES shiraz
REGION Geelong, Vic.
CELLAR 🍷 1–5
ALC./VOL. 12.5%
RRP $20.00

This wine has improved remarkably in the '90s since winemaker Gary Farr began visiting Rhône winemaker Alain Graillot.

Previous outstanding vintages: '91, '92

CURRENT RELEASE 1993 This is a step behind the '91 and '92, perhaps due to a cool year. There are strong spice/black peppercorn and vegetal characters in a leaner, meaner style without the sweet fruit of the ripe years. It's tight 'n tense, and drinks well with a meat and vegie hotpot.

Barwang Cabernet Sauvignon

This cool-area vineyard at Young was bought by McWilliam's from its founders in 1989 and radically increased in size. Maker Jim Brayne. Previous outstanding vintages: '91, '92

CURRENT RELEASE 1993 What a cracker! The orchestra really comes together with a crescendo that raises the roof here. Like the Moody Blues in search of the lost chord. Marvellous concentration and elegance, fruit uppermost, and cedary oak well harmonised with a whiff of mint. It's tightly structured and the harmony thrills the tastebuds. The finish carries an authoritative grip. Drink with venison cutlets.

QUALITY 🍷🍷🍷🍷🍷
VALUE ★★★★★
GRAPES cabernet sauvignon
REGION Young, NSW
CELLAR 🍷 10
ALC./VOL. 13.5%
RRP $15.00 ⓢ

Barwang Shiraz

The first three vintages from Barwang have made everyone sit up and take notice. The wines are made at McWilliam's at Griffith.
Previous outstanding vintages: '89, '91

CURRENT RELEASE 1993 Tight and a little unyielding in its youth, this wine needs time. The shy nose has cherry and spice with a twist of the pepper grinder. It builds mintiness as it airs. In the mouth, it's austere and restrained with a dry finish. Cellar, then drink with hard cheese.

QUALITY 🍷🍷🍷🍷
VALUE ★★★½
GRAPES shiraz
REGION Young, NSW
CELLAR ⟻ 2–7+
ALC./VOL. 13.5%
RRP $15.00 ⓢ

Basedow Oscar's Heritage

Oscar Basedow is commemorated by this new brand from the stable of Grant Burge. He was a nephew of the founder, and was the driving force behind Basedow's establishing itself. The company turns 100 in 1996.

CURRENT RELEASE 1993 This is good value: a soft, fruity, open style with little oak evident. It is an up-front red designed for early drinking. Pleasant, if straightforward, cherry flavour and fruit sweetness. Try it with veal.

QUALITY 🍷🍷🍷🍷
VALUE ★★★★
GRAPES grenache, cabernet sauvignon
REGION Barossa Valley, SA
CELLAR 🍷 6
ALC./VOL. 13.0%
RRP $10.00

Basedow Shiraz

QUALITY ♛♛♛♛
VALUE ★★★½
GRAPES shiraz
REGION Barossa Valley, SA
CELLAR 🍾 4
ALC./VOL. 13.5%
RRP $14.50 ⓢ

When Peter Lehmann went public and divested Basedow, the contract bottling business went to mail-order specialists Cellarmaster, and the winery and brand to the burgeoning Grant Burge. He's repackaged and relaunched the wines.

CURRENT RELEASE 1992 This wine is a typical Barossa fraulein: buxom, friendly and easy to like. The colour and bouquet show a touch of aged development, with a trace of gumleaf. There's stacks of smooth, rich flavour, and the wine is very drinkable already. Try it with Barossa mettwurst.

Bazzani

QUALITY ♛♛♛♛
VALUE ★★★½
GRAPES cabernet sauvignon, shiraz, dolcetto
REGION Pyrenees, Vic.
CELLAR 🍾 4
ALC./VOL. 12.5%
RRP $19.00

This is labelled after the proprietor of Warrenmang vineyards, Luigi Bazzani, who has a distinguished reputation as a restaurateur. The wine is as individual as the personality.

CURRENT RELEASE 1993 This is an interesting mix of flavours and aromas. There's an Italian slant to it with a nose that shows some tart raisin and raspberry aromas. The palate is complex with tart fruit characters that mingle with discreet oak. The finish shows some strong acid. It goes well with osso bucco.

Best's Shiraz Bin 0

The Thomson family, owners of Best's since 1920, are now into their fifth generation of winemakers, with Chris and Viv's sons Bart, Ben and Marcus and daughter Yvette all involved. Maker Simon Clayfield.

Previous outstanding vintages: '66, '67, '71, '80, '82, '84, '86, '88, '90, '91

CURRENT RELEASE 1992 Little change since last year's review: the wine is still fairly shy and developing slowly, the oak is yet to fully integrate, giving a coconutty edge to a nose of mixed spice and sweet berries. Although undeveloped, it's well balanced and already approachable. But those who cellar it won't be disappointed. Try a peppery beef stew.

QUALITY ★★★★
VALUE ★★★★
GRAPES shiraz
REGION Great Western, Vic.
CELLAR 2–6+
ALC./VOL. 14.0%
RRP $19.30

Best's Thomson Centenary Shiraz

On 13 November 1893, William Thomson, vigneron, who was described as a temperance man, signed the title to St Andrews, a vineyard at Rhymney. Later, the family moved to Best's, and to celebrate a century of Thomson winemaking, a 200-case special blend was bottled from Henry Best's 1860s vines.

CURRENT RELEASE 1992 This is a strapping young red that would bring a tear to old William Thomson's eye. It is quite unready in its raw youth, and drinking it now would be a crime. Floral scented and fruit-driven, it has ripe aromas with little of the region's usual pepper. A big, grunty red, a powerhouse of spices and berries over supple ripe tannins.

QUALITY ★★★★★
VALUE ★★★★
GRAPES shiraz
REGION Great Western, Vic.
CELLAR 4–12+
ALC./VOL. 13.5%
RRP $35.00

Bethany Cabernet Merlot

QUALITY ♥♥♥♥♥
VALUE ★★★★
GRAPES cabernet sauvignon, merlot
REGION Barossa Valley, SA
CELLAR 🍾 5+
ALC./VOL. 14.0%
RRP $17.00

The Schrapel family winery is a picturesque spot with a panoramic view over the village of Bethany and its vineyards. The winery itself is snugly fitted into an old hillside quarry.
Previous outstanding vintages: '91
CURRENT RELEASE 1992 Yum-oh! This is a smooth, rich, chunky red that epitomises the best of the Barossa. It is vinous and complex, dry but supple, deep and compact. Ideal food style and works well with beef casserole.

Bethany Grenache Pressings

QUALITY ♥♥♥♥
VALUE ★★★½
GRAPES grenache
REGION Barossa Valley, SA
CELLAR 🍾 1
ALC./VOL. 14.5%
RRP $15.00

This unusual wine is made as a by-product of port material, and is not wood-matured.
Previous outstanding vintages: '93
CURRENT RELEASE 1994 This is like a tubby infant, all puppy fat but not all that interesting to talk to. The nose is very young and fruity, the taste very sweet in ultra-ripe fruit with a tannin finish, but lacking enough complexity to challenge one's attention span. Try it with beef casserole.

Bethany Shiraz

Bethany's shiraz is crafted in the modern Barossa Valley idiom, with high alcohol, stacks of vanillary American oak; and while this style is appealing young, we wonder about its long-term potential. Maker Geoff and Robert Schrapel. Previous outstanding vintages: '90

CURRENT RELEASE 1992 High-toast oak dominates the wine on nose and palate, giving vanilla, coconut and chocolate flavours that will appeal to many. The alcohol fights a little as it goes down, but the final impression is of a decent, if straightforward, drinking red. Try it with steak and kidney pie.

QUALITY 🍷🍷🍷
VALUE ★★★
GRAPES shiraz
REGION Barossa Valley, SA
CELLAR 🍾 5+
ALC./VOL. 14.0%
RRP $17.40

CURRENT RELEASE 1993 Typical Barossa shiraz: a nose of Violet Crumble (chocolate, vanilla and honey) and a big rich sweet-fruit palate. It's a friendly wine with lots of interest: traces of garden mint, green peppercorns and lashings of liquorice and dark berries. Lots happening here: it's one of the best from this maker. Drink with wiener schnitzel.

QUALITY 🍷🍷🍷🍷
VALUE ★★★★
GRAPES shiraz
REGION Barossa Valley, SA
CELLAR 🍾 7
ALC./VOL. 13.5%
RRP $18.40 ⓢ

Blackjack Shiraz

Blackjack takes its name from a road near the vineyard at Harcourt which commemorates a colourful American sailor who jumped ship in the 1850s gold rush and went to the Castlemaine goldfields.

CURRENT RELEASE 1993 Typical of the Bendigo region, this is a lush wine of extravagant proportions, chock-full of spice, pepper, blackberry and plum flavours. It is big yet elegant, full of personality and fruit sweetness, and has a nice full finish. Serve with kangaroo.

QUALITY 🍷🍷🍷🍷
VALUE ★★★★½
GRAPES shiraz
REGION Bendigo, Vic.
CELLAR 🍾 8+
ALC./VOL. 13.0%
RRP $16.00 (cellar door)

Bloodwood Cabernet Merlot

QUALITY 🍷🍷🍷🍷
VALUE ★★★½
GRAPES cabernet sauvignon, merlot
REGION Orange, NSW
CELLAR 🍾 5+
ALC./VOL. 12.5%
RRP $15.00 (cellar door) 🍾

Orange is a chilly place and this vineyard sits at about 850 metres. Maker Jon Reynolds.
CURRENT RELEASE 1993 An oak-driven style which smells of coffee, vanilla and toast. The tannin stands out, making the palate savoury rather than fruity, with mainly secondary flavours. The finish is quite firm, with a lingering echo of cinnamon. A very agreeable drink. Try smoked lamb.

Blue Pyrenees Estate

QUALITY 🍷🍷🍷🍷
VALUE ★★★
GRAPES cabernet sauvignon, merlot, shiraz
REGION Pyrenees, Vic.
CELLAR 🍾 7+
ALC./VOL. 13.1%
RRP $23.50 🍾

In a certain light, the eucalypt-cloaked hills of Victoria's Pyrenees district look distinctly blue. Hence the name of this wine, which is so much better than the old Chateau Remy.
Previous outstanding vintages: '82, '88, '90, '91
CURRENT RELEASE 1992 This is a serious food wine which has swallowed up a lot of oak during its maturation. The nose is subdued with toasty oak and a slightly feral gamey aspect; the taste is lean and savoury with some firm tannin. Drink with char-grilled steak.

Botobolar Shiraz

QUALITY 🍷🍷🍷
VALUE ★★★
GRAPES shiraz
REGION Mudgee, NSW
CELLAR 🍾 3
ALC./VOL. 13.7%
RRP $13.00 ❂

This is one of the country's few organic vineyards, and was recently sold by the founding Wahlquists to the Karstroms.
CURRENT RELEASE 1991 This is a dusty, earthy, slightly dried-out wine which nevertheless drinks well, with a chunky, full-flavoured palate and smooth tannins. A savoury style that would go well with a casserole.

Bowen Estate Cabernet Sauvignon

Bowen Estate was established in 1972 by Doug and Joy Bowen. It has developed a well-deserved reputation for quality and authenticity, and the production seems to be on an exponential growth curve. Makers Doug and Emma Bowen.

Previous outstanding vintages: '84, '85, '86, '87, '88, '89, '90, '92

CURRENT RELEASE 1993 Quite often straight cabernet can be full of holes and stumbles. Not so this wine, which is the goods. The nose is complex with strong cassis and spice aromas. The palate is also complex with dark cherry flavours and hints of blackberry. Lifted spice graces the finish and there's plenty of grip. It will age spectacularly but now it goes well with minted lamb.

QUALITY 🍷🍷🍷🍷🍷
VALUE ★★★★★
GRAPES cabernet sauvignon
REGION Coonawarra, SA
CELLAR 🍾 3–7
ALC./VOL. 14.5%
RRP $15.95

Bowen Estate Cabernet Sauvignon Merlot Cabernet Franc

This might be a Bordeaux-style blend but when you visit Bowen Estate it is about as un-Bordeaux as you can get – very laid back Oz, but the wines would be the envy of Bordeaux.

Previous outstanding vintages: '92

CURRENT RELEASE 1994 High style in a vinous equivalent to art deco. There are lots of things happening on the nose and the palate: the former is highly perfumed with violets and a bouquet of ripe fruit while the latter offers complex mulberry, blackberry and dark cherry flavours that conjoin with well-shaped oak on an astringent finish. It will be a wine that rewards the cellar hounds. At the moment it is great with casseroled kid.

QUALITY 🍷🍷🍷🍷
VALUE ★★★★
GRAPES cabernet sauvignon, merlot, cabernet franc
REGION Coonawarra, SA
CELLAR 🍾 2–8
ALC./VOL. 14.5%
RRP $17.45

Bowen Estate Shiraz

QUALITY ★★★★★
VALUE ★★★★★
GRAPES shiraz
REGION Coonawarra, SA
CELLAR 8
ALC./VOL. 14.5%
RRP $15.95

Doug 'Bogger' Bowen is convinced that the south end (his end) of Coonawarra is quite different to the north. It ripens later and is less prone to hot 'sensations' when the alcohol is high. Makers Doug and Emma Bowen.

Previous outstanding vintages: '86, '87, '88, '89, '90, '91

CURRENT RELEASE 1992 Great stuff that doesn't want for alcohol or flavour. The nose is spicy and there are ripe berry flavours. The palate is rich with dark cherry and raspberry flavours plus loads of spice. The finish is long with attractive astringency and grip. It drinks very well now but cellaring will surely reward. Decant and try it with confit of duck.

Brands Laira Cabernet Sauvignon

QUALITY ★★★★
VALUE ★★★½
GRAPES cabernet sauvignon
REGION Coonawarra, SA
CELLAR 5
ALC./VOL. 13.5%
RRP $17.00

The *Laira* was a square-rigger that is said to have brought the first vine cuttings to Coonawarra in 1896. Some still survive in the Brands' vineyards. Maker Jim Brand.

CURRENT RELEASE 1993 This wine does its elegant new livery proud. With a deep purple-red hue, it shows a complex nose of oak and typical Coonawarra blackcurrant fruit. It's elegant and suave, mediumweight and quite tasty on the mid-palate. It would go well with roast lamb.

Brands Laira Shiraz

QUALITY ★★★
VALUE ★★½
GRAPES shiraz
REGION Coonawarra, SA
CELLAR 2
ALC./VOL. 13.0%
RRP $12.90

Brands, although operated by the Brand family, is now wholly owned by McWilliam's. For the trivia buffs: founder Eric Brand was a baker before he turned his yeasts to a more liquid purpose. Maker Jim Brand.

CURRENT RELEASE 1992 This a rather woody shiraz which lacks a little in the fruit concentration department, falling away to a shortish finish. Could appeal with spaghetti bolognaise.

Bremerton Blend Shiraz Cabernet Merlot

Bremerton Lodge is a very new small brand emanating from Langhorne Creek, although the vineyard is a handy 44 hectares.

CURRENT RELEASE 1992 An oak-driven style, with plentiful savoury, cedary dark berry flavours and lots of furry tannins on the finish. A wine of good depth and character, which just needs a year or two for the oak to soften. Try it with game pie.

QUALITY ♛♛♛♛
VALUE ★★★★
GRAPES shiraz, cabernet sauvignon, merlot
REGION Langhorne Creek, SA
CELLAR 🍾 6+
ALC./VOL. 13.1%
RRP $12.00 (cellar door)

Briar Ridge Cabernet Sauvignon

This is the former Murray Robson vineyard at Mount View. Hunter legend Karl Stockhausen has a hand in the winemaking.

Previous outstanding vintages: '89

CURRENT RELEASE 1993 Lashings of toasty vanillan oak keep this one together. While driven by toasty oak, it has good depth of pleasant berry flavours as well and will drink fairly soon with beef hotpot.

QUALITY ♛♛♛♛
VALUE ★★★
GRAPES cabernet sauvignon
REGION Hunter Valley, NSW
CELLAR 🍾 5+
ALC./VOL. 12.6%
RRP $17.70

Brindabella Hills Cabernets

Roger and Fay Harris's vineyard is in a picturesque location just outside Canberra, where their house has a stunning view over the Murrumbidgee River.

Previous outstanding vintages: '91

CURRENT RELEASE 1993 This is a lean, mild-mannered red with sweet blackcurrant aromas and good depth of ripe cabernet fruit on the tongue. The wood is well balanced and the finish is firmed up by good tannin. A good partner for pink lamb.

QUALITY ♛♛♛♛
VALUE ★★★½
GRAPES cabernet sauvignon, cabernet franc, merlot
REGION Canberra district, NSW
CELLAR 🍾 5+
ALC./VOL. 12.5%
RRP $15.50 (cellar door)

Brokenwood Cabernet Sauvignon

QUALITY ♉♉♉♉⚇
VALUE ★★★★
GRAPES cabernet sauvignon
REGION 46% Coonawarra, 46% McLaren Vale, SA & 8% Yarra Valley, Vic.
CELLAR 🍾 10
ALC./VOL. 13.5%
RRP $20.50

Brokenwood's Iain Riggs is an eclectic blender. Only 1000 cases of this were produced.
Previous outstanding vintages: '91
CURRENT RELEASE 1993 Coonawarra dominates the nose with blackcurrant, mint and mulberry aromas, while McLaren Vale holds sway on the palate, which has lashings of rich ripe liquorice and berry flavours. The oak is subtly spicy and the fruit concentrated, with firm tannin and good length. Goes well with smoked pork.

Brokenwood Cricket Pitch

QUALITY ♉♉♉⚇
VALUE ★★★½
GRAPES merlot 66%, shiraz 17%, cabernet sauvignon 17%
REGION 83% McLaren Vale, SA & 17% Yarra Valley, Vic.
CELLAR 🍾 5
ALC./VOL. 13.0%
RRP $16.10

They're a sporty lot at Brokenwood and the partners get together for an annual cricket match against Rothbury. The cricket pitch referred to is imaginary, however.
CURRENT RELEASE 1993 The merlot shows through in a soft, sweet, plummy fruit character. The wine is rich and smooth and very user-friendly, although not ultra-complex. Try it with pork ribs in plum sauce.

Brokenwood Graveyard Vineyard

From the '93 vintage the name becomes simply the above, without hermitage or shiraz. It sells out quickly every year, but we record the '93 for interest's sake. There was no '92 release. Maker Iain Riggs.

Previous outstanding vintages: '83, '85, '86, '87, '88, '89, '90, '91

CURRENT RELEASE 1993 Very deep, dark colour and powerful 'linseed' aroma with stacks of coconut/vanilla oak, as well as vegetal, pepper/spice and floral notes. The fruit is sweet, deep and powerful as usual, but we wonder if this won't be peaking sooner than the massive '91. Drink with venison.

QUALITY 🍷🍷🍷🍷?
VALUE ★★★★
GRAPES shiraz
REGION Hunter Valley, NSW
CELLAR 🍾 2–8+
ALC./VOL. 13.5%
RRP $35.00

CURRENT RELEASE 1994 Much more austere than the Rayner, with typical Graveyard clove-like spiciness, liberal oak and gripping tannin. This is all about structure: it's dry and savoury, deep and powerful with hints of coffee on the palate. A serious red wine which demands cellaring. Then drink with venison.

QUALITY 🍷🍷🍷🍷?
VALUE ★★★★
GRAPES shiraz
REGION Hunter Valley, NSW
CELLAR 🍾 6–20
ALC./VOL. 13.5%
RRP $35.00

Brokenwood Hermitage

QUALITY 🍷🍷🍷🍷
VALUE ★★★½
GRAPES shiraz
REGION Hunter Valley, NSW
CELLAR ⬤ 1–5+
ALC./VOL. 13.5%
RRP $16.10

Old habits die hard and there are pockets of the Hunter where the shiraz still answers to its traditional name (that's hermitage ...). Maker Iain Riggs.

CURRENT RELEASE 1992 This is quite a full-bodied, rich red that's firm in its youth and driven by coconutty, vanillan American oak. The structure is tight and it should develop well with short-term cellaring. Drink with Thai beef salad.

QUALITY 🍷🍷🍷🍷
VALUE ★★★★
GRAPES shiraz
REGION McLaren Vale, SA; Hunter Valley, NSW; Stanthorpe, Qld
CELLAR 🍾 6+
ALC./VOL. 13.5%
RRP $16.00

CURRENT RELEASE 1993 The hermitage is named shiraz from 1993. A charming, soft, berryish shiraz with some cool-area pepper on the nose and some cherry and liquorice in the mouth. Very friendly with no sharp edges. Drink with rissoles.

Brokenwood Rayner Vineyard Shiraz

QUALITY 🍷🍷🍷🍷🍷
VALUE ★★★★★
GRAPES shiraz
REGION McLaren Vale, SA
CELLAR 🍾 10
ALC./VOL. 13.5%
RRP $25.00

This Sydney Show trophy-winner comes from 50-year-old untrellised, unirrigated vines on deep, sandy Blewitt Springs soil.

CURRENT RELEASE 1993 Astonishing stuff and a great alter-ego to the Graveyard shiraz. Very complex spice, toast and plum nose. In the mouth, it's rich, soft and full-bodied with lots of liquorice, plum, chocolate, vanilla and spice. Remarkably open and accessible. Try it with kangaroo.

Brookland Valley Cabernet Sauvignon Merlot Cabernet Franc

Perhaps the best way to enjoy Brookland Valley wines is to sit in Flutes Café at the winery and drink them with lunch.

CURRENT RELEASE 1992 This is quite a Bordeaux-like young red with lots of toasty oak and gripping tannins. There is good fruit weight and an interesting gamey note. A serious wine which should cellar well. Try it with venison.

QUALITY ★★★★★
VALUE ★★★★
GRAPES cabernet sauvignon, merlot, cabernet franc
REGION Margaret River, WA
CELLAR 1–6+
ALC./VOL. 13.3%
RRP $21.00

Brown Brothers Barbera

This Piedmontese grape variety has found a good home in the King Valley, where many of the growers are of Italian descent.

CURRENT RELEASE 1993 This is an improvement on the previous vintage, which featured rather heavy-handed American oak. It has a youthful colour and a plummy, earthy nose with more than an echo of Italy. The oak is well in the background and the taste is smooth, supple and mediumweight. A good pasta wine.

QUALITY ★★★★
VALUE ★★★½
GRAPES barbera
REGION King Valley, Vic.
CELLAR 3
ALC./VOL. 13.5%
RRP $12.60 $

Brown Brothers Cabernet Sauvignon

Brown's have done away with their cabernet shiraz blend and now have just the single varietal shiraz and cabernet sauvignon. Makers Roland Wahlquist, Terry Barnett and team.

CURRENT RELEASE 1993 While it doesn't have sharply defined varietal character, this is a pleasant red wine with deliberate commercial appeal. The nose is soft vanilla and mulberry, the palate smooth and well put together with a light grip to the finish. Very much a drink-now style, with a herby game pie.

QUALITY ★★★★
VALUE ★★★½
GRAPES cabernet sauvignon
REGION King Valley, Vic.
CELLAR 4
ALC./VOL. 12.5%
RRP $15.50 $

Brown Brothers Classic Vintage Release Cabernet Sauvignon

QUALITY ♆♆♆♆⸮
VALUE ★★★★½
GRAPES cabernet sauvignon
REGION King Valley, Vic.
CELLAR 🍾 2
ALC./VOL. 13.0%
RRP $24.85 ⓢ 🍾

Classic Vintage Release cabernet is the same wine that was released young, only it's been cellared at Milawa for many years. This is simply the best we've ever tasted in the series.

CURRENT RELEASE 1982 A lovely, mellow, aged cabernet from a fine vintage, showing classic cigar-box maturity on the nose and a svelte, beautifully balanced mediumweight flavour, finishing with soft tannins. A wine of finesse, at its peak now. Serve with aged hard cheeses at the end of a meal.

Brown Brothers Shiraz

QUALITY ♆♆♆♆
VALUE ★★★★
GRAPES shiraz 95%, cabernet sauvignon 5%
REGION Milawa, Murray Valley & King Valley, Vic.
CELLAR 🍾 4+
ALC./VOL. 12.5%
RRP $12.20 ⓢ

Brown's Milawa cellar door sales and tasting facility is one of the best in the land and does a roaring trade. Recently they have added a restaurant which features local produce.

Previous outstanding vintages: '80, '82, '86, '90, '92

CURRENT RELEASE 1993 In the King Valley, 1993 may not have been much of a year but this wine is a success nonetheless: fruit-driven aromas of black pepper, mixed spices and berries which translate to a very lively, fresh palate that shows a cool-grown spicy tang. Goes well with kangaroo and pepperberries.

Brown Brothers Tarrango

QUALITY ♆♆♆
VALUE ★★★
GRAPES tarrango
REGION Murray Valley, Vic.
CELLAR 🍾
ALC./VOL. 12.0%
RRP $9.45 ⓢ

A tribute to Aussie inventiveness, this variety was bred by the CSIRO at Merbein by crossing touriga with sultana. It was designed to thrive in hot climates.

CURRENT RELEASE 1994 With a medium-light purple-red colour, this is like a strong rosé style. It smells softly cherry/plummy and while it's a light, simple wine, it is what the Poms would call 'very gulpable'. Best served chilled in summery weather with antipasto.

Buller Classic Red

There's something disarmingly nostalgic about a company calling itself R.L. Buller & Son in the 1990s.

CURRENT RELEASE 1992 The first thing that hits you is the spirity high-alcohol nose and a certain portiness to the fruit. There are liquorice flavours to this rustic red and a pretty rough tannin grip, but it's fair value at the price. Try spaghetti bolognese.

QUALITY 🍷🍷🍷
VALUE ★★★
GRAPES not stated
REGION not stated
CELLAR 🍷 3
ALC./VOL. 13.9%
RRP $9.65

Burge Family Draycott Shiraz

Rick Burge sells his wines from the winery or by mail order. He is related to Grant Burge in blood but not in business.

Previous outstanding vintages: '92

CURRENT RELEASE 1993 In the style of the '92, this is an oak-driven wine which packs plenty of flavour and drinkability into the bottle. The nose is spicy with oak to the fore; the palate quite elegant with good oaky complexity and a dry, puckering tannin finish. Suits a rich casserole.

QUALITY 🍷🍷🍷🍷
VALUE ★★★★
GRAPES shiraz
REGION Barossa Valley, SA
CELLAR 🍷 6
ALC./VOL. 13.5%
RRP $13.80 (cellar door)

Campbells Barkly (The)

A new line with very sexy packaging. Campbells seemed to have recently shifted into top gear and are really motoring. This is an exciting wine.

CURRENT RELEASE 1992 Big and bold and, truth be told, you probably will be if you finish the bottle. The colour is dense and the nose has strong raspberry aromas. The palate is very rich with sweet raspberry and redcurrant fruit flavours and a lot of mouthfeel. The finish is typically north-east Victorian with slabs of tannin and lots of grip. It needs a big meal – try it with game pie.

QUALITY 🍷🍷🍷🍷
VALUE ★★★★½
GRAPES durif
REGION Rutherglen, Vic.
CELLAR ⟃ 2–8
ALC./VOL. 14.0%
RRP $22.00

Campbells Bobbie Burns Shiraz

QUALITY ♗♗♗♗♗
VALUE ★★★★★
GRAPES shiraz
REGION Rutherglen, Vic.
CELLAR ➡ 3–8
ALC./VOL. 14.5%
RRP $14.00

Bobbie Burns is one of those traditional styles that's as comfortable as well-worn slippers. These days there seems to be a tad more finesse in the making. Maker Colin Campbell.

CURRENT RELEASE 1993 Hallelujah! Keep the faith, brothers and sisters – this is the way it's meant to be. The colour is a mid-ruby and the nose has ripe fruit, pepper and spice aromas. The palate is chewy with rich, complex shiraz flavours that show intense concentration and slabs of tannin and a glow of alcohol. Great with smoked kangaroo.

Campbells Cabernet Merlot

QUALITY ♗♗♗♗
VALUE ★★★½
GRAPES cabernet sauvignon, merlot
REGION Rutherglen, Vic.
CELLAR ◊ 4
ALC./VOL. 13.5%
RRP $12.50

It seems this blend has been adopted by the Rutherglen district as a drink-now utility style.

CURRENT RELEASE 1994 This a fruit-driven style with a nose that's bursting with berry aroma. The palate is soft with ripe cherry and raspberry flavours, but the finish betrays its regional origins, revealing slabs of black tea-like tannins. It drinks well with pasta and a meat sauce.

Canobolas-Smith Alchemy

QUALITY ♗♗♗♗
VALUE ★★★★
GRAPES merlot & cabernet franc 50%, cabernet sauvignon 45%, shiraz 5%
REGION Orange, NSW
CELLAR ➡ 2–10
ALC./VOL. 13.5%
RRP $17.00

The startling blue and purple label is full of mysterious symbols and, given the complex blend of varieties, the name Alchemy is most appropriate. Maker Murray Smith.

CURRENT RELEASE 1993 A solid lump of a wine of excellent ripeness and concentration that reflects low-yielding vines. A tad straightforward at this stage but should be a lovely rich wine in time. Drink with rare roast beef.

Cape Mentelle Shiraz

It's an irresistible temptation to avoid the 'Rhône Ranger' cliché. The maker, David Hohnen, seems to be paying homage to that district in France. Previous outstanding vintages: '83, '86, '87, '88, '89, '90, '91, '92

CURRENT RELEASE 1993 A very polished style that is a little lighter than last year's. In this case, light doesn't mean less: the nose is very spicy and the palate is complex following considerable winemaking application such as whole bunch fermentation. This ups the berry ante and the fruit is matched by some fine-grained tannins on a lingering finish. It drinks well now, as long as you have it with a robust dish. Try steak and kidney pie.

QUALITY ★★★★★
VALUE ★★★★½
GRAPES shiraz, grenache
REGION Margaret River, WA
CELLAR 2–6
ALC./VOL. 13.0%
RRP $19.25

Cape Mentelle Trinders

Although not a second label per se, this is an early drinking style. Trinders is the name of a vineyard. Previous outstanding vintages: '90, '91, '92

CURRENT RELEASE 1993 A soft middleweight style with some charming fruit. The colour is dense and there are berry and leaf aromas with a hint of coffee oak on the nose. The palate offers dark cherry flavours plus hints of pepper and spice. The finish shows fine-grained tannins and good length. This goes well with roast lamb.

QUALITY ★★★★
VALUE ★★★★
GRAPES cabernet sauvignon, merlot
REGION Margaret River, WA
CELLAR 4
ALC./VOL. 13.0%
RRP $16.00

Cape Mentelle Zinfandel

QUALITY ♛♛♛♛♗
VALUE ★★★★½
GRAPES zinfandel
REGION Margaret River, WA
CELLAR 🍷 6
ALC./VOL. 14.5%
RRP $18.90

This is one of the curiosity wines in Australia's inventory. Zinfandel is a popular variety in the USA; in Australia this wine stands out from all the rest. Maker David Hohnen.

Previous outstanding vintages: '81, '82, '84, '88, '90, '91, '92

CURRENT RELEASE 1993 Perhaps just a skerrick lighter in flavour than usual but still a big mutha. The colour is intense and the nose has earth, ripe berry and eucalypt aromas. The palate has a slippery feel thanks to the alcohol, and the main flavour is a tart raspberry. The finish shows soft oak and a warmth of alcohol. It needs a gutsy dish like hare stew.

Cassegrain Merlot

QUALITY ♛♛♛♛
VALUE ★★★★
GRAPES 100% merlot
REGION Hastings, NSW
CELLAR 🍷 4
ALC./VOL. 12.3%
RRP $13.50

Cassegrain is hardly a hobby farm – it's a large venture by the family of the same name on the central coast of northern New South Wales. Maker John Cassegrain.

CURRENT RELEASE 1993 The colour is a deep ruby and the nose has rose-garden, ripe cherry and chocolate aromas. The middleweight palate offers intense cherry/berry characters followed by some discreet tannins on a soft finish. Try it with barbecued lamb straps.

Cassegrain Shiraz

The viticultural demands of this area are steep; humidity and high rainfall mean sophisticated viticultural techniques are applied. Maker John Cassegrain.

CURRENT RELEASE 1993 The colour is a deep crimson and the nose has mint aplenty plus a backdrop of pepper. The palate is a light heavyweight with an attractive dark plum flavour and a pinch of pepper supported by strapping tannin and acid. It has enough power to handle a slightly spicy dish like granny's bean curd.

QUALITY ?????
VALUE ★★★★½
GRAPES shiraz
CELLAR Hastings, NSW
CELLAR 3–6
ALC./VOL. 12.6%
RRP $14.00

Castle Crossing Bin CC1

Castle Crossing is one of the many labels to emanate from the Alambie Wine Company in Mildura.

CURRENT RELEASE 1993 This is a middleweight drink-now style. The colour is mid-ruby and the nose offers soft fruit aromas. There is plenty of ripe berry flavour on the palate followed by some soft tannins on a clean finish. It would go with a pasta disaster.

QUALITY ????
VALUE ★★★★
GRAPES shiraz 49%, malbec 33%, mourvèdre 17%
REGION Mildura, Vic.
CELLAR
ALC./VOL. 12.0%
RRP $8.00

Charles Cimicky Signature Shiraz

The 1991 version made the top ten in last year's edition. The richness continues, thanks to a marvellous vintage. Maker Charles Cimicky.
Previous outstanding vintages: '91

CURRENT RELEASE 1993 Skating close to the edge, thanks to the high alcohol – they don't come much richer than this! The colour is dense and the nose is porty with sweet ripe plum flavours. The palate has a slippery mouthfilling texture and sweet ripe fruit flavours with hints of spice. The finish is characterised by surprisingly soft tannins. It drinks well now with osso bucco.

QUALITY ?????
VALUE ★★★★
GRAPES shiraz
REGION Barossa Valley, SA
CELLAR 2–5+
ALC./VOL. 14.5%
RRP $17.50

Charles Melton Cabernet Sauvignon

QUALITY ♛♛♛♛
VALUE ★★★★
GRAPES cabernet sauvignon
REGION Barossa Valley, SA
CELLAR 🍾 3–6
ALC./VOL. 12.5%
RRP $16.00

A visit to this cellar door is a delight, but be warned: you'll be greeted by Wedgwood the dog whose capacity to emit gas might fool you into thinking the wines have H_2S problems.

CURRENT RELEASE 1994 A very polished style with great structure. The nose has dark cherry aromas plus a hint of spice. The palate is austere at the moment, with mulberry and cassis flavours followed by some attractive new oak. The wine needs time – try it with rare roast beef.

Charles Melton Nine Popes

QUALITY ♛♛♛♛♛
VALUE ★★★★½
GRAPES grenache, shiraz
REGION Barossa Valley, SA
CELLAR 🍾 5
ALC./VOL. 14.5%
RRP $16.00

This is the darling of the wine world. It was meant to be a play on Châteauneuf-du-Pape but these days it is a boot scooter's delight in London and Paris. Maker Graham Melton.

Previous outstanding vintages: '89, '90, '91, '92, '93

CURRENT RELEASE 1994 Big, rich and sensuous, this is all about flavour. The colour is dense and the nose is porty with ripe raspberry flavours. The palate is sweet and rich with strong raspberry and cherry flavours tinged by spice. Delicate tannins on a well-balanced finish. It goes well with a rich casserole.

Charles Melton Rose of Virginia

QUALITY ♛♛♛♛
VALUE ★★★★
GRAPES grenache, cabernet sauvignon
REGION Barossa Valley, SA
CELLAR 🍾 1
ALC./VOL. 12.0%
RRP $12.00

Named after Mrs Virginia Melton, who is a rose by any other name.

CURRENT RELEASE 1995 The colour is a blushing ruby. The nose has a strong lolly component with hints of raspberry. The palate is soft with sweet fruit flavours matched by clean acid. It should be served well chilled with cold cuts.

Charles Melton Shiraz

The confusion over Graham Melton's name comes from the days when he worked for Peter Lehmann. Peter declared he wouldn't have a Graham working in the winery so he called him Charlie. The young Melton refused to answer to the name but when he left to start his own business he named it Charles Melton.

CURRENT RELEASE 1994 Big varietal definition and lots of colour here. The nose has ripe plums and spice aromas. The palate is medium-bodied with taut plum-flavoured fruit and white-pepper spice. The oak treatment is subtle yet supportive. Try it with rare kangaroo.

QUALITY ♛♛♛♛♛
VALUE ★★★★½
GRAPES shiraz
REGION Barossa Valley, SA
CELLAR ➡ 2–6
ALC./VOL. 13.0%
RRP $16.00

Chateau Reynella Cabernet Merlot

Made in the old-fashioned way (basket press, etc.) and it shows. There is a lovely softness and generosity. Last year it was one of the stars of this guide.

Previous outstanding vintages: '92

CURRENT RELEASE 1993 Wonderfully fruity and rich. The colour is a mid-ruby and the nose has mint and primary ferment aromas. The palate is juicy with ripe mulberry and raspberry flavours followed by soft tannins on a gentle finish. It is a smooth, almost seamless product that goes well with pasta and a meat sauce.

QUALITY ♛♛♛♛
VALUE ★★★★
GRAPES cabernet sauvignon, merlot
REGION McLaren Vale, SA
CELLAR ↓ 6
ALC./VOL. 14.0%
RRP $16.00

Chateau Xanadu Cabernet Franc

QUALITY 🍷🍷🍷⟨
VALUE ★★★
GRAPES cabernet franc
REGION Margaret River, WA
CELLAR 🍷 3
ALC./VOL. 13.5%
RRP $20.00

There is an eccentricity about this place: '... weave a circle round him thrice and close your eyes in holy dread ...' Sometimes it is hard to take the place and proprietor seriously. (MS wants to be 'included out!' and would rather just review the wines.)

CURRENT RELEASE 1993 An intense wine with attractive packaging, but the question about nude cabernet franc needs to be asked – why? The nose is highly perfumed and the colour is a mid-ruby. The medium-bodied palate has sweet cherry/berry fruit that is almost immediately swamped by brand-spanking-new French oak. Interesting as a contrast with osso bucco.

Chateau Xanadu Cabernet Sauvignon

QUALITY 🍷🍷🍷🍷
VALUE ★★★
GRAPES cabernet sauvignon
REGION Margaret River, WA
CELLAR ⟶ 2–6
ALC./VOL. 13.0%
RRP $20.00

This winery-cum-vineyard was established in 1977 and the production now is in the order of 10,000 cases.

CURRENT RELEASE 1993 A tough, youthful style that has a dense colour and a nose with a strong hint of ripe berries plus talcum-powder oak characters. The palate is intense with dark cherry flavours followed by some awkward tannins and an aggressive finish. An astringent style that can be drunk with buffalo steaks.

Clonakilla Shiraz

This is one of the many vineyards dotted around the ACT region. It was established in 1971 by Dr John Kirk. Production is around 600 cases.

CURRENT RELEASE 1993 Because of the cool climate this would have to be a marginal area for ripening this variety. The colour is dense and the nose is loaded with pepper spice. The palate is lean and austere, and again the spice dominates. The finish is astringent with heavy tannins. A hard wine that needs time. Try it with sharp cheese.

QUALITY ♀♀♀
VALUE ★★★
GRAPES shiraz
REGION Canberra district, NSW
CELLAR ← 4–6
ALC./VOL. 12.7%
RRP $17.00 (cellar door)

Coldstream Hills Cabernet Merlot

Proprietor James Halliday is known around the world as a wine writer and commentator. Originally committed to the Hunter Valley, James defected to Victoria in 1985.

CURRENT RELEASE 1993 An elegant style that is a little less ripe. The nose has leaf and cassis aromas and the medium-bodied palate has raspberry and cherry flavours that combine with well-directed oak on an astringent finish. Try it with a veal goulash.

QUALITY ♀♀♀♀
VALUE ★★★½
GRAPES cabernet sauvignon, merlot, cabernet franc
REGION Yarra Valley, Vic.
CELLAR ↕ 4
ALC./VOL. 12.5%
RRP $19.00

Coldstream Hills Pinot Noir

QUALITY ♟♟♟♟♙
VALUE ★★★★
GRAPES pinot noir
REGION Yarra Valley, Vic.
CELLAR 🍾 4
ALC./VOL. 13.0%
RRP $20.00

It's a dream writing about Coldstream Hills because all the research is on the back label. The home vineyard is 25 hectares and produces 3500 cases. The winery was established in 1985 and total production is 21,000 cases. Maker Phillip Dowell.

Previous outstanding vintages: '93

CURRENT RELEASE 1994 A charming wine that is at the string quartet end of the pinot spectrum. It has a clean cherry-scented nose and the palate offers abundant sweet dark cherry flavours. The finish shows off some politically correct oak that adds discreet grip. Drinks well with char-grilled quail.

Coriole Cabernet Sauvignon

QUALITY ♟♟♟♟
VALUE ★★★★
GRAPES cabernet sauvignon
REGION McLaren Vale, SA
CELLAR 🍾 4
ALC./VOL. 13.0%
RRP $16.50

Founded in 1969, this was one of the first renaissance vineyards. Today it is an established label with a production of 12,000 cases a year. Maker Stephen Hall.

Previous outstanding vintages: '90, '91

CURRENT RELEASE 1992 A very well balanced style that gives substance to the saying 'McLaren Vale is the middle palate of Australian wine'. The nose is fragrant with strong cassis aromas. The palate has generous blackberry flavours plus hints of earth. This is attuned to some well-integrated oak on a long finish. It drinks well now with oxtail stew.

Coriole Mary Kathleen

A wine named after the matriarch of the founding Lloyd family. Mary Kathleen is responsible for the naïve paintings seen on the white wine labels. CURRENT RELEASE 1993 A classy, stylish wine that trades on complexity. The structure is the key. It is indeed a fine wine with a fragrant nose of strong cassis aromas. The palate is complex with strong red berry flavours tuned to an oak treatment that adds structure and grip. It drinks well now with venison steak.

QUALITY 🍷🍷🍷🍷?
VALUE ★★★★
GRAPES cabernet sauvignon, merlot, cabernet franc
REGION McLaren Vale, SA
CELLAR 🍾 2–6
ALC./VOL. 13.0%
RRP $18.00

Coriole Redstone

This is Coriole's fighting brand, meant to capture the hearts and minds of the bistro bunnies. It should do well.
CURRENT RELEASE 1994 Lots of fun by the glass. The alcohol and flavour make this an ideal bistro style. The nose has plenty of sweet ripe-fruit aromas. The ample palate has plenty of fruit flavours augmented by supportive oak on a well-adjusted finish. Great value for money – let the pasta roll!

QUALITY 🍷🍷🍷🍷?
VALUE ★★★★½
GRAPES cabernet sauvignon, shiraz
REGION McLaren Vale, SA
CELLAR 🍾 3
ALC./VOL. 14.0%
RRP $11.95

Coriole Sangiovese

Coriole is a far-sighted venture – for years this winery has been pioneering the cause for sangiovese. It's a good bet they are well on target, because there is growing interest in such varieties. CURRENT RELEASE 1993 The colour is deceptively light with a bright ruby colour. The nose is packed full of ripe berries. The middleweight palate has an interesting mix of wild fruit with a cocoa undertone. Bracing acid follows on a crisp, dry finish. It could be served chilled with antipasto.

QUALITY 🍷🍷🍷🍷
VALUE ★★★★
GRAPES sangiovese
REGION McLaren Vale, SA
CELLAR 🍾 3
ALC./VOL. 14.0%
RRP $13.00

Coriole Shiraz

QUALITY ♛♛♛♛
VALUE ★★★★
GRAPES shiraz
REGION McLaren Vale, SA
CELLAR 🍾 6
ALC./VOL. 14.0%
RRP $14.00

This is the mother lode from this vineyard, and the first examples in the early '70s captured the punters' attention. (In those days they sold for $1.60 a bottle ...)
Previous outstanding vintages: '88, '91
CURRENT RELEASE 1993 Let the good times roll – this is the right stuff! A big brawny style that has plenty of flavour. The nose has a down-and-dirty component with earth and sap aromas. The palate is robust with ripe plum and spice flavours matched by well-tuned oak on a dry, grippy finish. It is a lovable, faithful-hound style. Have it with a beef and mushroom pie.

Craigow Pinot Noir

QUALITY ♛♛♛♛
VALUE ★★★½
GRAPES pinot noir
REGION Coal River Valley, Tas.
CELLAR 🍾 3+
ALC./VOL. 13.2%
RRP $20.00 (mail order)

A spectacular convict-built stone house sits atop a hill beside this vineyard, and both are the property of Hobart surgeon Barry Edwards, whose main plantings are pinot noir, with some riesling. Maker Andrew Hood.
CURRENT RELEASE 1994 A promising early release from this young vineyard, with the arresting dark colour typical of the Tasmanian '94 vintage pinots. This is a big-fruit wine, full of sweet cherry flavour but not especially complex, although it may build interest with a year or so in bottle. Char-grilled squab would work well.

Crawford River Cabernet Sauvignon

This is a Western District vineyard and winery that belongs to the Thomson family. It was founded in 1982 and the annual production is around 3000 cases. Maker John Thomson.

CURRENT RELEASE 1991 Starting to show some bottle development and a considerable crust. The colour is dense and the nose has strong raspberry jam aromas. The palate is tight with muted berry flavours and bracken characters matched by some fine-grained tannins on a dry, grippy finish. It goes very well with steak and kidney.

QUALITY ♛♛♛♛
VALUE ★★★
GRAPES cabernet sauvignon, cabernet franc, merlot
REGION Western District, Vic.
CELLAR ⊕ 3–6
ALC./VOL. 13.0%
RRP $19.00

CURRENT RELEASE 1993 A tough unyielding style with a dense colour and perfumed nose. The palate is tight and lean. Heavy metal wood seems to dominate a slightly stalky finish. This is still very youthful and for the time being it's better in the cellar than in the glass.

QUALITY ♛♛♛
VALUE ★★★
GRAPES cabernet sauvignon, cabernet franc, merlot
REGION Western District, Vic.
CELLAR ⊕ 4–8
ALC./VOL. 13.5%
RRP $19.00

Dalwhinnie Cabernet

Very low yields enable Dalwhinnie to produce very concentrated, profound reds from their blessed pocket of soil adjacent to Taltarni. Maker David Jones.

Previous outstanding vintages: '80, '84, '86, '88, '90, '92

CURRENT RELEASE 1993 Another superb red from Dalwhinnie, who seem to have worked out the secret of their vines. The colour, nose and palate all show concentration and masses of toasty oak, and ripe dark berry fruit permeate the wine. The fruit rises above the substantial tannins, which are nice and supple. A superbly structured wine of incredible length. Drink with hard cheeses.

QUALITY ♛♛♛♛♛
VALUE ★★★★★
GRAPES cabernet sauvignon
REGION Pyrenees, Vic.
CELLAR ⊕ 2–10+
ALC./VOL. 14.0%
RRP $23.50

Dalwhinnie Shiraz

QUALITY 🍷🍷🍷🍷🍷
VALUE ★★★★½
GRAPES shiraz
REGION Pyrenees, Vic.
CELLAR 2–10+
ALC./VOL. 14.0%
RRP $26.00

Founded by Ballarat architect Ewan Jones and family in 1976, Dalwhinnie is a small planting of very low-yielding vines which give concentrated, serious wines. They seem to get better each year. Maker David Jones.

Previous outstanding vintages: '80, '85, '88, '90, '91, '92

CURRENT RELEASE 1993 Dalwhinnie can do no wrong in recent times: this is another sensational shiraz and a contender for the title of best in Australia. The flavours are an irresistible combination of pepper, spices and toasty oak with cedar and vanilla highlights. There's great weight of sweet fruit and a firm structure that avoids mouth-numbing tannin. A wonderful red wine, remarkably complex even in infancy. Cellar or drink with barbecued kangaroo.

David Traeger Cabernet Sauvignon

QUALITY 🍷🍷🍷
VALUE ★★★
GRAPES cabernet sauvignon, cabernet franc, merlot
REGION Nagambie & King Valley, Vic.
CELLAR 4+
ALC./VOL. 12.5%
RRP $15.30

Traeger worked for Mitchelton for a number of years before striking out on his own. He crafts wines from other people's grapes, sourced from around the Nagambie region.

CURRENT RELEASE 1992 A pleasant mediumweight cabernet with toasty/cedary oak, a hint of gaminess, and some flesh and sweetness on the palate. A trace of astringency on the finish doesn't prevent it from being drink-now in style. Try it with braised lamb shanks.

David Wynn Patriarch Shiraz

David Wynn was the patriarch of the distinguished Wynn family and hopefully it will continue now that he's passed away. Maker Adam Wynn.

Previous outstanding vintages: '92

CURRENT RELEASE 1993 A big, liquorice/plummy ripe style of Barossa shiraz, perhaps a bit more rustic than the stylish '92. The fruit has a plum-jam quality and the flavour is robust, generous and intense with a very full, long finish. Needs a hearty game pie.

QUALITY ♥♥♥♥
VALUE ★★★½
GRAPES shiraz
REGION Barossa & Eden Valleys, SA
CELLAR 6+
ALC./VOL. 13.5%
RRP $19.35

David Wynn Shiraz

David Wynn was one of the delightful gentlemen of the wine business, who was also a marketing and financial genius. He died aged 80 in February 1995, leaving an indelible mark on the arts as well as the wine industry. Maker Adam Wynn.

CURRENT RELEASE 1994 A fruit style with lots of sweet, berryish fruit out front and a certain curranty aspect, underlined by some floral, coconutty oak. The wine is fairly simple and has a firm tannin finish. It would team well with civet of hare, made with a little of the wine in the sauce.

QUALITY ♥♥♥♥
VALUE ★★★½
GRAPES shiraz
REGION Barossa & Eden Valleys, SA
CELLAR 4
ALC./VOL. 13.0%
RRP $12.90

De Bortoli Montage Red Blend

The label depicts scenes from the De Bortoli Yarra Valley property, where an excellent restaurant serves northern Italian food.

CURRENT RELEASE 1993 A gentle, innocuous red which, as the title suggests, avoids varietal identity. The nose is nondescript; the taste is smooth with light tannins and an easy drinkability, if lacking personality. Try veal scalloppine.

QUALITY ♥♥♥
VALUE ★★★
GRAPES not stated
REGION Southern Victoria
CELLAR 1
ALC./VOL. 12.5%
RRP $11.60 ⓢ

De Bortoli Sacred Hill Shiraz Cabernet

QUALITY 🍷🍷🍷
VALUE ★★★½
GRAPES shiraz, cabernet sauvignon
REGION Riverina, NSW
CELLAR 🍾 1
ALC./VOL. 12.0%
RRP $5.80 ⓢ

According to legend, a paranoid recluse, acting on the orders of a 'white lady' in a vision, retired to defend his sacred hill against an enemy. The hill overlooks the De Bortoli complex near Griffith.

CURRENT RELEASE 1993 This is a light-bodied, straight-up-and-down red with little apparent wood but adequate sweet-berry and green-leafy fruit. Not a wine for close analysis but decent quaffing value. Would suit toad in the hole.

De Bortoli Windy Peak Cabernets Shiraz Merlot

QUALITY 🍷🍷🍷🍷
VALUE ★★★★
GRAPES cabernet sauvignon, cabernet franc, shiraz, merlot
REGION Yarra & King Valleys, Vic.
CELLAR 🍾 4
ALC./VOL. 13.0%
RRP $12.20 ⓢ

With today's labelling laws, this is the sort of convoluted name you get when you blend four grape varieties.

Previous outstanding vintages: '91, '92

CURRENT RELEASE 1993 Designed as a drink-now which can be cellared, this hits the bull's-eye. An elegant wine with leafy cedary cabernet aromas and a fruit-sweet complement of blackberry and raspberry in the mouth. It is quite full with some tannin but the balance makes it approachable now. Try it with steak and kidney pie.

De Bortoli Yarra Valley Cabernet Merlot

QUALITY 🍷🍷🍷⸱
VALUE ★★★
GRAPES cabernet sauvignon, cabernet franc, merlot
REGION Yarra Valley, SA
CELLAR 🍾 3+
ALC./VOL. 12.5%
RRP $19.30 ⓢ

Blends of cabernet and merlot have well and truly supplanted the traditional Aussie cab-shiraz blend these days.

CURRENT RELEASE 1992 This has excellent colour and a pungent aroma of Ribena/cassis. The same character flows through to the palate, where it's mediumweight with some concentration and a slight gap in the middle. Fine with meaty lasagne.

De Bortoli Yarra Valley Pinot Noir

The pinots grown on the warmer side of the Yarra Valley, where De Bortoli lies, are a different style to the cooler Seville-Coldstream's side.
Previous outstanding vintages: '89
CURRENT RELEASE 1992 A nice minty, soft dry red, rather than a definitive pinot. It has good colour depth, a hint of gumleaf on the dark berry/mint nose and a fruit-sweet middle palate with good persistence and smooth tannin. Try with lamb kebabs.

QUALITY ▼▼▼▼
VALUE ★★★
GRAPES pinot noir
REGION Yarra Valley, Vic.
CELLAR 2
ALC./VOL. 12.5%
RRP $19.30

De Bortoli Yarra Valley Shiraz

This is one of the few shirazes in the Yarra. It's surprising that a wine of this calibre is still lingering on the shop shelves. Makers Steve Webber and David Slingsby-Smith.
CURRENT RELEASE 1992 Here's a stylish red with cedary/toasty oak and spicy cool-grown shiraz fruit superbly entwined. The depth and balance are most impressive. The palate is smooth and lush with oodles of fruit. Drink with peppered steak.

QUALITY ▼▼▼▼▼
VALUE ★★★★
GRAPES shiraz
REGION Yarra Valley, Vic.
CELLAR 6+
ALC./VOL. 12.5%
RRP $20.30 ⓢ

Deen De Bortoli Vat 8 Shiraz

This range of wines draws on grapes from the Riverina and several other regions, such as the King Valley. Makers Darren De Bortoli and Nick Guy.
CURRENT RELEASE 1994 A fruit-driven shiraz which smells of slightly stewed fruit, although varietal notes of spice and plum chime in as well. There's good depth of fruit and some astringency to finish. While it's straightforward, a year or two in the cellar won't hurt and it's well priced. Grill some spicy sausages for this one.

QUALITY ▼▼▼▼
VALUE ★★★★
GRAPES shiraz
REGION King Valley, Vic.
CELLAR 5
ALC./VOL. 12.5%
RRP $9.00 ⓢ

Delamere Pinot Noir

QUALITY ♛♛♛
VALUE ★★★
GRAPES pinot noir
REGION Pipers Brook, Tas.
CELLAR 🍶 3
ALC./VOL. 12.5%
RRP $23.00

Richard and Dallas Richardson have decided to move on, and Delamere, sadly, is for sale. Richardson's chardonnays and pinot noirs have been nothing if not individual: sometimes superb and often challenging.

Previous outstanding vintages: '90

CURRENT RELEASE 1993 Pale colour shows premature development, but that is par for the course with this maker. Again, typically, the nose has a lot of sappy, stalky character as well as spice and cherry, which translate onto a lightweight palate. A pleasant rather than great vintage. Try spaghetti marinara.

Delatite Pinot Noir

QUALITY ♛♛♛♛½
VALUE ★★★★½
GRAPES pinot noir
REGION Mansfield, Vic.
CELLAR 🍶 3+
ALC./VOL. 14.0%
RRP $17.40

The Ritchie family's reds are often laced with mint character which tends to dominate proceedings, but this one happily is not.

CURRENT RELEASE 1994 An impressive pinot, showing strawberry and cherry fruit aromas with true varietal character and charm. The palate has stylish brandied cherry, vanilla, and hints of liquorice with good concentration and length. More, please!

Dennis Cabernet Sauvignon

QUALITY ♛♛♛♛
VALUE ★★★★
GRAPES cabernet sauvignon
REGION McLaren Vale, SA
CELLAR 🍶 8+
ALC./VOL. 14.0%
RRP $13.50

They say McLaren Vale is the middle palate of Australian red wine, and this wine shows why.

CURRENT RELEASE 1993 This is a big rich chunky regional style, smelling of dark berries and ripe plums, with excellent penetrating chocolatey, berry flavours in the mouth. A warm, rich wine with a good future. Drink it with veal kidneys.

Dennis Shiraz

This small winery with its 20-hectare vineyard makes some superb but low-profile wines. Maker Peter Dennis.

CURRENT RELEASE 1992 Super-ripe, concentrated pepper/spice and plummy fruit is the hallmark of this rich, fleshy shiraz. The palate has liquorice and ripe berry flavours and there's a whiff of mint. Still youthful and will repay cellaring. Try it with goulash.

QUALITY ♛♛♛♛♛
VALUE ★★★★½
GRAPES shiraz
REGION McLaren Vale, SA
CELLAR 🍷 7+
ALC./VOL. 14.0%
RRP $13.50

Devil's Lair Cabernet Merlot

This vineyard is at the southern end of the Margaret River region. A few locals have been heard to say it grows some of the region's best grapes.

CURRENT RELEASE 1992 The colour and flavour suggest concentrated grapes. Dense blackberry and green-leafy fruit are nicely partnered by cedary French oak. The palate is intense, lively and astringent, with oak in good support. A hint of volatility does not worry. Needs time, then drink with lamb and pesto sauce.

QUALITY ♛♛♛♛
VALUE ★★★½
GRAPES cabernet sauvignon, merlot
REGION Margaret River, WA
CELLAR 🍷 2–6+
ALC./VOL. 13.0%
RRP $22.50

Devil's Lair Cabernet Sauvignon

This is a relatively new (and very attractive) label and its makers know how to charge. They justify the prices by way of low yields and expensive French oak.

CURRENT RELEASE 1993 This fresh and rather raw youngster has quite a green-leafy nose but there are scents of flowers and berries too, making for a captivating sniff. The mid-palate is nice and full with callow astringency and a lively farewell. Cellar, then try with barbecued lamb fillet.

QUALITY ♛♛♛♛
VALUE ★★★
GRAPES cabernet sauvignon 85%, merlot 10%, cabernet franc 5%
REGION Margaret River, WA
CELLAR 🍷 3–7+
ALC./VOL. 13.5%
RRP $25.00

Diamond Valley Blue Label Cabernet Sauvignon

QUALITY ♛♛♛
VALUE ★★★
GRAPES cabernet sauvignon
REGION Yarra Valley, Vic.
CELLAR 🍷 2
ALC./VOL. 13.1%
RRP $16.40

This maker's cabernet style tends to the leafier end of the Yarra Valley spectrum. Maker David Lance.
CURRENT RELEASE 1992 An intriguing blend of sweet berry and leafy/capsicum aromas greets the nose. The wine is smooth, supple and very approachable now, with a soft finish and the lightest of tannins. Not a wine to keep, but enjoy with veal.

Diamond Valley Blue Label Pinot Noir

QUALITY ♛♛♛♛
VALUE ★★★
GRAPES pinot noir
REGION Yarra Valley, Vic.
CELLAR 🍷 2
ALC./VOL. 13.1%
RRP $18.70

David Lance has carved out a name as one of the best producers of pinot noir in Australia, a reputation greatly helped along by considerable show success. This one's made from bought-in grapes.
Previous outstanding vintages: '92
CURRENT RELEASE 1993 This is the 'Bourgogne pinot noir' or lesser Burgundy of the Lance range. The colour is rather pale and developed, but don't be fooled: this is a wine of subtle charms. It has a developed fungal earthy bouquet with vegetal and gamey complexities. The weight is lightish but there is good flavour intensity: a style cut out for pasta.

Diamond Valley Estate Pinot Noir

The Lances of Diamond Valley have just two acres of pinot noir vines, but since they were planted in 1976 that little patch has won 24 trophies at major wine shows, which gives an idea of just how blessed a piece of dirt it is.
Previous outstanding vintages: '86, '87, '90, '91, '92
CURRENT RELEASE 1993 Simply, a great pinot! Unlike some other Yarra '93 pinots this has extraordinary depth of colour, matching its wonderful concentration and sweetness. There's an intoxicating complex of vanilla, cherry and gamey flavours, without stalkiness; the lush fruit and subtle oak carrying a powerful palate to a long, lingering finish. Celebrate with spit-roasted quail.

QUALITY ▼▼▼▼▼
VALUE ★★★★★
GRAPES pinot noir
REGION Yarra Valley, Vic.
CELLAR 🍷 4+
ALC./VOL. 13.5%
RRP $33.50

Best Pinot Noir

Doonkuna Estate Shiraz

The motto of this winery is a hearty 'Furth, fortune and fill the fetters' – a nice touch of alliteration – and the label has a bold and striking design.
CURRENT RELEASE 1992 This vineyard has a severe case of almost-central Victorian gumleaf/mintiness. The nose is subdued pepper/spice and eucalyptus with peppermint growing as it airs. It has a stylish palate with lively, elegant peppermint and berry flavours and a smooth, pleasing harmony. Try it with kangaroo.

QUALITY ▼▼▼▼
VALUE ★★★½
GRAPES shiraz
REGION Canberra district, NSW
CELLAR 🍷 6+
ALC./VOL. 12.6%
RRP $17.70

Doonkuna Pinot Noir

QUALITY 🍷🍷🍷
VALUE ★★★
GRAPES pinot noir
REGION Canberra district, NSW
CELLAR 🍾 3
ALC./VOL. 12.6%
RRP $13.00 (cellar door)

The Canberra district has the potential to be at the forefront of Australian pinot noir, but it still has a way to go.
CURRENT RELEASE 1992 A big, blood-and-guts style that packs plenty of flavour but precious little authentic pinot finesse. The nose is all gumleaf/mint and the palate is tannic and somewhat tough. For those who like a boots-and-all pinot. Try lamb with mint sauce.

Dromana Estate Pinot Noir

QUALITY 🍷🍷🍷
VALUE ★★½
GRAPES pinot noir
REGION Mornington Peninsula, Vic.
CELLAR 🍾 2
ALC./VOL. 13.0%
RRP $19.30

Garry Crittenden is a former nurseryman who turned his green thumbs to grapegrowing at Dromana, which used to be better known as a beach holiday destination.
Previous outstanding vintages: '91
CURRENT RELEASE 1994 In keeping with the maker's style, this is a simple, light-bodied pinot with a decided lack of concentration. What flavour there is, is good: sweet cherry/strawberry. But the wine is short and wispy and stands comparison only with Beaujolais. Enjoyable with smoked salmon.

Eaglehawk Shiraz Merlot Cabernet Sauvignon

QUALITY 🍷🍷🍷🍷
VALUE ★★★★
GRAPES shiraz, merlot, cabernet sauvignon
REGION various, SA
CELLAR 🍾 2
ALC./VOL. 12.0%
RRP $8.95

Mildara Blass scored a coup when they acquired the services of David O'Leary who now looks after this brand. O'Leary made his reputation at Chateau Reynella.
CURRENT RELEASE 1993 An easy-drinking style that has leaf and tobacco aromas on the nose. The palate is soft and fruity with some cherry flavours balanced by clean acid and gentle tannin on a dry finish. Great with a cornish pastie.

Eden Ridge Cabernet Sauvignon

This is the organic label from Mountadam. Maker 'Up and Adam' Wynn believes there will be a growing market for such wines.

CURRENT RELEASE 1993 The colour is an intense purple-ruby and the nose has strong berry aromas plus some smoky oak. The substantial palate shows sweet ripe fruit flavours with a hint of spice. Well-tuned oak completes the finish by adding grip from fine-grained tannins. It needs a cuddly casserole.

QUALITY ♟♟♟♟
VALUE ★★★★
GRAPES cabernet sauvignon
REGION Barossa Valley, SA
CELLAR 🍷 4
ALC./VOL. 12.5%
RRP $15.00 ✪

Elderton Cabernet Sauvignon

This winery was part of the new-guard revolution that swept through the Barossa in the early '80s. The '92 vintage was a Jimmy Watson Memorial Trophy Winner in 1993.

CURRENT RELEASE 1993 This wine is all about fruit, oak and alcohol, in large measures. The nose has ripe fruit aromas plus some high-tone toasty oak. The palate is massive with slabs of fruit supported by lively oak adding a vanillan lift. At present the oak is a little oppressive but time in the bottle will settle that – try it with rare roast beef and Yorkshire pud.

QUALITY ♟♟♟♟♟
VALUE ★★★★★
GRAPES cabernet sauvignon
REGION Barossa Valley, SA
CELLAR ➴ 3–7
ALC./VOL. 14.5%
RRP $19.00

Eldredge Cabernet Sauvignon

This is a new label in the Clare Valley. It was made by Tim Adams, as a consultant, for long-established grapegrowers.

CURRENT RELEASE 1992 The colour is a mid-ruby and the vinous nose has ripe berry characters plus a whisper of wood. The middleweight palate offers clean berry flavours with raspberry dominant. Fine-grained tannins follow on a finish that is spiced by oak. It's very well balanced and ready to drink now. Try it with pasta and a meat sauce.

QUALITY ♟♟♟♟
VALUE ★★★★
GRAPES cabernet sauvignon, shiraz
REGION Clare Valley, SA
CELLAR 🍷 3
ALC./VOL. 13.0%
RRP $15.00

Elsewhere Pinot Noir

QUALITY 🍷🍷🍷🍷🍷
VALUE ★★★★
GRAPES pinot noir
REGION Huon Valley, Tas.
CELLAR 🍾 3+
ALC./VOL. 12.5%
RRP $15.00 (cellar door)

Eric and Jette Phillips's aptly named vineyard is in the remote channel country, south of Hobart, where one might expect it to be too cold and wet to grow grapes. Not so! Maker Andrew Hood. Previous outstanding vintages: '91, '93

CURRENT RELEASE 1994 A major success here, with a gold medal at the Tasmanian Wine Show. Deep colour; rich plum and vanilla aromas; full, fruit-sweet palate with chocolatey flavours and appropriate tannin to finish. Serve with country-style terrine.

Evans & Tate Barrique 61

QUALITY 🍷🍷🍷🍷
VALUE ★★★★
GRAPES cabernet sauvignon, merlot
REGION Great Southern, WA
CELLAR 🍾 3
ALC./VOL. 13.0%
RRP $15.00

There are no clues to the significance of Barrique 61 – is it like Brazil 66? Maker Brian Fletcher.

CURRENT RELEASE 1993 This is a well-made drink-now style. It has an attractive blackberry nose. There is a complex mix of cherries and blackberries on a middleweight palate supported by discreet oak on a well-integrated finish. It goes well with pink lamb and mint sauce.

Evans & Tate Margaret River Hermitage

QUALITY 🍷🍷🍷🍷
VALUE ★★★★
GRAPES shiraz
REGION Margaret River, WA
CELLAR 🍾 5
ALC./VOL. 13.0%
RRP $16.00

This is a very progressive company that markets aggressively. There are some very fine wines in the stable. Maker Brian Fletcher.

CURRENT RELEASE 1992 Rhône on the range – this is a very French style with a deep red-purple colour and a spicy varietal nose. A sweet berry character on the mouthfilling palate is balanced by dusty oak on a firm dry finish. It should cellar well. Try it with a hearty casserole.

Evans & Tate Margaret River Merlot

If you could bottle hype this company would have a limitless supply. Mind you, they don't do a bad job of making wine either. Maker Brian Fletcher.

CURRENT RELEASE 1993 Very merlot with a strong varietal nose. There are cherry, talcum-powder and rose-petal aromas on the nose with plums and cherries on the palate that has a hint of chocolate. Soft tannins make for a benign finish. It drinks well now with lamb chops.

QUALITY ♥♥♥
VALUE ★★½
GRAPES merlot
REGION Margaret River, WA
CELLAR 🍷 4
ALC./VOL. 14.0%
RRP $25.00

Eyton on Yarra Cabernet Merlot

The Yarra Valley is proving to have quite a benign climate. Less prone to drought than most areas and with moderate temperatures, it seems a logical place for vineyard expansion.

CURRENT RELEASE 1993 A youthful style that already has drinkability and softness. The nose shows sap, leaf and cherry aromas. The palate is medium-bodied but doesn't want for fruit flavour. There are cassis and dark cherry touches that are graced by soft tannins on a gentle finish. It drinks well with pink lamb chops.

QUALITY ♥♥♥
VALUE ★★★★
GRAPES cabernet sauvignon, merlot
REGION Yarra Valley, Vic.
CELLAR 🍷 4
ALC./VOL. 13.0%
RRP $18.00

Eyton on Yarra Merlot

Yet another label from the burgeoning Yarra Valley. They are playing for keeps here and we can expect some spectacular wines. Pity about the toffee name. Maker Tony Royal.

CURRENT RELEASE 1994 More satisfying than most merlots, this wine has substance and style. The colour is deep and the nose has strong berry aromas. The palate is a light heavyweight with strong berry character balanced by some well-integrated oak on a lively finish. Perfect with tandoori lamb.

QUALITY ♥♥♥♥
VALUE ★★★★½
GRAPES merlot
REGION Yarra Valley, Vic.
CELLAR 🍷 3
ALC./VOL. 12.5%
RRP $18.00

Fern Hill Estate Cabernet Sauvignon

QUALITY ♥♥♥♥
VALUE ★★★★
GRAPES cabernet sauvignon
REGION McLaren Vale, SA
CELLAR 🍷 6
ALC./VOL. 14.0%
RRP $18.00

Trivia buffs will know that Tyrrell's red winemaker Andrew Thomas is the son of Fern Hill's founder Wayne Thomas. Present owner is Terry Hill.

CURRENT RELEASE 1992 This is a generous lump of a wine with some forward development that does no harm to the leathery, earthy regional characters and rich, fruit-sweet middle palate. The nice dry tannin finish lingers well. A food wine with loads of character. Try it with saddle of hare.

Fern Hill Estate Shiraz

QUALITY ♥♥♥♥
VALUE ★★★
GRAPES shiraz
REGION McLaren Vale, SA
CELLAR 🍷 4+
ALC./VOL. 14.5%
RRP $18.00

Wayne Thomas has sold Thomas's Fern Hill at McLaren Vale and this is the first of the new regime's wines. New owner is aptly-named wine marketer Terry Hill. Maker Grant Burge.

CURRENT RELEASE 1992 A rich, fleshy, generous red with somewhat domineering oakiness. Toasty, savoury, woody nose with some attractive spice peeping through; good depth and length with plenty of smooth tannin. Suits traditional French cassoulet.

Fiddlers Creek Cabernet Shiraz

QUALITY ♥♥♥
VALUE ★★★½
GRAPES cabernet sauvignon, shiraz
REGION Pyrenees, Vic.
CELLAR 🍷 3
ALC./VOL. 12.5%
RRP $8.85 Ⓢ

Dare we say this is the second string of Chateau Remy's red wine repertoire? It's named after a creek where musical gold-miners camped during Avoca's gold-mining days. Maker Vincent Gere.

CURRENT RELEASE 1994 This is certainly no fiddle: it's good value, in fact. Youthful, fragrant cherry and vanilla aromas; lightweight but pleasant, simple flavour with a gentle tannin finish. A fine pasta wine.

Fire Gully Cabernets Merlot

The Fire Gully label, with its violent red and orange colours, leaves one in no doubt how the place got its name.

CURRENT RELEASE 1992 This is a mild, drink-now red with leafy, tobacco-like aromas, and a lean palate with some fruit sweetness and respectable depth of ripe, yet herbaceous flavour. Try it with lamb and pesto sauce.

QUALITY ♛♛♛
VALUE ★★★
GRAPES cabernet sauvignon, cabernet franc, merlot
REGION Margaret River, WA
CELLAR 🍷 3
ALC./VOL. 12.0%
RRP $17.00

Fire Gully Pinot Noir

Mike Peterkin, an accomplished full-time physician as well as the distinguished winemaker of Pierro, buys grapes from his neighbours' vineyards for the Fire Gully wines.

CURRENT RELEASE 1993 A straightforward pinot which relies on oak and tannin to carry the day. The flavour is dominated by vanilla and there is some grunt to the palate, mainly thanks to wood. Suits pasta with a mushroom sauce.

QUALITY ♛♛♛
VALUE ★★★
GRAPES pinot noir
REGION Margaret River, WA
CELLAR 🍷 2
ALC./VOL. 13.5%
RRP $13.70

Frankland Estate Olmo's Reward

American viticulturist Prof. Harold Olmo had a hand in selecting the Frankland River region of WA for grapegrowing, after a visit in 1955. This is a way of saying 'Ta, Harold'.

CURRENT RELEASE 1992 Not a lot has happened with this wine since last year's review: it's a big fruit style without overt oak. There's a linseed character on the nose and the mouth has straightforward plummy flavour and assertive tannin. Don't be in a hurry to drink it, then serve with lamb.

QUALITY ♛♛♛♛
VALUE ★★★½
GRAPES cabernet franc 43%, merlot 43%, cabernet sauvignon 10.5%, malbec 3.5%
REGION Frankland River, WA
CELLAR ⊸ 2–5+
ALC./VOL. 13.0%
RRP $24.00

Freycinet Cabernet Sauvignon

QUALITY 🍷🍷🍷🍷
VALUE ★★★★
GRAPES cabernet sauvignon, cabernet franc, merlot
REGION East coast, Tas.
CELLAR 🍷 1–6+
ALC./VOL. 13.5%
RRP $35.00

Freycinet's well-chosen site in a suntrap and rain shadow on the east coast of Tassie is one of the few places on the island where cabernet ripens well and regularly. Owner Geoff Bull is a former newspaper photographer who made his fortune diving for abalone.

Previous outstanding vintages: '91

CURRENT RELEASE 1993 This is a surprisingly concentrated wine for a Taswegian cab: rich, muscular dark berries and vanilla, plenty of fruit sweetness and tannin. A major success and should go well with rare rack of venison.

Freycinet Pinot Noir

QUALITY 🍷🍷🍷🍷🍷
VALUE ★★★★
GRAPES pinot noir
REGION East Coast, Tas.
CELLAR 🍷 4
ALC./VOL. 13.5%
RRP $35.00

The east coast of Tassie near the Freycinet Peninsula is a special location: this vineyard achieves healthy yields as well as remarkable depth of flavour. Makers Lindy Bull and Claudio Radenti.

Previous outstanding vintages: '91, '92, '93

CURRENT RELEASE 1994 A slightly lighter and less structured wine than the monster '93 but yet another cracking pinot from this impressive vineyard. Sweet, complex strawberry/cherry aromas, with a sappy overtone. In the mouth it's smooth and balanced with brandied-cherry flavour. Would suit spit-roasted quail.

Galafrey Pinot Noir

Galafrey is the land of origin for the Time Lords from the TV series *Dr Who*. (MS believes Tom Baker was the best Dr Who.) Maker Ian Tyrer.

CURRENT RELEASE 1992 An interesting style with a strong resinous nose with hints of floor polish. The palate is a contrast, with sweet strawberry flavour followed by a firm, almost splintery finish. Try it with quail.

QUALITY 🍷🍷🍷
VALUE ★★★
GRAPES pinot noir
REGION Great Southern, WA
CELLAR 🍾 3
ALC./VOL. 12.0%
RRP $15.00

Galafrey Shiraz

The winery and cellar door were until recently located in a converted 100-year-old wool store on the waterfront at Albany, Western Australia. They have since moved the whole operation to the vineyard. Maker Ian Tyrer.

CURRENT RELEASE 1992 An elegant style that shows restrained power. There're plenty of pepper and spice aromas; the palate offers sweet fruit with ample ripe plum flavour balanced by discreet oak providing fine-grained tannin and a positive grip. It is *bella* with pink lamb.

QUALITY 🍷🍷🍷🍷
VALUE ★★★★
GRAPES shiraz
REGION Great Southern, WA
CELLAR 🍾 3
ALC./VOL. 12.0%
RRP $15.50

Galah Wine Red

Don't let the label and the parrot on it put you off. Galah is the second label from Ashton Hills and it's normally a very tasty drop. Maker Steve George.

CURRENT RELEASE 1992 This unlikely blend has plenty of flavour and good balance. The colour is dense and the nose combines fruit, earth and leaf aromas. The palate is full of berry flavour with concentrated fruit characters balanced by well-matched oak. It drinks well with pasta and a meat sauce.

QUALITY 🍷🍷🍷🍷
VALUE ★★★★
GRAPES shiraz, cabernet franc, mataro
REGION Clare Valley, SA
CELLAR 🍾 3
ALC./VOL. 13.0%
RRP $12.00

Garden Gully Shiraz

QUALITY ♛♛♛♛
VALUE ★★★★
GRAPES shiraz
REGION Great Western, Vic.
CELLAR 🍷 3–8
ALC./VOL. 13.0%
RRP $14.90

This is a small winery on the outskirts of Victoria's Great Western. Among the partners the names Brian Fletcher and Warren Randall can be found. Maker Brian Fletcher.

CURRENT RELEASE 1993 This is an authentic regional style that will probably age long and well. The nose shows typical pepper and spice. The palate is complex with a mixture of pepper, plum and liquorice. It's a steely style with a backbone of acid and positive grip on the finish. Try it with duck.

Gehrig Shiraz

QUALITY ♛♛♛♛
VALUE ★★★★
GRAPES shiraz
REGION Rutherglen, Vic.
CELLAR 🍷 5
ALC./VOL. 12.5%
RRP $13.00

This is a famous name in the north-east of Victoria. They continue to make traditional styles that are largely sold through cellar door. Maker Brian Gehrig.

CURRENT RELEASE 1992 A spicy style that shows it is possible to find elegance in the north-east. The nose is spicy with hints of sap, and the elegant palate has sweet cherry fruit balanced by dry, gripping tannins on an astringent finish. A good beef style.

Geoff Merrill Cabernet Sauvignon

QUALITY ♛♛♛♛♛
VALUE ★★★★
GRAPES cabernet sauvignon, cabernet franc
REGION Coonawarra 72%, McLaren Vale 28%, SA
CELLAR 🍷 5
ALC./VOL. 13.0%
RRP $20.00

There has been some quiet repackaging to this label. The result is very stylish indeed.

CURRENT RELEASE 1990 Very smart and starting to show the benefits of bottle-age. The colour is a dark ruby and the nose has scented cherry aromas. The palate has sweet maraschino fruit and plenty of spice. Oak imparts fine-grained tannins to the finish. A very well balanced wine that's fun to drink. Try it with roast pheasant.

Giesen Marlborough Pinot Noir

Surprisingly, this wine was made from vines which were just four years old, and cropping at 3.5 tonnes an acre.

CURRENT RELEASE 1994 This is an 'essence of pinot noir' style, fruit-driven with a light red-purple hue and a hi-fi fresh cherry pinot nose. The mouth is intense and lively, with light tannins, subtle oak and a clean, lingering aftertaste. A promising wine indeed. Have it with beef carpaccio.

QUALITY ▼▼▼▼
VALUE ★★★½
GRAPES pinot noir
REGION Marlborough, NZ
CELLAR 🍷 3
ALC./VOL. 13.0%
RRP $18.50

Goundrey Shiraz

This is a winery of considerable size – the production is over 30,000 cases and there is evidence of a new marketing thrust with the new labelling.

CURRENT RELEASE 1992 A distinguished Rhône-like style that offers subtlety and grace. The nose has ripe plum and pepper aromas and the palate is medium-bodied with plum flavour dominating. Spice and pepper augment these, followed by a brisk finish of well-integrated oak. It goes well with a char-grilled eye fillet.

QUALITY ▼▼▼▼▼
VALUE ★★★★
GRAPES shiraz
REGION Mount Barker, WA
CELLAR 🍷 3
ALC./VOL. 12.5%
RRP $15.00

Grant Burge Meshach

The Burge relatives tend to have grand names and grand loves. Meshach Burge lived to a ripe old age. The vines that provided the grapes were 70 years old, a lot younger than Meshach. Previous outstanding vintages: '90

CURRENT RELEASE 1991 A rich and succulent style that shows the Barossa's red prowess to the full. The colour is dense and the nose has ripe plum and spice aromas. The palate is juicy and floods the mouth with ripe berry flavours. These are followed by soft yet substantial tannins on a long dry finish. Just the thing for pink lamb straps.

QUALITY ▼▼▼▼▼
VALUE ★★★½
GRAPES shiraz
REGION Barossa Valley, SA
CELLAR ↔ 2–8
ALC./VOL. 14.0%
RRP $34.00

Grosset Gaia

QUALITY ????
VALUE ★★★★
GRAPES cabernet sauvignon 90%, cabernet franc 5%, merlot 5%
REGION Clare Valley, SA
CELLAR ➡ 3–6
ALC./VOL. 13.5%
RRP $23.90

Top of the tree for Jeffrey Grosset and an attempt to make a thinking person's wine. Space doesn't permit an explanation of the philosophy, better ask the maker Jeffrey himself.

CURRENT RELEASE 1993 A dark and brooding style that brooks no compromise. The nose is vinous with some bracken and smoky oak. The palate is complex and a tad bound up. There are cherry and raspberry flavours that are attached to tight oak. Black tea-like tannins offer strong grip on the finish. It needs time. Try it with baked squab.

Hardys Bankside Grenache

QUALITY ????
VALUE ★★★★½
GRAPES grenache
REGION McLaren Vale, SA
CELLAR ▯ 5+
ALC./VOL. 14.5%
RRP $12.00 ⓢ

Yet another varietal grenache catering to the revival of Rhône Valley grape varieties. It's named after Thomas Hardy's original cellars in Adelaide which were razed by fire in 1905.

CURRENT RELEASE 1993 This is a marvellously concentrated red, issuing plum/cherry/berry fruit and coffee, vanilla, dusty oak aromas nicely interwoven. It's a solid mouthful: savoury, rich, spicy, big and rustic with plenty of grip. Try it with game.

Hardys Bankside Shiraz

QUALITY ????
VALUE ★★★½
GRAPES shiraz
REGION McLaren Vale, SA
CELLAR ▯ 5
ALC./VOL. 14.5%
RRP $12.00 ⓢ

The red wines at Hardys are now in the hands of young Stephen Pannell, but in '93 David O'Leary, who did much to raise the level of Hardys' reds, was in charge.

CURRENT RELEASE 1993 An unusual bouquet of peppery, spicy cool-year shiraz together with vanillary oak and a salami overtone. The palate is intense and lively – the French might say nervous – with a tightly focused flavour that doesn't linger quite long enough. Good with gourmet bangers.

Hardys Eileen Hardy Shiraz

This was made by David O'Leary before he defected to the Mildara Blass camp in 1994, and reflects his passion for old styles and methods: open fermenters, basket press, big solid reds.
Previous outstanding vintages: '70, '71, '75, '79, '81, '82, '86, '87, '88, '89, '90
CURRENT RELEASE 1991 What a sensational wine! This is one of the finds of the past year: a great full-bodied Aussie red which begs to be cellared long-term. The bouquet has a myriad scents: liquorice, tar, toasty oak, mint and a fruit salad of dark berries. It is massively structured, high in ripe tannins and incredibly long. Strong cheeses, if you must drink it now.

QUALITY ♟♟♟♟♟
VALUE ★★★★★
GRAPES shiraz
REGION McLaren Vale 60%, Padthaway 25%, Clare 15%, SA
CELLAR ☛ 2–10+
ALC./VOL. 13.5%
RRP $25.00

CURRENT RELEASE 1992 This is still all arms and legs, and too young to leave its mother. Very deep colour, an unresolved nose of garden mint, liquorice and plums, and a massively tannic palate that really packs a wallop. Come back in four or five years, with pepper steak.

QUALITY ♟♟♟♟♟
VALUE ★★★★
GRAPES shiraz
REGION McLaren Vale, Padthaway, Clare Valley, SA
CELLAR ☛ 4–15
ALC./VOL. 14.0%
RRP $26.00

Hardys McLaren Vale Hermitage

This is an old favourite that's provided good-value drinking for many years.
CURRENT RELEASE 1993 This light to mediumweight red has attractive fresh spicy shiraz aromas without much complicating oak. The up-front, easy-drinking taste has some leafy characters and is light on tannin. Good value. Try it with goulash.

QUALITY ♟♟♟♟
VALUE ★★★★
GRAPES shiraz
REGION McLaren Vale, SA
CELLAR ᶦ 3
ALC./VOL. 13.5%
RRP $7.70 ⓢ

Hardys Regional Collection Cabernet Sauvignon

QUALITY 🍷🍷🍷
VALUE ★★★
GRAPES cabernet sauvignon
REGION Coonawarra, SA
CELLAR ☛ 1–5
ALC./VOL. 14.0%
RRP $14.50 ⓢ

The Hardy Collection, complete with picture labels, is now the Regional Collection. In this case the region is Coonawarra.

CURRENT RELEASE 1993 Slightly inky style with liquorice, spice, dark berry and chocolate nuances. Somewhat extracted, it has a solid feral feel and slightly rough tannins. Will be better when that astringency softens. Try it with meatballs.

Hardys RR Traditional Dry Red

QUALITY 🍷🍷🍷
VALUE ★★★½
GRAPES shiraz, cabernet franc
REGION Padthaway & Clare Valley, SA
CELLAR 🍾 2
ALC./VOL. 13.5%
RRP $6.75 ⓢ

This is part of a new series from Hardys which began with a rhine riesling disguised as 'RR' to hide it from people who thought they disliked riesling.

CURRENT RELEASE 1993 A whiff of hydrogen sulphide mars the nose of this wine, which is otherwise flavoursome and racy with some cool-grown peppery flavour. To 90 per cent of drinkers this would be no problem, and the generous flavour is all that matters.

Hardys Thomas Hardy Cabernet Sauvignon

This has been a big winner on the show circuit, ending up with a Stodart Trophy and five gold medals. It's named after the founder of Hardys and is a running mate for the Eileen Hardy chardonnay and shiraz.

Previous outstanding vintages: '89

CURRENT RELEASE 1990 A most impressive wine which bears the stamp of former chief red winemaker David O'Leary. It's a big, concentrated and very oaky wine in youth, but we'll bet London to a brick it develops into a classic. Rich, savoury, toasty oak and liquorice fruit of great power and length. Venison here.

QUALITY 🍷🍷🍷🍷🍷
VALUE ★★★★½
GRAPES cabernet sauvignon
REGION Coonawarra, SA
CELLAR 🍾 10+
ALC./VOL. 13.5%
RRP $25.00

CURRENT RELEASE 1991 This is saying 'go away and let me be'. It's a big, serious brooding giant with lots of alcohol and oak. It is very ripe and liquoricey, with concentrated fruit and mouth-coating tannins. Leave it alone to sort out its difficult adolescence, then drink with hard cheeses.

QUALITY 🍷🍷🍷🍷
VALUE ★★★★
GRAPES cabernet sauvignon
REGION Coonawarra, SA
CELLAR ➥ 2–9+
ALC./VOL. 13.5%
RRP $26.00

Haselgrove Futures Shiraz

As a futures wine, this one seems to have been selected for cellaring potential. Maker Nick Haselgrove.

CURRENT RELEASE 1993 Coconutty American oak dominates the nose at first (decanting will help), and the palate has a rather firm tannin grip which needs time to mellow. There's abundant sweet fruit flavour as well, and the wine has good cellar potential. Try it with a mixed grill.

QUALITY 🍷🍷🍷🍷
VALUE ★★★½
GRAPES shiraz
REGION McLaren Vale, SA
CELLAR 🍾 7+
ALC./VOL. 14.0%
RRP $18.50 (cellar door)

Haselgrove Grenache Shiraz

QUALITY 🍷🍷🍷
VALUE ★★★
GRAPES grenache, shiraz
REGION McLaren Vale, SA
CELLAR 🍾 4+
ALC./VOL. 13.5%
RRP $11.90 (cellar door)

Grenache has been a stalwart of the Southern Vales since the first days. After a few decades in the wilderness, it's suddenly fashionable and wines like this have a ready market.

CURRENT RELEASE 1993 A solid red, with dusty, dried herb and earthy regional characters in the bouquet. Ample tannin puckers the finish and balances the sweet-cherry grenache fruit. Good drinking now, with corned beef.

Haselgrove McLaren Vale Cabernet Merlot

QUALITY 🍷🍷🍷
VALUE ★★★
GRAPES cabernet sauvignon, merlot
REGION McLaren Vale, SA
CELLAR 🍾 3+
ALC./VOL. 13.5%
RRP $12.90 (cellar door)

Cabernet merlot is now a standard item in almost every winery's repertoire. The merlot is supposed to soften the wine and fill out the mid-palate.

CURRENT RELEASE 1992 Fairly oak-driven, this wine smells strongly of vanilla and chocolate. The palate is middleweight and freshened by lively acid. It lacks a little fruit intensity to balance the wood, but it's a decent drink with sausages.

Haselgrove Reserve Coonawarra Cabernet Sauvignon

QUALITY 🍷🍷🍷
VALUE ★★★
GRAPES cabernet sauvignon
REGION Coonawarra, SA
CELLAR 🍾 5+
ALC./VOL. 12.5%
RRP $18.90 (cellar door)

Reserve bottlings are all the rage these days, but they don't always deliver the sort of extra flavour and character they promise.

CURRENT RELEASE 1992 This lighter-bodied cabernet has a lean profile and leafy, tobacco-like bouquet. The finish carries plenty of grip but there seems to be a slight hollow in the mid-palate. A year or two more age may bring it into better harmony. Try it with duck.

Heggies Pinot Noir

Colin Heggie was a friend of the Hill Smiths of Yalumba, a farmer from whom they bought the land for the vineyard. Maker Simon Adams.

CURRENT RELEASE 1993 A turn-up for the books! This is a pretty serious pinot, breathing to show an excellent, slightly feral pinot nose, while the palate reveals excellent concentration, fruit sweetness, depth and structure. It lingers well and generally satisfies. Drink with turkey.

QUALITY ?????
VALUE ★★★★
GRAPES pinot noir
REGION Eden Valley, SA
CELLAR 2+
ALC./VOL. 14.0%
RRP $19.30 ⓢ

Henschke Abbott's Prayer

Henschke, the master red winemakers, point the way for the Bordeaux-style reds in the cool Adelaide Hills with this merlot-dominant blend. It always avoids the greenness of straight cabernet sauvignon. Maker Stephen Henschke. Previous outstanding vintages: '89, '90, '91

CURRENT RELEASE 1992 This is a benchmark style for the Adelaide Hills. The nose is an exquisite combo of toasty oak and ripe blackcurranty fruit, the taste is rich and fleshy, with good weight and balance, and lingers long. Pink roast lamb here.

QUALITY ?????
VALUE ★★★★
GRAPES merlot 60%, cabernet sauvignon 40%
REGION Adelaide Hills, SA
CELLAR 6+
ALC./VOL. 13.5%
RRP $27.00

CURRENT RELEASE 1993 No prayers needed here: this is a serious wine that shows its peers in the Hills a clean pair of heels. This very elegant red has good concentration as well as subtlety, with herbal leafy notes on the nose among the cherry and dark berry. The flavours are fruit-led and concentrated in all regards, the merlot rendering it smooth and supple. Try it with veal sweetbreads.

QUALITY ?????
VALUE ★★★★½
GRAPES cabernet sauvignon 55%, merlot 45%
REGION Adelaide Hills, SA
CELLAR 8+
ALC./VOL. 15.0%
RRP $33.00

Penguin Wine of the Year; Best Red Wine

Henschke Cyril Henschke Cabernet Sauvignon

QUALITY 🍷🍷🍷🍷🍷
VALUE ★★★★★
GRAPES cabernet sauvignon
REGION Eden Valley, SA
CELLAR 🍾 3–12+
ALC./VOL. 13.0%
RRP $35.40

Cyril Henschke was the present winemaker Stephen's father: a Churchill Fellow who was acknowledged in his time as a leading winemaker.

Previous outstanding vintages: '81, '86, '88, '90, '91

CURRENT RELEASE 1992 This is a monster! Very deep, dark colour; slightly shy, dusty oak and latent cabernet fruit nose; great power and concentration in the mouth. The style is impressively grand, and the tannins pucker the mouth. Don't drink for at least three years, then have it with beef.

Henschke Hill of Grace

QUALITY 🍷🍷🍷🍷🍷
VALUE ★★★★½
GRAPES shiraz
REGION Eden Valley, SA
CELLAR 🍾 2–12+
ALC./VOL. 13.5%
RRP $64.40

The oldest vines in this vineyard date back to the 1860s, and Prue Henschke is ensuring that any replanting is done with stock from the best of the original vines. The wine is widely regarded as second only to Grange.

Previous outstanding vintages: '82, '86, '88, '89, '90

CURRENT RELEASE 1991 This is fabulous stuff, and no wonder it's expensive. It is very seductive, multi-layered and profound, with great power and length. The flavours are of liquorice, berries and coffee with an earthy, truffle background; the sweetness from ripe fruit balanced by a dry savoury tannin finish. Aged cheeses here.

Henschke Keyneton Estate

Keyneton, where the Henschke winery is located, has been producing wine since Henry Evans was at Evandale in the 1840s. After he died, his wife turned teetotal and destroyed his vines.

CURRENT RELEASE 1993 Even the drink-now Henschke is a serious red that's been beefed up in recent vintages. Lovely depth of cherry flavours with subtle oak, the palate stacked with sweet plummy, vanilla flavours and positive tannin. Good structure and could be cellared. Drink with barbecued kebabs.

QUALITY 🍷🍷🍷🍷🍷
VALUE ★★★★
GRAPES shiraz, cabernet sauvignon, malbec
REGION Eden Valley, SA
CELLAR 🍷 5+
ALC./VOL. 14.4%
RRP $20.30

Henschke Mount Edelstone

Early Barossa surveyor Johann Menge found precious stones on an outcrop of land that became christened Mount Edelstone, meaning noble stone. Maker Stephen Henschke.

Previous outstanding vintages: '78, '80, '84, '86, '88, '90, '91

CURRENT RELEASE 1992 A very good but not outstanding Mount Edelstone. The nose has impressive aromatics: sweet, ripe oak/fruit marriage that recalls mint, cedar and dark berries. The palate is slightly lean and finishes with firm tannins, but the mouth aromas are hauntingly good. Try it with aged cheddar.

QUALITY 🍷🍷🍷🍷🍷
VALUE ★★★★
GRAPES shiraz
REGION Eden Valley, SA
CELLAR 🍷 6+
ALC./VOL. 13.5%
RRP $25.75

CURRENT RELEASE 1993 This is a much more butch style than the '92, its big, overripe plum/liquorice nose developing a marvellous perfume in the glass. Very ripe fruit-sweet flavours cram a powerfully structured wine which is quite dense and solid. Built for the long haul. Try it with venison.

QUALITY 🍷🍷🍷🍷🍷
VALUE ★★★★★
GRAPES shiraz
REGION Eden Valley, SA
CELLAR ⬤ 3–10+
ALC./VOL. 14.6%
RRP $33.00

Hillstowe Buxton Cabernet Merlot

QUALITY 🍷🍷🍷🍷
VALUE ★★★½
GRAPES cabernet sauvignon & cabernet franc 85%, merlot 15%
REGION McLaren Vale, SA
CELLAR 🍾 2
ALC./VOL. 12.0%
RRP $16.90

This is named after founder Dr Christie Laurie's great grandfather, Buxton Forbes Laurie, who had a pioneering vineyard on the South Australian south coast near Goolwa.
CURRENT RELEASE 1991 This has a developed colour and a full, soft, earthy, typical McLaren Vale regional – rather than varietal – character. There's some stalkiness and the palate is soft, rich and full, and it's probably already at its best. Drink with a lamb casserole.

Hollick Coonawarra

QUALITY 🍷🍷🍷🍷🍷
VALUE ★★★★½
GRAPES cabernet sauvignon 75%, merlot 15%, cabernet franc 10%
REGION Coonawarra, SA
CELLAR 🍾 10+
ALC./VOL. 12.5%
RRP $18.00

Ian Hollick and Pat Tocaciu have followed Petaluma in naming their red blend simply Coonawarra.
Previous outstanding vintages: '84, '88, '90, '91
CURRENT RELEASE 1992 Essence of Coonawarra here! Intense blackcurrant/mulberry nose, superbly fruity with nice background oak. Smooth and pure, as poised as a ballerina, this is Coonawarra cab writ large. Made for pink lamb.

Hollick Ravenswood

QUALITY 🍷🍷🍷🍷🍷
VALUE ★★★★
GRAPES cabernet sauvignon
REGION Coonawarra, SA
CELLAR ➞ 6–10+
ALC./VOL. 13.0%
RRP $40.00 🍷

This was one of the first such branded 'reserve' wines on the market, and still shines a light for others to follow. Maker Pat Tocaciu.
Previous outstanding vintages: '88, '89, '90
CURRENT RELEASE 1991 A serious red for the long haul. This is concentrated, mildly tannic and the lush fruit is allowed to dominate the stylish oak. The texture is quite dense, reflecting low-yielding vines. A wine to cellar. It's not cheap, so to get your money's worth, come back in 2001 and serve with roast lamb.

Holm Oak Cabernet Sauvignon

This vineyard takes its name from the massive holm oak trees beside the vines. It's appropriate because the cabernets always show plenty of American oak character. Maker Nick Butler.
Previous outstanding vintages: '90
CURRENT RELEASE 1992 This slow-ageing wine has not changed a lot since last year's review. It has very good weight for a Tassie cab and smells of coffee, vanilla and chocolate, thanks to generous use of oak cooperage. Uncommonly good mid-palate flavour and fruit concentration. Bring on the beef wellington.

QUALITY ♀♀♀♀
VALUE ★★★½
GRAPES cabernet sauvignon
REGION West Tamar, Tas.
CELLAR 🍷 6+
ALC./VOL. 12.5%
RRP $18.90

Houghton Cabernet Sauvignon

This wine's label carries a red stripe to echo the blue one on Houghton's most famous wine, the White Burgundy. Maker Paul Lapsley.
CURRENT RELEASE 1993 This is a light to medium-bodied red with a lightish, forward colour and a sweet, leafy/herbaceous nose. Its lean briary, sweet berry flavours fall away somewhat on the finish, but it's very fairly priced at around a tenner. Try it with pizza.

QUALITY ♀♀♀
VALUE ★★★½
GRAPES cabernet sauvignon
REGION Frankland River, Margaret River, Mount Barker, WA
CELLAR 🍷 3
ALC./VOL. 12.5%
RRP $11.60 ⑤

Houghton Gold Reserve Cabernet Sauvignon

Houghton is part of the BRL Hardy group. Its winery at Caversham near Perth is a major tourist destination, with access via paddleboat trips up the Swan River.
Previous outstanding vintages: '90
CURRENT RELEASE 1992 This is Houghton's top-line red, bursting with gamey and blackcurrant cabernet aroma and flavour, carefully matched with understated oak. It has elegance, firm structure and appealing balance. A good partner for steak and kidney pie.

QUALITY ♀♀♀♀
VALUE ★★★½
GRAPES cabernet sauvignon
REGION Frankland River & Manjimup, WA
CELLAR 🍷 8
ALC./VOL. 12.5%
RRP $17.40 ⑤

Houghton Rosé

QUALITY ♥♥♥
VALUE ★★★
GRAPES cabernet sauvignon
REGION Gingin & Frankland River, WA
CELLAR 🍷 1
ALC./VOL. 10.5%
RRP $11.60 ⓢ

Rosé is a bit of a dinosaur these days, and few companies persist with making one. Odd, because it does have a place, especially when chilled on a warm summer's evening.

CURRENT RELEASE 1994 The green, herbaceous early-harvested cabernet flavours are a little sharp-edged in this vintage, and it doesn't have the charm of some earlier versions. Quite a full purple-pink hue for a rosé, and the entry is sweetish with herbaceous/raspberry flavour and lots of acid on the finish.

Hungerford Hill Cabernet Sauvignon Merlot

QUALITY ♥♥♥♥
VALUE ★★★½
GRAPES cabernet sauvignon, merlot
REGION mainly Hunter Valley, NSW
CELLAR 🍷 4
ALC./VOL. 11.5%
RRP $13.00 ⓢ

Once a Hunter Valley-based company, owned for a time by Rothmans, Hungerford Hill is now a brand without a home as part of the Southcorp group. McGuigan Brothers now use the winery.

CURRENT RELEASE 1991 Age shows in a lighter, more developed colour and the smooth, mellowing style of the wine. The earthy fruit is matched by strong vanillan oaky scents and the palate holds sweet, mature, leathery Hunter flavours. The low-alcohol strength is reflected in a certain leanness. Try it with pork.

Hungerford Hill Shiraz

QUALITY ♥♥♥♥
VALUE ★★★★
GRAPES shiraz
REGION mainly Hunter Valley & Mudgee, NSW
CELLAR 🍷 4+
ALC./VOL. 12.5%
RRP $9.30 ⓢ

This brand has been kicked around the Southcorp office somewhat. It's now blended from various regions. But it does offer perhaps better value now than ever before. Maker Ian Walsh.

CURRENT RELEASE 1993 This is a very decent wine with drinkability and life, smelling of spices – true to the shiraz grape – with elegance and subtle but attractive oak. It's medium-bodied, not big, and would suit a beef stew.

Huntington Estate Cabernet Sauvignon

In the sleepy Mudgee region, this winery stands out as a red wine producer of real merit. Makers Bob and Susie Roberts.

Previous outstanding vintages: '79, '81, '82, '84, '85, '89, '90

CURRENT RELEASE 1991 Bin FB24 is a big, solid, old-fashioned 'fruit style' which has some bottle-age. The shy nose has latent berry and mint aromas, the palate has plenty of depth and concentration ending with a firm grip. The oak is underplayed and the wine will repay cellaring. Goes well with Lebanese yeeros.

QUALITY ♛♛♛♛
VALUE ★★★★½
GRAPES cabernet sauvignon
REGION Mudgee, NSW
CELLAR 7+
ALC./VOL. 13.5%
RRP $13.00 (cellar door)

Jamiesons Run

This is the label that went from a standing start to mega-case production in no time flat. It has been an outstanding success.

Previous outstanding vintages: '86, '88, '90, '91

CURRENT RELEASE 1993 Mint and spice and all things nice. The nose has a strong plum-pudding aroma, and the palate is full, rich, sweetly succulent with a mouthful of complex fruit flavours laced with spice. The finish shows a touch of anise and vanilla and the grip adds balance. Great with minted lamb chops.

QUALITY ♛♛♛♛♛
VALUE ★★★★★
GRAPES cabernet sauvignon, merlot, cabernet franc, malbec
REGION Coonawarra, SA
CELLAR 4
ALC./VOL. 13.5%
RRP $11.00

Jasper Hill Emily's Paddock Shiraz Cabernet Franc

QUALITY 🍷🍷🍷🍷
VALUE ★★★½
GRAPES shiraz, cabernet franc
REGION Heathcote, Vic.
CELLAR ➡ 2–8+
ALC./VOL. 13.5%
RRP $33.00

The novel blend of grape varieties really works, although they first came together by accident. Ron and Elva Laughton named their wines after their daughters.
Previous outstanding vintages: '86, '90, '91, '92
CURRENT RELEASE 1993 This one needs breathing, after which it starts to reveal shiraz pepper/spice as well as raspberry leafy aromas from the franc. True to house style it is a dense, dry, tannic but powerful red built for the long haul. There is cedary oak, plenty of dry grip and not quite the length of Georgia's. Drink with beef and demiglaze.

Jasper Hill Georgia's Paddock Shiraz

QUALITY 🍷🍷🍷🍷?
VALUE ★★★★
GRAPES shiraz
REGION Heathcote, Vic.
CELLAR ➡ 2–10+
ALC./VOL. 14.0%
RRP $24.15

There's something quaintly charming about the very Aussie word 'paddock'. A field, a block or a vineyard would mean so much less.
Previous outstanding vintages: '86, '90, '91, '92
CURRENT RELEASE 1993 The colour is very deep purple-red and the nose has good complexity of pungent pepper/spice and gamey shiraz characters. This is a serious wine, full of stuffing, the dusty/earthy aspects suggesting long wood-ageing. The taste is dry and savoury, chunky and very long, with mouth-coating tannins. Promising wine to cellar or drink with aged cheeses.

Jenke Cabernet Franc

QUALITY 🍷🍷🍷
VALUE ★★★★
GRAPES cabernet franc
REGION Barossa Valley, SA
CELLAR 🍾 4+
ALC./VOL. 13.8%
RRP $13.75

It's rare to see this grape standing alone. A good blend component, it seldom has the weight and interest to go solo.
CURRENT RELEASE 1993 A very spicy wine due to liberal use of quality oak, this has elegant medium-bodied berry fruit flavour, with spicy oak the main event again on the palate. An attractive red of good balance and style. Would go with tandoori chicken.

Jim Barry Armagh (The) Shiraz

This wine seems intent on chasing down Grange's price; it's already dearer than Henschke's Hill of Grace. Maker Mark Barry.

Previous outstanding vintages: '87, '88, '89, '90, '91

CURRENT RELEASE 1992 An impressive wine: enormously concentrated fruit and tannin complemented by liberal high-toast, coconutty American oak. Amazingly smooth considering its colossal weight and richness, with massive flavour and a finish that never ends. Great cellar potential. Drink with venison.

QUALITY 🍷🍷🍷🍷🍷
VALUE ★★★★
GRAPES shiraz
REGION Clare Valley, SA
CELLAR 2–10+
ALC./VOL. 14.0%
RRP $74.00

Jim Barry Cabernet Merlot

The blending of cabernet and merlot these days usually heralds a soft, ready-drinking red, and this is no exception.

CURRENT RELEASE 1992 Lovely deep purple-red colour introduces a fruit-driven wine laden with plum-skin aroma. It's a big, straightforward, fairly butch Clare style without a lot of varietal character and a firm tannin finish. Drink with lamb chops.

QUALITY 🍷🍷🍷
VALUE ★★★
GRAPES cabernet sauvignon, merlot
REGION Clare Valley, SA
CELLAR 5
ALC./VOL. 13.5%
RRP $10.40 Ⓢ

Jim Barry McRae Wood Shiraz

'In 1964 Jim Barry purchased 70 acres of land from Duncan McRae Wood for £50 an acre, in the Armagh area of Clare,' the label notes explain. If this wine's any guide, it was an inspired purchase.

CURRENT RELEASE 1992 Here's a red that's packed with personality. A big, rich, powerful brute with a complex spicy shiraz fruit and oak nose, some black pepper plus riper notes. The style reminds of Wendouree, with earthy, dried herb aspects and firm tannin balance. A keeper that teams well with game.

QUALITY 🍷🍷🍷🍷🍷
VALUE ★★★★½
GRAPES shiraz
REGION Clare Valley, SA
CELLAR 10+
ALC./VOL. 13.1%
RRP $23.30

Jim Barry Personal Selection Cabernet Sauvignon

QUALITY ????
VALUE ★★★½
GRAPES cabernet sauvignon
REGION Clare Valley, SA
CELLAR 2–8+
ALC./VOL. 12.7%
RRP $13.70 ⓢ

The label tells us this was born in the wettest year in Clare's recorded history, when 'half the average yield led to concentrated wines'. This doesn't quite make sense, but the wine is certainly not dilute. Maker Mark Barry.

CURRENT RELEASE 1993 Good varietal character, with a leafy aspect to the nose and a strong, gutsy palate with plenty of extraction and serious tannins. There's a solid slab of fruit on the mid-palate and it should age well. Drink with beef wellington.

Joseph Cabernet Sauvignon Merlot

QUALITY ?????
VALUE ★★★★½
GRAPES cabernet sauvignon 80%, merlot 20%
REGION McLaren Vale & Coonawarra, SA
CELLAR 2–10+
ALC./VOL. 14.0%
RRP $28.00

Joe Grilli makes this wine according to the Veronese amarone method: the grapes are partly air-dried before crushing.

CURRENT RELEASE 1993 This is a concentrated red of high potential. The colour is dark and the strong aromas are of dark berries and oak with undergrowth and fungal notes. It's superbly packed with fruit and tannin, the oak lurking in the background. A solid cellaring style that needs a few years; then drink it with aged parmesan.

Karriview Pinot Noir

QUALITY ????
VALUE ★★★½
GRAPES pinot noir
REGION Great Southern, WA
CELLAR 2
ALC./VOL. 12.7%
RRP $24.00

This is a small vineyard near Denmark in the Great Southern region of Western Australia. Karriview was founded in 1986. Maker John Wade (consultant).

CURRENT RELEASE 1993 The colour is a light brick-red and the nose has game, strawberry and stalk aromas. The elegant palate has sweet strawberry flavours and some Burgundian undertones. The finish shows clean acid and slightly stalky tannins. It drinks well now with char-grilled quail.

Katnook Cabernet Sauvignon

The total production from this company (including the labels of John Riddoch and Sunnycliff) is in the order of 25,000 cases. Maker Wayne Stehbens.

CURRENT RELEASE 1991 This is the product of a warm vintage where the grapes ripened quickly and the alcohol is high. The colour is dense ruby and the nose has strong blackberry aromas. The rich palate fills the mouth with the warmth of alcohol and sweet blackberry fruit, balanced by attractive oak that makes a discreet contribution of tannin on the finish. It drinks well now with a game pie.

QUALITY ♛♛♛♛⚬
VALUE ★★★★
GRAPES cabernet sauvignon
REGION Coonawarra, SA
CELLAR 🍷 4
ALC./VOL. 14.0%
RRP $21.00

Katnook Merlot

Yet another in the swelling ranks of merlot as a solo act. Merlot from Coonawarra usually shows more character than most. Maker Wayne Stehbens.

CURRENT RELEASE 1990 A scented nose opens out to cedar aromas while the palate is full with rich cherry flavours and a hint of tobacco. Well-tailored oak mortices into a long, grippy finish. There is also evidence of fresh acid. The wine goes well with a traditional mixed grill.

QUALITY ♛♛♛♛⚬
VALUE ★★★★
GRAPES merlot
REGION Coonawarra, SA
CELLAR 🍷 4
ALC./VOL. 13.5%
RRP $21.00

Kay's Amery Block 6 Shiraz

There are not many wineries that can mark their centenary by picking grapes from 100-year-old vines. Maker Colin Kay.

CURRENT RELEASE 1992 The colour is lovely, dark and deep, and like the poem, this wine has far to go before it sleeps. The nose is rich with a porty aroma and ripe plum smells, and the intense palate fills the mouth with concentrated shiraz flavour. Slabs of tannin impart a black tea-like character to the finish. It would go well with an aged cheddar.

QUALITY ♛♛♛♛♛
VALUE ★★★★★
GRAPES shiraz
REGION McLaren Vale, SA
CELLAR ⇥ 2–6
ALC./VOL. 14.2%
RRP $18.00

Kay's Amery Grenache

QUALITY 🍷🍷🍷?
VALUE ★★★
GRAPES grenache
REGION McLaren Vale, SA
CELLAR 🍾 2
ALC./VOL. 13.4%
RRP $15.00

Yet another grenache to come out of the closet. It is interesting to watch the revival of this once out-of-fashion variety. Maker Colin Kay.

CURRENT RELEASE 1994 A big fruity style that is not ashamed of flavour. There are strong raspberry aromas on the nose, and the same fruit – this time sweet and very berryish in character – features as the major palate flavour. Soft tannin makes for a gentle finish. Drinks well now with a steak and kidney pie.

Kay's Amery Shiraz

QUALITY 🍷🍷🍷🍷
VALUE ★★★★
GRAPES shiraz
REGION McLaren Vale, SA
CELLAR ➨ 2–8
ALC./VOL. 14.0%
RRP $12.00

Founded in 1890, this vineyard has shrunk in size since the early plantings yet has consolidated in terms of regional style. It produces around 6500 cases per year. Maker Colin Kay.

CURRENT RELEASE 1992 Big, rich and generous, the wine makes a discreet swerve to avoid being jammy. The colour is dense and the nose is alcoholic with tinges of spice. The palate shows sweet plum-flavoured fruit balanced by slabs of tannin on an assertive finish. A style that could handle a robust devilled kidney dish.

Killerby April Classic Red

QUALITY 🍷🍷🍷
VALUE ★★★
GRAPES shiraz
REGION Capel, WA
CELLAR 🍾 1
ALC./VOL. 13.0%
RRP $11.00

This is another example of the eternal tilt at a soft drink-now style. The Australian market is indeed perverse because it doesn't really support this style, despite its suitability to our climate.

CURRENT RELEASE 1995 The colour is a bright candy-coloured pink. The nose has a confectionery smell. There is sweet fruit on the palate with strong berry character matched by crisp acid on a clean finish. It could be served chilled with char-grilled tuna.

Killerby Shiraz

This label continues to impress with good viticulture and equally impressive winemaking. The vineyard was established in 1973 by Dr Barry Killerby. Maker Matt Aldridge.
Previous outstanding vintages: '90
CURRENT RELEASE 1993 A solid style with plenty of guts. The nose is spicy with a hint of alcohol and ripe berry fruit. The palate is rich with sweet fruit and a mouthfilling texture. The finish shows well-tuned oak and positive grip. This will cellar well. Try it with tandoori lamb.

QUALITY ♛♛♛♛
VALUE ★★★★
GRAPES shiraz
REGION Capel, WA
CELLAR ➡ 2–6
ALC./VOL. 13.9%
RRP $16.00

Kingston Estate Reserve Shiraz

This product was designed for export (witness the warning of the Surgeon General – what a killjoy that man!). Maker Bill Moularadellis.
CURRENT RELEASE 1991 A well-balanced style with a strong, concentrated nose of crushed black pepper aromas. The middleweight palate has sweet redcurrant flavours plus loads of pepper. The finish is well balanced and dry. A good style for minted lamb.

QUALITY ♛♛♛♛
VALUE ★★★½
GRAPES shiraz
REGION Riverland, SA
CELLAR ❖ 4
ALC./VOL. 13.5%
RRP $10.00

Krondorf Coonawarra Hermitage

This is a good value-for-money style that offers simple but enjoyable pleasure. Maker Nick Walker.
CURRENT RELEASE 1993 A fruit-driven style with an astringent finish. The nose has spice and plum aromas; the palate is all about big bopping berries, simple yet cheery. The tannins dry out the finish. Would be great with a meat pie.

QUALITY ♛♛♛♛
VALUE ★★★★
GRAPES shiraz
REGION Coonawarra, SA
CELLAR ❖ 3
ALC./VOL. 13.0%
RRP $8.95

Krondorf Show Cabernet Sauvignon Shiraz

QUALITY ♟♟♟♟
VALUE ★★★★
GRAPES cabernet sauvignon, shiraz
REGION Barossa Valley, Coonawarra, SA
CELLAR 🍾 5
ALC./VOL. 12.5%
RRP $18.00

It is timely to remember this label was founded as a legal argument between Dalgety and a small vineyard in Mudgee. The Augustine vineyard won and Dalgety had to drop their name and invent a new label. Crown village (Krondorf) is located below King's Seat (Kaiser Stuhl) in the Barossa Valley.

CURRENT RELEASE 1992 This is a well-composed style with considerable finesse. The nose shows both fresh wood and fruit, and the palate has an attractive berry quality. The finish shows off with expensive oak and good tannin grip. Drink it now with a hearty dish like casseroled rabbit and field mushrooms.

Lakes Folly Cabernet

QUALITY ♟♟♟♟♟
VALUE ★★★★½
GRAPES cabernet sauvignon, shiraz, petit verdot, merlot
REGION Hunter Valley, NSW
CELLAR 🍾 8+
ALC./VOL. 12.5%
RRP $29.00

Max Lake planted some cabernet vines on deep red volcanic loam soils opposite McWilliam's Rose Hill vineyard in 1963 and set the scene for the small winery revolution in Australia. Today the Folly is run by his son Stephen Lake.

Previous outstanding vintages: '87, '89, '91, '92

CURRENT RELEASE 1993 A classic Lakes Folly: elegant, cedary and harmonious with good fruit concentration, impeccable oak-fruit balance and a lingering aftertaste. Drink with roast lamb.

Leasingham Bin 56 Cabernet Malbec

Penfolds' Max Schubert, a great blender, had a hand in this wine's genesis. He berated his friend Mick Knappstein at Leasingham for not experimenting more with blends. He tasted a tank of each variety and said they'd both be better if blended.

Previous outstanding vintages: '71, '72, '75, '78, '80, '81, '84, '88, '90, '92

CURRENT RELEASE 1993 A knee-tremblingly good wine that continues the revitalisation of the brand. Marvellous deep, rich, smooth ripe flavours of blackberry and spices, toasty oak and layers of lush fruit. Tannins are assertive but supple. Fine balance and length. A class act to serve with beef casserole.

QUALITY 🍷🍷🍷🍷🍷
VALUE ★★★★★
GRAPES cabernet sauvignon, malbec
REGION Clare Valley, SA
CELLAR 🍾 8+
ALC./VOL. 13.5%
RRP $14.50 ⓢ

Best Red Blend

Leasingham Bin 61 Shiraz

This wine and its twin, Bin 56, represent some of the best and most consistent value in Australian wine today. Maker Richard Rowe.

Previous outstanding vintages: '90, '91, '92

CURRENT RELEASE 1993 A sumptuous wine! Wonderfully deep, rich and concentrated, smooth and rounded with skilfully interwoven fruit and oak flavours. Ripe spice, plum and toasty oak flavours turning minty with airing. Good firm tannic finish. Great value and very underrated. Does wonders for hamburgers.

QUALITY 🍷🍷🍷🍷🍷
VALUE ★★★★★
GRAPES shiraz
REGION Clare Valley, SA
CELLAR 🍾 9+
ALC./VOL. 13.0%
RRP $14.50 ⓢ

Leasingham Classic Clare Cabernet Sauvignon

QUALITY ♛♛♛♛♛
VALUE ★★★★½
GRAPES cabernet sauvignon
REGION Clare Valley, SA
CELLAR ⊷ 3–10+
ALC./VOL. 13.0%
RRP $19.30 Ⓢ

Leasingham's top-of-the-range label was introduced with the 1991 vintage in the winery's centenary year, 1993. Maker Richard Rowe.
Previous outstanding vintages: '91, '92
CURRENT RELEASE 1993 A thumper of a wine with high alcohol, bordering on porty, but gets away with it. Very rich ripe plummy/berry aromas, and some cedary oak. Very concentrated; big but supple tannins; a monster that needs cellaring. For those who like 'em huge. A steak and eggs wine.

Leasingham Classic Clare Shiraz

QUALITY ♛♛♛♛♛
VALUE ★★★★½
GRAPES shiraz
REGION Clare Valley, SA
CELLAR 🍷 10
ALC./VOL. 13.5%
RRP $19.30 Ⓢ

For once the term classic is used correctly. The Leasingham winemaker and vineyard boss have certainly got their acts together these days, as the wines are models for the region.
Previous outstanding vintages: '91, '92
CURRENT RELEASE 1993 A more elegant style compared to the cabernet, showing lovely sweet ripe berry, spice and peppermint aromas and some raspberry on the tongue. Lush, soft, mouthfilling flavour that is already smooth and approachable. Try it with meat and a fruity demiglaze.

Leconfield Cabernet Sauvignon

The late Sydney Hamilton, uncle of the present owner Richard, was an energetic man who was in his 80s when he decided to establish Leconfield. He planted its vines in some of the best terra rossa soils. Maker Ralph Fowler.

Previous outstanding vintages: '80, '82, '88, '90, '91, '92

CURRENT RELEASE 1993 This is impressive stuff, the nose being worth a detour by itself! It has an exquisite sniff of concentrated mint and dark berries, but that's not all – it's quite weighty in the mouth, backing up the extravagant claims for the '93 Coonawarra vintage. The emphasis is on fruit: oak and tannin are in the background. Big finish and very long. Drink with pink lamb chops.

QUALITY	▼▼▼▼▼
VALUE	★★★★★
GRAPES	cabernet sauvignon 89%, merlot 11%
REGION	Coonawarra, SA
CELLAR	🍾 10+
ALC./VOL.	13.0%
RRP	$19.30

Best Cabernet Sauvignon

Leconfield Shiraz

The Leconfield and Richard Hamilton reds, all made by Ralph Fowler at Coonawarra, seldom fail to impress, but we wonder at the wisdom of releasing them at a tender 18 months old.

CURRENT RELEASE 1993 A mere babe in arms, this pumps fresh and slightly raw aromas of herbaceous pepper/spice fruit and stylish oak from the glass, and seems a little hollow until aeration allows it to fill out. It is lean and firm with spice and grip to burn. Should be good with venison in a year or two.

QUALITY	▼▼▼▼
VALUE	★★★★
GRAPES	shiraz
REGION	Coonawarra, SA
CELLAR	➡ 2–8+
ALC./VOL.	12.5%
RRP	$15.40

Leeuwin Estate Art Series Cabernet Sauvignon

QUALITY ♛♛♛♛♛
VALUE ★★★★½
GRAPES cabernet sauvignon
REGION Margaret River, WA
CELLAR ⬤ 4–9+
ALC./VOL. 13.9%
RRP $26.60

The Leeuwin cabernets have been up, down and all around. This one is certainly 'up'. Makers Bob Cartwright and John Brocksopp.
Previous outstanding vintages: '79, '82, '87, '89
CURRENT RELEASE 1991 Miles ahead of the Prelude of the same vintage, this is a class act. The nose is gamey, cedary and oak-led; the taste is savoury and again oaky but cleverly integrated, and there's no trace of the vegetal character of some past vintages. The proportions are massive, with tight, dense, chunky structure and enormous length. Cellar, then enjoy with hard cheeses.

Lenswood Pinot Noir

QUALITY ♛♛♛♛♝
VALUE ★★★★
GRAPES pinot noir
REGION Adelaide Hills, SA
CELLAR ▮ 2
ALC./VOL. 14.0%
RRP $28.00

Lenswood is Tim Knappstein's exciting new vineyard in the Adelaide Hills, cheek by jowl with Stafford Ridge and Henschke. Knappstein says his next challenge is to make pinots that live for 10 or 15 years, like good Burgundy.
Previous outstanding vintages: '91, '92
CURRENT RELEASE 1993 A superb pinot noir, deep-hued, with a stalky, sappy bouquet that turns to multi-layered flavours of sweet, ripe cherry in the mouth, with a sneaky veneer of subtle oak. A delicious wine for pinot sceptics, to drink with any roasted game bird.

Leo Buring DR 150 Cabernet Sauvignon

This is the junior cabernet in the Buring range and thankfully the bin number stays the same every year nowadays. Maker Geoff Henriks.

CURRENT RELEASE 1993 This charmingly fruity, cassisy cabernet is soft and smooth and ready to drink, and offers terrific value for money. Very much a cabernet, it has blackberry, cherry and leafy aspects and offers excellent depth of flavour, usually for under ten bucks. Try it with beef and mushroom and cream.

QUALITY ♛♛♛♛
VALUE ★★★★½
GRAPES cabernet sauvignon
REGION various, SA
CELLAR 🍾 4
ALC./VOL. 12.5%
RRP $11.30 Ⓢ

Lindemans Bin 50 Shiraz

This is the running-mate of Bin 65 chardonnay, a huge seller especially in the US. Lindemans' bin range has made such an impact that at least one major American winery has admitted it's using the Aussie wines as a model.

CURRENT RELEASE 1992 Slightly subdued in aroma, this wine is simple and fairly basic, but provides good honest flavour at the price. The fruit is slightly peppery and there's some acid tartness on the finish, which suggests it would taste better with food. We'd favour barbecued snags.

QUALITY ♛♛♝
VALUE ★★★
GRAPES shiraz
REGION mainly Padthaway & Barossa Valley, SA
CELLAR 🍾 2
ALC./VOL. 12.5%
RRP $8.80 Ⓢ

CURRENT RELEASE 1993 It would be easy to think this had some cabernet blended in, because of a certain blackcurrant aroma. The nose is sweet and ripe – almost jammy – with a trace of leafiness. The palate has heaps of up-front, uncomplicated berry flavour that's well balanced. This is a very fruity red that's great value for money. Try beef stroganoff.

QUALITY ♛♛♛♝
VALUE ★★★★
GRAPES shiraz
REGION mainly Padthaway & Barossa Valley, SA
CELLAR 🍾 3
ALC./VOL. 13.0%
RRP $8.80 Ⓢ

Lindemans Cawarra Shiraz Cabernet

QUALITY ▼▼▼
VALUE ★★★½
GRAPES shiraz, cabernet sauvignon
REGION not stated
CELLAR 2
ALC./VOL. 12.5%
RRP $6.90 ⓢ

Dr Henry Lindeman gave the name Cawarra to his original vineyard at Gresford in the Hunter Valley, presumably a name used by the local Aborigines.

CURRENT RELEASE 1994 This is a lean and lightweight, fruit-driven red which has a meaty/gamey aspect that mightn't appeal to purists, but there is more than adequate flavour and character at this price – even better when it's discounted to $5.95. Pair it with rissoles.

Lindemans Hunter River Burgundy

QUALITY ▼▼▼
VALUE ★★★
GRAPES shiraz
REGION Hunter Valley, NSW
CELLAR ➞ 2–6+
ALC./VOL. 11.5%
RRP $18.00 ⓢ

Some great wines have appeared under this label in the past, but it's a style that time has passed by. The best of them need several years cellaring to show their true colours. Maker Pat Auld.

Previous outstanding vintages: '59, '65, '67, '68, '73, '79, '80, '83, '86, '87

CURRENT RELEASE 1991 *Bin 8203* Strangely peppery and low in alcohol for what was touted as a great red year in the Hunter. There are leathery regional characters too, and the wine is slightly hollow and astringent in the mouth. Give it the benefit of the doubt and cellar, then drink with a mature cheese.

Lindemans Hunter River Steven Hermitage

QUALITY ▼▼▼⸜
VALUE ★★★
GRAPES shiraz
REGION Hunter Valley, NSW
CELLAR 3+
ALC./VOL. 12.0%
RRP $18.75 ⓢ

This is an individual vineyard wine: Karl Stockhausen established this vineyard for Lindemans when he was winemaker at Ben Ean between 1959 and 1985. Maker Patrick Auld.

CURRENT RELEASE 1990 *Bin 8025* Strong Hunter identity leaps from the glass here! If you like that old-bandages scent, tinged with ancient leather armchairs, this is for you. Earthy, spicy, leathery developed Hunter flavours. Medium-bodied, mature and well balanced with a trace of liquorice on the finish. Beaut with rabbit stew.

Lindemans Limestone Ridge

This blend of roughly one-fifth cabernet with shiraz is the most popular of Lindemans' Coonawarra trio, and deservedly so. They are wines for people who don't mind a bit of oak in their reds. Maker Greg Clayfield.

Previous outstanding vintages: '82, '86, '88, '90

CURRENT RELEASE 1991 A sophisticated combination of oak and intense fruit gives a fine floral scent to the nose. This is a deep, lush, concentrated red tasting of coffee, vanilla and dark berries. It has real structure and length. Good with barbecued red meats.

QUALITY 🍷🍷🍷🍷🍷
VALUE ★★★★
GRAPES shiraz 80%, cabernet sauvignon 20%
REGION Coonawarra, SA
CELLAR 8+
ALC./VOL. 13.0%
RRP $29.00

CURRENT RELEASE 1992 A subdued, toasty, coconut American oak nose introduces a soft, rich, broad flavour that carries a lot of oak and shows signs of integrating further with more time. There's plenty of flavour, concluded by a dry, savoury, slightly earthy tannin finish. Barbecued steak would suit.

QUALITY 🍷🍷🍷🍷
VALUE ★★★
GRAPES shiraz, cabernet sauvignon
REGION Coonawarra, SA
CELLAR 2–6+
ALC./VOL. 12.5%
RRP $29.00 ⓢ

Lindemans Nyrang Hermitage

QUALITY ♟♟♟
VALUE ★★★
GRAPES shiraz
REGION Barossa, Clare, Langhorne Creek, Coonawarra & Eden Valley, SA
CELLAR 🍷 3
ALC./VOL. 13.0%
RRP $10.35 ⓢ

Lindemans used to have its cellars and offices in Nyrang Street, Lidcombe – a Sydney suburb. Hence the name of this 'cellar style' inter-regional blend.
CURRENT RELEASE 1992 This is a lively, somewhat boisterous youngster. It has a fresh, youthful purplish colour and a brash, fruity flavour with a crisp acid finish. There's a trace of tannin on the finish and it would team well with a spicy pasta sauce.

QUALITY ♟♟♟♟
VALUE ★★★★
GRAPES shiraz
REGION Clare, Barossa Valley, McLaren Vale, SA
CELLAR 🍷 4
ALC./VOL. 13.0%
RRP $10.40 ⓢ

CURRENT RELEASE 1993 Yet another damn good value red from Lindemans, with a nice full purple-red hue, fresh plummy shiraz fruit and nutty oak aromas. The palate has plenty of weight and the oak and tannins dry off the finish nicely. A savoury food style that would do justice to lasagna.

Lindemans Padthaway Cabernet Merlot

QUALITY ♟♟♟♟
VALUE ★★★★½
GRAPES cabernet sauvignon 89%, merlot 11%
REGION Padthaway, SA
CELLAR 🍷 4
ALC./VOL. 13.0%
RRP $13.30 ⓢ

Padthaway has proved itself a mecca for white wines, but fine reds have been slower coming. This wine changes all that. Maker Greg Clayfield.
CURRENT RELEASE 1992 This hi-fidelity cabernet proudly struts its stuff with all the aplomb of a Moulin Rouge dancer. It's generously endowed with blackcurrant fruit and is nice and soft on the finish. It's lively, intense and fresh: just the thing for pink lamb.

QUALITY ♟♟♟♟
VALUE ★★★★½
GRAPES cabernet sauvignon, merlot
REGION Padthaway, SA
CELLAR ⇌ 1–6+
ALC./VOL. 12.5%
RRP $13.30 ⓢ 🍷

CURRENT RELEASE 1993 Yet more evidence that Padthaway reds are coming of age. Strong toasty oak on the nose gives way in the mouth to smooth, rich, round cabernet flavours with fruit winning the tussle over wood. Ripe and harmonious in the mouth with supple tannins. Good value, and a fine choice with kassler.

Lindemans Padthaway Pinot Noir

The grocery marketers at Lindemans have been at it again, changing the labels. At least the new ones look good. Maker Greg Clayfield.

CURRENT RELEASE 1993 If it wasn't for the distracting gumleaf/mint overtones and excessive oak vanillan, this would be a pretty handy pinot. There's a velvety smooth richness, nice tannin and flesh, but the wine is oak-driven in every regard. It has length and balance but the vanilla flavour dominates the longer it's in the glass.

QUALITY 🍷🍷🍷🍷
VALUE ★★★½
GRAPES pinot noir
REGION Padthaway, SA
CELLAR 🍷 3
ALC./VOL. 13.5%
RRP $13.30 ⓢ

Lindemans Pyrus

The Southcorp umbrella casts a long shadow these days: the Lindeman Coonawarras, especially this one, are looking increasingly like Penfolds reds. Maker Greg Clayfield.

Previous outstanding vintages: '85, '86, '88, '90

CURRENT RELEASE 1991 Excellent deep purple-red colour and the nose is very oaky and concentrated, with toasty, earthy and minty characters. It's a big, gutsy, powerful red with stacks of oak but it all manages to stay in balance. Solid, rich, chewy: a good Penfolds impersonation. Drink with a juicy steak.

QUALITY 🍷🍷🍷🍷🍷
VALUE ★★★★
GRAPES cabernet sauvignon, merlot, malbec, cabernet franc
REGION Coonawarra, SA
CELLAR 🍷 8+
ALC./VOL. 13.0%
RRP $29.00 ⓢ

CURRENT RELEASE 1992 Assertive toasty oak permeates this wine, giving a dusty, biscuity nose and a cedary, slightly hollow, dry tannin palate. May just need a little time to sort itself out. Slightly confused and hard to assess at present.

QUALITY 🍷🍷🍷🍷
VALUE ★★★
GRAPES cabernet sauvignon, merlot, malbec, cabernet franc
REGION Coonawarra, SA
CELLAR ⊷ 2–5+
ALC./VOL. 12.5%
RRP $29.00 ⓢ

Lindemans St George Cabernet Sauvignon

QUALITY 🍷🍷🍷
VALUE ★★½
GRAPES cabernet sauvignon
REGION Coonawarra, SA
CELLAR 🍾 3+
ALC./VOL. 13.0%
RRP $29.00 💲🍾

Named after Major General Hinton St George, one of the early 'wine doctors' who retired to a vineyard in Coonawarra. This is usually the least impressive of the Lindemans Coonawarra trio. Previous outstanding vintages: '86, '88

CURRENT RELEASE 1991 This is true to style, showing dominant oak on the nose and palate. Very toasty with grainy tannins and a slightly short finish. We're not sure whether the fruit concentration is there for age to confer harmony. Try it with wiener schnitzel.

QUALITY 🍷🍷🍷🍷
VALUE ★★★½
GRAPES cabernet sauvignon
REGION Coonawarra, SA
CELLAR ⇌ 2–10+
ALC./VOL. 13.0%
RRP $29.00 💲🍾

CURRENT RELEASE 1992 Again true to style, with lots of cedary French oak and a lean, dry palate which has tight concentration and balance. Ripe cherry, currant and oak on the bouquet. Needs a little time to come together, then drink with guinea fowl.

Marienberg Cabernet Sauvignon

QUALITY 🍷🍷🍷🍷
VALUE ★★★½
GRAPES cabernet sauvignon
REGION McLaren Vale, SA
CELLAR 🍾 3
ALC./VOL. 13.1%
RRP $13.00

The vineyard was founded in 1966 by Geoff and Ursula Pridham. It is now owned by the Hill group of companies and produces around 20,000 cases per annum.

CURRENT RELEASE 1991 Starting to show signs of maturity, the nose offers concentrated developed fruit aromas while the palate is quite rich with medium-bodied fruit. The main flavour is plum, and there's an astringent finish with robust tannins. It would be a good osso bucco style.

Marion's Vineyard Cabernet Sauvignon

Marion and Mark Semmens are American imports whose vineyard has one of the most stunning settings overlooking the Tamar River estuary. They are known to throw the occasional party at the winery, which is in demand as a function venue.

Previous outstanding vintages: '88

CURRENT RELEASE 1990 This is a late starter, coming onto the market at nearly five years old – which is a bonus. The wine is deeply coloured and smells very ripe: dark berry and mint aromas allied to vanilla and caramel from oak. There is a lot of oak tannin which could still use time to soften. Drink with pan-fried calf's liver.

QUALITY 🍷🍷🍷🍷
VALUE ★★★★
GRAPES cabernet sauvignon
REGION West Tamar, Tas.
CELLAR ➡ 1–5+
ALC./VOL. 13.0%
RRP $18.00 (cellar door)

Maxwell Cabernet Merlot

This is the economy package from Maxwell. It represents reasonable drinking at an affordable price.

CURRENT RELEASE 1992 A lean wine that is dominated by an astringent finish. The nose is vinous with a hint of rose-petal. The palate is tight with redcurrant flavours followed by a slightly stalky finish and some assertive tannins. A tough wine that goes well with a meat pie.

QUALITY 🍷🍷🍷
VALUE ★★★
GRAPES cabernet sauvignon, merlot
REGION McLaren Vale, SA
CELLAR 🍾 2
ALC./VOL. 12.5%
RRP $9.95

Maxwell Ellen Street Shiraz

Ellen Street is the name of a vineyard in McLaren Vale that features very old shiraz vines.

CURRENT RELEASE 1993 This is a charming yet robust style. The colour is deep and the nose has succulent ripe fruit aromas and attractive spice. The palate is rich with ripe fruit, a hint of iron tonic and more spice. The finish shows well-integrated oak and positive tannin grip. It goes well with rare roast beef.

QUALITY 🍷🍷🍷🍷?
VALUE ★★★★½
GRAPES shiraz
REGION McLaren Vale, SA
CELLAR 🍾 6
ALC./VOL. 13.5%
RRP $11.50

Maxwell Lime Cave Cabernet Sauvignon

QUALITY 🍷🍷🍷🍷
VALUE ★★★★
GRAPES cabernet sauvignon
REGION McLaren Vale, SA
CELLAR 🍾 2–6
ALC./VOL. 12.5%
RRP $13.50

The lime cave in question is located at the bottom of the vineyard and was hand dug in 1912 for the commercial production of mushrooms. It is currently being turned into a storage cellar. Maker Mark Maxwell.

CURRENT RELEASE 1992 A very elegant and well-made style with plenty of development to come. The colour is deep crimson and the nose is full of fruit. The palate has strong blackberry flavour bound to assertive oak on an astringent finish. It would go well with rare beef.

Maxwell Reserve Shiraz

QUALITY 🍷🍷🍷🍷½
VALUE ★★★★½
GRAPES shiraz
REGION McLaren Vale, SA
CELLAR 🍾 4
ALC./VOL. 13.5%
RRP $14.00

This long-established winery is typical of the small-sized producers in the Southern Vales. The production is around 4000 cases. Maker Mark Maxwell.

CURRENT RELEASE 1991 A complete and almost seamless wine that has authentic regional characters. The colour is dark red and the nose has herb and plum aromas. The full palate is rich and sensuous with a warmth of alcohol. Plum flavour dominates with a lift of spice, while the finish has ample soft tannins making the wine perfect for a shepherd's pie.

Meadowbank Pinot Noir

QUALITY 🍷🍷🍷🍷
VALUE ★★★★
GRAPES pinot noir
REGION Southern Tasmania
CELLAR 🍾 3
ALC./VOL. 12.5%
RRP $20.00

This vineyard is one of the few (perhaps only) Tasmanian vineyards that isn't influenced by the sea. It is landlocked north of Hobart. Maker Greg O'Keefe.

CURRENT RELEASE 1994 This has an impressively dense colour and there are berry aromas on the nose with hints of cherry. The palate is tight with restrained dark cherry flavours tinged by spice and followed by firm oak on a dry finish. Try it with rabbit.

Merricks Estate Shiraz

This vineyard and winery was established in 1978 and today (vintage permitting) it produces around 2000 cases.

CURRENT RELEASE 1993 Who said they didn't get grapes ripe on the Mornington Peninsula? This is a big, rich wine by any standards. The colour is dense and the nose intense with strong mulberry and bracken aromas. The palate is complex with concentrated dark cherry flavours framed by black tea-like tannins and high acid on a strong finish. It needs time but if you drink it now, it requires a robust dish like jugged hare.

QUALITY ♛♛♛♛♛
VALUE ★★★★
GRAPES shiraz
REGION Mornington Peninsula, Vic.
CELLAR ☐ 3–8
ALC./VOL. 14.0%
RRP $22.25

Mildara Alexanders

This is Mildara's top Coonawarra red. It is a well-sorted style that introduces the best fruit to the finest oak. Maker 'Gifted' Gavin Hogg.
Previous outstanding vintages: '85, '86, '87, '88, '90

CURRENT RELEASE 1991 This has all the hallmarks of a classic Coonawarra red, showing great style with a leaf, mint and cassis nose and a taut palate, but with an impressive depth of sweet raspberry. The finish is elegant, subtle in oak and fine-grained tannins. The result is grip, balance, and just the thing for slightly spicy bratwurst sausages.

QUALITY ♛♛♛♛♛
VALUE ★★★★
GRAPES cabernet sauvignon
REGION Coonawarra, SA
CELLAR ☐ 2–8
ALC./VOL. 12.5%
RRP $24.00

Mildara Coonawarra Cabernet Sauvignon

QUALITY ♛♛♛♛♛
VALUE ★★★★★
GRAPES cabernet sauvignon
REGION Coonawarra, SA
CELLAR ➡ 4–8
ALC./VOL. 13.5%
RRP $18.95

Ever since the legendary 'Peppermint Patty' in 1963, this label has been revered by wine buffs. Rightly so.
Previous outstanding vintages: '63, '71, '76, '80, '86, '88, '90, '91
CURRENT RELEASE 1993 A very fine style that brings out the Bordeaux in Coonawarra. The nose has classy oak and sweet cassis aromas. The palate is lean and fine. Cassis is the main flavour and there are hints of tobacco and leaf supported by some fine-grained tannins on a very long finish. A style that needs time; try it with roast squab.

Mildara Hermitage

QUALITY ♛♛♛♛
VALUE ★★★★½
GRAPES shiraz
REGION Coonawarra, Barossa Valley, SA
CELLAR 🍷 4
ALC./VOL. 13.5%
RRP $7.95

The style of this wine is always dictated by Mother Nature. In cool years it will be lean, but in years of even ripening it will have plenty of body.
CURRENT RELEASE 1993 A fuller style than usual with a minty nose and a blackberry undertone. The palate is full of berries and tinged with spice. Subtle oak and clean acid makes for a soft finish. A good wine for goulash.

Miranda Rovalley Ridge Shiraz

QUALITY ♛♛♛♛
VALUE ★★★½
GRAPES shiraz
REGION Barossa Valley, SA
CELLAR 🍷 4
ALC./VOL. 13.0%
RRP $14.00

The new label is less confusing. Miranda is a large wine company in Griffith and they purchased Rovalley in the Barossa Valley. Maker Shayne Cunningham.
CURRENT RELEASE 1992 This has rich, almost porty aromas and plenty of ripe plum as well. There are dense plum and gentle spice flavours on a lightweight palate that's supported by gentle acid and soft tannin. A good regional style that drinks well now.

Mitchell Growers Grenache

Another arrow in the ever expanding grenache quiver. Grenache has experienced a miraculous return to grace.

CURRENT RELEASE 1994 Ripe, ripe, ripe! Turn up the Dervish music with the Eastern hypnotics, this wine is an experience not to be missed. The nose has strong raspberry aromas plus a waft of alcohol. The palate is slinky and mouthfilling. A sensuous experience of ripe raspberry flavour and a warmth of alcohol. The finish is alcohol-driven, and there's been no oak treatment. A fantasy wine that needs liver and bacon.

QUALITY 🍷🍷🍷🍷🍷
VALUE ★★★★★
GRAPES grenache
REGION Clare Valley, SA
CELLAR 🍾 3
ALC./VOL. 15.0%
RRP $16.50

Mitchell Pepper Tree Vineyard Shiraz

A distinctive cellar style that has captured the hearts and wallets of Clare Valley devotees. Maker Andrew Mitchell.

Previous outstanding vintages: '88, '89, '90, '91

CURRENT RELEASE 1993 A very faithful rendition of the style. It's slightly finer than other years but no less substantial. The nose is spicy with macerated plum aromas. The plum theme is continued on a juicy palate, which is matched by supportive oak on a dry finish with substantial grip. It drinks well now with devilled kidneys.

QUALITY 🍷🍷🍷🍷🍷
VALUE ★★★★
GRAPES shiraz
REGION Clare Valley, SA
CELLAR 🍾 4
ALC./VOL. 13.5%
RRP $16.50

Mitchelton III Shiraz Mourvèdre Grenache

This is a relatively new development in the Mitchelton portfolio. It is a Rhône style with very interesting flavours. Maker Don Lewis.

CURRENT RELEASE 1993 A rich style that drinks well now. The colour is a deep crimson and the nose is dominated by spice. The palate is full-bodied and there are cherry and berry flavours plus plenty of spice. The finish is well matched with some fine-grained tannins and attractive grip. It goes well with pan-fried kangaroo.

QUALITY 🍷🍷🍷🍷
VALUE ★★★★
GRAPES shiraz, mourvèdre, grenache
REGION Goulburn Valley, Vic.
CELLAR 🍾 3
ALC./VOL. 13.5%
RRP $19.95 Ⓢ

Mitchelton Chinaman's Bridge Merlot

QUALITY 🍷🍷🍷🍷
VALUE ★★★★
GRAPES merlot
REGION Goulburn Valley, Vic.
CELLAR 🍾 3
ALC./VOL. 12.5%
RRP $12.90

You wouldn't miss this one on a dark night – the label is as striking as a baseball bat. Mitchelton is now part of Petaluma, so it will be interesting to watch future developments. Maker Don Lewis.

CURRENT RELEASE 1993 The emphasis is on elegance. The colour is a mid-ruby and the nose has some rose petal aromas. The middleweight palate offers attractive cherry flavours backed up by subtle oak. The finish is dry and adds balance. It goes well with a rabbit stew.

Moondah Brook Cabernet Sauvignon

QUALITY 🍷🍷🍷🍷
VALUE ★★★★
GRAPES cabernet sauvignon
REGION Gingin, WA
CELLAR 🍾 3
ALC./VOL. 13.0%
RRP $13.00

This location in the Darling Ranges north of Perth is serviced by the Fremantle Doctor (a local trade wind) that comes in much earlier than in southern locations. The zephyr cools the fruit in the vineyard.

CURRENT RELEASE 1992 The colour is a deep ruby and the nose is vinous with ripe cherry and raspberry flavours. The palate is complex, with berry and spice flavours mingled with early oak. The oak continues on the finish and adds grip and astringency. It is a drink-now style that goes well with haggis.

Mount Avoca Cabernet

This vineyard was established in 1978 and now the second generation is at the marketing helm. Proprietor John Barry remains helmsman and son Matthew is calling the marketing shots. Maker Rod Morrish.

Previous outstanding vintages: '84, '86, '87, '90, '91

CURRENT RELEASE 1992 This is proof that the Pyrenees doesn't have to be about blood-and-guts reds. The wine is no wimp but there is a touch of elegance. The nose has marked berry and cigar-box characters while the palate is satisfying but not overbearing. Sweet berry fruit is augmented by French oak that gives a firm tannin grip. Try it with a standing rib roast of beef.

QUALITY ♛♛♛♛
VALUE ★★★★
GRAPES cabernet sauvignon, merlot, cabernet franc
REGION Pyrenees, Vic.
CELLAR 🍾 4
ALC./VOL. 13.0%
RRP $17.80

Mount Avoca Shiraz

Shiraz is a point of pride in this district and with good reason. Mount Avoca is increasing plantings, as are many of the wineries in the region.

CURRENT RELEASE 1992 This is a civilised wine that drinks well now. The colour is a mid-ruby and the nose has plenty of pepper spice. The medium-bodied palate has ripe plum and cherry flavours tuned to discreet French oak. Try it with doner kebab.

QUALITY ♛♛♛♛
VALUE ★★★★
GRAPES shiraz
REGION Pyrenees, Vic.
CELLAR 🍾 4
ALC./VOL. 12.5%
RRP $14.80

Mount Bold Shiraz

QUALITY ♛♛♛♛♛
VALUE ★★★★½
GRAPES shiraz
REGION McLaren Vale, SA
CELLAR ⌑ 2–6
ALC./VOL. 13.5%
RRP $15.30

Mount Bold is the export/restaurant label at the top of the tree for Maxwell in McLaren Vale. The packaging is very attractive. Maker Mark Maxwell.

CURRENT RELEASE 1992 A fine wine with plenty of style. The colour is intense and the nose has spiced and ripe shiraz aromas. The palate is tight with classic plum and red-cherry flavours. The oak enters stage left without any commotion – a finely tuned wine with a well-tailored finish. Goes well with char-grilled side fillet of kangaroo.

Mount Horrocks Cabernet Merlot

QUALITY ♛♛♛♛
VALUE ★★★★
GRAPES cabernet sauvignon 75%, merlot 25%
REGION Clare Valley, SA
CELLAR ▮ 4
ALC./VOL. 13.0%
RRP $15.50

Mount Horrocks was established in 1982 as a tiny vineyard with a production in the order of 3500 cases. The wines are made at Grosset.

CURRENT RELEASE 1992 This is a handsome middleweight from Clare. The nose has intense mint aromas and the palate offers sweet berry flavours with a trace of mint. Fine-grained tannins adorn the long dry finish. It will cellar well and it could handle mildly spiced bratwurst sausages.

QUALITY ♛♛♛♛
VALUE ★★★★
GRAPES cabernet sauvignon 75%, merlot 25%
REGION Clare Valley, SA
CELLAR ⌑ 2–6
ALC./VOL. 13.5%
RRP $16.00

CURRENT RELEASE 1993 This is a wine that takes time to open up. At first it tastes quite firm and the nose is reserved, but with air it blossoms. The colour is dark crimson and the nose has rosewater and berry aromas. The palate offers ripe fruit and dense wood with plenty of tannin grip on the finish. It goes well with steak and kidney pudding.

Mount Hurtle Cabernet Merlot

Amaze your friends at dinner parties. The illustration on the label is entitled 'Three black ducks' yet there are only two ducks visible. Look closely under the ripples ...

CURRENT RELEASE 1992 The colour is a mid-ruby and the nose has plenty of spice and capsicum aroma. The palate is medium-bodied, with sweet fruit and a light cherry flavour plus hints of raspberry. The finish shows very deft oak treatment that imparts a positive tannin grip. It drinks well now with a pepper steak.

QUALITY ♛♛♛♛
VALUE ★★★★
GRAPES cabernet sauvignon, merlot
REGION Goulburn Valley 54%, Vic. & McLaren Vale 33%, Coonawarra 13%, SA
CELLAR 🍾 3
ALC./VOL. 13.0%
RRP $11.50

Mount Hurtle Grenache

There is a story to this wine that dates back many years. MS was always criticising Geoff Merrill about the price of his wine. The grenache style was invented for 'cheapskate Shield'. Little could he know he was reviving a flagging variety.

CURRENT RELEASE 1994 This is a rosé by any other name. It has soft raspberry aromas and a pretty pink colour. The palate has a hint of sweetness plus typical varietal raspberry balanced by cleansing acid on a lingering finish. It tastes deceptively un-alcoholic. Serve well chilled with antipasto.

QUALITY ♛♛♛♛
VALUE ★★★★
GRAPES grenache
REGION McLaren Vale, SA
CELLAR 🍾 1
ALC./VOL. 13.5%
RRP $9.50

Mount Hurtle Shiraz

Pay attention to the top of the capsule. It's a Geoffrey Lewis quirk. You are dealing with a complex character who vacillates between Forrest Gump and Albert Einstein.

CURRENT RELEASE 1992 The colour is a medium ruby and the nose has strong ripe fruit and plum aromas. The palate is fruity with some ironstone/regional characters plus peppers. The finish shows unobtrusive oak. It goes well with a veal goulash.

QUALITY ♛♛♛♖
VALUE ★★★½
GRAPES shiraz, cabernet sauvignon
REGION McLaren Vale 86%, Coonawarra 6%, SA & Goulburn Valley, Vic.
CELLAR 🍾 4
ALC./VOL. 12.5%
RRP $11.50

Mount Ida Shiraz

QUALITY 🍷🍷🍷🍷
VALUE ★★★½
GRAPES shiraz
REGION Heathcote, Vic.
CELLAR 🍷 2–6+
ALC./VOL. 13.0%
RRP $17.00 ⓢ 🍷

Originally started by Len French, Mount Ida was acquired by Tisdall, now part of the Mildara Blass group, which has grown to such a size that it's spawned a second distribution company (Southern Cross Wines) to handle the overflow. Maker Toni Stockhausen.

CURRENT RELEASE 1991 At first taste, this is all about high-toast American oak, relegating the normally impressive Heathcote fruit to the background. But let it breathe and the fruit richness shines through – it transforms into a yummy velvety smooth red. Cellar, or decant and air thoroughly, then try it with smoked meats.

Mount Langi Ghiran Cabernet Merlot

QUALITY 🍷🍷🍷🍷
VALUE ★★★½
GRAPES cabernet sauvignon, merlot
REGION Grampians District, Vic.
CELLAR 🍷 2–6
ALC./VOL. 13.0%
RRP $14.00 🍷

This winery has an up-town underground following. It appeals to organic dudes as well as the street-smart who know a good wine when they have a glass in front of them. Maker Trevor Mast.

CURRENT RELEASE 1992 The dense colour and spicy nose with *sotto voce* berry are followed by a palate that is a little bit sulky and reluctant – it seems to be in bondage to some rather dominating oak. Time might restore a sunny disposition. Try it with emu fillet fried with olive oil.

Mount Langi Ghiran Shiraz

Learning his winemaking in Germany did a lot for Trevor Mast: he's been back there recently selling wine to the biggest German liquor chain, Jacques Wine Depot. This vintage was picked in May and the crop was down 30 per cent.

Previous outstanding vintages: '84, '86, '88, '89, '90, '91, '92

CURRENT RELEASE 1993 This is 750 ml of bottled excitement, a wine that rises to any occasion. A typical Langi, fresh and fruit-driven, with pepper and spice coupled with dark berry fruit aromas. The palate has superb depth of cool, elegant flavour. It's less forbidding than some earlier vintages, but right up to the mark and drinks well already. Try it with aged parmesan cheese.

QUALITY ★★★★★
VALUE ★★★★★
GRAPES shiraz
REGION Grampians, Vic.
CELLAR 10+
ALC./VOL. 13.5%
RRP $21.00

Best Shiraz

Mountadam Pinot Noir

Could Eden Valley/Eden Hills be the place where the great Australian pinot noirs will be made? There is ever-increasing evidence to suspect this will be the case. Maker Adam Wynn.

Previous outstanding vintages: '89, '90, '91

CURRENT RELEASE 1993 Big, buxom, slinky and sexy! The colour is a 'come hither' ruby and the nose has sap, cherry and game aromas. The palate is rich with an impressive depth of dark cherry fruit flavour married to some well-integrated oak that supplies a positive grip. Full marks for the tannin grip and the voluptuous structure. Try it with venison sausages.

QUALITY ★★★★½
VALUE ★★★★½
GRAPES pinot noir
REGION Eden Valley, SA
CELLAR 5
ALC./VOL. 14.0%
RRP $26.00

Mountadam The Red

QUALITY ▼▼▼▼
VALUE ★★★
GRAPES cabernet sauvignon 50%, merlot 50%
REGION Eden Valley, SA
REGION 🍷 2–10
ALC./VOL. 13.0%
RRP $34.00

It's a bit like *Superman: The Movie*: this is the top of the ziggurat for the Mountadam winery which has a total annual production of 30,000 cases. Maker Adam Wynn.

Previous outstanding vintages: '89, '90

CURRENT RELEASE 1991 As ever, an individual wine which has its own statement on style. The colour is deep ruby and the nose offers crushed rose-petals and hints of cedar. The palate is complex, with cassis flavour plus hints of cedar and briar followed by some toasty oak on a long and astringent finish. A very sophisticated wine. Try it with pheasant in a reduction sauce.

Murrindindi Vineyards Cabernets

QUALITY ▼▼▼▼⸸
VALUE ★★★★½
GRAPES cabernet sauvignon, cabernet franc
REGION Murrindindi, Vic.
CELLAR 🍷 2–6+
ALC./VOL. 12.5%
RRP $20.00

The Murrindindi Vineyards are located in between the head of the Yarra Valley and the Strathbogie Ranges. It is beautiful country and the vineyard is a labour of love for the Cuthbertson family. Maker Hugh Cuthbertson.

CURRENT RELEASE 1992 Little has changed since the last review. The wine seems to be hastening slowly towards maturity. The nose is complex with berry, leaf and smoky aromas. The palate is tight with concentrated blackberry flavours bound to fine-grained tannins on an astringent finish. Be patient and cellar, or drink now with a char-grilled piece of eye fillet in red wine sauce.

Normans Chais Clarendon Cabernet Sauvignon

Chais is French for winery, and Clarendon is where this one's located. The groovy minimalist label serves as Normans' prestige brand.
CURRENT RELEASE 1991 This is a good Penfolds imitation, which is no back-handed compliment. Slightly closed and austere, it will benefit from age before opening. The shy nose carries toasty oak, dark berry and nutmeg/vanilla, and opens up with airing. In the mouth one finds a tight structure and firm tannin finish. Cellar, then serve with venison.

QUALITY 🍷🍷🍷🍷
VALUE ★★★★
GRAPES cabernet sauvignon
REGION not stated
CELLAR ➡ 2–8+
ALC./VOL. 13.0%
RRP $25.00 ⑤

Normans Chais Clarendon Shiraz

This major winery was owned by Adelaide's Horlin Smith family until they launched a public float in 1994. Maker Brian Light.
CURRENT RELEASE 1993 Oak has been cleverly used here to pump up a wine without overpowering its fruit. The nose is all vanilla and sweet berry-jam, echoing ultra-ripe fruit and high alcohol. The palate is smooth and rich and very vanillary. Try it with a rich game dish with chocolate in the sauce.

QUALITY 🍷🍷🍷
VALUE ★★★
GRAPES shiraz
REGION not stated
CELLAR 🍾 5+
ALC./VOL. 14.0%
RRP $24.00 ⑤

Normans Family Reserve Cabernet Sauvignon

This label consistently heralds good value for money wines. The Normans winery is near Clarendon in the foothills north of McLaren Vale. Maker Brian Light.
CURRENT RELEASE 1993 Dangerously easy to drink. This has a captivating soft-berry and liquorice aroma and the palate is medium-bodied with lots of fruit, negligible oak and gentle tannins. A straightforward easy-drinking red.

QUALITY 🍷🍷🍷
VALUE ★★★½
GRAPES cabernet sauvignon
REGION not stated
CELLAR 🍾 5
ALC./VOL. 13.0%
RRP $15.00 ⑤

Oakland Cabernet Mataro Grenache

QUALITY ♥♥♥♥
VALUE ★★★★½
GRAPES cabernet sauvignon 55%, mataro 25%, grenache 20%
REGION Barossa Valley, SA
CELLAR 🍷 3
ALC./VOL. 13.0%
RRP $10.00 $

This is the economy label from the Grant Burge stable. It makes use of the some stalwart Barossa grape varieties. Maker Grant Burge.

CURRENT RELEASE 1993 No threats here, this is a soft fruity wine that is ready to drink. There are excellent berry characters on the nose and the palate has plenty of raspberry flavour and sweet fruit backed by some gentle tannin and acid on a clean dry finish. A good pasta style.

Old Kent River Pinot Noir

QUALITY ♥♥♥♥½
VALUE ★★★★½
GRAPES pinot noir
REGION Frankland River, WA
CELLAR 🍷 4+
ALC./VOL. 12.0%
RRP $12.00 (cellar door)

This newcomer in the Frankland region has a five-hectare vineyard and the wines are made at Alkoomi. The '93s were made by Kim Hart.

CURRENT RELEASE 1993 A most impressive full-bodied pinot, with a deep colour, rich oak/fruit nose and concentrated palate flavour matched by serious tannin. This is a label to watch. Drink with a coq au vin made with the same wine.

Orlando Lawson's Shiraz

QUALITY ♥♥♥♥½
VALUE ★★★★
GRAPES shiraz
REGION Padthaway, SA
CELLAR 🍷 5
ALC./VOL. 12.5%
RRP $23.00

According to the winemakers the trick to making good red at Padthaway is stressing the fruit. Judging by the result they are on the right track. Robert Lawson was the pioneer of Padthaway. Maker Team Effort.

Previous outstanding vintages: '88, '89, '90

CURRENT RELEASE 1992 Possibly the best Lawson yet. The nose has strong ripe berry aromas and plenty of pepper. The palate displays a concentrated fruit character but with ripeness while still remaining firm. The finish cavorts about with zingy oak. A well-made and perfectly balanced Australian shiraz style. Try it with roast saddle of hare.

Pankhurst Cabernet Merlot

Pankhurst is a tiny vineyard and its wines aren't easy to find. With boutique wineries, sometimes the only way is to phone or write direct. See the directory at the end of this book.

CURRENT RELEASE 1993 The flavours here lean rather heavily towards vanilla, caramel and chocolate, suggesting a long time in wood. There are dark berries as well, sweet and ripe on the tongue, and smooth on the finish. Not so complex, but very drinkable. Try it with any meat and a rich demiglaze.

QUALITY ★★★
VALUE ★★★½
GRAPES cabernet sauvignon, merlot
REGION Canberra district, NSW
CELLAR 5+
ALC./VOL. 12.5%
RRP $13.00 (cellar door)

Pankhurst Pinot Noir

This three-hectare vineyard at Hall, near Canberra, was started in 1986. The wines are made by other local wineries, recently Roger Harris at Brindabella Hills.

CURRENT RELEASE 1992 This is a promising effort, with hints of stalk and mint on the nose, and a palate of serious weight and flavour depth. It has been worked hard, resulting in fairly firm tannins, and it may benefit from some time to soften. Try it with moussaka.

QUALITY ★★★★
VALUE ★★★★
GRAPES pinot noir
REGION Canberra district, NSW
CELLAR 1–3+
ALC./VOL. 12.5%
RRP $13.00 (cellar door)

Paracombe Cabernet Franc

Paracombe is the site of an old shiraz vineyard which provided John Davoren with grapes for his early Penfolds St Henri Clarets. Like merlot, cabernet franc may be better suited to the hills than cabernet sauvignon.

CURRENT RELEASE 1993 Attractive sweet, leafy, tobacco-ish bouquet leads into a fine red of lighter body but good flavour and mid-palate. A well-balanced wine that shows cabernet franc can stand up by itself. Try it with spaghetti marinara.

QUALITY ★★★★
VALUE ★★★★
GRAPES cabernet franc
REGION Adelaide Hills, SA
CELLAR 3
ALC./VOL. 12.7%
RRP $13.00 (ex-winery)

Paringa Estate Pinot Noir

QUALITY ★★★★★
VALUE ★★★★
GRAPES pinot noir
REGION Mornington Peninsula, Vic.
CELLAR 🍷 3+
ALC./VOL. 13.8%
RRP $25.00 (cellar door)

Lindsay McCall's small vineyard is one of the most exciting new names in Victoria, with pinot and shiraz that have turned our heads on several occasions.

CURRENT RELEASE 1993 What a seducer! This sensuous pinot brings forth delightful aromas of sweet, ripe brandied cherries backlit by dusty, stalky hints. The palate is silky smooth, fruit-sweet and bursting with vibrant, authentic pinot flavour, backed by subtle oak and gentle tannins. Barbecue some tuna steaks.

Paringa Estate Shiraz

QUALITY ★★★★★
VALUE ★★★★½
GRAPES shiraz
REGION Mornington Peninsula, Vic.
CELLAR 🍷 6+
ALC./VOL. 12.7%
RRP $25.00 (cellar door)

On paper, Mornington is not the area you'd probably choose to plant shiraz, but this small four-hectare vineyard seems to be well suited. The wines are not easy to find. Maker Lindsay McCall.

Previous outstanding vintages: '91

CURRENT RELEASE 1993 A concentrated yet very elegant shiraz, with superb dark colour, pungent pepper/spice and classy oak bouquet, and stacks of delicious sweet-berry flavour in the mouth. The finish is soft with plenty of supple tannin. Try it with mild Indian curry.

Passing Clouds Shiraz Cabernet

QUALITY ★★★★★
VALUE ★★★★½
GRAPES shiraz 60%, cabernet sauvignon 40%
REGION Bendigo, Vic.
CELLAR 🍷 2–10+
ALC./VOL. 13.5%
RRP $17.70 🍷

The name refers to the moisture status of this arid spot 50 km north-west of Bendigo. This particular wine is estate-grown, although there are other reds made from other people's grapes.

CURRENT RELEASE 1991 Deep purple-red colour and a powerful peppermint, blackberry, central Victorian nose are the first impressions. There is huge depth of fruit and flavour, excellent concentration, lightly played oak, and good tannin grip. This wine has handsome style and is a delicious drink with roast lamb.

Peel Estate Shiraz

This winery's specialty is an unusual wood-matured chenin blanc. Maker Will Nairn.

CURRENT RELEASE 1990 This is showing some maturity now, with a green vegetal edge to the peppery fruit underlined by some slightly suspect oak, and winds up with furry tannins. Try it with steak and kidney pie.

QUALITY ♛♛♛
VALUE ★★★
GRAPES shiraz
REGION South-west Coastal Plain, WA
CELLAR 🍷 2
ALC./VOL. 13.5%
RRP $17.70

Penfolds Bin 28 Kalimna Shiraz

Kalimna is the jewel in Penfolds' crown, a large vineyard in the northern Barossa Valley which provides the basis for Grange and all the premium Penfolds reds. Maker John Duval.

Previous outstanding vintages: '82, '83, '86, '87, '88, '90, '91

CURRENT RELEASE 1992 Ever reliable, this '92 Kalimna is a very good vintage, very much in the Penfolds style with plum, spice, earthy ripe fruit and well-integrated oak flavours. It is very generous in the mouth: full, deep, rich, with lashings of sweet fruit and finishing solid, chunky and dry, with length and the ability to age. Try it with osso bucco.

QUALITY ♛♛♛♛
VALUE ★★★★
GRAPES shiraz
REGION Barossa Valley, Padthaway, McLaren Vale, SA
CELLAR 🍷 6+
ALC./VOL. 13.5%
RRP $15.50 ⓢ 🍷

Penfolds Bin 389 Cabernet Shiraz

QUALITY ♥♥♥♥⸰
VALUE ★★★★½
GRAPES cabernet sauvignon, shiraz
REGION Padthaway, Barossa Valley, Coonawarra & McLaren Vale, SA
CELLAR ← 3–10+
ALC./VOL. 13.5%
RRP $19.60

Max Schubert created this wine in the 1950s when cabernet grapes were a scarce commodity. It's nicknamed the Poor Man's Grange because it goes into the previous vintage Grange barrels.
Previous outstanding vintages: '66, '71, '80, '82, '83, '86, '87, '90, '91
CURRENT RELEASE 1992 Typically dominated in its youth by toasty Penfolds-style American oak, this vintage has a touch of mint and the usual high-extract palate finishing with mouth-puckering tannin. Full-bodied and grainy textured, it's a gutsy wine that demands patience. Cellar, then serve with game meats.

Penfolds Bin 407 Cabernet Sauvignon

QUALITY ♥♥♥♥
VALUE ★★★★
GRAPES cabernet sauvignon
REGION Padthaway, Coonawarra, McLaren Vale, SA
CELLAR ← 1–5+
ALC./VOL. 13.5%
RRP $19.60

This new wine was created to fill the gap that was left as Bin 707 cabernet got increasingly expensive and difficult to get. Maker John Duval and team.
Previous outstanding vintages: '90, '91
CURRENT RELEASE 1992 This tastes as though Coonawarra played a big part in its creation: the nose shows refined blackcurrant cabernet fruit, smoky/toasty oak and a whisper of volatility that doesn't mar. The palate is dry, lean and medium-bodied – perhaps lighter than prior vintages. A fine, subtle wine with well-judged tannin. Drink with lamb chops.

Penfolds Bin 707 Cabernet Sauvignon

Penfolds is hyping this up to be regarded as the cabernet equivalent of Grange. In the blurb, it boldly declares 'Australia's benchmark cabernet'. It seems to be harder to get and more expensive every year.
Previous outstanding vintages: '64, '76, '80, '83, '84, '86, '87, '90, '91
CURRENT RELEASE 1992 A very tightly structured Bin 707, bursting with concentrated cedar, mint and dark berry flavours. The wine is solid and high in extract, with skilfully melded oak and fruit, and enough tannin to see it age happily for many years. Cellar, then serve with roast beef and yorkshire pud.

QUALITY 🍷🍷🍷🍷🍷
VALUE ★★★★½
GRAPES cabernet sauvignon
REGION Padthaway, Coonawarra, Barossa Valley, SA
CELLAR 3–15+
ALC./VOL. 13.4%
RRP $55.00

Penfolds Clare Estate

The land for this 120-hectare vineyard was selected by the late Max Schubert, with the help of his friend Mick Knappstein. Part of it is organically managed for export wines.
Previous outstanding vintages: '86, '90, '91
CURRENT RELEASE 1992 A very woody wine, lean and tough with lots of tannin that turns bitter on the finish. May come good with time in the cellar. The flavours are of vanilla and coffee rather than fruit. If you're drinking it now, decant and breathe it well first. (Our bottle was much better four days later!) A match for steak and kidney pie.

QUALITY 🍷🍷🍷
VALUE ★★★
GRAPES cabernet sauvignon, merlot, malbec, cabernet franc
REGION Clare Valley, SA
CELLAR 1–5+
ALC./VOL. 12.5%
RRP $16.35

CURRENT RELEASE 1993 Could just be the best wine yet under this label. The nose is perfumed with mint, blackcurrant and high-char oak. In the mouth it's lush with fruit, smooth tannin and liberal oak. It's a big, fruit-sweet wine that promises more with time. Great value. Try it with steak and a blackcurrant demiglaze.

QUALITY 🍷🍷🍷🍷🍷
VALUE ★★★★★
GRAPES cabernet sauvignon, merlot, malbec, cabernet franc
REGION Clare Valley, SA
CELLAR 2–10+
ALC./VOL. 13.0%
RRP $16.35

Penfolds Grange

QUALITY ♆♆♆♆♆
VALUE ★★★★★
GRAPES shiraz
REGION Barossa & Clare Valleys, Coonawarra, SA
CELLAR ➡ 5–15+
ALC./VOL. 13.8%
RRP $130.00 ⓢ

At a rare 1994 tasting of every Grange, 40 vintages up to the 1990, it was apparent that the wines of the '80s are more consistent than ever before. The queue started years ago for this one. Maker John Duval and team.

Previous outstanding vintages: '52, '53, '55, '62, '63, '66, '71, '76, '83, '86, '88

CURRENT RELEASE 1990 This is simply the most keenly awaited Grange ever, as '90 was a great vintage, especially for Penfolds. It has all the hallmarks of a great young Grange, only more of them: more intense aroma, more richness and fruit weight on the palate, more complexity despite its youth, more harmony between the oak, tannin, fruit and other components. A mind-bending wine that lives up to the hype. Cellar at least five years, then serve with aged cheese.

Penfolds Koonunga Hill Shiraz Cabernet

QUALITY ♆♆♆♆
VALUE ★★★★★
GRAPES shiraz, cabernet sauvignon
REGION various 'dryland', SA
CELLAR 🍾 4
ALC./VOL. 13.5%
RRP $10.35 ⓢ

Best Bargain Red

We think this is the best value in inexpensive quality red wine. Every drop of it sees the inside of small oak barrels, which is unusual these days for a red of its price. Maker John Duval and team.

Previous outstanding vintages: '76, '82, '86, '89, '90, '91, '92

CURRENT RELEASE 1993 Quality fruit and winemaking in evidence here: rich, ripe plummy nose with a whisper of spice and currant. The palate is stylish with good medium weight, berries and cedar, surprising tannin and fruit sweetness. Very generous flavour: at around $9 (usually) you should feel guilty. Try a hamburger with plenty of herbs and fried onion.

Penfolds Magill Estate

This was designed by Max Schubert and Don Ditter in the early '80s to justify retaining the last of Penfolds' Magill vines, whence came half the grapes for the first Granges. The only wine still made entirely at the old Magill winery, by John Bird.

Previous outstanding vintages: '83, '86, '87, '88, '89

CURRENT RELEASE 1990 From a peak vintage for Penfolds reds, this is a powerful but reticent wine which promises much for the patient. Tightly structured and somewhat astringent with plenty of oak tannins, it has a bouquet of pencil-wood and savoury, spicy shiraz. There's concentration and length aplenty, and it will ultimately be a fine accompaniment to game and red meats.

QUALITY ♟♟♟♟
VALUE ★★★
GRAPES shiraz
REGION Adelaide foothills, SA
CELLAR ← 1–10
ALC./VOL. 13.5%
RRP $35.00

CURRENT RELEASE 1991 A complex shiraz, with intriguing spicy, violet-scented fruit and toasty cedar/cigarbox oak-matured characters. It's quite lively in the mouth with plenty of acid, intense flavour and obvious potential for cellaring. Drink with barbecued marinated lamb.

QUALITY ♟♟♟♟♟
VALUE ★★★½
GRAPES shiraz
REGION Adelaide foothills, SA
CELLAR ▮ 7+
ALC./VOL. 13.0%
RRP $35.90 ⓢ

Penfolds Old Vine Mourvèdre Grenache Shiraz

This is a new release in '95, created to appeal to the sudden new interest in the Cinderella varieties grenache and mataro (mourvèdre).

CURRENT RELEASE 1992 This opens with typical Penfolds wood-matured bouquet, giving the nose a strong toasty, nutty, dry quality that needs more fruit for balance. The mouth has plenty of oak tannin and a rather lean profile. For wood lovers. Try it with smoked meats.

QUALITY ♟♟♟
VALUE ★★★
GRAPES mataro 51%, grenache 26%, shiraz 23%
REGION Barossa Valley, SA
CELLAR ← 1–5+
ALC./VOL. 13.5%
RRP $17.00 ⓢ

Penfolds St Henri Shiraz

QUALITY 🍷🍷🍷🍷
VALUE ★★★
GRAPES shiraz
REGION McLaren Vale, Barossa Valley, Coonawarra, Padthaway & Clare, SA
CELLAR 🍾 6+
ALC./VOL. 13.5%
RRP $25.00 ⓢ 🍾

This is one of the few top Penfolds reds that wasn't created by Max Schubert, but at least he inspired it. His fellow winemaker John Davoren made it as a reaction to Grange, which he didn't like.

Previous outstanding vintages: '76, '80, '82, '83, '85, '86, '87, '89, '90

CURRENT RELEASE 1991 This is a very dry, savoury style with plenty of fruit but not in the modern grapey idiom. The nose displays wood and developed characters of leather, earth, toast and vanilla, the palate is full and not especially complex but with a long, lingering dry finish. Definitely a food style. Needs smoky barbecued steak.

Penley Estate Cabernet Sauvignon

QUALITY 🍷🍷🍷🍷🍷
VALUE ★★★★
GRAPES cabernet sauvignon
REGION Coonawarra, SA
CELLAR 🍾 10
ALC./VOL. 13.5%
RRP $37.00 🍾

Kym Tolley is something of a blue-blood in the South Australian oenostocracy: his mother was a Penfold and his dad a Tolley, so he put the two together in Penley.

Previous outstanding vintages: '89, '90, '91

CURRENT RELEASE 1992 This lad can do no wrong, at least with his straight cabernet. It is a charming wine and encapsulates the essence of Coonawarra. Gloriously perfumed nose of flowers, berries, cedar and spices. Pure fruit and classy French oak well melded, and elegant weight in the mouth. This calls for pink lamb.

Penley Estate Shiraz Cabernet

Normally when shiraz is the first-named variety, it means it exceeds cabernet by a fair margin in the wine's makeup. Not so in this case.

CURRENT RELEASE 1992 This is a delicious wine, streets ahead of the '93 Hyland Shiraz, showing excellent aromatic cassis/mulberry regional Coonawarra fruit, and cabernet dominating the shiraz. It is smooth, graceful, and approachable now. Oak leaves a twist of coffee on the finish. Enjoy with a lunch of cold rare beef, mustard and salad.

QUALITY ♛♛♛♛♛
VALUE ★★★★
GRAPES shiraz 50%, cabernet sauvignon 50%
REGION Coonawarra 90%, McLaren Vale 10%, SA
CELLAR 7
ALC./VOL. 13.5%
RRP $21.00

Petaluma Coonawarra

Brian Croser and his winemaker Andrew Hardy craft this wine to be a long-term keeper. There are no concessions to up-front accessibility and the wine is not easy to appreciate when young. Previous outstanding vintages: '79, '82, '86, '87, '88, '90, '91

CURRENT RELEASE 1992 This is a wine for the true believers: you have to punt on its future and cellar it. At present it's closed, massively tannic and its flavours are locked away in hibernation. The right ingredients seem to be there; all it needs is time. Cellar, then drink with beef in a blackcurrant demiglaze.

QUALITY ♛♛♛♛
VALUE ★★★½
GRAPES cabernet sauvignon, merlot
REGION Coonawarra, SA
CELLAR 5–12+
ALC./VOL. 13.0%
RRP $35.00

Petaluma Merlot

QUALITY 🍷🍷🍷🍷🍷
VALUE ★★★★
GRAPES merlot
REGION Coonawarra, SA
CELLAR 🍾 3–8+
ALC./VOL. 13.0%
RRP $28.20 🍷

This wine is sold on indent, i.e. certificates of ownership are sold before the wine is available, which is a clever marketing gimmick and an act of faith by the consumer.
Previous outstanding vintages: '90, '91
CURRENT RELEASE 1992 This is a very fresh, raw, undeveloped wine which seems to need quite a bit of time. The colour has dense purples and reds, the nose and palate show concentrated young fruit which is quite astringent and closed. Come back in three or four years with duck.

Peter Lehmann Cabernet Sauvignon

QUALITY 🍷🍷🍷🍷🍷
VALUE ★★★★★
GRAPES cabernet sauvignon
REGION Barossa Valley, SA
CELLAR 🍷 7+
ALC./VOL. 13.0%
RRP $13.70 ⓢ

This won the Arthur Kelman Trophy at the Sydney Wine Show and it's hard to believe that it's so inexpensive. Maker Andrew Wigan, Peter Scholz and team.
Previous outstanding vintages: '88, '89, '90
CURRENT RELEASE 1992 This is a sensational value-for-money wine! An extra year in the bottle has improved it even further: the oak has integrated better and the generous quota of chocolate, vanilla, toast and berry flavours is smoother. It remains lively in the mouth and very satisfying with rare roast beef.

QUALITY 🍷🍷🍷🍷
VALUE ★★★★
GRAPES cabernet sauvignon
REGION Barossa Valley, SA
CELLAR 🍾 1–7+
ALC./VOL. 14.0%
RRP $13.70 ⓢ

CURRENT RELEASE 1993 Made from a reduced crop, this is a worthy follow-up to the '92: herbal fruit, leather, linseed and berries, with a savoury wood-matured aspect. The palate features a generous dollop of sweet fruit countered by dry tannin, then a long follow-through warmed by alcohol. Drink with aged cheese.

Peter Lehmann Cellar Collection Cabernet Malbec

The grapes of about 150 Barossa Valley growers pass over Lehmann's famous weighbridge every year. This wine is sourced from growers in the Stonewell, Ebenezer and Light Pass sub-regions.
CURRENT RELEASE 1990 An exceptional wine: dark red hue; rich plum, vanilla, chocolate nose; very intense, penetrating flavours of complex coconut, plum and chocolate. There's great power and length: terrific now but even better in three years. Drink with a rich game casserole.

QUALITY ★★★★★
VALUE ★★★★★
GRAPES cabernet sauvignon, malbec
REGION Barossa Valley, SA
CELLAR 8+
ALC./VOL. 12.5%
RRP $20.00

Peter Lehmann Cellar Collection Stonewell Shiraz

The Stonewell vineyard, which encircles the Hermitage, the Barossa's best place to bed down, provides the fruit for this, Lehmann's flagship wine. It's the only vineyard the company actually owns. The '89 won the Jimmy Watson. Maker Andrew Wigan.
Previous outstanding vintages: '87, '88
CURRENT RELEASE 1989 A dense, power-packed shiraz with a youthful purply colour, rich sweet plummy fruit and sweet vanillan oak which after six years is beautifully melded into the wine. An intense, lively, youthful red that promises to be with us for the long haul, a trait enhanced by the magnum-only presentation. Drink with Barossa mettwurst.

QUALITY ★★★★★
VALUE ★★★★
GRAPES shiraz
REGION Barossa Valley, SA
CELLAR 10+
ALC./VOL. 13.5%
RRP $100.00 (1.5 litre)

Peter Lehmann Shiraz

This is every bit as good as the '92 cabernet but with less new oak. It's even cheaper than that wine, often selling sub-$10.
CURRENT RELEASE 1992 This is a very sexy wine, multi-layered and fleshy, with seductive fruit and almost fathomless depths. The nose is big on spice and liquorice, the palate smooth and lush, fruit-driven and supple. Spicy sausages here.

QUALITY ★★★★★
VALUE ★★★★★
GRAPES shiraz
REGION Barossa Valley, SA
CELLAR 8+
ALC./VOL. 13.5%
RRP $12.00 $

Pikes Cabernet Sauvignon

QUALITY ▉▉▉▉
VALUE ★★★½
GRAPES cabernet sauvignon
REGION Clare Valley, SA
CELLAR 🍷 1–6+
ALC./VOL. 13.5%
RRP $19.00

Neil Pike was the winemaker at Mitchell's while getting his own vineyard and winery up and running. It's located in the Polish Hill River sub-region.
Previous outstanding vintages: '86, '90, '91
CURRENT RELEASE 1992 More oaky than the same maker's shiraz, this has a big, aromatic vanilla/dark berry nose. In the mouth it's full-bodied, with dusty tannins and a firm, dry finish. Serve it with a robust, homely casserole.

Pikes Shiraz

QUALITY ▉▉▉▉▉
VALUE ★★★★
GRAPES shiraz
REGION Clare Valley, SA
CELLAR 🍷 2–7+
ALC./VOL. 14.0%
RRP $19.00

Neil Pike's forebear Henry Pike was a brewer back in the 1880s. Neil's white wine labels show an impression of a piscatorial pike taken from the beer label.
Previous outstanding vintages: '90, '91
CURRENT RELEASE 1993 This is a big, concentrated shiraz with plenty of alcohol and solid structure. The flavours are of spices, plums and liquorice with a whiff of mint. A delicious drop for those who like 'em big. Try it with kangaroo.

Pirramimma Hillsview Cabernet Merlot

QUALITY ▉▉▉
VALUE ★★★½
GRAPES cabernet sauvignon 60%, merlot 40%
REGION McLaren Vale, SA
CELLAR 🍷 3+
ALC./VOL. 12.5%
RRP $11.60 ⓢ

The Johnston family of Pirramimma celebrated their centenary recently with an excellent 1990 shiraz reviewed in last year's edition. This is very much the little brother. Maker Geoff Johnston.
CURRENT RELEASE 1990 McLaren Vale is known as the middle palate of Australian wine, and this is a good illustration. The nose is up-front sweet berries; the taste, although straightforward, is fruity and soft with a firm grip on the finish. At five years it's ready to fly. Try it with wiener schnitzel.

Plantagenet Cabernet Sauvignon

This senior Mount Barker winery goes from strength to strength despite the loss of John Wade as chief winemaker. His deputy Gavin Berry seems to be maintaining the quality.
Previous outstanding vintages: '76, '79, '81, '83, '85, '86, '89, '90, '91
CURRENT RELEASE 1992 The Plantagenet style emphasises fresh mixed-berry fruit with subtle oak and this is right in the groove. Fresh aromas of cherry, raspberry and blackberry on an elegant framework; although not a big wine it has good concentration. Well-trimmed tannin and good length. Drink with pink lamb and mint sauce.

QUALITY ★★★★★
VALUE ★★★★½
GRAPES cabernet sauvignon 83%, cabernet franc 9%, merlot 8%
REGION Mount Barker 95%, Pemberton 5%, WA
CELLAR 8+
ALC./VOL. 13.0%
RRP $21.75

Plantagenet Pinot Noir

The Lower Great Southern of WA is fast establishing itself as one of the three or four best regions in Australia for pinot noir. Made by John Wade and Gavin Berry.
Previous outstanding vintages: '90, '91, '92
CURRENT RELEASE 1993 A lovely wine which is further evidence of John Wade's mastery of the difficult grape. It has good depth of colour, a complex cherry, strawberry, toasty and vanillan bouquet with depth and intensity, and that elusive component – a silky fruit-sweet mid-palate. Drink with spaghetti marinara.

QUALITY ★★★★?
VALUE ★★★★½
GRAPES pinot noir
REGION Mount Barker, WA
CELLAR 4+
ALC./VOL. 13.5%
RRP $20.00

Plantagenet Shiraz

QUALITY 🍷🍷🍷🍷🍷
VALUE ★★★★
GRAPES shiraz
REGION Mount Barker, WA
CELLAR 🍷 8
ALC./VOL. 12.5%
RRP $20.00

The reds of Plantagenet are seldom included in lists of the country's best, but they are very underrated. Founder and owner is English migrant Tony Smith.

Previous outstanding vintages: '76, '77, '83, '84, '85, '88, '90 '91, '92

CURRENT RELEASE 1993 Totally typical of the vineyard, this is an intensely peppery style with vegetable overtones and subtle French oak. The elegant palate shows real poise. It is chunky, fleshy, with stacks of fruit but also restraint: a good contrast to the porty South Australian styles. Try it with meat and vegie lasagne.

Plunkett Cabernet Merlot

QUALITY 🍷🍷🍷🍷
VALUE ★★★
GRAPES cabernet sauvignon, merlot
REGION Strathbogie Ranges, Vic.
CELLAR 🍷 2
ALC./VOL. 12.8%
RRP $16.00 (cellar door)

Sam Plunkett's parents planted their first vines back in 1968 but he didn't venture into the rat-race of marketing his own wines till 1992.

CURRENT RELEASE 1992 This wine won a gold medal at the Victorian Wines Show in 1993, and we can only surmise the judges saw a cask-sample. This is a decent wine but the earth won't move. It has a leafy/mulberry aroma, is of modest weight and falls away somewhat on the finish. Try it with veal.

Preece Cabernet Sauvignon

QUALITY 🍷🍷🍷🍷
VALUE ★★★½
GRAPES cabernet sauvignon
REGION mainly Goulburn Valley, Vic.
CELLAR 🍷 3
ALC./VOL. 12.5%
RRP $12.85 ⑤

Named after Mitchelton's first winemaker/manager, the legendary Seppelt Great Western winemaker Colin Preece, this is Mitchelton's bistro-style soft red. Maker Don Lewis.

CURRENT RELEASE 1993 This is a crafty wine: a real crowd-pleaser that should lay them in the aisles of the trendy trattorias. It's an easy-drinking red filled with soft, sweet raspberry flavours, little oak and a gentle, rounded finish. Try it with veal saltimbocca.

Primo Estate Adelaide Shiraz

Joe Grilli believes this is one of the biggest shirazes he has produced, and to make the most of the vintage he refrained from fining or filtering it.

CURRENT RELEASE 1992 The colour is profound and the nose is stacked with coffee, vanilla, coconutty American oak scents. In the mouth it is big, slightly extractive and not exactly a model of refinement, although there is flavour aplenty and it should age well. Match it with char-grilled meats.

QUALITY 🍷🍷🍷
VALUE ★★★
GRAPES shiraz
REGION Adelaide Plains, SA
CELLAR ⬤ 1–8
ALC./VOL. 13.5%
RRP $15.30

Queen Adelaide Pinot Noir

As well as the vapours, dear old Adelaide has had an attack of the varietals. Here's yet another one.
CURRENT RELEASE 1994 This is almost a nouveau style that could be served chilled if you wish. The colour is a light ruby and the nose has strawberry and cherry aromas, while the palate is more about plums and cherries which are followed by clean acid and minimal (if any) oak.

QUALITY 🍷🍷🍷
VALUE ★★★
GRAPES pinot noir
REGION Barossa Valley, SA
CELLAR 🍾 1
ALC./VOL. 13.0%
RRP $8.00 ⓢ

Queen Adelaide Ruby Cabernet Cabernet Sauvignon

Ruby cabernet is a hybrid variety designed to grow well in hot climates. What ever happened to Queen Adelaide claret?
CURRENT RELEASE 1993 A pleasing wine that makes much of the fruit. The nose has strong berry aromas and the palate is quite rich. A pleasantly tart raspberry flavour dominates, followed by soft oak on a clean finish.

QUALITY 🍷🍷🍷🍷
VALUE ★★★★
GRAPES ruby cabernet, cabernet sauvignon
REGION not stated
CELLAR 🍾 3
ALC./VOL. 12.5%
RRP $8.00 ⓢ

Redbank Long Paddock Shiraz

QUALITY 🍷🍷🍷
VALUE ★★★
GRAPES shiraz
REGION Pyrenees, Vic.
CELLAR 🍾 3
ALC./VOL. 13.0%
RRP $11.60

Maker/proprietor Neill Robb is on record as saying he doesn't like fruity red wines and tries to avoid varietal characters. This is a good example of his style.

CURRENT RELEASE 1992 The wine shows some development in colour and bouquet, being slightly nondescript, and the palate is dry, savoury, non-fruity and medium-bodied. There are earthy, walnutty characters throughout. Definitely a food wine; try spicy sausages.

Redbank Sally's Paddock

QUALITY 🍷🍷🍷🍷
VALUE ★★½
GRAPES cabernet sauvignon, shiraz, cabernet franc, malbec, merlot
REGION Pyrenees, Vic.
CELLAR 🍾 4+
ALC./VOL. 12.0%
RRP $33.00

This is a fruit-salad blend of grapes that has become Redbank's signature wine. It is named after winemaker Neill Robb's wife.

Previous outstanding vintages: '80, '81, '82, '86, '88, '90, '91, '92

CURRENT RELEASE 1993 A decent but not outstanding Sally's: its deep rich hue, and complex earth, spice, plum and pepper nose are appealing, while the palate lacks a little intensity and seems a tad hollow. Typical Redbank savoury finish. Try it with kangaroo.

Redman Cabernet Merlot

QUALITY 🍷🍷🍷
VALUE ★★½
GRAPES cabernet sauvignon 55%, merlot 45%
REGION Coonawarra, SA
CELLAR ⇌ 2–5+
ALC./VOL. 13.0%
RRP $18.35 ⓢ

This is a new blend from a traditional family winery. The Redmans have a distinguished past: Bill Redman, grandfather of present winemaker Bruce, was the only winemaker in the area for most of the '30s and '40s.

CURRENT RELEASE 1991 This is aggressively oaky in its youth and may just need some time in a cool, dark place. There's also some bitterness on the finish that may soften out as well. If you must drink it now, decant and give it plenty of air first. Try a char-grilled steak.

Redman Cabernet Sauvignon

Redmans have been making wine in the 'warra since 1908, which is a lot longer than anyone else. These days brothers Bruce and Malcolm both sign the label.

CURRENT RELEASE 1992 Definite Coonawarra regional blackcurrant and mulberry aromas here, ripe and liquorice/minty and laced with good oak. A bigger more generous style than father Owen used to make. Very good intensity, weight, extract and tannin. A roast beef style.

QUALITY 🍷🍷🍷🍷🍷
VALUE ★★★★
GRAPES cabernet sauvignon
REGION Coonawarra, SA
CELLAR 🍾 8
ALC./VOL. 12.5%
RRP $18.35 $

Redman Shiraz

The Redman Claret is now all politically correct. This is a long-running ready-drinking style that won't break the bank.

CURRENT RELEASE 1993 A straightforward red, with fruit-driven cherry and lollyish aromas without apparent oak. The palate is light and simple and falls away on the finish. A decent quaffing red that's in a different class from the same maker's cabernet. Try ham steak and pineapple.

QUALITY 🍷🍷🍷
VALUE ★★★
GRAPES shiraz
REGION Coonawarra, SA
CELLAR 🍾 3
ALC./VOL. 12.5%
RRP $12.60 $

Renmano Chairman's Selection Cabernet Sauvignon

The level of oak has been challenging in past vintages, but it seems to have been moderated in '93. Maker Fiona Donald.

CURRENT RELEASE 1993 This is more reserved than usual, a big, bold style that could be cellared a few years. It has an excellent purple-red colour and slightly reserved, cherry-stone aromas. The palate is full-bodied and firmly structured, with sweet ripe-fruit flavours. Good value. Serve with gourmet bangers.

QUALITY 🍷🍷🍷🍷
VALUE ★★★★★
GRAPES cabernet sauvignon
REGION Riverland, SA
CELLAR ⇨ 1–5+
ALC./VOL. 12.0%
RRP $11.00 $

Renmano Chairman's Selection Hermitage

QUALITY ♀♀♀
VALUE ★★★
GRAPES shiraz
REGION Riverland, SA
CELLAR 🍾 3
ALC./VOL. 13.0%
RRP $11.10 ⓢ 🍾

Renmano creams off the best grapes from its enormous crush every year to funnel into its chairman's selection wines.

CURRENT RELEASE 1993 Here's one for the lumberjacks. Smells like oak. Tastes like oak. Somehow it manages to be smooth on the tongue and not splintery. It's quite rich and high in extract, with a dry, furry tannin finish. Could be paired with kebabs (leave the skewers in!).

Richard Hamilton Burton's Vineyard

QUALITY ♀♀♀♀
VALUE ★★★★
GRAPES grenache, shiraz
REGION McLaren Vale, SA
CELLAR 🍾 6
ALC./VOL. 13.0%
RRP $15.50

Burton Hamilton is a good advertisement for wine in moderation: he was born in 1904 and died in 1994.

CURRENT RELEASE 1993 This is a different style to many of the fad grenaches, being savoury, complex, dry and non-grapey. The nose has feral earthy characters with plenty of oak and definite terroir. It's a wine of character: spicy, earthy/dusty and somewhat old fashioned, but not in a negative way. It's well endowed with fruit and nicely balanced. Try gourmet bangers.

Richard Hamilton Cabernet Sauvignon Merlot

QUALITY ♀♀♀
VALUE ★★½
GRAPES cabernet sauvignon, merlot
REGION Coonawarra, SA
CELLAR 🍾 2+
ALC./VOL. 13.0%
RRP $25.00 🍾

The Richard Hamilton wines, mostly made from McLaren Vale grapes, are made at Coonawarra along with the Leconfield wines, so perhaps it was inevitable that there would come a Richard Hamilton Coonawarra. Only 300 cases of this limited release were bottled. Maker Ralph Fowler.

CURRENT RELEASE 1993 Not a great nor typical Coonawarra, this suffers from green flavours that give it a peppery spiciness on the plus side, but also some astringency and leanness on the negative. The finish is slightly short. Anything with a pesto sauce should work.

Richard Hamilton Hut Block Cabernet Sauvignon

The grapes come from a vineyard which features a very unglamorous shed, hence the name. Not half as romantic as a genuine ol' bark hut. Maker Ralph Fowler.

CURRENT RELEASE 1993 This is a lovely red that tastes more like Coonawarra than McLaren Vale. The colour is excitingly dark and it's very aromatic, with pungent violet, blackcurrant and blackberry. The fruit triumphs over the oak. The wine oozes seductive sweet ripe berry flavours but also has structure and grip. Cries out for pink lamb.

QUALITY ♛♛♛♛♛
VALUE ★★★★★
GRAPES cabernet sauvignon
REGION McLaren Vale, SA
CELLAR 🍾 10+
ALC./VOL. 12.5%
RRP $15.45

Richard Hamilton Old Vines Shiraz

Dr Richard Hamilton is a plastic surgeon descended from one of the first people ever to make wine in South Australia. This is made from 100-year-old vines. Maker Ralph Fowler.

CURRENT RELEASE 1993 This sumptuous, fruity red really opens up with breathing. The captivating nose has lashings of sweet, ripe berry fruit and the palate is medium-bodied, elegant and intense, with fairly lively acid. Try it with steak tartare.

QUALITY ♛♛♛♛♝
VALUE ★★★★
GRAPES shiraz
REGION McLaren Vale, SA
CELLAR 🍾 5
ALC./VOL. 13.0%
RRP $19.30

Riddoch Cabernet Shiraz

Not to be confused with Wynns' John Riddoch or Rymill's Riddoch Run, this is the second label of Katnook. Maker Wayne Stehbens.

CURRENT RELEASE 1992 This one doesn't challenge the tastebuds, but aims fairly low as an affordable everyday-drinking red. The nose has slightly funky, animal overtones and the taste is smooth and uncomplicated, if slightly short. The finish has minimal tannin. Good pasta wine.

QUALITY ♛♛♛
VALUE ★★½
GRAPES cabernet sauvignon, shiraz
REGION Coonawarra, SA
CELLAR 🍾 2
ALC./VOL. 13.0%
RRP $12.90

Riddoch Run (The) Cabernet Sauvignon

QUALITY ♥♥♥♥♥
VALUE ★★★★½
GRAPES cabernet sauvignon
REGION Coonawarra, SA
CELLAR 🍷 7+
ALC./VOL. 13.5%
RRP $14.50 🍷

A run is an early outback Aussie term for a sheep station. John Riddoch of course was the father of Coonawarra.
Previous outstanding vintages: '91
CURRENT RELEASE 1992 This is a lovely wine from an average year: typically Coonawarra blackberryish aromas, fruit-driven with lashings of minty, berry cabernet flavour that's chunky, deep and smooth in the mouth. The balance has a seamless quality to it. Drink with pink lamb.

Riddoch Run (The) Shiraz

QUALITY ♥♥♥♥♪
VALUE ★★★★½
GRAPES shiraz
REGION Coonawarra, SA
CELLAR 🍷 6+
ALC./VOL. 13.4%
RRP $14.50 🍷

This is the secondary, cheaper label of the Rymill winery and often gives exceptional value for money. Maker John Innes.
Previous outstanding vintages: '91
CURRENT RELEASE 1992 This has similar generous fruit weight and style to the cabernet, albeit with the difference in aroma and flavour of the shiraz grape. The nose is forest floor, bayleaf, shiraz spice; the palate full with good intensity and length balanced by well-judged tannin. Satisfying. Try it with kassler.

Robertson's Well Cabernet Sauvignon

QUALITY ♥♥♥♥♪
VALUE ★★★★½
GRAPES cabernet sauvignon
REGION Coonawarra, SA
CELLAR 🍷 5
ALC./VOL. 13.5
RRP $15.95

This is a newish label that is a cousin to Jamiesons Run. Ignore the flash designer sheep-dip label. Label designers don't make wine – thank God! Maker Gavin Hogg.
CURRENT RELEASE 1993 A very stylish elegant wine that was obviously made to a formula. The nose has a full-on berry character and the medium-bodied palate shows cherry and cassis flavours. Well-integrated oak and acid make for a balanced finish. It drinks well now with barbecue lamb straps.

Rockford Basket Press Shiraz

If any wine started the Barossa stampede to rediscover old vines, shiraz and traditional full-bodied red wines, this is it. Made by confirmed individualist and preserver of history, Robert O'Callaghan.

CURRENT RELEASE 1992 An old-fashioned style which is more about richness, smoothness, flavour and cellarability than primary fruit or hi-fi varietal character. The colour is dark and dense, the subdued bouquet is woodsy and earthy, but the mouth is chock-full of flavour: deep, chunky, supple and seamless. A treat with Linke's meat pies.

QUALITY ★★★★★
VALUE ★★★★★
GRAPES shiraz
REGION Barossa Valley, SA
CELLAR 10+
ALC./VOL. 14.5%
RRP $18.00 (cellar door)

Rockford Dry Country Grenache

Made from 80-year-old struggling grapevines grown without irrigation. 'Barossa folklore says that vines only give their best if they struggle,' says maker Rob O'Callaghan.

CURRENT RELEASE 1993 An old-fashioned style in every way, this has a leathery, tarry nose with aged characters and a nice chunky, full, fleshy palate. The weight is medium and the finish has a pleasant tannin grip. This would go well with roast squab.

QUALITY ★★★★
VALUE ★★★★
GRAPES grenache
REGION Barossa Valley, SA
CELLAR 5
ALC./VOL. 13.0%
RRP $9.50 (cellar door)

Rosemount Balmoral Syrah

QUALITY ♙♙♙♙♙
VALUE ★★★★½
GRAPES shiraz
REGION McLaren Vale, SA
CELLAR ☞ 2–10+
ALC./VOL. 14.0%
RRP $40.00

Balmoral is the name of the Oatley family's 1852 Hunter Valley homestead, and this wine is the renamed Show Reserve McLaren Vale Syrah. It probably owes its existence to demands from the Americans, who love it. Maker Philip Shaw.
Previous outstanding vintages: '89, '90, '91
CURRENT RELEASE 1992 An inky purple in colour, this is a concentrated, dense shiraz with a pronounced gamey/spicy nose. The palate has sweet liquorice, plum and oaky flavours with alcohol and tannin to burn. A voluptuous wine, based on a 100-year-old block of vines at Ryecroft. Try saddle of hare.

Rosemount Cabernet Sauvignon

QUALITY ♙♙♙♙
VALUE ★★★½
GRAPES cabernet sauvignon
REGION McLaren Vale, SA & Hunter Valley & Mudgee, NSW
CELLAR 6
ALC./VOL. 12.5%
RRP $13.85 ⓢ

Rosemount chief winemaker Philip Shaw has won ample recognition but the contribution of managing director Chris Hancock, once a senior winemaker at Penfolds, is probably underestimated.
CURRENT RELEASE 1994 The sweet, curranty, berry cabernet fruit has a dusty, leafy overlay and the mouth is smooth and round, tailored for ready drinking. Good depth of ripe, friendly cabernet flavour. Try it with roast kid.

Rosemount McLaren Vale Shiraz

The 'rose label' series was begun two years ago by Rosemount, with an Orange chardonnay followed by a Coonawarra cabernet. This wine confirms our theory that first-releases are often exceptional value. Maker Philip Shaw and team.
CURRENT RELEASE 1992 The colour is so concentrated it stains the glass, presaging a very intense wine. The nose is a riot of berries, nutty oak scents, spices and dried herbs and it doesn't disappoint in the mouth: rich and fleshy, with guts and grip. Lovely smooth tannins and long finish. Beef casserole here.

QUALITY ♕♕♕♕♕
VALUE ★★★★★
GRAPES shiraz
REGION McLaren Vale, SA
CELLAR 🍾 10
ALC./VOL. 14.0%
RRP $20.00 ⓢ 🍾

Rosemount Shiraz

Founder Bob Oatley celebrated 25 years of winemaking at Rosemount during the 1995 vintage.
CURRENT RELEASE 1994 This soft, gentle, ready-drinking red dips as low as $10 and is among the best-value drinking reds each year. The nose offers dark cherry, vanilla and currants with a gamey/spicy aspect and it's smooth and rich in the mouth with subtle oak. Try it with rabbit casserole.

QUALITY ♕♕♕♕
VALUE ★★★½
GRAPES shiraz
REGION McLaren Vale, SA & Hunter Valley & Mudgee, NSW
CELLAR 🍾 4
ALC./VOL. 12.5%
RRP $13.85 ⓢ

Rosemount Shiraz Cabernet

Rosemount is a sponsor of the 2000 Sydney Olympic Games: a small percentage of sales is donated to the fund.
CURRENT RELEASE 1994 This is a fruit-driven cherry/plum flavoured, straight-up-and-down red. It's soft, fairly light and doesn't test the faculties too much. Slips down without a fight and leaves an agreeably soft, dry finish. Good with a ham sandwich.

QUALITY ♕♕♕
VALUE ★★★
GRAPES shiraz, cabernet sauvignon
REGION South-eastern Australia
CELLAR 🍾 2
ALC./VOL. 12.5%
RRP $11.90 ⓢ

Rosemount Show Reserve Cabernet Sauvignon

QUALITY 🍷🍷🍷🍷🍷
VALUE ★★★★½
GRAPES cabernet sauvignon
REGION Coonawarra, SA
CELLAR 🍷 8+
ALC./VOL. 14.0%
RRP $23.35 ⓢ 🍷

Rosemount winemaker Philip Shaw is best known for chardonnay but in fact he is multi-talented and has perfected many varietals during his long tenure at Rosemount.
Previous outstanding vintages: '88, '89, '90, '91
CURRENT RELEASE 1992 This is a complex Bordeaux style with a tobacco-leaf and cigarbox cabernet bouquet, seriously concentrated flavour and well-structured tannin. Excellent length – the finish goes on and on. Try it with a leg of lamb.

Rothbury Estate Hunter Valley Shiraz

QUALITY 🍷🍷🍷🍷🍷
VALUE ★★★★½
GRAPES shiraz
REGION Hunter Valley, NSW
CELLAR ← 1–6+
ALC./VOL. 12.6%
RRP $15.60

The Rothbury Estate is now part of the large publicly listed group Rothbury Wines, which encompasses Bailey's, St Huberts and Saltram. Maker Keith Tulloch.
Previous outstanding vintages: '79, '83, '86, '87, '91
CURRENT RELEASE 1993 A luscious, lovely wine with a perfumed oak-fruit combination on the nose, which has a trace of meatiness typical of '93 Hunters, and deep cherry/plum flavours with some tannin on the palate. Would team well with game meats.

Rothbury Estate Reserve Shiraz

This reserve bottling of straight Hunter shiraz has been produced only since 1989. Len Evans believes the '93 to be a great wine, one of the best Rothbury has ever made, and compares it to the '59 Lindemans Bin 1590. Makers Peter Hall and Keith Tulloch.

Previous outstanding vintages: '89, '91

CURRENT RELEASE 1993 This is a voluptuous, decadently rich wine. The nose is scented, floral and spicy with some gamey accents; the palate is very rich and smooth with lots of well-married American oak, fine but powerful. A superb wine that has a big future. Pair with barbecued roo fillets.

QUALITY ♛♛♛♛♛
VALUE ★★★★★
GRAPES shiraz
REGION Hunter Valley, NSW
CELLAR 🍷 2–8+
ALC./VOL. 12.0%
RRP $30.00

Rothbury Estate South-eastern Australia Shiraz

This blend of regions was begun in 1992 when the Hunter material wasn't up to a separate bottling. The '93 is a quantum leap up from that wine.

CURRENT RELEASE 1993 Another lovely Rothbury '93 red: pepper, spice, liquorice and toasty oak greet the nose. Excellent depth of spicy and cherry/plum fruit on the palate has depth and length over and above what you'd expect at the price.

QUALITY ♛♛♛♛?
VALUE ★★★★½
GRAPES shiraz
REGION Hunter Valley, NSW & McLaren Vale, SA
CELLAR 🍷 5+
ALC./VOL. 12.5%
RRP $13.30

Rotherhythe Cabernet Sauvignon

QUALITY 🍷🍷🍷🍷
VALUE ★★★½
GRAPES cabernet sauvignon, merlot
REGION West Tamar, Tas.
CELLAR 🍾 5+
ALC./VOL. 13.0%
RRP $18.00

Rotherhythe is situated on the west bank of the Tamar River estuary, near Launceston, where views are breathtaking and the population amazingly sparse for such a beautiful spot. Maker Steve Hyde.

Previous outstanding vintages: '86, '92

CURRENT RELEASE 1993 This tastes riper and fruitier than some of the previous releases, still with some of the dusty leafy overtones typical of the region, but pleasingly full and smooth on the tongue, with an almost Italianate savoury aspect. Pair it with beef.

Rouge Homme Cabernet Sauvignon

QUALITY 🍷🍷🍷🍷
VALUE ★★★½
GRAPES cabernet sauvignon
REGION Coonawarra, SA
CELLAR 🍾 5
ALC./VOL. 13.0%
RRP $16.00 ⓢ

This brand was started by the Redman family in the 1950s. It's a reliable label but seldom scales the pinnacles. Maker Paul Gordon.

CURRENT RELEASE 1992 A decent wine that happily avoids the porty characters of the early '80s, this is a much more savoury style, with nutmeg-like oak and nutty aromas that translate to a smooth, dry palate with suggestions of mint and plum. The balance is agreeable if a tad short, and it drinks well with osso bucco.

Rouge Homme Richardson's Red Block

QUALITY 🍷🍷🍷🍷🍷
VALUE ★★★★★
GRAPES cabernet sauvignon, malbec, merlot
REGION Coonawarra, SA
CELLAR 🍷 1–7+
ALC./VOL. 12.7%
RRP $17.70 ⓢ

This won the Jimmy Watson Trophy – an award we love to hate – so we were secretly hoping it would be awful. But we got the shock of our lives. Maker Paul Gordon.

CURRENT RELEASE 1993 This sumptuous red is top value and on another plane to the 1992 debut vintage. The colour is profound and the aroma is fresh, penetrating and fruit-driven with dark berry, curranty, spicy accents. The palate has superb concentration with layers of well-married fruit/oak flavours and balanced tannin. A worthy Watson.

Ryecroft Flame Tree Red

The Flame Tree label boasts a very colourful flaming red tree that will appeal to the botanically minded.

CURRENT RELEASE 1994 This is not far above Beaujolais weight. The colour is light red-purple, the nose reminiscent of chocolate-dipped cherries. It's light-bodied, soft and easy on the gums. As the Poms would say, very gulpable. Drink chilled as a summer red with pork.

QUALITY ♛♛♛
VALUE ★★★
GRAPES various
REGION not stated
CELLAR 🍶 1
ALC./VOL. 12.5%
RRP $8.85 ⓢ

Ryecroft Flame Tree Shiraz

This winery, founded in 1888, was bought by Rosemount owner Bob Oatley in 1991 and is now a mid-to-lower market brand.

CURRENT RELEASE 1992 This is good value in a ripely regional, almost porty sort of way. The nose intrigues with inky, alcoholic and jammy notes as well as some varietal spice. The palate is soft, round and unctuous with liquorice, spice and plum flavours. Somewhat rustic but a generous crowd-pleaser at a very fair price. Barbecue some rissoles.

QUALITY ♛♛♛♝
VALUE ★★★½
GRAPES shiraz
REGION McLaren Vale, SA
CELLAR 🍶 3
ALC./VOL. 13.0%
RRP $11.60 ⓢ

Ryecroft Traditional

Since the Rosemount takeover, this old McLaren Vale warhorse has finally found stability. The wines are much more consistent now, if lacking excitement.

CURRENT RELEASE 1992 The nose is dominated by sappy, somewhat green American oak but the spicy/liquorice fruit comes to the fore when the wine's in the mouth. It's sweet, smooth, spicy and the finish packs some alcohol warmth and a fair tannin bite. A lovely chunky wine, not without elegance. Try braised steak and onions.

QUALITY ♛♛♛♛
VALUE ★★★★
GRAPES cabernet sauvignon, shiraz, merlot
REGION McLaren Vale, SA
CELLAR 🍶 5+
ALC./VOL. 14.0%
RRP $13.50 ⓢ

Rymill Shiraz

QUALITY 🍷🍷🍷🍷?
VALUE ★★★★½
GRAPES shiraz
REGION Coonawarra, SA
CELLAR ➡ 2–10
ALC./VOL. 13.5%
RRP $14.50 ⑤

The plan is to phase out the Riddoch Run brand locally and keep it for export. Then the new crop of wines will be all labelled 'Rymill' and all except the cabernet will drop to the Riddoch Run's price-point.

CURRENT RELEASE 1993 This is a stunner in baby clothes! A deep, concentrated wine with amazing purple hue and pungent spicy fruit/oak nose which needs time to resolve. The flavour is youthful and very powerful, packed with plum and spice, already beautifully balanced but needing time to mellow a little. Cellar, then drink with game pie.

Salisbury Estate Cabernet Sauvignon

QUALITY 🍷🍷🍷
VALUE ★★★
GRAPES cabernet sauvignon
REGION Mildura, Vic.
CELLAR 🍾 2
ALC./VOL. 12.5%
RRP $9.90

The Chaffey brothers turned what was a desert into a salad bowl, thanks to irrigation. Ironically this company is using a technique called deficit (restricted) watering to viticultural advantage.

CURRENT RELEASE 1993 The big plummy nose is a tease because the palate is quite conservative in terms of flavour. There are soft cherry/berry flavours which are matched by well-tuned oak. It drinks well now with a steak sandwich.

QUALITY 🍷🍷🍷
VALUE ★★★
GRAPES cabernet sauvignon
REGION Mildura, Vic.
CELLAR 🍾 3
ALC./VOL. 12.5%
RRP $9.90

CURRENT RELEASE 1994 Identical nose to the 1993 vintage and the palate also bears a resemblance. There is a little more spice but it carries the same weight and fruit flavours. Attractive tannins lead to a mildly grippy finish. It drinks well now with liver and bacon.

Salisbury Estate Cabernet Sauvignon Merlot

Fine wines from the dry lands, this drop owes its existence to the presence of the irrigation scheme and the Murray River.

CURRENT RELEASE 1994 The colour is a deep ruby and the nose has strong merlot aromas. The palate is quite rich with well-defined berry flavours. Raspberry is the main flavour and there are some black tea-like tannins on a long dry finish. It drinks well now with a chilli con carne.

QUALITY 🍷🍷🍷
VALUE ★★★
GRAPES cabernet sauvignon, merlot
REGION Mildura, Vic.
CELLAR 🍾 2
ALC./VOL. 12.0%
RRP $9.90

Salitage Pinot Noir

Salitage is an exciting project established by John and Jenny Horgan (related to Denis Horgan who set up Leeuwin Estate). Maker John Wade (consultant).

CURRENT RELEASE 1994 This is still tight and needs time. The colour is an impressive deep crimson and the nose has dark cherry and smoky wood aromas. The palate is tight with dark cherry flavours tied to brooding oak. The oak is a little oppressive and adds a toasty element. A wine that goes well with duck in soy sauce.

QUALITY 🍷🍷🍷🍷
VALUE ★★★
GRAPES pinot noir
REGION Great Southern, WA
CELLAR ⇌ 2–6
ALC./VOL. 13.3%
RRP $30.00

Sandalford Shiraz

New (almost twee) label for this marque that claims establishment in 1840. Today's production is around 40,000 cases. Maker Bill Crappsley.

CURRENT RELEASE 1993 A very elegant style with lots of charm. The nose is full of pepper and sweet fruit aromas and the middleweight palate has well-defined varietal character. There are plum and blackberry flavours which are also mingled with an iron tonic character. The finish shows happily married oak. Try it with hard cheese.

QUALITY 🍷🍷🍷🍷
VALUE ★★★★
GRAPES shiraz
REGION Margaret River, Mount Barker, WA
CELLAR 🍾 4
ALC./VOL. 12.0%
RRP $12.00

Schinus Cabernet

QUALITY ♙♙♙♙
VALUE ★★★½
GRAPES cabernet sauvignon
REGION King Valley, Vic.
CELLAR 🍷 3
ALC./VOL. 13.0%
RRP $15.00

The combined production of Dromana Estate wines and the Schinus label is in the order of 10,000 cases.

CURRENT RELEASE 1993 The colour is a mid-ruby and the nose is very herbal and leafy. The palate offers some attractive sweet redcurrant flavour followed by modest tannin and acid on a clean and well-balanced finish. It drinks well now with a casserole.

Schinus Dolcetto

QUALITY ♙♙♙♙
VALUE ★★★½
GRAPES dolcetto
REGION King Valley, Vic.
CELLAR 🍷 2
ALC./VOL. 13.0%
RRP $14.00

Full marks for the pop-up capsule (have you noticed the number of waiters with cut fingers these days?). The label is so named because the proprietor, Garry Crittenden, made his mark as a horticulturist growing peppercorn trees.

CURRENT RELEASE 1993 An Italianesque style with a brick-red colour. The nose has hints of tart raisins and the palate is an explosion of sweet berry fruit lifted by a tart grace note while discreet oak provides the finish. Chilling is not out of the question. Try it with cotechino and lentils.

Schinus Nebbiolo

QUALITY ♙♙♙♙
VALUE ★★★★
GRAPES nebbiolo
REGION King Valley, Vic.
CELLAR 🍷 2
ALC./VOL. 13.5%
RRP $14.00

Schinus (the botanical name for the peppercorn tree) is the second label to Dromana Estate. While Dromana wines are sourced from the property, the Schinus label covers fruit from other districts. Maker Garry Crittenden.

CURRENT RELEASE 1993 Nice change of pace. The colour is a mid-brick red and the nose is dominated by spice. The palate is structure rather than fruit-driven with stays of acid beneath middleweight cherry flavours followed up by a chalky dry finish. In keeping with the style, it would go well with antipasto.

Seaview Edwards & Chaffey Cabernet Sauvignon

This is a new label to commemorate two pioneers who made Seaview famous. The Chaffey brothers were also pioneers of irrigation in the Riverland. Maker Mike Farmilo.

CURRENT RELEASE 1992 A very impressive debut. This is a fruit-driven style that shows what flavours the district can supply. The colour is dense and the nose has intense blackberry aromas plus a hint of wood. The palate is loaded with sweet blackberry fruit supported by spicy oak on a long dry finish. It drinks well now with pink lamb chops.

QUALITY 🍷🍷🍷🍷🍷
VALUE ★★★★★
GRAPES cabernet sauvignon
REGION McLaren Vale, SA
CELLAR 🍷 6
ALC./VOL. 13.5%
RRP $22.00

Seaview Edwards & Chaffey Shiraz

This is the other bookend in the revival special releases. Seaview has long been a bargain basement line and now it's about to return to superstar status.

CURRENT RELEASE 1992 Less impressive than its cabernet cousin, but still an impressive wine. There is a concentrated character which smacks of a Lindemans winemaking technique. The colour is dense and the nose offers high-tone oak and ripe plum flavours. The palate is a bombshell of concentrated fruit followed by lifted oak on a finish that adds a chalky character. Try it with kranski sausages.

QUALITY 🍷🍷🍷🍷
VALUE ★★★★
GRAPES shiraz
REGION McLaren Vale, SA
CELLAR 🍷 4
ALC./VOL. 13.5%
RRP $22.00

Seppelt Chalambar Shiraz

VALUE 🍷🍷🍷🍷◐
REGION ★★★★½
GRAPES shiraz
REGION Great Western, Geelong, Ovens Valley, Vic.
CELLAR 🍾 4
ALC./VOL. 12.5%
RRP $13.00 🍾

This series of labels marks a worrying trend. Chalambar is a geographical location but the grapes come from three different regions. Maker Ian McKenzie (chief winemaker).

CURRENT RELEASE 1992 The colour is a mid-ruby and the nose has pepper and spice aromas. Pepper and spice are again encountered on the palate, as are intense black cherry fruit flavours matched by well-integrated oak on a dry grippy finish. It goes well with char-grilled kangaroo.

Seppelt Drumborg Cabernet Sauvignon

QUALITY 🍷🍷🍷◐
VALUE ★★★
GRAPES cabernet sauvignon
REGION Drumborg, Vic.
CELLAR 🍾 3
ALC./VOL. 12.5%
RRP $22.50

No geography lesson necessary with this label – the grapes come from the vineyard named on the label. Maker Ian McKenzie.

CURRENT RELEASE 1989 This wine is a bit like New Age music – it doesn't seem to get anywhere. The nose is leafy with hints of bracken, the middleweight palate offers clean cassis flavour supported by clean oak on a dry astringent finish. It goes well with pasta.

Seppelt Harpers Range Cabernet Sauvignon

QUALITY 🍷🍷🍷◐
VALUE ★★★½
GRAPES cabernet sauvignon
REGION Yarra Valley, Mornington Peninsula, Great Western, Vic.
CELLAR 🍾 3
ALC./VOL. 12.5%
RRP $17.50

Where exactly is Harpers Range? More geographical confusion! A previous model won the Jimmy Watson Memorial Trophy. Maker Ian McKenzie.

CURRENT RELEASE 1992 The wine has a deep brick-red colour and the nose offers ripe fruit aromas. The palate is a middleweight with sweet blackberry flavour balanced by soft oak on a mild-mannered finish. A good casserole style.

Seppelt Sunday Creek Pinot Noir

Believe it or not, Sunday Creek actually is a trickle of water that runs through the Drumborg vineyard.

CURRENT RELEASE 1993 An interesting style that makes much of regional mixing. The wine is medium-bodied with a distinct cherry/berry nose. The palate has cherry and strawberry flavours matched by discreet oak on a soft finish. It drinks well now with char-grilled tuna.

QUALITY 🍷🍷🍷🍷
VALUE ★★★½
GRAPES pinot noir
REGION Ballarat, Mornington, Drumborg, Vic.
CELLAR 🍷 3
ALC./VOL. 13.0%
RRP $16.00

Shottesbrooke Merlot

Yet another solo merlot. Shottesbrooke is the personal label of hired gun winemaker Nick Holmes, who works for Rosemount and Ryecroft.

CURRENT RELEASE 1994 This is an easy-to-drink style with lots of charm. The nose is scented with rosewater aromas, the palate has soft redcurrant flavours balanced by fine-grained tannins on a mildly astringent finish, and it's great with pasta and a meat sauce.

QUALITY 🍷🍷🍷🍷
VALUE ★★★★
GRAPES merlot
REGION McLaren Vale, SA
CELLAR 🍷 3
ALC./VOL. 12.0%
RRP $18.00

Smithbrook Pinot Noir

Smithbrook is a syndicate of businessmen including David Clarke (Poole's Rock) and various others who also overlap with the ownership of Burgundy's Domaine de la Pousse d'Or. WA's stand-out winemaker John Wade does the honours.

CURRENT RELEASE 1993 A most impressive wine from young vines. Although unashamedly oak-driven, it has the fruit depth to handle this level of wood. Cedar, vanilla, and coconut aromas entwine with dark cherry and a hint of sap. Excellent length and harmony. A portent for the Pemberton region. Drink with Peking duck.

QUALITY 🍷🍷🍷🍷?
VALUE ★★★★
GRAPES pinot noir
REGION Pemberton, WA
CELLAR 🍷 4
ALC./VOL. 13.5%
RRP $20.00 (cellar door)

Sorrenberg Cabernet Sauvignon

QUALITY 🍷🍷🍷🍷
VALUE ★★★½
GRAPES cabernet sauvignon 70%, cabernet franc 15%, malbec 15%
REGION Beechworth, Vic.
CELLAR 🍾 3–6
ALC./VOL. 12.9%
RRP $20.00

This is a 1000-case winery located in the high country near Beechworth in north-east Victoria. Maker Barry Morey.

CURRENT RELEASE 1993 A high acid wine from the high country. The nose has leaf, tobacco and briar aromas. The palate is tight with muted blackberry fruit bound to strongly expressed smoky oak that offers long grip. High acid is also obvious. Serve with smoked kangaroo.

Sorrenberg Gamay

QUALITY 🍷🍷🍷
VALUE ★★½
GRAPES gamay
REGION Beechworth, Vic.
CELLAR 🍾 2
ALC./VOL. 12.7%
RRP $18.00

This is one of the few commercial gamays on the market. Thus far the examples have been far removed from the wine of Beaujolais.

CURRENT RELEASE 1994 An interesting yet disturbing style. The wine has a bright cherry red colour and the nose shows obvious primary ferment characters. The palate is raw with sweet berry and youthful ferment characters. The finish is characterised by soft acid. Serve chilled with cold meats.

St Hallett Cabernet Merlot

QUALITY 🍷🍷🍷🍷
VALUE ★★★★
GRAPES cabernet sauvignon, merlot
REGION Barossa Valley, SA
CELLAR 🍾 3
ALC./VOL. 13.5%
REGION $15.00

This is a very approachable style that was made for drinking now. It is a cut above the average commercial style.

CURRENT RELEASE 1993 A big, soft and juicy wine. The nose is rich and vinous with rose-water and sweet berry aromas. The palate is heavy with sweet berry fruit matched by discreet oak on a well-balanced finish. It drinks well now with lamb steaks.

St Hallett Old Block Shiraz

Old Block is made from shiraz vines 80 years old. It is meant to capture the essence of the Barossa Valley. Maker Stuart Blackwell.

Previous outstanding vintages: '80, '86, '88, '89, '90

CURRENT RELEASE 1992 Stylistically this is a tighter style than normally. There is plenty of pepper and spice on the nose. The palate is firm with ripe fruit flavours attended by lively spice. There is also a hint of chocolate and soft acid. The finish shows attractive oak that imparts fine-grained tannins and substantial grip. There's great cellar potential here, but if you drink it now try it with a piece of rare rump steak.

QUALITY ♕♕♕♕♕
VALUE ★★★★
GRAPES shiraz
REGION Barossa Valley, SA
CELLAR ⇨ 3–7
ALC./VOL. 13.5%
RRP $23.95

Stanley Brothers Thoroughbred Cabernet Sauvignon

This is a new label from the Barossa Valley and if you disregard the verbosity on the back label, the wine is pretty smart.

CURRENT RELEASE 1991 The colour is mid-ruby and the nose has some cherry-pip characters as well as dusty oak aromas. The middleweight palate offers excellent berry characters matched by complex oak. The finish has positive tannin grip. It goes well with a mature cheddar.

QUALITY ♕♕♕♕♕
VALUE ★★★★½
GRAPES cabernet sauvignon
REGION Barossa Valley, SA
CELLAR ▯ 5
ALC./VOL. 12.5%
RRP $16.50

Stanton & Killeen Moodemere Dry Red

'Stomp it and Kill it' as it is affectionately known, was established in 1875 and the annual production is around 8000 cases. Maker Chris Killeen.

CURRENT RELEASE 1991 A well-balanced style with more than just a tad of elegance. The nose has hints of ripe fruit and smoky oak. The palate offers rich berry flavours with cherry and cassis characters backed up by typical black tea-like tannins on a dry gripping finish. It goes well with duck.

QUALITY ♕♕♕♕♕
VALUE ★★★★½
GRAPES shiraz 50%, cabernet sauvignon 50%
REGION Rutherglen, Vic.
CELLAR ⇨ 2–5
ALC./VOL. 13.0%
RRP $13.50

Stanton & Killeen Moodemere Red Shiraz

QUALITY ▼▼▼▼
VALUE ★★★★
GRAPES shiraz
REGION Rutherglen, Vic.
CELLAR ☛ 2–6
ALC./VOL. 13.1%
RRP $12.00

In Rutherglen they pronounce the variety *shy-raz*, but there is usually nothing shy about it!
CURRENT RELEASE 1991 Rutherglen right to the last ounce of flavour. It is rich, lusty but not porty. The colour is a very dark ruby and the nose is full of ripe plums and spice. The palate has intense plum flavours and spices balanced by strong tannins on a vigorous finish. This is a wine that needs time, but right now it's perfect with a simple plate of steak and eggs.

Stonyfell Metala

QUALITY ▼▼▼▼
VALUE ★★★½
GRAPES cabernet sauvignon, shiraz
REGION Langhorne Creek, SA
CELLAR ▮ 3
ALC./VOL. 13.2%
RRP $14.00 ⓢ

This traditional style started life by winning the first Jimmy Watson Memorial Trophy in 1962. It is now part of the Rothbury group. Maker Nigel Dolan.
Previous outstanding vintages: '61, '66, '71, '83, '84, '86
CURRENT RELEASE 1993 A solid wine, and although the earth won't move it is a nice drink. The colour is a mid-ruby and the nose has cedar and ripe fruit smells. The medium-bodied palate has sweet ripe raspberry flavours balanced by well-tailored oak on a dry finish. It drinks well now with a hearty lamb and barley casserole.

Summerfield Cabernet Sauvignon

QUALITY ▼▼▼▼
VALUE ★★★★
GRAPES cabernet sauvignon
REGION Pyrenees, Vic.
CELLAR ▮ 4
ALC./VOL. 13.0%
RRP $16.00

Summerfield has the distinction of having the only airstrip in the region. If you know Moonambel, you'll know that's a big deal.
CURRENT RELEASE 1992 The colour is impressively deep and the nose offers abundant berry character. The palate is dominated by dark cherry and redcurrant characters framed against dry oak on an astringent finish. It is a youthful style. Try it with rare rump steak.

Summerfield Shiraz

This is a small winery/vineyard near Moonambel that was established in 1979. The annual production is 2000 cases. Maker Ian Summerfield.

CURRENT RELEASE 1992 The colour is a deep ruby and the nose has a distinct talcum powder and perfumed aroma. The middleweight palate has a dark cherry flavour attached to a grippy finish with fine-grained tannin. A good match for roast squab.

QUALITY ♈♈♈♈
VALUE ★★★★
GRAPES shiraz
REGION Pyrenees, Vic.
CELLAR 4
ALC./VOL. 13.0%
RRP $16.00

Taltarni Cabernet Sauvignon

The Taltarni reds have always demanded patience and generally reward those who cellar them. This is only seven years young but it's already mellowed nicely. Makers Greg Gallagher and Dominique Portet.

Previous outstanding vintages: '78, '79, '81, '82, '84, '86, '88, '90

CURRENT RELEASE 1988 There's some tawny development in the hue and it's acquired a complex bouquet of leather, chocolate and coffee. The flavour is full-bodied, warm and rich with ample flesh, tannin and concentration. A lovely mature glass of red to have with aged cheeses.

QUALITY ♈♈♈♈♉
VALUE ★★★½
GRAPES cabernet sauvignon 85%, merlot 8%, cabernet franc 7%
REGION Pyrenees, Vic.
CELLAR 4+
ALC./VOL. 13.2%
RRP $28.00

CURRENT RELEASE 1992 The titanic Taltarni has issued a real sleeper for its 20th anniversary vintage. The wine seems quite unready – closed and needing time to develop. This is typical Taltarni: difficult to appreciate in its youth, subdued, tight and somewhat forbidding. But if there are doubts about how they develop, refer to the current re-release, the excellent 1988. Give it plenty of air, and serve with game.

QUALITY ♈♈♈♉
VALUE ★★★
GRAPES cabernet sauvignon 87%, merlot 9%, cabernet franc 4%
REGION Pyrenees, Vic.
CELLAR 2–8+
ALC./VOL. 13.0%
RRP $19.50

Taltarni Merlot

QUALITY 🍷🍷🍷🍷⁽
VALUE ★★★★
GRAPES merlot 96%, cabernet franc 4%
REGION Pyrenees, Vic.
CELLAR 🍾 7+
ALC./VOL. 13.6%
RRP $20.00 ⓢ 🍷

The vintage for this wine, 1992, was the 20th anniversary of Taltarni's foundation, hence the inscription on all their '92 reds. Makers Greg Gallagher and Dominique Portet.

CURRENT RELEASE 1992 This is a cracker of a merlot, showing depth and completeness not normally found in this grape in Australia. The nose is subdued, earthy, dry, with plum and oaky notes. It comes into its own in the mouth, with serious weight and richness, complex mellow cabernet-like flavours, power and length. Try it with guinea fowl.

Taltarni Shiraz

QUALITY 🍷🍷🍷🍷⁽
VALUE ★★★★
GRAPES shiraz 98%, malbec 2%
REGION Pyrenees, Vic.
CELLAR 🍾 10
ALC./VOL. 13.3%
RRP $19.50 🍷

It's amazing how many people still think Taltarni reds are heavy and tannic. They should try a bottle, as the wines are much more approachable these days. The shiraz is regularly our pick of the litter. Against the current trend to American oak, it is always aged in French.

Previous outstanding vintages: '77, '81, '82, '84, '86, '88, '90, '91

CURRENT RELEASE 1992 A 'big-fruit' wine, exuding pepper and spice aromas coupled with vanilla and caramel scents from extended oak maturation. A serious red in a savoury, dry-finishing style that's quite removed from the sweet and berryish Barossa styles. Perfect with gourmet bangers and mash.

Tapestry Cabernet Sauvignon

This brand comes from the Merrivale winery, which has fallen into the hands of talented Normans winemaker Brian Light. The Light family's Bakers Gully vineyard is the main grape source.

CURRENT RELEASE 1992 This has a rich, deep colour and a concentrated cherry/plum aroma which indicates a fruit-driven style with subtle oak. Medium weight and elegant, it has the character of a good red wine rather than a definitive cabernet. A good partner for veal scalloppine.

QUALITY ????
VALUE ★★★½
GRAPES cabernet sauvignon
REGION McLaren Vale, SA
CELLAR 5
ALC./VOL. 13.5%
RRP $17.70

Tarrawarra Pinot Noir

David Wollan established Tarrawarra's as one of the leading pinots in Victoria. Unfortunately, most of its wines are sold through restaurants, which makes them hard to find in off-licences. Previous outstanding vintages: '88, '90, '91

CURRENT RELEASE 1992 A very serious pinot: complex and powerful. The colour is deep and the wine is ageing slowly, promising to cellar well. The nose has rich cherry and spices with well-married oak. The palate is profound and superbly structured, with flesh, weight, and tannin. It climaxes in a resounding finish that goes on and on. Try it with spit-roasted quail.

QUALITY ?????
VALUE ★★★★½
GRAPES pinot noir
REGION Yarra Valley, Vic.
CELLAR 5+
ALC./VOL. 14.2%
RRP $28.00

Tatachilla Keystone

Keystone has become something of a fashion plate around McLaren Vale. In fact it's been in existence for yonks but disguised under the banner of 'dry red'.

CURRENT RELEASE 1994 The nose is forceful with strong raspberry aromas. The palate offers sweetness and succulent fruit flavours, particularly raspberry. These are matched by a finely tuned oak treatment and modest astringency. It drinks well now with a goat stew.

QUALITY ????
VALUE ★★★★
GRAPES grenache, shiraz
REGION McLaren Vale, SA
CELLAR 2
ALC./VOL. 14.1%
RRP $16.00

Tatachilla Partners

QUALITY ♛♛♛♛
VALUE ★★★★
GRAPES shiraz, cabernet sauvignon
REGION McLaren Vale, SA
CELLAR 🍷 4
ALC./VOL. 13.7%
RRP $18.00

This blend was minted for the partners of the rekindled company, and as such is an 'after boardmeeting' tipple. Tatachilla was established in 1901 and has seen many changes of management.

CURRENT RELEASE 1994 Very easy to drink, this is a fruit-driven style with shiraz to the fore. The nose has plum and spice aromas. The palate is a middleweight with sweet berry characters framed by soft oak on a gentle, dry finish. It drinks well now with underdone lamb chops.

Temple Bruer Cornucopia Grenache

QUALITY ♛♛♛♛
VALUE ★★★½
GRAPES grenache
REGION Langhorne Creek, SA
CELLAR 🍷 3
ALC./VOL. 14.8%
RRP $12.90

David Bruer, a one-time wine chemistry lecturer at Roseworthy College, now devotes his energy and technical knowledge to making the stuff. He produces small quantities from his own vineyard at Langhorne Creek.

CURRENT RELEASE 1993 This is a most appealing light-to-mediumweight red which comes in a clear bottle for extra effect. It's a clean, spicy, grapey, fruit-driven style with plenty of flavour that lingers well. Good with veal and could be chilled to sip as a summer red.

T'Gallant Holystone

Kevin McCarthy and Kathleen Quealy are two of the most adventurous vignerons on the Mornington Peninsula. T'Gallant refers to the top-gallant sail of a square-rigged sailing ship, silly.
Previous outstanding vintages: '93
CURRENT RELEASE 1994 Very pale pink, this is like a delicate rosé but it finishes dry as a bone and its smoky, vanilla, candy pinot noir flavours are better than your average rosé. It's a delicious wine with light-flavoured entrées or hors d'oeuvres and you'll have a lot of fun with the label.

QUALITY 🍷🍷🍷
VALUE ★★★½
GRAPES pinot noir, chardonnay
REGION Mornington Peninsula, Vic.
CELLAR 2
ALC./VOL. 13.5%
RRP $15.00

Tim Adams Aberfeldy

The Aberfeldy vineyard was first planted by the Birks family of Wendouree in 1904. It was sold separately from Wendouree when that winery changed hands about 20 years ago. Present owners are the McDowells.
Previous outstanding vintages: '90, '92
CURRENT RELEASE 1993 This is a powerful red in trad Clare style, the nose full of spicy, nutmeg and oaky nuances. It has excellent flavour concentration with superb fruit-oak harmony and a long, smooth aftertaste. Should be even better with time. Perfect with saddle of hare.

QUALITY 🍷🍷🍷🍷
VALUE ★★★★
GRAPES shiraz
REGION Clare Valley, SA
CELLAR ⮕ 2–8+
ALC./VOL. 14.0%
RRP $20.00

Tim Adams (The) Fergus

QUALITY 🍷🍷🍷🍷
VALUE ★★★★
GRAPES grenache, cabernet sauvignon, cabernet franc, malbec
REGION Clare Valley, SA
CELLAR 🍾 5
ALC./VOL. 14.0%
RRP $14.50

The grapes were grown mainly on the property of Ferg and Vyv Mahon out the back of Wendouree, near Sevenhill. Maker Tim Adams.

CURRENT RELEASE 1994 Takes you way back to childhood with the booming scent of Steamrollers peppermints! This is a lovely drink: smooth, full and packed with fruit and tannin, gutsy albeit not very complex, and that mint gets into every pore of every tastebud. Try it with braised lamb shanks.

Tim Adams Shiraz

QUALITY 🍷🍷🍷
VALUE ★★★
GRAPES shiraz
REGION Clare Valley, SA
CELLAR 🍾 5
ALC./VOL. 13.0%
RRP $15.00

Adams is a winemaker with considerable experience in the Clare region, having worked at Leasingham and Eaglehawk. He owns very little vineyard and buys most of his fruit.
Previous outstanding vintages: '88, '90, '92

CURRENT RELEASE 1993 This is like a junior version of the Aberfeldy, with similar earthy, nutmeg-spice bouquet and dry tannin finish, but lacks the mid-palate intensity of its big sibling. A more approachable wine to drink sooner. Try a rabbit casserole.

Tim Gramp Shiraz

Tim Gramp is descended from the founding family of Orlando. He burst onto the scene with a stunning first-release 1991 shiraz, which is still unbeaten to date.

Previous outstanding vintages: '91, '92

CURRENT RELEASE 1993 This needs to be left alone for a couple of years. It's an obstreperous youngster with a sappy, coconutty oak-dominant nose and although there's heaps of weight and depth, it's a tad raw and rough at this point. The finish is stacked with oak and tannin and there's alcohol heat to keep you warm on a cold winter's night, when a rich beef casserole would be in order.

QUALITY ♛♛♛♛
VALUE ★★★★
GRAPES shiraz
REGION McLaren Vale, SA
CELLAR ⬤ 2–5+
ALC./VOL. 14.0%
RRP $17.70

Tim Knappstein Cabernet Merlot

Knappstein makes two cabernet-based reds: this is his drink-now bistro wine, while the straight cabernet is a more serious, cellarable style. The '93 is the first to include Lenswood fruit.

CURRENT RELEASE 1993 This light-mediumweight red is a little firmer to finish than usual, although the mulberry, herbal fruit is soft and up-front. There's a little oak vanilla and the general impression is a straightforward red that's ready to go. Try it with scalloppine.

QUALITY ♛♛♛♛
VALUE ★★★
GRAPES cabernet sauvignon 68%, merlot 28%, malbec 4%
REGION Clare 82%, Lenswood 18%, SA
CELLAR 🍷 4
ALC./VOL. 13.8%
RRP $18.00 Ⓢ

Tim Knappstein Cabernet Sauvignon

QUALITY ♀♀♀♀
VALUE ★★★
GRAPES cabernet sauvignon 91%, cabernet franc 6%, merlot 3%
REGION Clare, SA
CELLAR 🍷 4+
ALC./VOL. 13.2%
RRP $19.50

This company, though still headed up by its founder, Tim K. himself, is now part of the Petaluma Wines group. The vineyard is high for Clare, at 450 metres. Maker Tim Knappstein.

CURRENT RELEASE 1990 Bottle-age is a bonus here: the colour and nose show development, with brick-red tints and a leathery, earthy aspect to the soft plum/berry fruit bouquet. The palate is smooth, mellow and fruit-sweet and finishes with dry, grainy tannins. Good with food: try an aged cheese.

Tisdall Cabernet Merlot

QUALITY ♀♀♀♀
VALUE ★★★★
GRAPES cabernet sauvignon, merlot
REGION Echuca, Vic.
CELLAR 🍷 4
ALC./VOL. 13.5%
RRP $10.00 $

Now that it's part of the bullish Mildara Blass empire, the Tisdall brand, which languished under the previous ownership, is set to build a higher profile. Maker Toni Stockhausen.

CURRENT RELEASE 1992 A most attractive wine at an everyday price. Blackcurrant fruit and vanillan oak are skilfully melded and a hint of volatility does not bother. Good flavour, structure and length: a must for grilled lamb chops.

Tollana Bin TR 222 Cabernet Sauvignon

QUALITY ♀♀♀♀
VALUE ★★★★
GRAPES cabernet sauvignon
REGION Eden Valley, SA
CELLAR 🍷 5
ALC./VOL. 13.5%
RRP $16.50 $

Tollana, a quiet achiever that was put on the map by a not-so-quiet achiever, Wolf Blass, is based on the large Woodbury vineyard in the Eden Valley ranges. Maker Neville Falkenberg.

Previous outstanding vintages: '82, '84, '87, '88, '90, '91

CURRENT RELEASE 1992 As usual, this is a well-concentrated, chunky style infused with an abundance of oak and finishing with smooth, grainy tannins. It has a high-extract palate filled with currant/dark berry flavours. Try it with barbecued kebabs.

Tollana Eden Valley Hermitage Bin TR 16

Lesson number one for most people new to the arcane world of wine is that hermitage is the same as shiraz. In the not so distant future it will be illegal to use the h-word.

CURRENT RELEASE 1991 This is very much in the Penfolds mould, with dominant vanilla/coconut oak and ripe, rich developed plum and currant flavours. A friendly wine with stacks of flavour, the mid-palate fruit drying into a long arid tail. Try it with rare venison cutlets.

QUALITY ♛♛♛♛
VALUE ★★★★
GRAPES shiraz
REGION Eden Valley, SA
CELLAR 🍾 5+
ALC./VOL. 12.5%
RRP $15.00 Ⓢ 🍾

Tolley Cellar Reserve Shiraz Cabernet

Cellar Reserve sounds like it's a special stash just for the boss, but nothing could be further from the truth: it's the bottom of the range.

CURRENT RELEASE 1993 This is a perfectly acceptable wine at the price, somewhat nondescript, but a light, lean and inoffensive red with some jammy ripe-fruit aromas, and a mild dash of tannin on the finish. Try it with minestrone.

QUALITY ♛♛♝
VALUE ★★★
GRAPES shiraz, cabernet sauvignon
REGION Padthaway, Barossa Valley, Riverland, SA
CELLAR 🍾 2
ALC./VOL. 13.0%
RRP $8.50 Ⓢ

Tolley Hope Valley Cellars Barossa Shiraz

Another new release from Tolley, made from selected old, low-yielding shiraz vines in their Barossa vineyards. It bears the stylish old Hope Valley Burgundy label.

CURRENT RELEASE 1992 Needs quite a bit of airing to show its full worth. There's an off-putting oak character on the nose at first, which later reveals pepper, plum, liquorice and dark chocolate aromas. The palate is big and brawny, with slightly unkempt tannin astringency which will soften with cellaring. Rump steak here.

QUALITY ♛♛♛♝
VALUE ★★★
GRAPES shiraz
REGION Barossa Valley, SA
CELLAR ⇌ 2–7
ALC./VOL. 12.5%
RRP $19.50 🍾

Tolley Pedare Cabernet Sauvignon

QUALITY ♛♛♛♛½
VALUE ★★★½
GRAPES cabernet sauvignon
REGION Barossa Valley 82%, Padthaway 18%, SA
CELLAR 🍶 6
ALC./VOL. 12.5%
RRP $13.85 Ⓢ

Tolley is a family affair, with winemaker Chris, marketing manager Jon and managing director Reg, but the recent sale to Mildara will ring in some changes.

CURRENT RELEASE 1992 This is a typical Barossa style of red, loaded with peppermint, chocolate, berry and liquorice flavours. The colour is nice and deep and there's good quality oak in fine balance. It finishes with a well-judged grip. Drink with barbecued lamb kebabs.

Tolley Pedare Shiraz Cabernet Merlot

QUALITY ♛♛♛
VALUE ★★★
GRAPES shiraz 65%, cabernet sauvignon 27%, merlot 8%
REGION Barossa Valley & Padthaway, SA
CELLAR 🍶 3+
ALC./VOL. 13.0%
RRP $13.85 Ⓢ

A new blend from Tolley. Pedare is their mid-priced range, while – oddly enough – Cellar Reserve is their cheaper line.

CURRENT RELEASE 1993 This wine reminds of the drover's dog: it's a bit lean in the middle. It's a decent drink although we'd like to see more flesh and smoothness. The flavours are attractive: plum, vanilla and coconut with a lacing of peppermint. Drink with gourmet sausages.

Trentham Estate Merlot

Trentham turns out a very competent range of wines at most agreeable prices. This gold medal winner is one of its best value wines. Maker Tony Murphy.

CURRENT RELEASE 1993 A stylish, oak-driven merlot that impresses with its complex flavours and coffee, gamey, toasty-oak characters. The nose is very inviting and develops more coffee overtones as the wine breathes. Slightly lean and perhaps a trifle oak-reliant, it has a lot of appeal and a soft finish. Try it with rabbit casserole.

QUALITY ▼▼▼▼
VALUE ★★★★½
GRAPES merlot
REGION Murray River, NSW
CELLAR 🍷 3
ALC./VOL. 13.5%
RRP $12.00

Trentham Estate Shiraz

The fact that Trentham wines are often outstanding value must be a function of being located in an unfashionable district. There is a restaurant at Trentham and tourists are well looked after.

CURRENT RELEASE 1992 This is a real surprise: a rich, intense, oak-driven red which aims to please and succeeds. Toasty oak combines with ripe fruit to give chocolate, coffee flavours. A trace of volatility does not intrude; the wine is mouthfilling, gutsy, stacked with flavour and the finish is long. Should go well with calf's liver.

QUALITY ▼▼▼▼
VALUE ★★★★½
GRAPES shiraz
REGION Murray River, NSW
CELLAR 🍷 5+
ALC./VOL. 14.0%
RRP $13.70 ⓢ

Tunnel Hill Pinot Noir

QUALITY ♈♈♈
VALUE ★★½
GRAPES pinot noir
REGION Yarra Valley, Vic.
CELLAR 🍾 2
ALC./VOL. 13.4%
RRP $16.90

The second label of Tarrawarra. Owner Marc Besen is an art collector and the Tunnel Hill label is modelled on a painting of the winery by William Delafield Cook.

CURRENT RELEASE 1993 The pale colour belies a quite pleasant pinot. The dusty nose has some resiny oak and matured characters. In the mouth it is dry, mediumweight and shows a little tannin firmness. Ready to drink, with spaghetti bolognaise.

QUALITY ♈♈♈♈
VALUE ★★★½
GRAPES pinot noir
REGION Yarra Valley, Vic.
CELLAR 🍾 2+
ALC./VOL. 13.1%
RRP $18.00

CURRENT RELEASE 1994 This wine, made as a drink-now pinot, has loads of up-front charm. Medium-light purple-red hue and a fragrant strawberry/cherry aromatic nose. The palate is light to medium bodied, soft and fruity with low tannins. Good with barbecued tuna steaks.

Turkey Flat Grenache Noir

QUALITY ♈♈♈♈♈
VALUE ★★★★★
GRAPES grenache
REGION Barossa Valley, SA
CELLAR 🍾 5+
ALC./VOL. 14.3%
RRP $17.00 🍾

The Schulzes have done it again with another superb red. It just goes to show how critical a good, mature vineyard is in the quality equation. Made by Chris Ringland at Rockford.

CURRENT RELEASE 1993 This opens up with all guns firing: a seductive nose of high toast oak and lovely sweet, plum-jam fruit. The flavour is layered and concentrated, with superb depth and structure. The palate is warm, round, sweet and very persistent. Yum! Try it with civet of hare.

Turkey Flat Rosé

This is made by rosé specialist, Charlie Melton.
CURRENT RELEASE 1995 Deepish colour for a rosé, with a slightly subdued herbal, cherry nose and plenty of structure on the palate. There is a trace of sweetness, and tannin dries the finish. Very much a modern Barossa style of rosé that is closer to beaujolais in style. Try it with spag bol.

QUALITY ♛♛♛♕
VALUE ★★★½
GRAPES grenache, shiraz, cabernet sauvignon
REGION Barossa Valley, SA
CELLAR 🍷 3
ALC./VOL. 11.0%
RRP $14.00

Turkey Flat Shiraz

The Schulz family have been growing grapes for other winemakers for many years, only recently venturing into the winemaking and marketing rat-race. The original vines are nearly 150 years old, making them some of the oldest shiraz vines in the world. Maker Peter Schulz.

CURRENT RELEASE 1992 Made from vines planted in 1847, this is a delightfully rich, round, silky-smooth red, showing genuine old-vine concentration. The flavour is a skilful juxtaposition of spicy and vanillan elements laced with liquorice and dark chocolate – the epitome of Barossa shiraz. Delicious with Thai beef salad (easy on the chilli!).

QUALITY ♛♛♛♛♛
VALUE ★★★★★
GRAPES shiraz
REGION Barossa Valley, SA
CELLAR 🍷 7+
ALC./VOL. 14.3%
RRP $23.00 🍾

Tyrrell's Old Winery Cabernet Merlot

The name of Tyrrell's popular, ready-drinking brand evokes the old dirt-floored winery and ancestral home which visitors can see at Tyrrell's on Broke Road, Pokolbin. Maker Andrew Spinaze.

CURRENT RELEASE 1993 One-room slab hut meets Double Bay brasserie! This is a very drinkable, soft cabernet showing a leafy/blackcurrant varietal nose and lashings of sweet, dark berry fruit flavour. Not hugely complex but full of charm and ready to party.

QUALITY ♛♛♛♛
VALUE ★★★★½
GRAPES cabernet sauvignon 80%, merlot 20%
REGION mainly McLaren Vale & Coonawarra, SA
CELLAR 🍷 5
ALC./VOL. 13.3%
RRP $13.00 Ⓢ

Tyrrell's Old Winery Pinot Noir

QUALITY ♕♕♕♔
VALUE ★★★½
GRAPES pinot noir
REGION Hunter Valley, NSW
CELLAR 🍷 3
ALC./VOL. 12.5%
RRP $14.00 Ⓢ

Murray Tyrrell pioneered pinot noir in Australia, which is an irony because the cooler, more southerly regions have conclusively wrested the mantle from him. This is Tyrrell's second-string pinot.
Previous outstanding vintages: '89
CURRENT RELEASE 1994 A very handy pinot at around $12, offering authentic cherry/plum fruit aromas and a trace of vanilla. The finish is firmed up by some nicely judged tannin and the wine is well balanced although not exactly complex. Drink now with duck.

Tyrrell's Old Winery Shiraz

QUALITY ♕♕♕♕
VALUE ★★★★
GRAPES shiraz
REGION Hunter Valley, NSW
CELLAR 🍷 4+
ALC./VOL. 13.0%
RRP $14.00 Ⓢ

This won the Arthur Kelman trophy at the '95 Sydney Wine Show, which meant a great deal to patriarch Murray Tyrrell, as the trophy was named in memory of his uncle. Kelman married Florence, sister of Dan Tyrrell, Murray's mentor.
CURRENT RELEASE 1991 This is a wine of flavour, if not finesse. The nose offers gumleaf mint and earthy scents. The palate has fullness, flesh, tannin and body. The rich, long plummy flavours are satisfying and there's a nice grip to the finish. Drink with char-grilled meats.

Tyrrell's Stevens Shiraz

The grapegrower's name is Stevens, and this is one of several new releases in Tyrrell's new individual vineyard range. Maker Andrew Spinaze.

CURRENT RELEASE 1993 The Hunter terroir asserts itself strongly here. The wine has a quite unusual accent to its spicy, earthy bouquet, and there's a vanilla/caramel edge. The palate is more familiar, with sweet berry and oak undercurrents finishing firm and dry with good tannin grip. Serve with game.

QUALITY ♀♀♀♀
VALUE ★★★
GRAPES shiraz
REGION Hunter Valley, NSW
CELLAR 🍷 7+
ALC./VOL. 13.3%
RRP $29.00 ⓢ 🍷

Tyrrell's Vat 9 Shiraz

This has evolved into the flagship Tyrrell red in recent years, and is based on two blocks of very old vines near the winery, one planted in 1879 and one 1892, as well as the best fruit off the younger Brokenback vineyard.

Previous outstanding vintages: '79, '80, '81, '83, '85, '87, '90, '91, '92

CURRENT RELEASE 1993 This is a tightly structured, medium-bodied shiraz with a subdued, dusty but spicy/peppery nose with a trace of nutty oak. It's a lively, leaner style and should turn into a very good Vat 9. Drink it with duck a l'orange.

QUALITY ♀♀♀♀
VALUE ★★★★
GRAPES shiraz
REGION Hunter Valley, NSW
CELLAR 🍷 1–6+
ALC./VOL. 13.2%
RRP $25.00 🍷

Wa-de-Lock Vineyards Cabernet Sauvignon Merlot

There are plans to expand production and a further five hectares are now under vine. Maker Graeme Little.

CURRENT RELEASE 1993 The colour is a substantial deep ruby and the nose is strongly minty with hints of leaves. The palate has attractive berry characters, with blackberry and cherry to the fore, followed by black tea-like tannins on a firm finish. Try it with roast kid.

QUALITY ♀♀♀♀
VALUE ★★★★
GRAPES cabernet sauvignon 60%, merlot 40%
REGION Gippsland, Vic.
CELLAR 🍷 4
ALC./VOL. 12.0%
RRP $13.50

Wa-de-Lock Vineyards Pinot Noir

QUALITY 🍷🍷🍷🍷
VALUE ★★★½
GRAPES pinot noir
REGION Gippsland, Vic.
CELLAR 🍷 3
ALC./VOL. 12.7%
RRP $13.50

Funny name, you Australians. This vineyard was established in 1987 and production is around 850 cases. Maker Graeme Little.

CURRENT RELEASE 1993 The colour is a mid-ruby and the nose offers a mix of earth and mint aromas. The palate is quite intense with wild strawberry flavours followed by soft tannins and mild astringency on a very dry finish. Try it with quail.

Warrenmang Estate Shiraz

QUALITY 🍷🍷🍷🍷
VALUE ★★★★
GRAPES shiraz
REGION Pyrenees, Vic.
CELLAR ⇨ 2–6
ALC./VOL. 13.0%
RRP $16.50

Once upon a time this style was loaded with mint. It was thought to be a contribution from the local peppermint gums. These days this character is less obvious.

CURRENT RELEASE 1993 The colour has a typical regional density. The nose has just a trace of mint with ripe plum and underlying spice. The palate is rich with ripe plum flavours plus a hint of earth. Strong oak maintains a firm finish. A good wine for roast squab and wild rice.

Warrenmang Grand Pyrenees

QUALITY 🍷🍷🍷🍷
VALUE ★★★★
GRAPES not stated
REGION Pyrenees, Vic.
CELLAR 🍷 5
ALC./VOL. 13.5%
RRP $19.50

This is a generic style from the Moonambel district. The label maintains an element of mystery and gives no clue to the varieties used – *tres* Frog.

CURRENT RELEASE *non-vintage* Deep, dark colour and a very vinous nose. Fruit and oak have combined to make a strong wine aroma. The palate shows wild cherry flavours plus some slightly feral tinges followed by integrated oak on a dry finish. It drinks well now and needs a strong dish like oxtail stew to set it off.

Water Wheel Cabernet Sauvignon

Water Wheel was established in 1972 and made indifferent wines until it came into the hands of the love apple-growing Cumming family. These days the name is high in the wine firmament.
Maker Peter Cumming
Previous outstanding vintages: '91, '92
CURRENT RELEASE 1993 A very elegant style that defies the regional propensity to brutish wines. This is cherry country and it seems to be reflected in the wine: the colour is cherry red and there are oak and cherry smells on the nose. The mediumweight palate is all about dark cherries and there is a cherry pip character on the astringent finish. A very fine wine that goes well with a hearty casserole.

QUALITY ▼▼▼▼
VALUE ★★★★
GRAPES cabernet sauvignon
REGION Bendigo, Vic.
CELLAR 6
ALC./VOL. 13.5%
RRP $13.00

Weatherall Cabernet Sauvignon

When you visit Coonawarra make sure you nosh out at the Weatherall restaurant – it is one of the best of the Terra Rossa strip.
CURRENT RELEASE 1992 This wine is possibly reflective of the cool vintage. The nose is minty with a slightly musty background. The palate has a sweet cherry/berry flavour matched by soft tannins on a dry finish. Try it with veal schnitzel.

QUALITY ▼▼▼
VALUE ★★★
GRAPES cabernet sauvignon
REGION Coonawarra, SA
CELLAR 4
ALC./VOL. 12.5%
RRP $19.00

Weatherall Shiraz

This variety in Coonawarra can play devil's advocate depending on the weather. When years are cool, times are tough.
CURRENT RELEASE 1992 The nose is slightly minty with dusty oak and a musty background. The middleweight palate offers tart raspberry flavours followed by strong grip on a high acid finish. Try it with grilled lamb chops.

QUALITY ▼▼▼
VALUE ★★★
GRAPES shiraz
REGION Coonawarra, SA
CELLAR 3
ALC./VOL. 12.0%
RRP $14.00

Wellington Pinot Noir

QUALITY ♜♜♜♜
VALUE ★★★½
GRAPES pinot noir
REGION various, Tas.
CELLAR 🍷 3
ALC./VOL. 12.5%
RRP $16.95

There is a debate over where this wine comes from: the distributor has one version, HH another, and MS doesn't have a clue – he just likes to drink it!

CURRENT RELEASE 1993 A very interesting wine that has charm and complexity. The nose has tobacco, cherry and strawberry aromas. The palate is fruity with ripe cherry, strawberry and a hint of earth. Crisp acid fills out the finish and there is minimal oak. It goes well with char-grilled quail.

Wild Duck Creek Alan's Cabernets

QUALITY ♜♜♜
VALUE ★★★
GRAPES cabernet sauvignon, cabernet franc
REGION Heathcote, Vic.
CELLAR 🍷 3
ALC./VOL. 12.5%
RRP $16.00

The identity of Alan is not revealed in the label. This is a small vineyard in the Heathcote hills. Maker David Anderson.

CURRENT RELEASE 1993 Minty stuff; in fact the mint can drive you to distraction. Mint dominates the nose and there are some sweet berry flavours on the cherry flavoured palate, plus the ubiquitous mint. The finish shows firm oak and positive grip. Try it with sauer barton.

Wild Duck Creek Springflat Shiraz

QUALITY ♜♜♜♜↷
VALUE ★★★★½
GRAPES shiraz
REGION Heathcote, Vic.
CELLAR 🍷 5+
ALC./VOL. 13.0%
RRP $13.35 (cellar door)

This is a relative newcomer in Heathcote, an area that's proved itself – with panache – to be a great source of shiraz. Grown and made by David and Diana Anderson, who are also looking after Tyrrell's major new vineyard at Heathcote. Only 600 cases produced.

CURRENT RELEASE 1993 A wonderfully intense, fresh shiraz bubbling over with natural charm and complex spicy berry aromas. It is lively, medium-bodied and elegant in profile, with mild tannins. An opened bottle holds together for many days, which augurs well for cellaring. Drink with – what else? – wild duck.

Willow Creek Cabernet Sauvignon

This vineyard was established in 1989 and the production is about 2000 cases. Consultants are used to make the wine.
CURRENT RELEASE 1993 This is a bigger style from a region notorious for thin wines. The colour is deep and the nose has perfume and concentrated berry aromas. The palate is rich with sweet raspberry flavoured fruit and a distinct berry character. Toasty oak fills out the finish, adding a lot of grip. It would go well with guinea fowl.

QUALITY ▼▼▼▼⸱
VALUE ★★★★½
GRAPES cabernet sauvignon
REGION Mornington Peninsula, Vic.
CELLAR 🍷 5
ALC./VOL. 13.5%
RRP $19.00

Willows (The) Cabernet Sauvignon

Ancient river red gums and willows adorn the peaceful, picturesque vineyard of the Scholz family at Light Pass, hence the property's name.
CURRENT RELEASE 1991 The colour is rich red, still with a tinge of purple, and the developed bouquet shows earth and mint/eucalypt rustic Barossa characters, without strong varietal identity. The style is rich, chunky and soft, with big round chocolate, vanilla and berry flavours. The big finish reverberates around the mouth for a long time. Drink with saddle of hare.

QUALITY ▼▼▼▼
VALUE ★★★★
GRAPES cabernet sauvignon
REGION Barossa Valley, SA
CELLAR 🍷 5
ALC./VOL. 13.5%
RRP $15.30 🍾

Wilson Vineyard Cabernet Sauvignon

In an industry rich in characters there are few more interesting that Dr John Wilson, who established a vineyard in Clare in 1974. He is an outspoken advocate for wine and health. His production is 2800 cases. Maker John Wilson.
CURRENT RELEASE 1991 There is some bottle development evident in this elegant wine. The nose has soft mulberry and hints of leaf aromas. The palate is minty with mulberry dominating, followed by dry tannins on an astringent finish. It goes well with osso bucco.

QUALITY ▼▼▼▼
VALUE ★★★★
GRAPES cabernet sauvignon
REGION Clare Valley, SA
CELLAR 🍷 3
ALC./VOL. 12.5%
RRP $15.50 🍾

Wirra Wirra Vineyards The Angelus

QUALITY ★★★★½
VALUE ★★★★
GRAPES cabernet sauvignon
REGION McLaren Vale, SA
CELLAR 2–5
ALC./VOL. 14.0%
RRP $27.00

God bless proprietor Greg Trott. The Trott sense of humour is never far from the surface. The back label declares, 'This wine contains approximately 8.3 standard drinks at sea level.'
Previous outstanding vintages: '91, '92
CURRENT RELEASE 1993 The impressive quality continues with this relatively new line. The colour is a mid to deep ruby and the nose has a mixture of leaf, lantana and berry aromas. The medium-to-full-bodied palate has sweet redcurrant fruit flavours and cinnamon spice. The finish shows useful oak and balanced grip. Try it with osso bucco.

Wirra Wirra Vineyards Original Blend

QUALITY ★★★★★
VALUE ★★★★½
GRAPES grenache 70%, shiraz 30%
CELLAR 4
ALC./VOL. 14.5%
RRP $20.00

Once upon a time you would hide a blend like this behind the mask of 'Dry Red'. These days it is fashionable to come out of the vinous closet and announce the grape varieties on the label.
CURRENT RELEASE 1994 Ho, ho, ho, vertigo row! This has generous everything, including alcohol. The nose has a strong raspberry aroma, which is the main flavour encountered on the succulent palate. There is also a warmth of alcohol that adds a slippery texture. The finish shows discreet oak and soft tannin. It goes well with a hearty casserole of saltbush mutton.

Wirra Wirra Vineyards RSW Shiraz

RSW are the initials of Robert Strangways Wigley, who established Wirra Wirra in 1894. He was said to be an eccentric proprietor, and little seems to have changed since then (in the nicest possible way).
Previous outstanding vintages: '92
CURRENT RELEASE 1993 This is a full-frontal McLaren Vale style. The nose is plummy with hints of leaf and the palate is rich, mouthfilling and succulent of texture. There are plenty of sweet berry characters matched by well-integrated oak that imparts chalky tannins on an astringent finish. Try it with duck or game.

QUALITY ♆♆♆♆♆
VALUE ★★★★
GRAPES shiraz
REGION McLaren Vale, SA
CELLAR 🍷 6
ALC./VOL. 14.0%
RRP $22.50

Wolf Blass Black Label

Wolfgang Blass *über alles*, that's how it was when he won the Jimmy Watson Memorial for three consecutive years ('73, '74, '75, and at the time MS was selling Blass wines in Melbourne). The popularity went to his head and he started writing books! Maker John Glaetzer.
Previous outstanding vintages: '73, '74, '75, '78, '80, '82, '83, '84, '86, '87, '89
CURRENT RELEASE 1991 A worthy Black Label with all the richness of Aladdin's cave. The nose has blackcurrant and smoky oak aromas. The fruit on the palate is positively explosive with incredible depth. Blackberry, mulberry and dark cherry flavours vie for the palate's attention, and there's some very sophisticated wood on a dry and astringent finish. It drinks well now and cellar gains will probably be marginal. Try it with beef casserole.

QUALITY ♆♆♆♆♆
VALUE ★★★★
GRAPES cabernet sauvignon, shiraz
REGION Coonawarra, McLaren Vale, Clare, SA
CELLAR 🍷 4
ALC./VOL. 13.0%
RRP $38.00

Wolf Blass Brown Label Classic Shiraz

QUALITY 🍷🍷🍷🍷🍷
VALUE ★★★★½
GRAPES shiraz
REGION not stated
CELLAR 🍾 4
ALC./VOL. 13.5%
RRP $19.00

'Break on through to the other side,' as the late Jim Morrison would have lisped. This is a breakthrough wine that begs no pardons.

Previous outstanding vintages: '90, '91

CURRENT RELEASE 1992 Spice and all things nice, this is a well-balanced encounter between oak and fruit. The nose offers pepper and coconut. The palate is laden with sweet plum flavours and zesty spice. American oak enters like the 7th Cavalry to the rescue, adding a savoury nature and positive fine-grained tannins. There is also plenty of grip. It drinks well with roast duck.

Wolf Blass Grey Label

QUALITY 🍷🍷🍷🍷
VALUE ★★★★
GRAPES cabernet sauvignon, shiraz
REGION Langhorne Creek, SA
CELLAR 🍾 6
ALC./VOL. 14.0%
RRP $20.00

This has long been an essay in Langhorne Creek fruit. Through the years it has won many trophies and gongs.

Previous outstanding vintages: '81, '84, '85, '89, '90

CURRENT RELEASE 1991 Very interesting wine with some unique flavours and aromas. There are rose-petals and rock melons on the nose, yet the palate is dominated by ripe fruit with sweet berry flavours supported by lifted American oak. Old-fashioned in style and easy to love. Try it with a carpetbag steak.

Wolf Blass Red Label

QUALITY 🍷🍷🍷🍷
VALUE ★★★½
GRAPES shiraz, cabernet sauvignon
REGION McLaren Vale, Barossa Valley, SA
CELLAR 🍾 3
ALC./VOL. 12.5%
RRP $9.95

This is an enduring style that was made to drink now. A very good example of value for money.

CURRENT RELEASE 1993 A big plummy style that has plenty of cuddly fruit. The nose has soft berry aromas and the palate is medium-bodied with sweet raspberry flavours. The finish shows soft tannins and well-integrated oak. Try it with a lamb and barley casserole.

Wolf Blass Yellow Label

This is always a reliable commercial style that is made for drinking and not thinking. Value for money is always the other part of the equation. Maker John Glaetzer.

CURRENT RELEASE 1993 A little bigger and broader than the usual. The wine is fruit driven. The nose has ripe berry aromas and coconut oak smells. The palate has rich blackberry and raspberry flavours and there is a seamless transition to a mildly oaky finish. It drinks well with a shepherd's pie.

QUALITY 🍷🍷🍷
VALUE ★★★★
GRAPES cabernet sauvignon, shiraz
REGION Langhorne Creek, SA
CELLAR 🍾 2
ALC./VOL. 13.0%
RRP $12.95

Wood Ridge Classic Red

Wood Ridge, a name inherited from San Bernadino, is De Bortoli's el cheapo bottled range.

CURRENT RELEASE 1994 This is basic barbecue fodder indeed – dare we say cask quality in a bottle? But it's fair value at the price, offering a medium-light red colour, stewy, jammy hot-grown aromas and a lean, short and slightly astringent palate. Pork sausages here.

QUALITY 🍷🍷
VALUE ★★★
GRAPES not stated
REGION Riverina, NSW
CELLAR 🍾
ALC./VOL. 11.0%
RRP $4.85 Ⓢ

Woodstock Cabernet Sauvignon

The proprietor of this vineyard/winery/restaurant calls himself a 'red wine man' and it shows in his product. Maker Scott Collett.

CURRENT RELEASE 1992 A generous wine with lots of flavour. The nose has blackberry and chocolate aromas, and the palate is long and sinuous with blackberry flavour and earthy undertones matched by discreet wood and a warmth of alcohol. It goes very well with rare kangaroo.

QUALITY 🍷🍷🍷🍷
VALUE ★★★★
GRAPES cabernet sauvignon
REGION McLaren Vale, SA
CELLAR ⇀ 2–10
ALC./VOL. 14.0%
RRP $14.90

Woodstock The Stocks

QUALITY 🍷🍷🍷🍷½
VALUE ★★★★½
GRAPES shiraz
REGION McLaren Vale, SA
CELLAR 2–6
ALC./VOL. 12.5%
RRP $18.00

There is a set of ye olde English stocks in front of this winery. They seem to be a magnet to visitors, who insist on incarcerating each other.

CURRENT RELEASE 1991 A very well-made wine typical of McLaren Vale. The colour is dense and the nose has ripe plum, pepper and spice aromas. The palate is intense and complex with strong plum flavours and loads of spice. New wood contributes grip to the finish and the wine should cellar well. Try it with coarse beef sausages.

Wyndham Estate Bin 444 Cabernet Sauvignon

QUALITY 🍷🍷🍷
VALUE ★★★
GRAPES cabernet sauvignon
REGION Hunter Valley, NSW
CELLAR 🍾 2
ALC./VOL. 12.5%
RRP $11.00 (S)

The Wyndham range is the middle tier in terms of price. They are commercial styles that are easy to like.

CURRENT RELEASE 1993 The colour is a mid-ruby and the nose offers cherries and spice smells. The medium-bodied palate is lean with soft raspberry flavours backed by some obvious acid on a mildly astringent finish. It drinks well now with lamb shanks.

Wyndham Estate Bin 555 Selected Hermitage

QUALITY 🍷🍷🍷
VALUE ★★★
GRAPES shiraz
REGION Hunter Valley, NSW
CELLAR 🍾 1
ALC./VOL. 12.5%
RRP $11.00 (S)

What is a 'selected hermitage?' Never mind, while the marketers play you can assume it's Hunter Valley shiraz and drink accordingly.

CURRENT RELEASE 1993 The colour is a light ruby and the plummy nose shows some attractive spice. The palate is light with spicy fruit attached to a mildly astringent finish. It is easy to drink and/or take to a barbecue.

Wynns Cabernet Sauvignon Hermitage Merlot

A label change is a sure sign there is a new brand manager on the block. MS believes that a vertical tasting reveals the comings and goings of brand managers (by the label changes). In this case there will probably be another change very soon.
Previous outstanding vintages: '82, '86, '88, '90
CURRENT RELEASE 1992 The vintage is on record as a light year at Coonawarra but in this case light doesn't mean less. The nose has leaf, cigarbox and smoky oak. The palate is a middleweight with ripe berry flavours tinged with spices. The finish is beautifully integrated, conveying style and finesse. It drinks well now, so try it with marinated quail.

QUALITY ♥♥♥♥?
REGION ★★★★½
GRAPES cabernet sauvignon, shiraz, merlot
REGION Coonawarra, SA
CELLAR ← 2–6
ALC./VOL. 13.0%
RRP $11.90

Wynns Coonawarra Cabernet Sauvignon

The famous black label was demoted to the ranks with the advent of the John Riddoch label but it usually represents better value and more elegance.
Previous outstanding vintages: '62, '76, '82, '85, '86, '88, '90, '91
CURRENT RELEASE 1992 Lighter doesn't mean lesser. This is an elegant style with plenty of varietal character. The nose has cedar oak, leaf and cassis. The palate is a middleweight with sweet cassis and blackberry flavours matched by well-integrated oak on an astringent finish. This wine could be a sleeper and develop well. Try it with a steak and kidney pudding.

QUALITY ♥♥♥♥?
VALUE ★★★★½
GRAPES cabernet sauvignon
REGION Coonawarra, SA
CELLAR ← 2–10
ALC./VOL. 13.0%
RRP $18.00 Ⓢ

Wynns Coonawarra Hermitage

QUALITY 🍷🍷🍷🍷🍷
VALUE ★★★★★
GRAPES shiraz
REGION Coonawarra, SA
CELLAR 🍾 6
ALC./VOL. 13.5%
RRP $11.00 ⓢ

This wine is always a bargain and when the year is right it is one of the best on the market. Maker Peter Douglas.

Previous outstanding vintages: '86, '88, '90, '91

CURRENT RELEASE 1993 Bloody wonderful! This is the marque 'on song'. It has all the attributes of great Coonawarra shiraz, and look at the price! The colour is a bright ruby and the nose has ripe plum, pepper and spice aromas. The palate is complex with ripe plum flavours framed by spice and dusted with pepper. The finish is beautifully balanced with toasty oak and a fine-grained tannin grip. Great with char-grilled kangaroo.

Wynns John Riddoch Cabernet Sauvignon

QUALITY 🍷🍷🍷🍷
VALUE ★★★
GRAPES cabernet sauvignon
REGION Coonawarra, SA
CELLAR ➬ 3–8
ALC./VOL. 13.5%
RRP $35.00

This is the top of Wynns' ziggurat, and the best fruit is always used to make the flagship. It is invariably a powerpacked wine and you have to pay plenty.

Previous outstanding vintages: '82, '84, '85, '86, '88, '90, '91

CURRENT RELEASE 1992 This is where the nature of the year plays a vital part. The label demands maximum flavour and oak, and in this case the oak leads the dance. The wine is intense with sweet cassis fruit that is almost swamped by strong oak flavours. There's plenty of grip and more time in the cellar will help the drinkability. Try it with possum pie.

Yanwirra Cabernet Sauvignon

This is the second release from a small winery at Denmark, Western Australia. Maker John Wade (consultant).
CURRENT RELEASE 1993 A very sophisticated style that uses a blend of varieties to achieve complexity. The nose is vinous with fresh berry aromas. The medium-bodied palate shows a complex range of fruit flavours bound to some well-integrated oak on a dry, astringent finish. It drinks well now with a pink loin of lamb stuffed with apricot and spinach.

QUALITY ♛♛♛♛
VALUE ★★★★
GRAPES cabernet sauvignon 86%, cabernet franc 9%, merlot 5%
REGION Great Southern, WA
CELLAR 🍷 3
ALC./VOL. 12.5%
RRP $19.95

Yarra Edge Cabernets

Yet another vineyard with Yarra in its name. This one was established in 1984 and produces around 1200 cases.
CURRENT RELEASE 1992 An elegant and stylish blend that shows complexity. The nose is intense with strong berry aromas and hints of tobacco. The palate continues the complexity with wild cherry and blackberry while the finish is a bit of an anticlimax: the oak is discreet and the finish is soft. It drinks well now with char-grilled kangaroo.

QUALITY ♛♛♛♛
VALUE ★★★★
GRAPES cabernet sauvignon, cabernet franc, merlot
REGION Yarra Valley, Vic.
CELLAR 🍷 3
ALC./VOL. 12.4%
RRP $13.50

Yarra Ridge Shiraz

This is one of the best examples of minimalist labelling. It's a bit like the string bikini but what's inside is handsome and lean. Maker Rob Dolan.
CURRENT RELEASE 1993 Lean but not mean, this is a tight wine with some obvious oak. The colour is dense and the nose has bracken, spice and coffee oak aromas. The palate is tight with restrained blackberry and caramel oak flavours. The oak tends to steal the show at the moment but time might bring changes. Goes well with pink loin of lamb.

QUALITY ♛♛♛♛
VALUE ★★
GRAPES shiraz
REGION Yarra Valley, Vic.
CELLAR 🍷 2–5
ALC./VOL. 12.0%
RRP $28.95

Yarra Valley Hills Pinot Noir

QUALITY ▼▼▼▫
VALUE ★★★½
GRAPES pinot noir
REGION Yarra Valley, Vic.
CELLAR 🍷 3
ALC./VOL. 12.5%
RRP $15.00

The number of labels starting with 'Yarra' is beginning to rival the Jones section of the phone book. Here's another new one.

CURRENT RELEASE 1993 This is a serious (almost sombre) style which puts structure ahead of fruit. The nose offers wood and dark cherry smells, and the palate is a middleweight with tight fruit and muted cherry flavour followed by well-integrated oak. Try it with pink lamb chops.

QUALITY ▼▼▼▫
VALUE ★★★½
GRAPES pinot noir
REGION Yarra Valley, Vic.
CELLAR 🍷 2
ALC./VOL. 12.5%
RRP $15.00

CURRENT RELEASE 1994 A fresh friendly style that drinks well now. The colour is a mid-ruby and the nose has cherry and spice aromas. The palate is a middleweight with some charming dark cherry flavour which is enhanced by attractive spice. The finish offers modest tannins. It could be served chilled with char-grilled tuna.

Yering Station Cabernet Merlot

QUALITY ▼▼▼
VALUE ★★★
GRAPES cabernet sauvignon, merlot, cabernet franc
REGION Yarra Valley, Vic.
CELLAR 🍷 3
ALC./VOL. 11.7%
RRP $15.00

The Yarra Valley is expanding at an extraordinary pace. This winery is a reconstruction on the original site of Victoria's pioneer viticulturalist Paul de Castella.

CURRENT RELEASE 1992 The colour is deep and the nose is herbal with a slightly wet bracken tinge. The palate is elegant with muted berry characters followed by obvious acid on an astringent finish. Try it with pan-fried quail.

Yering Station Pinot Noir

How do you classify the current crop of Yarra Valley pinot noirs? Call them wimpy and the makers will say you don't understand elegance.

CURRENT RELEASE 1994 The colour is a very light ruby and the nose has a light strawberry aroma. There are sweet fruit flavours, mainly strawberry on the palate, backed up by some strong acid on the finish. It goes well with chicken.

QUALITY 🍷🍷🍷
VALUE ★★★
GRAPES pinot noir
REGION Yarra Valley, Vic.
CELLAR 🍾 2
ALC./VOL. 13.3%
RRP $17.90

White Wines

Alkoomi Mount Frankland Classic White

This is quite a large winery (15,000 cases) set in splendid isolation on Wingeballup Road at Frankland. Maker Kim Hart.

CURRENT RELEASE 1994 The nose offers fresh honeysuckle aromas that foreshadow a crisp palate of tropical fruit and peach flavours backed up by firm acid on a clean finish. Serve well chilled with a spaghetti marinara.

QUALITY ♛♛♛♙
VALUE ★★★½
GRAPES semillon, chardonnay, sauvignon blanc
REGION Frankland, WA
CELLAR 🍾 2
ALC./VOL. 12.0%
RRP $12.95

All Saints Chardonnay

If you get the chance to visit the winery at Wahgunyah, you'll be impressed by the care and attention lavished on the old castle. It has been done with taste and flair.

CURRENT RELEASE 1992 The nose is positively toasty and bristles with strong oak aromas. The palate shows equally strong peach flavours followed by a 'strength through joy' style oak on a robust finish. Don't overchill, and try it with pâté.

QUALITY ♛♛♛♙
VALUE ★★★½
GRAPES chardonnay
REGION Rutherglen, Vic.
CELLAR 🍾 3
ALC./VOL. 14.0%
RRP $13.00

All Saints Chenin Blanc

QUALITY ▼▼▼▼
VALUE ★★★★
GRAPES chenin blanc
GRAPES Rutherglen, Vic.
CELLAR 2
ALC./VOL. 13.5%
RRP $12.00

Chenin blanc seems to do quite well around Rutherglen. It's a pity it can't find a place in the marketing sun.
CURRENT RELEASE 1992 The wine shows little impact from bottle-age. The colour is pale and the nose is highly aromatic. The palate shows sweetness balanced by a tart green-apple character. The finish adds crispness. Serve well chilled with pork satay.

All Saints Late Harvest Semillon

QUALITY ▼▼▼▼▼
VALUE ★★★★½
GRAPES semillon
REGION Rutherglen, Vic.
CELLAR 3
ALC./VOL. 11.4%
RRP $12.50 (375ml)

All Saints is now in the hands of the Brown brethren, who have worked with a will to restore the place to its rightful glory. Maker Neil Jericho.
CURRENT RELEASE 1994 This is 375 ml of cuteness. There is an impressive green-gold colour and the nose has honey and dried fruit-peel aromas. The palate is a rich honeyed dried apricot and citrus followed by a marmalade character with a dry, cleansing finish. Serve well chilled as an entrée with smoked Atlantic salmon.

All Saints Marsanne

QUALITY ▼▼▼▼
VALUE ★★★★
GRAPES marsanne
REGION Rutherglen, Vic.
CELLAR 4
ALC./VOL. 12.9%
RRP $12.90

The previous owners, the Sutherland Smith family, put much store in this variety and Brown Brothers are continuing the tradition.
CURRENT RELEASE 1994 The nose shows honeysuckle and straw aromas. The palate is ample with a mouthfilling honeyed quality and grassy flavours, balanced by crisp acid on a clean finish. It should age well. Try it with rabbit terrine.

All Saints Orange Muscat

All Saints now belongs to Brown Brothers, and the Bros Brown are besotted with obscure grape varieties. Maker Neil Jericho.

CURRENT RELEASE 1994 No, the colour isn't bright orange but rather pale straw. The nose is subdued with soft aromatics and hints of grapes. The palate has a hint of sweetness and muscat flavours followed by clean acid on a dry finish. Serve well chilled with a rich fish soup.

QUALITY ▼▼▼▼
VALUE ★★★½
GRAPES orange muscat
REGION Rutherglen, Vic.
CELLAR 1
ALC./VOL. 13.5%
RRP $9.90

Allandale Chardonnay

Allandale is a medium-sized vineyard that was founded in 1977, and produces around 15,000 cases. Maker Bill Sneddon.

CURRENT RELEASE 1994 It's all about barrel ferment and classy oak. The nose has melon and caramel aromas, and the palate a mouth-coating quality of peach and melon flavours framed by dry French oak on a firm finish. Minimal chilling is recommended to match a designer warm chicken salad.

QUALITY ▼▼▼▼
VALUE ★★★★
GRAPES chardonnay
REGION Hunter Valley, NSW
CELLAR 3
ALC./VOL. 13.0%
RRP $14.50

Alta Sauvignon Blanc

This is a new label from the Endeavour wine company that is Australian based but dedicated to making wine internationally. Maker Don Lewis.

CURRENT RELEASE 1994 This is a carefully assembled style with a hint of green-pea and tomato-leaf aroma on the nose. The palate is a middleweight with herbal fruit that displays grassy characters balanced by clean acid on a crisp finish. Serve well chilled with white asparagus.

QUALITY ▼▼▼▼
VALUE ★★★★
GRAPES sauvignon blanc
REGION King Valley, Strathbogie Ranges, Vic.
CELLAR 2
ALC./VOL. 12.1%
RRP $12.00

Amberley Semillon Sauvignon Blanc

QUALITY ????
VALUE ★★★★
GRAPES semillon, sauvignon blanc
REGION Margaret River, WA
CELLAR 1
ALC./VOL. 12.5%
RRP $14.95

This is a big project that started in 1987 and the production is around 24,000 cases per annum. Maker Eddie Price.
CURRENT RELEASE 1994 A full-frontal style with an emphatic nose that shows tinned-pea and tomato-plant character. The palate is rich with gooseberry and tropical flavours balanced by crisp acid and gentle oak on a long finish. It can be served well chilled with an onion tart.

Andrew Garrett Chardonnay

QUALITY ????
VALUE ★★★★
GRAPES chardonnay
REGION Padthaway, McLaren Vale, SA; Mornington, Vic. & Cowra, NSW
CELLAR 3
ALC./VOL. 13.0%
RRP $10.95

Andrew Garrett is now part of the Mildara Blass stable and the portfolio has been incorporated within the many Mildara labels.
Previous outstanding vintages: '93
CURRENT RELEASE 1994 Padthaway dominates the blend. It is a rich style with obvious barrel-ferment character. There is sappy oak on the nose, while creamy peach and citrus flavours dominate the palate. Well-integrated oak fills out the finish. Don't overchill, and try it with stir-fried chicken.

Andrew Garrett Fumé Blanc

QUALITY ????
VALUE ★★★½
GRAPES sauvignon blanc
REGION McLaren Vale, Padthaway, SA
CELLAR 1
ALC./VOL. 13.0%
RRP $10.95

What is a fumé blanc? Provide us a clear definition and we'll buy you lunch with a bottle of red to avoid any further argument.
CURRENT RELEASE 1994 This is a big herbal style with lots of tropical characters. There are herbs and tropical fruit flavours on a full-bodied palate. The finish shows strong acid and good balance. It can be served well chilled with a quiche.

Andrew Garrett Riesling

'Thunderbirds are GO!' This label used to be gung-ho but now it's part of a more refined corporate culture. Maker Warren Dean Randall.
CURRENT RELEASE 1994 This is a typical Padthaway style with a floral, zesty nose. There is also a hint of botrytis. The palate is sweet but not cloying, thanks to a shock of lime. The finish shows fresh acid and good length. It can be served well chilled with grilled prawns.

QUALITY ♛♛♛♛
VALUE ★★★★
GRAPES riesling
REGION Padthaway, SA
CELLAR 🍷 2
ALC./VOL. 11.5%
RRP $10.95

Andrew Garrett Wood Aged Semillon

This used to be a bold, brash style but civilisation seems to have arrived with the new management. Less wood and more early drinking.
Previous outstanding vintages: '90, '91, '92
CURRENT RELEASE 1994 Oh what a lovely nose with its lanolin and gooseberry aromas! (The back label calls it a 'zesty style'.) The palate strays towards the sauvignon blanc spectrum of the variety, and there is some smoky wood on a robust finish with a big acid lift. Serve medium chilled with roast turkey.

QUALITY ♛♛♛♛
VALUE ★★★★
GRAPES semillon
REGION McLaren Vale, Padthaway, SA
CELLAR 🍷 5
ALC./VOL. 13.0%
RRP $10.95

Angoves Butterfly Ridge Chablis

The butterfly collection is a budget range made for the commercial market.
CURRENT RELEASE 1994 This wine is meant for everyday drinking. The nose has grape and tropical fruit aromas and the palate continues the same theme. The finish is soft and a tad short. Well chilled with KFC will fit the bill.

QUALITY ♛♛♛
VALUE ★★★
GRAPES colombard, chardonnay
REGION Renmark, SA
CELLAR 🍷
ALC./VOL. 12.0%
RRP $6.50

Angoves Colombard

QUALITY ▇▇▇▇
VALUE ★★★★½
GRAPES colombard
REGION Renmark, Vic.
CELLAR 🍾 1
ALC./VOL. 12.0%
RRP $8.80 Ⓢ

No one could accuse Angoves of being a hobby farm. It was established in 1886 and the annual production is 800,000 cases. Maker Frank Newman.

CURRENT RELEASE 1994 Colombard is a variety that does well in hot climates. The nose is toasty with hints of tropical fruit, the palate quite rich with pineapple and passionfruit flavours balanced by crisp acid on a lingering finish. Serve well chilled with a warm salad of chicken and pesto dressing.

Angoves Rhine Riesling

QUALITY ▇▇▇▇
VALUE ★★★★½
GRAPES riesling
REGION Renmark, SA
CELLAR 🍾 1
ALC./VOL. 11.5%
RRP $8.80 Ⓢ

This company makes a reliable range of varietal wines from grapes grown in their very large (over 1000 hectares) Nanya Vineyard near Renmark, SA. Maker Frank Newman.

CURRENT RELEASE 1994 There is authentic varietal character in this wine. The nose has lime and citrus aromas with a hint of spice. The palate is a middleweight with keen lime flavours braced by acid on a crisp finish. It can be served well chilled with oysters natural.

Angoves Sarnia Farm Chardonnay

QUALITY ▇▇▇▐
VALUE ★★★½
GRAPES chardonnay
REGION Padthaway, SA
CELLAR 🍾 2
ALC./VOL. 12.5%
RRP $15.50

Sarnia farm was one of the earliest Angove vineyards located in the Adelaide Hills. The fact that the grapes don't come from Sarnia Farm makes this label a tad confusing. Maker Frank J. Newman.

CURRENT RELEASE 1993 This wine is starting to show its age. The colour is quite gold and there are bottle-development keynotes on the nose. The palate is a middleweight with developed peach flavours and a creamy texture. The finish adds balance and discreet oak characters. Don't overchill.

Antipodean

Hill Smith Wines (Yalumba, Heggies, Pewsey Vale and Hill Smith Estate) is a perplexing company. Every time you think they've gone to sleep they seem to come up with something startling. The packaging is spectacular! Maker Brian Walsh and team.

CURRENT RELEASE 1994 The nose is dominated by sauvignon blanc smells, while the palate has complex tropical fruit flavours matched by crisp acid on a clean, bracing finish. A very refreshing style that can be served well chilled. Try it with mud crab.

QUALITY ♛♛♛♛♛
VALUE ★★★★★
GRAPES sauvignon blanc, semillon, viognier
REGION Eden Valley, SA
CELLAR 🍷 2
ALC./VOL. 11.0%
RRP $17.00

Aquila Estate Chardonnay

This is a new label/winery/vineyard from the Chittering district in Western Australia.

CURRENT RELEASE 1993 The colour is pale yellow and the nose dominated by toasty oak. The palate is complex with peach and melon flavours but toasty oak tends to override them. The finish is confronting and robust. Lightly chill only. Try it with smoked meat.

QUALITY ♛♛♛
VALUE ★★★
GRAPES chardonnay
REGION Perth Hills, WA
CELLAR 🍷 3
ALC./VOL. 12.7%
RRP $18.00

Aquila Estate Reflections

This is a curious blend, and what exactly it is supposed to reflect remains unclear. It is a real fruit salad.

CURRENT RELEASE 1994 The wine smells like a winery at vintage when fermentation is taking place. The palate is grapey with some hints of sweetness matched by a dry, chalky finish. Serve medium chilled with whitebait fritters.

QUALITY ♛♛♛
VALUE ★★★
GRAPES verdelho, semillon, sauvignon blanc, riesling
REGION Margaret River, WA
CELLAR 🍷 1
ALC./VOL. 12.5%
RRP $18.00

Arrowfield Chardonnay

QUALITY �杯♯♯♯
VALUE ★★★½
GRAPES chardonnay
REGION Upper Hunter Valley, NSW
CELLAR 🍾 3
ALC./VOL. 12.5%
RRP $13.00

This label has had more starts than the infamous Laughton. Arrowfield was a huge vineyard in the early '70s but has been shrinking ever since. As the acreage decreases, the quality seems to increase. Maker Simon Gilbert.

CURRENT RELEASE 1994 Big melon aroma and a bright gold colour; this is a full-flavoured mouth-filling drop. The palate has melon and peach flavours backed by some attractive oak that leaves the mouth feeling dry and clean. It goes well with a light chill and chicken involtini.

Ashton Hills Chardonnay

QUALITY ♯♯♯♯
VALUE ★★★★
GRAPES chardonnay
REGION Adelaide Hills, SA
CELLAR 🍷 2–6
ALC./VOL. 12.8%
RRP $15.00

Chardonnay can be a mirror of the region. In warm climates it is usually generous and buttery. This is an example of a cold-climate chardonnay.

CURRENT RELEASE 1992 Shows little evidence of bottle-age – it remains flinty and taut. The nose has strong citrus aromas and the palate has intense grapefruit flavour matched by bracing acid on a refreshing finish. It drinks like a French chablis. Try it well chilled with pan-fried calamari.

Ashton Hills Riesling

QUALITY ♯♯♯♯
VALUE ★★★★
GRAPES riesling
REGION Adelaide Hills, SA
CELLAR 🍾 4
ALC./VOL. 12.5%
RRP $12.00

This vineyard was founded in 1982 and has a small and sought-after production of 1200 cases. Maker Steve George.

CURRENT RELEASE 1994 The cool-climate location seems to have produced intense aromatics on the nose. The palate has a serious lime flavour followed by crisp acid on a lingering finish. Serve well chilled with oysters.

Augustine Chardonnay

This vineyard was established in 1918. The Mudgee district was the seed lot for chardonnay in Australia.

CURRENT RELEASE 1994 The nose has grass and grapefruit aromas and the palate is elegant with peach, citrus and melon flavours showing through. There is a lift of American oak on the finish. Try lightly chilled with veal in a cream sauce.

QUALITY ♛♛♛♛
VALUE ★★★½
GRAPES chardonnay
REGION Mudgee, NSW
CELLAR 🍾 2
ALC./VOL. 12.7%
RRP $12.50

Baldivis Estate Classic

The Kailis family is big in the WA fishing industry, and this small vineyard is part of their mixed farm at Baldivis on the southern coast. Maker John Smith.

CURRENT RELEASE 1994 This is a rather green, herbal-flavoured white which smells attractively nutty, peachy and straw-like. It is very light, green, and rather wispy on the tongue. Still, a presentable light dry white for general-purpose quaffing.

QUALITY ♛♛♛
VALUE ★★★
GRAPES sauvignon blanc, semillon, chardonnay
REGION South-west Coastal, WA
CELLAR 🍾
ALC./VOL. 12.8%
RRP $13.70

Balgownie Premier Cuvée Chardonnay

Unhappily, Balgownie is no longer selling an estate chardonnay. They were wines of very individual character. This is a regional blend.

CURRENT RELEASE 1994 Savoury spicy aromas from the oak are coupled with peach and nectarine fruit, giving a wine of good depth and smoothness. A well-balanced, middle-of-the-road style but it won't excite. Goes well with calamari.

QUALITY ♛♛♛
VALUE ★★★
GRAPES chardonnay
REGION Bendigo, North-western Vic. & Coonawarra, SA
CELLAR 🍾 2
ALC./VOL. 12.5%
RRP $11.70 Ⓢ

Bannockburn Chardonnay

QUALITY 🍷🍷🍷🍷🍷
VALUE ★★★★½
GRAPES chardonnay
REGION Geelong, Vic.
CELLAR 🍷 5
ALC./VOL. 14.0%
RRP $31.00

Despite its haggis-in-the-heather Scottish handle, this winery's technique is very French-influenced. The chardonnay has steadily improved and is now among the best in the country. Maker Gary Farr.

Previous outstanding vintages: '86, '87, '88, '90, '91, '92

CURRENT RELEASE 1993 This is a wine to take to a desert island. It's a stunner and a meal in itself. Very complex, with a focus and structure that can only be described as seamless. Lots of honey and melon flavours; refined, tight and crisp. The adjectives don't do it justice. Drink with crayfish.

Barossa Valley Estate Gewüztraminer

QUALITY 🍷🍷🍷
VALUE ★★★
GRAPES gewürztraminer
REGION Barossa Valley, SA
CELLAR 🍷 1
ALC./VOL. 11.5%
RRP $9.60 Ⓢ

This winery is owned by one of the last winemaking co-operatives left in Australia: the Valley Growers Co-operative. All its wines are 100 per cent Barossa. Maker Colin Glaetzer.

CURRENT RELEASE 1994 This is a typical warm-area Australian traminer, with a rich, ripe, lolly-shop bouquet which is already starting to show development. The flavour is big, broad and generous, with obvious sweetness but good balance. Try it with lychees and ice-cream.

Barwang Chardonnay

QUALITY 🍷🍷🍷🍷
VALUE ★★★★
GRAPES chardonnay
REGION Young, NSW
CELLAR ➞ 2–4+
ALC./VOL. 13.5%
RRP $14.00 Ⓢ

Barwang is McWilliam's cool-climate vineyard in the foothills of the Great Divide near Young, in eastern New South Wales. Maker Jim Brayne.

CURRENT RELEASE 1994 This is a shrinking violet, with pale hue and fruit-dominant nose. But the wine seems to need time. It is tightly focused, intense and undeveloped; a matter of potential rather than drink-now appeal. Aromas of nectarine and honey, and a long, firm finish. Not offering a lot yet, but may with time.

Basedow Chardonnay

This is the first Basedow chardonnay made by Grant Burge since he bought this winery in late '93. He believes '94 was the best white wine vintage in the Barossa for 20 years.

CURRENT RELEASE 1994 A big, soft, full-bodied wine from grapes picked riper than normal for this label. Fig, vanilla and honey greet the nose, and there is plenty of flavour, even if it lacks a little liveliness. A very respectable drink with roast chicken.

QUALITY ♥♥♥♥
VALUE ★★★
GRAPES chardonnay
REGION Barossa Valley, SA
CELLAR 🍷 2
ALC./VOL. 13.8%
RRP $14.50 ⓢ

Basedow White Burgundy

Basedow was bought by Grant Burge last year after McLeod's off-loaded Peter Lehmann and Lehmann went public. The wines are very fair value.

CURRENT RELEASE 1994 This popular wine is true to its past, showing a lot of coconutty American oak rather than semillon fruit, but that's what its fans want. It smells of peppermint Lifesavers and has some astringency on the finish. Drink it with smoked chicken.

QUALITY ♥♥♥
VALUE ★★★½
GRAPES semillon
REGION Barossa Valley, SA
CELLAR 🍷 3
ALC./VOL. 13.5%
RRP $10.80 ⓢ

Best's Chardonnay

William, the first Thomson to make wine at Best's, was once described in an 1887 newspaper article as a 'temperance caterer' ... Makers Viv Thomson and Simon Clayfield.

Previous outstanding vintages: '79, '81, '84, '89

CURRENT RELEASE 1994 Something of a contradiction, this chardonnay is high in alcohol but seems quite restrained in the flavour department. It has subdued nutty, toasty aromas coupled with a lean, acid-lively palate which just lacks a little fruit depth. Perhaps it will fill out with more bottle-age.

QUALITY ♥♥♥
VALUE ★★½
GRAPES chardonnay
REGION Great Western, Vic.
CELLAR 🍷 1–5
ALC./VOL. 14.0%
RRP $19.30

Best's Rhine Riesling

QUALITY 🍷🍷🍷🍷𝆑
VALUE ★★★★½
GRAPES riesling
REGION Great Western, Vic.
CELLAR 🍴 10+
ALC./VOL. 12.0%
RRP $13.65

Best's has always turned out some fine rieslings, but they seem to have become more consistent of late. Some of the vines are quite old, dating back to the '40s. Maker Simon Clayfield.

Previous outstanding vintages: '72, '81, '82, '85, '88, '90, '91, '92

CURRENT RELEASE 1994 Pale colour, a refined fragrance of lemon and lime, and a delicate, tangy palate which is reserved and almost austere. It's a lovely wine, delicious now but seems to have all the ingredients to age superbly. Pan-fried whiting here.

Bethany Late Harvest-Cut Riesling

QUALITY 🍷🍷🍷
VALUE ★★★
GRAPES riesling
REGION Barossa Valley, SA
CELLAR 🍴 2
ALC./VOL. 9.5%
RRP $15.00

This wine is made by cutting the vine's canes and leaving the grapes to shrivel slightly before picking.

CURRENT RELEASE 1994 Honey, peach, slightly yeasty and perhaps a hint of botrytis. The palate is moderately sweet and a trifle short but there is good vanillary flavour and balance. Try it with fruit salad.

Bethany Riesling (Dry)

QUALITY 🍷🍷🍷
VALUE ★★★
GRAPES riesling
REGION Barossa Valley, SA
CELLAR 🍴 5+
ALC./VOL. 12.0%
RRP $13.50

The 'dry' qualification is to set this apart from the other Bethany rieslings, which have varying degrees of sweetness.

CURRENT RELEASE 1994 A whiff of sulphur and a dry tobacco-like nose suggest that this needs time to settle down. The palate is high in acid and could do with more varietal fruit, but as a crisp food wine it has merit. Try it with fish and chips.

Bethany Steinbruch Riesling

In days gone by this would have been labelled a spätlese, but such European names are passing into extinction.
CURRENT RELEASE 1994 This sweet riesling smells of orange peel, which may be an indication of botrytis-affected grapes. The palate is full and generously flavoured, and will appeal to the sweet-tooths. Drink with a fresh peach.

QUALITY 🍷🍷🍷
VALUE ★★★
GRAPES riesling
REGION Barossa Valley, SA
CELLAR 🍾 3
ALC./VOL. 12.0%
RRP $11.70

Bethany Wood-Aged Semillon

The back label informs us that this wine was grown on old Barossa bush vines, ie. untrellised vines. Makers Rob and Geoff Schrapel.
CURRENT RELEASE 1994 This is a slightly grumpy semillon that has a kick in its tail. The nose offers subtle green-stick and sappy oak aromas while the palate is gutsy and dry, grassy/lemony in flavour with a snort of tannin to finish. Not a wine of finesse, but could profit from short-term keeping. Try sweetbreads.

QUALITY 🍷🍷🍷
VALUE ★★★
GRAPES semillon
REGION Barossa Valley, SA
CELLAR 🍾 1–4
ALC./VOL. 13.0%
RRP $16.00

Birdwood Estate Chardonnay

This five-hectare vineyard is named after a pretty little town in the Adelaide Hills and the wines are made by Colin Glaetzer at Barossa Valley Estate.
CURRENT RELEASE 1994 This is an unwooded chardonnay with crystal clear cool-grown chardonnay fruit flavours in the peach/fig spectrum. It's soft, ripe and full, with richness and a solid finish. Serve with pan-fried blue-eye cod.

QUALITY 🍷🍷🍷🍷
VALUE ★★★★
GRAPES chardonnay
REGION Adelaide Hills, SA
CELLAR 🍾 2+
ALC./VOL. 13.0%
RRP $13.00 (cellar door)

Bloodwood Chardonnay

QUALITY 🍷🍷🍷
VALUE ★★★
GRAPES chardonnay
REGION Orange, NSW
CELLAR 🍾 4
ALC./VOL. 12.5%
RRP $15.00 (cellar door)

The Bloodwood wines are made by Jon Reynolds in his Upper Hunter winery for Stephen and Rhonda Doyle, who own the vineyard at Orange.
CURRENT RELEASE 1994 Fairly delicate, restrained fruit allows the oak to dominate this wine. The nose is all toasty, spicy oak and there are clove and nutmeg nuances. A fair effort but we liked the '93 better. Try it with smoked chicken.

Bloodwood Ice Riesling

QUALITY 🍷🍷🍷🍷
VALUE ★★★½
GRAPES riesling
REGION Orange, NSW
CELLAR 🍾 3
ALC./VOL. 11.5%
RRP $17.00 (375ml, cellar door)

Forget the trendy ice beers, this is not just a marketing ploy. The grapes were picked after an April frost and early winter snow, on 5 July 1994, which could be a record.
CURRENT RELEASE 1994 This has aromas way out of left field, a lanolin hand-cream scent dominating. It comes into its own on the palate, with good concentration of flavour and sugar. The intense citrus vanilla flavours linger long on the finish. Try it with pavlova.

Blue Pyrenees Estate Chardonnay

QUALITY 🍷🍷🍷🍷
VALUE ★★★½
GRAPES chardonnay
REGION Pyrenees, Vic.
CELLAR 🍾 5
ALC./VOL. 13.1%
RRP $21.75

Chateau Remy's French winemaker Vincent Gere is careful not to make the mistake of so many Aussies and overwood his chardonnay. He succeeds.
CURRENT RELEASE 1994 The nose is very shy, but the wine is better on the palate. It is restrained, lightly nutty and spicy, with plenty of fruit-dominant flavour and a round, well-balanced palate. Try it with a frittata.

Bowen Estate Chardonnay

This leading Coonawarra small maker is best known for sterling reds, but its whites can surprise. Maker Doug Bowen.

CURRENT RELEASE 1993 A soft, fruit-sweet, generous wine that carries an unusual ginger aroma among the powder-puff and fig characters. There's a nice full middle palate which would marry well with a rich fish pie.

QUALITY 🍷🍷🍷🍷
VALUE ★★★★
GRAPES chardonnay
REGION Coonawarra, SA
CELLAR 🍾 3
ALC./VOL. 13.2%
RRP $14.50

CURRENT RELEASE 1994 This is as fresh as a primary-school debutante. Pale of hue, delicate, estery and fruit-driven, It's a cool-climate chardonnay without a lot of oak, the nose revealing peppermint and melon and the taste restrained yet intense. Good value! Try it with cold poultry.

QUALITY 🍷🍷🍷🍷
VALUE ★★★★½
GRAPES chardonnay
REGION Coonawarra, SA
CELLAR 🍾 5+
ALC./VOL. 13.0%
RRP $14.50

Brian Barry Jud's Hill Riesling

Brian Barry is one of this country's most experienced show judges, and he's listed his record on the back label to prove it. His wines are made at Petaluma.

CURRENT RELEASE 1994 A very smart wine, with softly floral, doughy aromas and rich smooth fruit on a fullish palate. Lovely ripe, round mouthfeel: a voluptuous riesling that drinks well now. Try it with flounder.

QUALITY 🍷🍷🍷🍷🍷
VALUE ★★★★★
GRAPES riesling
REGION Clare Valley, SA
CELLAR 🍾 5+
ALC./VOL. 13.1%
RRP $16.45

Briar Ridge Semillon Traditional

Neil McGuigan left McGuigan Brothers to take over as chief winemaker here during 1995.

CURRENT RELEASE 1994 A real charmer, this! Slightly full colour, but a traditional creamy, lanolin nose with hints of cashew nut and lemon. The palate is soft and full of flavour, yet has delicacy and tightness of structure that should see it age well. Drinks well now with seafood.

QUALITY 🍷🍷🍷🍷
VALUE ★★★★
GRAPES semillon
REGION Hunter Valley, NSW
CELLAR 🍾 5
ALC./VOL. 11.5%
RRP $17.70

Bridgewater Mill Chardonnay

QUALITY ♛♛♛♛
VALUE ★★★★
GRAPES chardonnay
REGION Clare & Coonawarra, SA
CELLAR 🍾 3
ALC./VOL. 13.5%
RRP $17.70

The mill is the public face of Petaluma, a lovingly restored 19th-century flour mill complete with waterwheel. It houses a sales and tasting room, and one of South Australia's best restaurants.
CURRENT RELEASE 1992 This is a fine wine indeed: even at three years it's reserved and retains its dignity. The nose offers discreet peach and nectarine with keenly tuned oak and a whiff of butterscotchy malolactic character. Goes well with most vegetarian foods.

Bridgewater Mill Sauvignon Blanc

QUALITY ♛♛♛♛
VALUE ★★★½
GRAPES sauvignon blanc
REGION Currency Creek, Coonawarra, Adelaide Hills and McLaren Vale, SA
CELLAR 🍾 2
ALC./VOL. 12.0%
RRP $18.00

This wine, under Petaluma's second label, is always one of the first whites of the new vintage to hit the shops. Maker Brian Croser.
CURRENT RELEASE 1995 The colour is pale yellow and the aroma is light, herbaceous/green fruit which is distinctly varietal. The palate is light, fresh and lean, perhaps lacking some of the fruity charm of the '94 at the same age, but a very handy drink all the same. Try it with asparagus and bearnaise.

Brokenwood Chardonnay

QUALITY ♛♛♛
VALUE ★★½
GRAPES chardonnay
REGION Hunter Valley, NSW
CELLAR ⇥ 1–3+
ALC./VOL. 13.0%
RRP $21.00

Once a quirky, small partnership of weekend lawyer/hobby-winemakers, Brokenwood is now a highly professional and successful business. Maker Iain Riggs.
CURRENT RELEASE 1994 The colour is quite a full buttercup yellow and the general tenor is forward in development. The nose suggests fig-jam and resiny oak and there is some astringency from wood on the palate. A little cellaring might see the wine come together more. Smoked chicken here.

Brokenwood Cricket Pitch Sauvignon Blanc Semillon

On the old parish plans, the area around the Brokenwood winery was earmarked for a sportsground, hence the evocative name of this blend.

CURRENT RELEASE 1994 Tasted in the bloom of its youth, this has confectionery notes from sauvignon fruit and esters from the fermentation yeast. The lolly flavours will give way to tropical fruit after a few months. It's a light, fresh, fruity soft white that's adaptable with salads and seafood.

QUALITY 🍷🍷🍷🍷
VALUE ★★★★
GRAPES sauvignon blanc, semillon
REGION McLaren Vale, SA & Hunter Valley, NSW
CELLAR 🍾 2
ALC./VOL. 13.0%
RRP $15.50

CURRENT RELEASE 1995 **Fragrant grassy/gooseberry aromas with suggestions of tropical fruit and some feline overtones; good depth of soft, aromatic flavour and a gentle grip on the finish. Perhaps a little lighter than the '94 but the flavours are equally delicious. Drink with vegetable dishes.**

QUALITY 🍷🍷🍷🍷🍷
VALUE ★★★★
GRAPES sauvignon blanc 86%, semillon 14%
REGION 81% McLaren Vale, SA; 11% Cowra, NSW; 8% King Valley, Vic.
CELLAR 🍾 2
ALC./VOL. 13.0%
RRP $15.00

Best Sauvignon Blanc

Brokenwood Semillon

This has a name as an up-front semillon that drinks nicely young. What's less well known is that it also ages superbly. Maker Iain Riggs.
Previous outstanding vintages: '83, '85, '86, '91, '92, '93

CURRENT RELEASE 1994 This is a delicate, grassy-scented, light-bodied semillon which tastes crisply acid and green in its youth, but everything's there for it to age well. While it's young, serve it with seafood.

QUALITY 🍷🍷🍷🍷
VALUE ★★★★
GRAPES semillon
REGION Hunter Valley, NSW
CELLAR 🍾 1–8+
ALC./VOL. 10.8%
RRP $16.50

Brook Eden Chardonnay

QUALITY 🍷🍷🍷🍷🍷
VALUE ★★★★
GRAPES chardonnay
REGION Pipers Brook, Tas.
CELLAR 🍾 4+
ALC./VOL. 12.5%
RRP $18.00

John Bezemer has 2.4 hectares of pinot noir and chardonnay in the Pipers Brook region, but his first vintage is in very limited supply. Made at Delamere winery.

CURRENT RELEASE 1993 This is a highly promising wine, oozing complexity and charm. The nose offers honey, butter and nuts, the palate is firm and dry with liberal use of oak and ample weight. It would partner barbecued chicken.

Brookland Valley Sauvignon Blanc

QUALITY 🍷🍷🍷🍷🍷
VALUE ★★★★
GRAPES sauvignon blanc
REGION Margaret River, WA
CELLAR 🍾 3+
ALC./VOL. 12.5%
RRP $17.70

What do vegans eat with red wine if they can't have meat or cheese? Perhaps they just drink a lot of white wine. This one would go with a lot of vegetarian dishes.

CURRENT RELEASE 1994 An impressive wine, jammed with gooseberry, grassy/ herbaceous and tropical fruit aromas and flavours that fill the mouth. It is jumpy, with acid on the tongue and zesty on the finish. Model sauvignon blanc. Try asparagus salad.

Brown Brothers Chardonnay

QUALITY 🍷🍷🍷🍷
VALUE ★★★½
GRAPES chardonnay
REGION King Valley, Vic.
CELLAR 🍾 2
ALC./VOL. 13.5%
RRP $15.00 ⓢ

It's nice to see chardonnays in this affordable price range emphasising fruit and not dominated by oak chips. Makers Roland Wahlquist and Terry Barnett.

CURRENT RELEASE 1994 A shy wine with little or no apparent oak, giving rather reluctant aromas of butter, melon and cashew. It's a mild, smooth wine in the mouth, fairly straightforward but pleasing, and finishes dry. Try it with flathead in beer batter.

Brown Brothers Colombard

Colombard is a minor grape in Cognac and Armagnac, but in Gascony some of the Armagnac grapes are today used to make high-quality fruity whites like this one.

CURRENT RELEASE 1994 Attractive fruity nose of citrus and tropical fruits with almost an overtone of sauvignon blanc. It's lively, light-bodied and fresh; a simple, easy-drinking white. Try it with Niçoise salad.

QUALITY ♟♟♟
VALUE ★★★
GRAPES colombard
REGION Murray Valley, Vic.
CELLAR 🍾 1
ALC./VOL. 13.0%
RRP $11.50 ⓢ

Brown Brothers Dry Muscat Blanc

This has proved something of a surprise hit for Browns, especially in the UK export market. Muscat of Alexandria is one of many permutations of the muscat varieties.

CURRENT RELEASE 1994 This is a bigger, stronger wine than the same maker's traminer, with a very flowery muscat aroma and a rich, dry lingering finish that cleverly avoids astringency. An excellent aperitif served chilled and solo.

QUALITY ♟♟♟♟
VALUE ★★★½
GRAPES muscat gordo blanco (muscat of Alexandria)
REGION Murray Valley, Vic.
CELLAR 🍾 1
ALC./VOL. 12.5%
RRP $9.85 ⓢ

Brown Brothers Gewürztraminer

Also known as traminer (*gewürz* is German for spicy), this is a captivating grape that is responsible for sparking a lot of people's interest in wine.

CURRENT RELEASE 1994 This has a fine, floral/spicy nose, typical of traminer, that will remind a lot of tasters of rose-petals. It's full and quite rich in the mouth and the ample flavour finishes dry. Perfect with a duck and rocket salad with fresh lychees.

QUALITY ♟♟♟♟
VALUE ★★★½
GRAPES gewürztraminer
REGION King Valley, Vic.
CELLAR 🍾 2
ALC./VOL. 13.0%
RRP $12.20 ⓢ

Brown Brothers Family Reserve Chardonnay

QUALITY 🍷🍷🍷🍷🍷
VALUE ★★★★
GRAPES chardonnay
REGION King Valley, Vic.
CELLAR 🍾 3
ALC./VOL. 13.5%
RRP $20.70 ⓢ

This is where Brown's winemakers really get to stretch out and go for their shots. They select the best batches of grapes and lavish them with TLC, as well as the full gamut of technical wizardry. Previous outstanding vintages: '90, '91

CURRENT RELEASE 1992 With a full buttercup yellow colour, this is a super-complex style of considerable character. Butterscotch, toast, peachy fruit and barrel-fermented complexities result in a rich style that fills the mouth with lingering flavour. It's oaky but in no way overdone. Could handle pork chops with mustard sauce.

Brown Brothers Late Harvest Orange Muscat & Flora

QUALITY 🍷🍷🍷🍷
VALUE ★★★½
GRAPES orange muscat 52%, flora 48%
REGION Murray Valley, Vic.
CELLAR 🍾 2
ALC./VOL. 10.0%
RRP $15.20 ⓢ

Browns are nothing if not great experimenters with oddball varieties. Here they fit two into one bottle. Orange muscat is a variation on a theme; flora is a Californian hybrid, bred from semillon and traminer.

CURRENT RELEASE 1994 Golden yellow in hue, this is a sweet but essentially straightforward dessert style without botrytis influence. It has an intense nose of honey and spices, and there's plenty of sweetness on the tongue, cleaned up by fresh acid. Goes well with fresh fruit salad and most cheeses.

Brown Brothers Noble Riesling

The previous release of this was the '88: Browns have always marketed it as an aged wine, until now. It was a distinctive style, but seemed to miss the primary appeal of botrytis wines – their fresh, sweet, fruity exuberance.

CURRENT RELEASE 1992 Plenty of exuberance here. The colour is a golden amber and the nose is rich in vanilla, honey and caramel aromas. It's one of the richer, sweeter examples of the style, luscious in the mouth yet elegant and fine, with lively floral riesling flavours. Superb wine; drink with crème brûlée.

QUALITY ▼▼▼▼▼
VALUE ★★★★
GRAPES riesling
REGION Milawa, Vic.
CELLAR ▮ 2+
ALC./VOL. 9.0%
RRP $28.35 ⑤

Brown Brothers Spätlese Lexia

The perennial crowd-pleaser, a wine almost every wine drinker has had a flirtation with at some stage.

CURRENT RELEASE 1994 Very clean, fresh, grapey muscat fruit jumps out of the glass. It is simple, cheerful and typical, with plenty of grape sweetness; a benchmark for its style. Try it with apple crumble.

QUALITY ▼▼▼
VALUE ★★★
GRAPES muscat gordo blanco
REGION Murray Valley, Vic.
CELLAR ▮ 1
ALC./VOL. 10.0%
RRP $10.15 ⑤

Buller Classic White

At Buller's, the whites are made by Richard Buller at Lake Boga while his brother Andrew looks after the reds and fortifieds at the Rutherglen winery.

CURRENT RELEASE 1994 This has a pale hue and does a good imitation of a lesser French white, with a certain whiff of sulphur and a lean, flinty palate that lacks the extroverted fruit of a typical Aussie. It has crisp, almost tart acidity and a sherbety finish. A respectable picnic white with salads. Chill well.

QUALITY ▼▼▼
VALUE ★★½
GRAPES not stated
REGION North-east Victoria
CELLAR ▮
ALC./VOL. 11.7%
RRP $9.60

Campbells Bobbie Burns Chardonnay

QUALITY 🍷🍷🍷🍷
VALUE ★★★½
GRAPES chardonnay
REGION Rutherglen, Vic.
CELLAR 🍾 4
ALC./VOL. 13.0%
RRP $15.00

Rutherglen can make a fairly convincing case in the chardonnay stakes. Campbells' marque is one of the leaders in the district.

CURRENT RELEASE 1994 An opulent style with lots of varietal flavour and obvious oak. The nose is herbal with tropical fruit aromas. The palate is rich and mouthfilling with peach to the fore. Oak gives a positive blast on the firm finish. Serve lightly chilled with pâté.

Campbells Limited Release Semillon

QUALITY 🍷🍷🍷🍷
VALUE ★★★
GRAPES semillon
REGION Rutherglen, Vic.
CELLAR 🍾 4
ALC./VOL. 12.0%
RRP $16.00

It is unusual to find this variety in these parts. Campbells has long been dedicated to forging a white wine persona. Maker Colin Campbell.

CURRENT RELEASE 1993 A distinctive style with a pronounced grassy lanolin aroma on the nose. The palate is mouthfilling with gooseberry and citrus flavours matched by drying oak characters on the finish. It gives the impression it should cellar well. Don't overchill, and serve with yabbies.

Campbells Pedro Ximenez

QUALITY 🍷🍷🍷🍷
VALUE ★★★
GRAPES pedro ximenez
REGION Rutherglen, Vic.
CELLAR 🍾 5
ALC./VOL. 12.5%
RRP $17.50

It is unusual to see pedro 'ham and eggs' used to make a dry white, but this style has long been an arrow in the Campbells quiver.

CURRENT RELEASE 1991 This is an old-fashioned chablis style that shows a very toasty nose and some bottle-developed fruit. The palate is quite complex with lime, kiwi fruit and tropical flavours followed by clean acid on a crisp finish. Served well chilled.

Campbells Semillon Chardonnay

Here's another example of an arranged marriage that works quite well. The best attributes of both varieties are captured.

CURRENT RELEASE 1994 The colour is a pale lemon yellow and the nose has plenty of peach with some underlying toast. The palate continues the peach theme but with a hint of citrus that adds complexity. Subtle oak dries out the finish. It should be served lightly chilled with chicken.

QUALITY 🍷🍷🍷?
VALUE ★★★½
GRAPES semillon, chardonnay
REGION Rutherglen, Vic.
CELLAR 🍾 1
ALC./VOL. 13.0%
RRP $12.00

Campbells Sliverburn

This wine takes its name from a vineyard near Rutherglen. There is no clue to the varieties used in the blend.

CURRENT RELEASE 1994 A straightforward style that could be classed as a utility wine. There are herbal aromas on the nose and the palate has grape characters and just a hint of sweetness. The acid on the finish is soft. Served well chilled with a chicken pie.

QUALITY 🍷🍷🍷
VALUE ★★★
GRAPES not stated
REGION Rutherglen, Vic.
CELLAR 🍾 1
ALC./VOL. 11.5%
RRP $12.00

Canobolas-Smith Chardonnay

This high-altitude, unirrigated vineyard is on deep, rich soils of volcanic origin on the slopes of Orange's Mount Canobolas. Maker Murray Smith.

Previous outstanding vintages: '92

CURRENT RELEASE 1993 This is a complex mouthful of chardonnay, showing good fruit concentration, nutty barrel-ferment and 'sur lie' characters. It has richness and weight enlivened by fresh acidity. A wine of power and substance which could cellar well. It calls for a rich yabbie dish.

QUALITY 🍷🍷🍷🍷?
VALUE ★★★★½
GRAPES chardonnay
REGION Orange, NSW
CELLAR 🍾 5+
ALC./VOL. 12.8%
RRP $17.00

Cape Mentelle Semillon Sauvignon Blanc

QUALITY ♀♀♀♀
VALUE ★★★
GRAPES semillon, sauvignon blanc
REGION Margaret River, WA
CELLAR 🍷 2
ALC./VOL. 13.0%
RRP $17.30

Cape Mentelle, established in 1970, is one of the pioneers of Margaret River. Production is 25,000 cases. Makers David Hohnen and John Durham.
CURRENT RELEASE 1994 A very stylish wine that has an almost seamless quality. The nose is grassy with a hint of lantana. The palate has a hint of sweetness and rich gooseberry flavour balanced by crisp acid. It can be served well chilled with pipis pesto.

Capel Vale CV Classic

QUALITY ♀♀♀
VALUE ★★★
GRAPES not stated
REGION various WA
CELLAR 🍷
ALC./VOL. 11.5%
RRP $11.60 Ⓢ

Rob Bowen crafts some very pleasant wines under this second-string Capel Vale label. This is one of the better-value wines from the west, where very little south of Perth is under $10 (on special, it can be had for as little as $9).
CURRENT RELEASE 1994 This is a real crowd-pleaser: sweet, peachy/fruity aromas and a soft, slightly floppy palate. Not much structure but there's lashings of fruit and a little sweetness to round it out. Good with salads and cold seafood.

Cassegrain Chardonnay

QUALITY ♀♀♀♀
VALUE ★★★★
GRAPES chardonnay
REGION Hastings Valley, NSW
CELLAR 🍷 5
ALC./VOL. 12.8%
RRP $14.50

Cassegrain winery and vineyard were established in 1980. It is a sophisticated venture with a production near 45,000 cases. Makers John Cassegrain and Drew Noon.
CURRENT RELEASE 1994 The nose offers melon and wet wood aromas and the palate has a creamy texture. The main flavour of grapefruit is matched by some drying oak on a firm finish. The wine should not be served too cold. Try it with a chowder.

Cassegrain Fromenteau Chardonnay

This is the top of the totem for Cassegrain. Fromenteau is the name of a vineyard near Port Macquarie.

CURRENT RELEASE 1991 Considering the bottle-age this is a very youthful style. The colour is bright lemon yellow and the nose is redolent of cedar and French oak aromas. The palate is taut with grapefruit and melon flavours conjoined by dry dusty oak on a lingering finish. Don't overchill, and serve with spaghetti marinara.

QUALITY ♛♛♛♛
VALUE ★★★½
GRAPES chardonnay
REGION Hastings, NSW
CELLAR 🍾 4
ALC./VOL. 12.3%
RRP $28.00

Cassegrain Semillon

It seems paradoxical that relatively low alcohol semillons (9.5–11%) are the ones that cellar with the best results.

CURRENT RELEASE 1993 The nose has strong gooseberry aromas and the palate exhibits distinctive varietal characters. Gooseberry is the dominant flavour and this is followed by some tinder dry oak on a long finish. Serve with a medium chill. Try it with veal.

QUALITY ♛♛♛♛
VALUE ★★★★
GRAPES semillon
REGION Hastings Valley, NSW
CELLAR 🍾 6
ALC./VOL. 11.0%
RRP $14.00

Castle Crossing Chenin Blanc

This is an economy label which is part of the Alambie Wine Company based at Mildura. Salisbury Estate is also part of the portfolio.

CURRENT RELEASE 1994 A sweet-and-sour style that offers refreshing flavours. The nose has green apple aromas and the palate is soft. There is some sweetness which is lifted by tart Granny Smith characters with soft acid on the finish. Serve well chilled. Try it with Singapore noodles.

QUALITY ♛♛♛
VALUE ★★★½
GRAPES chenin blanc
REGION Mildura, Vic.
CELLAR 🍾 1
ALC./VOL. 11.5%
RRP $7.00

Castle Crossing Colombard Chardonnay

QUALITY ▐▐▐▜
VALUE ★★★½
GRAPES colombard, chardonnay
REGION Mildura, Vic.
CELLAR ▐ 1
ALC./VOL. 11.5%
RRP $7.00

This company is one of the leaders in viticulture in warm to hot climates. The results are to be seen in their wines.

CURRENT RELEASE 1994 A very positive style where Australia struts its stuff. The nose shows distinct passionfruit characters plus hints of honey. Passionfruit and tropical flavours dominate the palate and there is soft acid on the finish. Serve well chilled with Vietnamese soup.

Chambers Botrytis Tokay

QUALITY ▐▐▐▐
VALUE ★★★★
GRAPES muscadelle
REGION Rutherglen, Vic.
CELLAR ▐ 1
ALC./VOL. 13.9%
RRP $11.00

This long-established Rutherglen winery is famous for fortified wines but the whites and reds should not be neglected. Maker Bill Chambers.

CURRENT RELEASE 1994 An oddball wine that is quite interesting. The nose has cold-tea aromas plus traces of botrytis. The palate is intense with an incredible depth of complex fruit flavours that include mandarin, lime and mango. A clean and lingering finish shows a crisp acid. Serve well chilled with a summer pudding.

Chateau Reynella Chardonnay

QUALITY ▐▐▐▐▜
VALUE ★★★★½
GRAPES chardonnay
REGION McLaren Vale, SA
CELLAR ▐ 5
ALC./VOL. 13.5%
RRP $16.40 ⓢ

Chateau Reynella was founded by John Reynell in 1838. It continues today as part of the BRL Hardy empire.

CURRENT RELEASE 1994 Well composed with plenty of style. The nose has rich nutty wood and fruit aromas. (The wood is 75 per cent American and 25 per cent French). The palate is complex with chewy textures and citrus and melon flavours. The finish shows a distinguished wood treatment and good balance. It should not be overchilled. Try it with smoked cod with a white sauce.

Chateau Xanadu Chardonnay

The vineyard was established in 1977 and today produces around 10,000 cases of both white and red.

CURRENT RELEASE 1994 A youthful style where wood looms large. The nose has grapefruit and vanilla aromas. Grapefruit again dominates the palate but is quickly followed by lively oak that bestows a caramel and vanilla flavour to the finish. It needs time in the cellar.

QUALITY ????
VALUE ★★★½
GRAPES chardonnay
REGION Margaret River, WA
CELLAR ⇌ 2–8
ALC./VOL. 13.5%
RRP $16.00

Cloudy Bay Chardonnay

Cloudy Bay is a bit like the pop group Abba: it was amazingly popular and it keeps making comebacks. *Mamma mia!* Maker Kevin Judd.

CURRENT RELEASE 1993 The wine has a very high alcohol by New Zealand standards. The nose is sappy with a hint of peach on a smoky background. The palate offers sweet peach and melon characters plus tropical fruit in the distance. French oak dominates a long finish. A little chill to thrill and serve with turkey and cranberry sauce.

QUALITY ????
VALUE ★★★
GRAPES chardonnay
REGION Marlborough, NZ
CELLAR ↓ 3
ALC./VOL. 14.0%
RRP $21.00

Coldstream Hills Chardonnay

Coldstream is wine-scribe/show-judge/wine-maker/author/lawyer James Halliday's labour of love. One of the partners in the business is the redoubtable Pom, Hugh Johnson. Maker Phillip Dowell.

CURRENT RELEASE 1994 A fine and complex wine that strikes a good balance between all components. The nose has grapefruit, melon and peach aromas with an underscore of oak. The palate shows grapefruit and peach flavour and a creamy texture. The finish has dry wood and good length. Chill lightly and serve with char-grilled octopus.

QUALITY ????
VALUE ★★★★
GRAPES chardonnay
REGION Yarra Valley, Vic.
CELLAR ⇌ 2–5
ALC./VOL. 13.0%
RRP $19.00

Coolangatta Estate Alexander Berry Chardonnay

QUALITY ♛♛♛♛
VALUE ★★★★
GRAPES chardonnay
REGION South coast, NSW
CELLAR 🍾 3
ALC./VOL. 13.3%
RRP $13.90 (cellar door)

Berry was one of the first settlers on the NSW south coast (in 1822). He built a settlement and named it Coolangatta, an Aboriginal word meaning good view. The resort on the north coast came later. The grapes were grown at Greg Bishop's six-hectare vineyard at Berry on the Shoalhaven.

CURRENT RELEASE 1994 This wine, made by chardonnay experts Tyrrell's, has a discreet but attractive nose and in the mouth there's plenty of melon and peach – typical chardonnay flavour. It has good finesse and balance. A good partner for seafood.

Coriole Chardonnay

QUALITY ♛♛♛♛♛
VALUE ★★★★
GRAPES chardonnay
REGION McLaren Vale, SA
CELLAR 🍾 5
ALC./VOL. 14.0%
RRP $16.95

The Coriole philosophy to making chardonnay seems to be to construct a white wine for red wine drinkers.

CURRENT RELEASE 1994 Ho ho ho – vertigo row. Jazz buffs will need no explanation but this wine is like Roland Kirk playing two horns at once. It is big, and what it lacks in finesse is made up for in exuberance. It has a powerful peach nose and the palate is rich with succulent peach flavour and a warmth of alcohol. The finish adds balance and length. It shouldn't be overchilled; try it with a cassoulet.

Coriole Chenin Blanc

This is one of the few wineries that make a feature of marketing chenin blanc with pride. Most others hide it in a blend or sell it as bulk. Maker Stephen Hall.

CURRENT RELEASE 1994 A big mutha – there are no beg-pardons here. The nose is herbal and the palate has a strong green-apple flavour. The most outstanding aspect is the mouthfilling texture which is balanced by crisp acid. It can be served well chilled with stir-fry pork.

QUALITY ♛♛♛♛
VALUE ★★★★
GRAPES chenin blanc
REGION McLaren Vale, SA
CELLAR 🍾 4
ALC./VOL. 13.5%
RRP $12.00

Coriole Late Harvest Riesling

'Say it ain't so, Joe.' This is a motherless child of a style that every winery has to get out of its system.

CURRENT RELEASE 1993 The nose shows sweet fruit characters and a hint of aromatics. The palate is tinged with sweetness and soft lime flavours. The finish shows clean acid. Serve well chilled. Try it as a pre-dinner drink.

QUALITY ♛♛♛
VALUE ★★★
GRAPES riesling
REGION McLaren Vale, SA
CELLAR 🍾 3
ALC./VOL. 12.5%
RRP $12.00

Coriole Semillon Sauvignon Blanc

In this case semillon gets to be on the top of the blend. Coriole tends to be known for its red wine and olive oil before its white wines.

CURRENT RELEASE 1994 This is a big wine with lots of flavour. The nose is grassy with hints of lanolin. The palate shows full-on gooseberry flavours plus herbal undertones followed by a very dry finish that helps qualify the wine as a food style. Try it with chicken casserole.

QUALITY ♛♛♛?
VALUE ★★★½
GRAPES semillon, sauvignon blanc
REGION McLaren Vale, SA
CELLAR 🍾 2
ALC./VOL. 13.5%
RRP $12.00

Cranswick Estate Autumn Gold Botrytis Semillon

QUALITY ♛♛♛♛♕
VALUE ★★★★½
GRAPES semillon
REGION Griffith, NSW
CELLAR 🍾 3
ALC./VOL. 10.5%
RRP $13.00

This is a large winery that was founded in 1977. Annual production is around a million cases. Maker Andrew Schulz.

CURRENT RELEASE 1993 A developing style that shows obvious botrytis character. The colour is a bright gold and the nose has honey and marmalade aromas. The palate is complex with dried apricot, marmalade and honey. The finish is very dry with pectin-like characters (must be the marmalade ...). Serve well chilled with smoked salmon.

Dalrymple Sauvignon Blanc

QUALITY ♛♛♛♛♛
VALUE ★★★★½
GRAPES sauvignon blanc
REGION Pipers Brook, Tas.
CELLAR 🍾 2
ALC./VOL. 13.0%
RRP $15.00

Launceston oncologist Bert Sundstrup with his wife Anne and sister-in-law Jill Mitchell were inspired to plant Dalrymple by their father and father-in-law Bill Mitchell's planting of Tamarway vineyard in the '60s. This is a rare wine made from a small first crop.

CURRENT RELEASE 1994 A cracker first-up success from such young vines! This is a superb sauvignon, crammed with lifted gooseberry, tropical fruit and herbaceous scents and offering a full, flavoursome yet racy palate that epitomises the best things about this grape. Perfect with spanner crab omelette.

Dalwhinnie Chardonnay

Dalwhinnie wines, especially the reds, are increasingly sought-after and made in tiny quantities. The chardonnay really pushes alcohol to the limits.
Previous outstanding vintages: '88, '90, '91, '92
CURRENT RELEASE 1994 The nose is slightly resiny with some edgy oak and leafy nuances, while the palate is smooth and complex with stacks of fruit, nice toasty oak and richness to burn. Not easy to match with food, but we'd try barbecued octopus.

QUALITY ♛♛♛♛
VALUE ★★★½
GRAPES chardonnay
REGION Pyrenees, Vic.
CELLAR 🍷 3
ALC./VOL. 14.5%
RRP $24.00

d'Arenberg Noble Riesling

Botrytis-affected stickies are increasingly labelled 'noble' as a result of the drift away from generic handles like sauternes and beerenauslese. It's a worthwhile trend. Maker Chester Osborn.
Previous outstanding vintages: '87, '89, '91
CURRENT RELEASE 1992 An elegant, restrained, well-harmonised wine which is coloured deep gold/amber and smells invitingly of honey, marmalade and vanilla. The palate has some tightness of structure, a clean finish and good length. Try it with crème brûlée.

QUALITY ♛♛♛♛♛
VALUE ★★★★½
GRAPES riesling
REGION McLaren Vale, SA
CELLAR 🍷 3+
ALC./VOL. 11.5%
RRP $20.15 (375ml)

David Wynn Riesling

Among the late David Wynn's many achievements was his work as founding chairman of the International Barossa Music Festival, from 1990 to 1994. Maker Adam Wynn.
CURRENT RELEASE 1994 The nose has scents of lemon and fresh green apple, and the flavour is light and delicate. There's a trace of sweetness on the finish but overall it's a dry wine. Serve with fish and a slice of lemon.

QUALITY ♛♛♛
VALUE ★★★
GRAPES riesling
REGION Eden Valley, SA
CELLAR 🍷 2
ALC./VOL. 11.5%
RRP $12.90 Ⓢ

De Bortoli Montage Dry White Blend

QUALITY 🍷🍷🍷
VALUE ★★★
GRAPES sauvignon blanc, semillon
REGION cooler regions of Victoria
CELLAR 🍾
ALC./VOL. 11.0%
RRP $11.60

The red and white blends under this label were conceived so the winemakers could construct the best blend for the price, without having to use the same varieties each year.

CURRENT RELEASE 1994 Green, grassy sauvignon blanc-like aromas introduce a light-weight, slightly short wine with early-picked green flavours, soft balance and quaffing appeal. Good with salads.

De Bortoli Noble One Botrytis Semillon

QUALITY 🍷🍷🍷🍷🍷
VALUE ★★★★★
GRAPES semillon
REGION Riverina, NSW
CELLAR 🍾 5+
ALC./VOL. 12.0%
RRP $21.25 (375ml)

Best Semillon

In 1982 Darren De Bortoli decided to leave some rotting semillon on the vines and see what happened. Much to the grower's horror he eventually picked it and made a great sticky wine that shook the world. Noble One so dominated the wine shows he's decided to stop exhibiting it. Previous outstanding vintages: '82, '84, '87, '90, '91

CURRENT RELEASE 1992 Still the leader in its field, and the '92 is right on form. Deep gold, with a staggeringly complex botrytis/fruit/oak nose of vanilla, toast, dried apricot and marmalade. These flavours are allied to luscious sweetness, giving a rich, unctuous, powerful and incredibly long palate. Try it with mango and apricot feuilleté.

De Bortoli Windy Peak Chardonnay

QUALITY 🍷🍷🍷🍷
VALUE ★★★★
GRAPES chardonnay
REGION King and Yarra Valleys, Vic.
CELLAR 🍾 2
ALC./VOL. 12.5%
RRP $12.20

Windy Peak wines are made at De Bortoli's Yarra Valley winery from grapes grown in southern Victorian regions, including the Yarra.

CURRENT RELEASE 1993 Buttery and slightly rubbery malolactic characters breathe to reveal some tropical fruit and a little toast. This is elegant, medium-bodied and well-rounded. There is a degree of complexity and it's a very attractive drink with calamari.

De Bortoli Yarra Valley Chardonnay

Last year we said this needed more time. Happily, it's come up to expectations, earning an extra half-point and is still available. Maker Steve Webber.

CURRENT RELEASE 1992 With a scrumptious butterscotch and peach nose, this wine is rich and smooth, filling the mouth with flavour. Bottle-age has enhanced its complexity and the finish lingers long. Try it with smoked chicken.

QUALITY ♛♛♛♛♝
VALUE ★★★★
GRAPES chardonnay
REGION Yarra Valley, Vic.
CELLAR 🍾 2+
ALC./VOL. 13.0%
RRP $19.30

Deen De Bortoli Vat 2 Sauvignon Blanc

This won a well-deserved gold medal in Melbourne, an impressive coup for a lowly priced wine. Maker Steve Webber.

CURRENT RELEASE 1994 A delicious wine showcasing the best features of this fickle grape. Lifted grassy, gooseberry aromas which follow onto the tongue, where it has excellent depth and fullness, and a lingering finish with the balance of a tightrope walker. Try asparagus quiche.

QUALITY ♛♛♛♛♝
VALUE ★★★★½
GRAPES sauvignon blanc
REGION cooler areas of Vic.
CELLAR 🍾 1+
ALC./VOL. 11.5
RRP $9.00

Best Bargain White

Deen De Bortoli Vat 7 Chardonnay

Deen De Bortoli, son of founder Vittorio, is the chairman of the company today and father of managing director Darren.

CURRENT RELEASE 1994 This has a forward yellow colour and strong bouquet featuring high-toast oak. It is more about oak and winemakerly complexities than primary fruit, and is soft and medium-bodied with a dry finish. A worthy partner for grilled pork chops.

QUALITY ♛♛♛♝
VALUE ★★★★
GRAPES chardonnay
REGION Riverina, NSW
CELLAR 🍾 1
ALC./VOL. 12.5%
RRP $9.00

Delatite Chardonnay

QUALITY ♛♛♛♛
VALUE ★★★½
GRAPES chardonnay
REGION Mansfield, Vic.
CELLAR 🍷 5
ALC./VOL. 13.5%
RRP $18.20

Isolation has never seemed a problem to the Ritchies at Delatite, up in the Great Divide near Mansfield. They have turned out fine white wines year after year. Maker Rosie Ritchie.
Previous outstanding vintages: '90, '91, '93
CURRENT RELEASE 1994 Unusual oak aromas here, of plasticene and spices with a hint of ginger. It is a good wine, with lots of fruit and flavour, deep in the mid-palate and with oak playing a supportive role. It finishes with balance and elegance. Try it with ginger chicken.

Delatite Dead Man's Hill Gewürztraminer

QUALITY ♛♛♛♛♛
VALUE ★★★★½
GRAPES gewürztraminer
REGION Mansfield, Vic.
CELLAR 🍷 5
ALC./VOL. 13.0%
RRP $15.00

Not an appealing name for a wine, and we hasten to add that wine in moderation has been shown to increase the average lifespan.
CURRENT RELEASE 1994 This is a definitive Aussie traminer, an exemplary style that's poles apart from its Alsace counterpart. Subtlety is the byword: the nose is doughy and discreet without this grape's usual pungency. The taste is spicy but restrained, with rose-petal hints and lovely balance. Delicious wine. Try a delicate quiche.

Delatite Riesling

QUALITY ♛♛♛♛?
VALUE ★★★★
GRAPES riesling
REGION Mansfield, Vic.
CELLAR 🍷 10
ALC./VOL. 13.0%
RRP $15.00

The '93 won our Penguin award last year for the top white wine and top riesling. It's a style that comes into its own with some time in the cellar. Maker Ros Ritchie.
Previous outstanding vintages: '82, '87, '91, '92, '93
CURRENT RELEASE 1994 This has greenish tints in its hue and an alpine tang to its nose and palate. Lifted aromatic citrusy, estery bouquet and a crisp, lively, high-acid taste that also carries a trace of firmness on the finish. Good now and will retain its freshness for several years. Try a Niçoise salad.

Diamond Ridge Classic Dry White

This label is Theo's Liquor Markets' own brand. The motto is 'simply brilliant'. Diamonds ... brilliant ... get it?

CURRENT RELEASE 1994 This is a soft, round, rather bland dry white with a dusty aroma and light, simple flavour. No distinctive attributes but will offend no one, and the price is very fair. Adaptable with salads and seafood.

QUALITY 🍷🍷🍷
VALUE ★★★½
GRAPES semillon, sauvignon blanc, chenin blanc
REGION McLaren Vale, SA
CELLAR 🍾
ALC./VOL. 12.0%
RRP $8.00

Diamond Valley Blue Label Chardonnay

Diamond Valley is a very small winery and vineyard producing just 5000 cases a year, but the wines are widely distributed. This is their second label, which uses bought-in grapes.

CURRENT RELEASE 1994 Jumps out of the glass with tropical/passionfruit aromas, and in the mouth it's light-bodied, crisply acidic and has some herbaceous undercurrents. Lightly wooded. Try it with scallops à la nage.

QUALITY 🍷🍷🍷🍷
VALUE ★★★
GRAPES chardonnay
REGION Yarra Valley, Vic.
CELLAR 🍾 2
ALC./VOL. 12.9%
RRP $17.30

Diamond Valley Blue Label Semillon Sauvignon Blanc

The blue label denotes a Diamond Valley wine made from grapes bought in from other Yarra Valley growers. Maker David Lance.

CURRENT RELEASE 1994 This has the sort of gooseberry flavours that appeal in wines of this type, rather than straight-out over-the-top vegetal character. The palate is light, crisp, perhaps a tad short, but the flavours are spot-on tropical and gooseberry and this is not submerged in residual sugar, but ends pleasingly arid. Prawns here.

QUALITY 🍷🍷🍷🍷
VALUE ★★★½
GRAPES semillon, sauvignon blanc
REGION Yarra Valley, Vic.
CELLAR 🍾 2
ALC./VOL. 12.2%
RRP $17.30

Doonkuna Chardonnay

QUALITY ♙♙♙♙♙
VALUE ★★★★★
GRAPES chardonnay
REGION Canberra district, NSW
CELLAR 🍷 5+
ALC./VOL. 12.7%
RRP $19.30

This 5.5-hectare vineyard at Murrumbateman is run by Lady Janette Murray, widow of former Victorian Governor Sir Brian Murray.

CURRENT RELEASE 1993 A very stylish wine, featuring clean cashewnut-fruit and cedary oak aromas, a mellifluous palate of intense, refined and complex flavours. The oak is skilfully employed and the finish lingers long. Partner with chicken and cashews.

Dromana Estate Chardonnay

QUALITY ♙♙♙♙
VALUE ★★★½
GRAPES chardonnay
REGION Mornington Peninsula, Vic.
CELLAR 🍷 3+
ALC./VOL. 14.0%
RRP $25.00

Proprietor Garry Crittenden has that rare combination of skills that small winery operators need but seldom have: he's a good grapegrower, winemaker, marketer and promoter.

Previous outstanding vintages: '90, '91, '92, '93

CURRENT RELEASE 1994 A typically delicate, restrained style which may be accused of lacking concentration, but it's certainly refined. Palish hue, a shy aroma of pear and butter, and a lightly wooded, tangy flavour that has lively acid and admirable finesse. Would suit oysters while young.

Eaglehawk Chardonnay

QUALITY ♙♙♙
VALUE ★★★★
GRAPES chardonnay
REGION various
CELLAR 🍷 4
ALC./VOL. 12.0%
RRP $8.95

This label has been revamped and now sports a new talent in the winemaking department. Watch this space. Maker David O'Leary.

CURRENT RELEASE 1994 An obvious style with rich peach and barrel-ferment characters. The nose has a creamy aroma plus some smoky wood. The palate is chewy with peach and melon flavours; dry wood characters adorn the finish. Chill lightly and serve with whitebait fritters.

Eaglehawk Rhine Riesling

Expect this commercial style to show some extra gloss due to new commitment to the estate.
CURRENT RELEASE 1994 A perfumed style with typical regional character and a price that would make Ned Kelly blush. The nose has lavender and lime aromas. The palate is citrus driven and the finish displays crisp acid. It can be served well chilled and should be drunk when young and fresh. Use it as a pre-dinner drink.

QUALITY 🍷🍷🍷
VALUE ★★★★
GRAPES riesling
REGION Clare Valley, SA
CELLAR 🍾 2
ALC./VOL. 11.0%
RRP $8.95

Eldredge Watervale Riesling

This is a new label from the Clare Valley. The presentation is a point of departure – the wine comes in a green claret bottle.
CURRENT RELEASE 1994 The nose has strong citrus aromas plus a hint of toast. The palate offers crisp lime flavours followed by fresh acid on a tingling finish. It can be served well chilled with yabbies.

QUALITY 🍷🍷🍷
VALUE ★★★½
GRAPES riesling
REGION Clare Valley, SA
CELLAR 🍾 5
ALC./VOL. 11.0%
RRP $13.50

Evans & Tate Margaret River Chardonnay

Evans & Tate is a very dynamic organisation that could be described as the best of the West. They have a no-nonsense approach and quality is the benchmark. Pity the price is a bit of a joke. Maker Brian Fletcher.
CURRENT RELEASE 1994 Put together by a master, this is a very polished style. The nose has peach, citrus and wood aromas. The palate is rich and complex with citrus, apricot and peach flavours that dovetail with a very neat oak treatment on a long finish. Serve slightly chilled with a seafood crêpe.

QUALITY 🍷🍷🍷🍷
VALUE ★★½
GRAPES chardonnay
REGION Margaret River, WA
CELLAR ⬌ 2–6
ALC./VOL. 13.0%
RRP $35.00

Evans & Tate Margaret River Semillon

QUALITY 🍷🍷🍷🍷🍷
VALUE ★★★★½
GRAPES semillon
REGION Margaret River, WA
CELLAR 🍶 5
ALC./VOL. 13.0%
RRP $18.50

The production here is around 20,000 cases and sales in Western Australia are very brisk indeed. CURRENT RELEASE 1994 The colour is pale and the nose is fresh and grassy. The palate is rich and mouthfilling with a gooseberry flavour dominant. A sensitive use of French oak pulls the wine together and gives it structure. Serve lightly chilled with tuna.

Evans & Tate Two Vineyards Chardonnay

QUALITY 🍷🍷🍷🍷
VALUE ★★★★
GRAPES chardonnay
REGION Swan Valley, Margaret River, WA
CELLAR 🍶 3
ALC./VOL. 13.0%
RRP $18.50

This might sound like a legal firm but it was founded in 1972 and has developed along a confident path since then. Maker Brian Fletcher. CURRENT RELEASE 1994 A pleasant drink-now style that makes much of the fruit and oak combination. The nose offers strong melon aromas and the palate has ripe melon and tropical fruit flavours underscored by some dry, smoky oak. The finish has a pleasant nuttiness. Don't overchill. It goes well with casuila de marasco.

Evans & Tate Western Australian Classic

In case you are wondering, a Western Australian classic is a 'skilful blend of semillon and sauvignon blanc', sourced from all over Western Australia.

CURRENT RELEASE 1994 The colour is a pale green-gold and the nose is pungent with sauvignon blanc dominating. There are herb and gooseberry flavours on the palate plus a hint of tinned peas. The finish shows off some crisp acid and dryness. Serve well chilled with yabbies.

QUALITY ♛♛♛♕
VALUE ★★★
GRAPES semillon, sauvignon blanc
REGION not stated
CELLAR 🍾 1
ALC./VOL. 12.5%
RRP $13.95

CURRENT RELEASE 1995 Pungent and herbal nose with a tomato-plant aroma. The palate is crisp with sauvignon blanc making the running; it's herbal and grassy with crisp acid on the finish. Get it while it is fresh and serve it well chilled with marron in a light dressing.

QUALITY ♛♛♛♛
VALUE ★★★
GRAPES semillon, sauvignon blanc, chardonnay, verdelho
REGION Swan Valley, Manjimup, Pemberton, Margaret River, WA
CELLAR 🍾 2
ALC./VOL. 13.0%
RRP $17.50

Evans Family Chardonnay

QUALITY ♛♛♛♛♛
VALUE ★★★★★
GRAPES chardonnay
REGION Hunter Valley, NSW
CELLAR 🍾 4+
ALC./VOL. 12.0%
RRP $21.00

As with all tiny, discrete vineyards, Len and Trish Evans's is prone to seasonal style variation. The '93 is a stunner, with more intensity and length than the '92. These limited-quantity wines are sold mainly from the cellar-door, so it helps to be on the mailing list. Maker Peter Hall.
Previous outstanding vintages: '91
CURRENT RELEASE 1993 An aromatic tropical-fruit nose is fruit-led and provides a preview of the taste, which is similarly stunning with concentrated fruit of great depth and vivacity. It has the three Ps: perfume, power and persistence, and would do a lobster proud.

QUALITY ♛♛♛♛
VALUE ★★★★
GRAPES chardonnay
REGION Hunter Valley, NSW
CELLAR 🍾 3+
ALC./VOL. 11.5%
RRP $18.50

CURRENT RELEASE 1994 A lighter wine than the '93, this is similarly fruit-powered and although it's more delicate, there's plenty of life, intensity and acid crispness. The nose offers fresh, doughy, melony scents and the wood is gently played. Yabbies here.

Eyton on Yarra Chardonnay

QUALITY ♛♛♛♛
VALUE ★★★★
GRAPES chardonnay
REGION Yarra Valley, Vic.
CELLAR 🍾 3
ALC./VOL. 13.0%
RRP $16.00

This is yet another new and lavish project in the Yarra Valley. It first saw the light of day as Yarra Vale and is now under new management. Maker Tony Royal.
CURRENT RELEASE 1993 An oak-driven style that should be served near room temperature. The nose has caramel and vanilla aromas, the palate peach and grapefruit flavours followed by vanilla lift on a firm finish.

Fire Gully Margaret River Classic

Made at Pierro from other growers' grapes by Michael Peterkin who, apart from being a GP, has a degree in oenology.

CURRENT RELEASE 1994 Maybe it won't set the world on fire, but it's a handy general-purpose white with a shy, slightly dusty nose and a hint of sweetness on the tongue. It's straightforward and undemanding, teaming well with spaghetti marinara.

QUALITY 🍷🍷🍷
VALUE ★★★
GRAPES various
REGION Margaret River, WA
CELLAR 🍾 2
ALC./VOL. 12.0%
RRP $13.70

Frankland Estate Chardonnay

This winery has just employed its second woman winemaker: Kiwi Jenny Dobson, who made quite a name for herself at Chateau Senejac, Bordeaux.

CURRENT RELEASE 1993 A delicate fruit-driven style which exhibits some passionfruit and melon aromas, but any oak that's been used is well hidden. A pleasant drink which needs a little more on the finish. Good with caesar salad.

QUALITY 🍷🍷🍷
VALUE ★★★
GRAPES chardonnay
REGION Lower Great Southern, WA
CELLAR 🍾 3
ALC./VOL. 13.3%
RRP $17.70

Frankland Estate Rhine Riesling

This vineyard is in one of the best places in Australia to grow riesling. Early results are promising. The address is Frankland Estate, Frankland Road, Frankland!

CURRENT RELEASE 1994 Good fragrant, floral varietal aromas, but the sweetness on the palate is slightly disappointing. It's a generous, ample, but slightly thick late-picked style with a broad finish. Chill well and serve with spicy prawns.

QUALITY 🍷🍷🍷
VALUE ★★★
GRAPES riesling
REGION Frankland River, WA
CELLAR 🍾 2
ALC./VOL. 13.0%
RRP $14.50

Freycinet Chardonnay

QUALITY 🍷🍷🍷🍷🍷
VALUE ★★★★½
GRAPES chardonnay
REGION East coast, Tas.
CELLAR 🍷 5+
ALC./VOL. 13.0%
RRP $26.50

This small but impressive vineyard on the Tassie east coast has views of the ocean and the Freycinet Peninsula, which was named after the cartographer from an early French expedition.

CURRENT RELEASE 1993 Freycinet's chardonnays are richer than most in Tassie, and the '93 may be their best yet. It is a wine of considerable density and gravity, bulging with quince and fig flavours, generously laced with high-toast oak and some buttery hints. A marvellous wine which really sings. Deserves a rich crayfish dish.

Galafrey Chardonnay

QUALITY 🍷🍷🍷🍷
VALUE ★★★½
GRAPES chardonnay
REGION Great Southern, WA
CELLAR 🍷 4
ALC./VOL. 13.0%
RRP $13.90

The production at Galafrey is around 4000 cases per annum and conventional wisdom says riesling should be the variety for the Great Southern. Chardonnay can make some interesting wines also.

CURRENT RELEASE 1993 There is no shortage of wood here in this oak-dominated wine. The nose is full of toasty oak and underscored by peach and melon aromas. The palate is rich with peach flavour dominating but quickly swamped by dusty oak on a firm finish. Don't overchill, and try it with pan-fried veal.

Galafrey Rhine Riesling

QUALITY 🍷🍷🍷🍷
VALUE ★★★★
GRAPES riesling
REGION Great Southern, WA
CELLAR 🍷 3
ALC./VOL. 12.0%
RRP $12.00

Apart from black sambuca and Mirage aircraft, winemaker Ian Tyrer's other passion is the TV show *Dr Who*, and a planet featured therein gives its name to the winery.

CURRENT RELEASE 1994 The colour is pale and the nose has floral talcum-powder aromas. The medium-bodied palate has lime/lemon flavours matched by crisp acid on a fresh finish. It can be served well chilled with marron.

Galafrey Unwooded Chardonnay

Unwooded chardonnay is shaping up as a battleground for many players. The style has yet to be defined – if it's a style at all. MS believes it is a marketing cash cow product. And although you can't drink labels, this is one of the worst on the market.

CURRENT RELEASE 1994 Not a lot of varietal character but this is a reasonable dry white. The nose is weak with some soft grapefruit aromas and there is a degree of residual sugar on the palate which gives body to an undistinguished palate. Soft acid fills out the finish. A KFC special.

QUALITY ♛♛♛
VALUE ★★½
GRAPES chardonnay
REGION Great Southern, WA
CELLAR 🍾 1
ALC./VOL. 12.0%
RRP $12.00

Garden Gully Sauvignon Blanc

Why does a small cellar door like this feel obliged to field every style? Maker Brian Fletcher.

CURRENT RELEASE 1994 Lacks varietal definition but is a very drinkable dry white. The nose has soft herbal aromas. The palate offers gooseberry flavours with some tropical underlay. The finish shows crisp acid. Serve well chilled with cabbage rolls.

QUALITY ♛♛♛
VALUE ★★★
GRAPES sauvignon blanc
REGION Padthaway, SA
CELLAR 🍾 1
ALC./VOL. 12.5%
RRP $14.00

Geoff Merrill Chardonnay

If you want a textbook example of oak influence and barrel fermentation try this! It's also interesting to see that Geoffrey Lewis Merrill has turned over a new leaf and is producing wines with higher alcohol.

CURRENT RELEASE 1990 The wine is starting to show bottle-age but the barrel-ferment character dominates with a nutty character. The palate is supple with peach flavours and rockmelon characters. The finish shows strong wood and good length. If lightly chilled it goes well with scampi in a light ginger sauce.

QUALITY ♛♛♛♛
VALUE ★★★★
GRAPES chardonnay 86%, semillon 14%
REGION McLaren Vale, Barossa Valley, SA
CELLAR 🍾 4
ALC./VOL. 13.0%
RRP $20.00

Giesen Marlborough Riesling

QUALITY ♛♛♛♛
VALUE ★★★★
GRAPES riesling
REGION Marlborough, NZ
CELLAR 🍾 5
ALC./VOL. 12.0%
RRP $15.30

Although Giesen is based in Canterbury in New Zealand's south, it seems to make most of its wines from Marlborough grapes, which may be a telling fact.

CURRENT RELEASE 1994 This has an intense slaty, minerally nose with an exotic chalky aspect. Floral characters lurk beneath. In the mouth it's full and soft with plenty of fruit, and finishes with marked acidity. Try it with fresh brook trout.

Giesen Marlborough Sauvignon Blanc

QUALITY ♛♛♛♛
VALUE ★★★½
GRAPES sauvignon blanc
REGION Marlborough, NZ
CELLAR 🍾 1
ALC./VOL. 12.5%
RRP $16.90

Marcel Giesen is a German-born winemaker who runs a winery in the Canterbury district of New Zealand's South Island.

CURRENT RELEASE 1994 This is a very impressive crisp, light-bodied sauvignon from a region famed for this grape. The nose is pungent gooseberry/tropical fruit with herbaceous, vegetal aspects. The palate is lighter than the nose suggests and falls away slightly, but what's there is delicious. Greenlip mussels here.

Gloucester Ridge Chardonnay

QUALITY ♛♛♛♛
VALUE ★★★
GRAPES chardonnay
REGION Pemberton, WA
CELLAR 🍾 3
ALC./VOL. 13.5%
RRP $ 17.50

The packaging is nothing if not arresting. You'll either love it or hate it but you won't overlook it. It's a stamp collector's delight.

CURRENT RELEASE 1994 No doubt about the wood – it simply bristles with fresh oak. The nose is ruled by toast, vanilla and caramel aromas. The palate shows distinct apricot and peach flavours balanced by assertive oak on a dry finish. Don't overchill it before you drink it with your chicken pie.

Gloucester Ridge Sauvignon Blanc

This West Australian vineyard is owned by Don and Sue Hancock. The wines are made under contract by John Wade.

CURRENT RELEASE 1994 A pungently strong style that leaves you in no doubt about the variety. The nose is grassy with hints of tinned peas. The palate is quite rich with tropical fruit characters and plenty of herbs. The finish offers crisp acid and a cleansing action. Serve well chilled with white asparagus.

QUALITY 🍷🍷🍷🍷
VALUE ★★★½
GRAPES sauvignon blanc
REGION Pemberton, WA
CELLAR 🍾 1
ALC./VOL. 13.0%
RRP $14.00

Grant Burge Chardonnay

Grant Burge boasts he used to ride a horse to school in the Barossa Valley. Barossa born and bred, he wears his heritage with pride. Maker Grant Burge.

CURRENT RELEASE 1994 A complex style that delivers the flavour. The nose is dominated by toasty oak plus hints of peach. The palate is complex with a creamy texture and plenty of barrel-ferment characters. Peach and grapefruit are the main flavours but are supported by savoury oak on a long finish. Don't overchill, and serve with pan-fried quail.

QUALITY 🍷🍷🍷🍷🍷
VALUE ★★★★½
GRAPES chardonnay
REGION Barossa Valley, SA
CELLAR 🍾 4
ALC./VOL. 13.6%
RRP $14.00

Grant Burge Riesling

For all his Barossa leanings, Grant Burge is not totally one-eyed. When it comes to riesling, he is willing to annex Eden Valley.

CURRENT RELEASE 1994 The nose has strong aromatics plus citrus followed up by lime and other citrus flavours on the palate. These are matched by crisp acid on a very clean finish. Served well chilled, it's a treat with oysters mornay.

QUALITY 🍷🍷🍷🍷🍷
VALUE ★★★★½
GRAPES riesling
REGION Eden Valley, SA
CELLAR 🍾 3
ALC./VOL. 12.0%
RRP $12.00

Grosset Piccadilly

QUALITY ♛♛♛♛♛
VALUE ★★★★★
GRAPES chardonnay
REGION Adelaide Hills, SA
CELLAR 🍾 5
ALC./VOL. 13.5%
RRP $23.95

Obviously Jeffrey Grosset is not a prisoner of his vineyard or the Clare Valley. Good things happen when he reaches beyond the boundaries.

CURRENT RELEASE 1994 Stirling style, this is a very exciting wine made from grapes grown in the Adelaide Hills – a wonderful chablis-like drink. The nose has grapefruit and citrus aromas. The palate is fine and complex with grapefruit, melon and peach. It is so fine and there is structured oak to continue the excitement. It should not be served too cold and goes well with scallops cooked in the shell with ginger.

Grosset Polish Hill

QUALITY ♛♛♛♛
VALUE ★★★★
GRAPES riesling
REGION Polish Hill River, SA
VALUE 🍾 5
ALC./VOL. 12.5%
RRP $14.50

Mr Grosset can be a tad thorny with scribes but he has firm and often good ideas, such as this attempt to make local generic labels.

CURRENT RELEASE 1994 A classic Clare style that has lots of style. The nose is aromatic with some dramatic citrus smells. The palate offers an impressive citrus/lime tang. The finish is crisp and acid. Great stuff with Coffin Bay scallops.

Hanging Rock Howqua River Riesling

QUALITY ♛♛♛♛
VALUE ★★★
GRAPES riesling
REGION Mansfield, Vic.
CELLAR 🍾 5+
ALC./VOL. 12.0%
RRP $18.15

Winemaker John Ellis buys grapes from several small growers in out-of-the-way places in the chilly parts of Victoria, such as this one near Mansfield.

CURRENT RELEASE 1994 Not a lot of riesling identity showing at this stage, as it's dominated by grassy herbaceous scents. It is delicate, lean, light-bodied and well endowed with fresh, crisp acid. Good with crab.

Hanging Rock Victoria Chardonnay

This winery was begun by John Ellis and his wife Anne Tyrrell in 1982. It produces about 10,000 cases of wine.

CURRENT RELEASE 1994 A delicate wine that doesn't burst forth with a fanfare, but creeps up from behind. It has a straightforward, lightly peachy taste and is as clean as a whistle, if a tad unexciting. Try it with caesar salad.

QUALITY ♥♥♥
VALUE ★★½
GRAPES chardonnay
REGION Murray Valley, Bendigo, Mansfield, Vic.
CELLAR 2
ALC./VOL. 13.0%
RRP $18.15

Hardys Eileen Hardy Chardonnay

Eileen Hardy was the matriarch of the family and was awarded an OBE in 1977 for services to the wine industry. Maker Tom Newton.

Previous outstanding vintages: '86, '89, '90, '92

CURRENT RELEASE 1994 A very stylish, complex, structured, rich yet subtle chardonnay with multi-faceted peach, nectarine, tropical, and vanilla flavours with sensitively handled cedary, toasty oak. Would reward cellaring. (Sorry about all the adjectives but it really is very complex!) Try it with crayfish.

QUALITY ♥♥♥♥♥
VALUE ★★★★★
GRAPES chardonnay
REGION Padthaway, SA & Yarra Valley, Vic.
CELLAR 5+
ALC./VOL. 13.5%
RRP $26.00 ⑤

Best White Wine/ Chardonnay

Hardys Nottage Hill Rhine Riesling

This is much better value than the chardonnay under the same label, which reflects fashion and the demand on grapes.

CURRENT RELEASE 1994 This is an authentic riesling that is very good value for money, especially when discounted. It has a light floral aroma, adequate flavour and a clean acid finish. Fry up a fishburger here.

QUALITY ♥♥♥
VALUE ★★★½
GRAPES riesling
REGION not stated
CELLAR 2
ALC./VOL. 12.5%
RRP $8.70 ⑤

Hardys RR Classic Dry White

QUALITY ♛♛♚
VALUE ★★★
GRAPES sauvignon blanc, semillon
REGION Clare & Padthaway, SA
CELLAR 🍶
ALC./VOL. 11.5%
RRP $6.75 ⑤

Hardys had better success marketing rhine riesling in Europe as RR. Then they decided to piggyback a few other wines and make RR a brand.
CURRENT RELEASE 1994 Pale coloured, this has a fragrant muscaty nose and is light, fresh, fruity and simple. Dry white is a misnomer, as it's actually fairly sweet. Very quaffable wine for the unfussy.

Hardys RR Medium Dry White

QUALITY ♛♛♚
VALUE ★★½
GRAPES riesling, gewürztraminer
REGION McLaren Vale & Padthaway, SA
CELLAR 🍶
ALC./VOL. 11.5%
RRP $6.75 ⑤

The RR back labels say 'great flavour and character', which could be said to be drawing a long bow.
CURRENT RELEASE 1994 As with the Classic Dry White, the name understates the sugar level. This has an oily, raisiny muscat nose and a fairly coarse, sweet, slightly gooey palate. But it's clean and technically well made.

Hardys Siegersdorf Chardonnay

QUALITY ♛♛♛
VALUE ★★★
GRAPES chardonnay
REGION mainly McLaren Vale & Padthaway, SA
CELLAR 🍶 2
ALC./VOL. 13.5%
RRP $11.70 ⑤

First came the riesling, then a red and a chardonnay piggybacking on it to create what the marketers call a family of wines. Maker Tom Newton.
CURRENT RELEASE 1994 Soft, straightforward, faintly peachy wine which is true to the variety and has good depth of flavour for its price. Slightly tropical on the finish, which is dry and lingers nicely. A fair match with fish fingers.

Hardys Siegersdorf Rhine Riesling

Siegersdorf is a place in the Barossa Valley where Hardys used to have a winery. It means a conqueror's village. This wine has had an all-conquering career.

CURRENT RELEASE 1994 A genuine riesling, without the aberrant flavours that one finds in so many modern cheaper rieslings, this has a pale colour, delicate floral/citrus nose and light, tangy acid palate. The finish is limes and lemons. It's fairly plain but crisp, dry and the real McCoy. Very adaptable with food.

QUALITY 🍷🍷🍷🍷
VALUE ★★★★
GRAPES riesling
REGION Clare Valley, Padthaway, SA
CELLAR 🍾 4
ALC./VOL. 12.0%
RRP $11.20 ⓢ

Haselgrove Sauvignon Blanc

This McLaren Vale winery used to be called James Haselgrove. Maker Nick Haselgrove.

CURRENT RELEASE 1994 This has a floral, limey aspect to the grassy/fruit aroma. The palate is crisp and lively with good balance and a touch of richness. The finish is dry and has good length assisted by alcohol. Try it with pasta and pesto.

QUALITY 🍷🍷🍷🍷
VALUE ★★★★
GRAPES sauvignon blanc
REGION McLaren Vale, SA
CELLAR 🍾 1
ALC./VOL. 12.5%
RRP $10.90 (cellar door)

Heemskerk Chardonnay

Big changes here, with the export-beef baron Joe Chromy buying Heemskerk along with Rochecombe and Buchanan and rolling them into a serious Tassie group with real clout. This was made by the previous winemaker, Jean-Baptiste Lecaillon.

Previous outstanding vintages: '91

CURRENT RELEASE 1992 Typical Heemskerk: very fine, tightly structured, reserved and slow ageing, with nectarine, peach and nutty aromas following through to a complex palate. Excellent liveliness from tingling acidity, and finishes with oak and dryness. A keeper that's also good now with food. Try it with Heidi gruyere.

QUALITY 🍷🍷🍷🍷🍷
VALUE ★★★★½
GRAPES chardonnay
REGION Pipers Brook, Tas.
CELLAR 🍾 6+
ALC./VOL. 12.9%
RRP $30.60

Heggies Chardonnay

QUALITY ♥♥♥♥
VALUE ★★★★
GRAPES chardonnay
REGION Eden Valley, SA
CELLAR 🍾 4
ALC./VOL. 14.0%
RRP $19.35 ⓢ

Heggies vineyard sits at a discrete 570 metres in the Eden Valley hills behind Angaston and is owned by Yalumba. It was developed in 1973. Maker Simon Adams.

CURRENT RELEASE 1994 A fine-boned, fruit-driven style with lightly handled wood and a slight sweetness on the forepalate which may come from the very ripe fruit. Despite that alcohol, it is a subtle wine, at least in youth. Restrained but deep spice flavours finish smooth and round. Good with vegetarian food.

Heggies Riesling

QUALITY ♥♥♥⚆
VALUE ★★★
GRAPES riesling
REGION Eden Valley, SA
CELLAR 🍾 4
ALC./VOL. 12.0%
RRP $15.45 ⓢ

Yalumba bought the land for this vineyard from Colin Heggie, whose name is on the bottle. But whether it's him up on the horse is unclear.

CURRENT RELEASE 1993 A distinctive style: not so much floral but tropical pineapple and citrus aromas come rocketing out of the glass. The citrusy palate is shot through with tart acid, and the finish is on the austere side, with a little astringency. Age will soften, but so will food. Try scallops.

Heggies Viognier

QUALITY ♥♥♥⚆
VALUE ★★★
GRAPES viognier
REGION Eden Valley, SA
CELLAR 🍾 3+
ALC./VOL. 13.5%
RRP $19.30 ⓢ

Viognier is a little-known grape that's highly regarded in France's Rhône Valley, where it's used for Condrieu.

CURRENT RELEASE 1994 A captivating alternative to oceans of chardonnay. The nose is very spicy, floral and slightly toasty from oak maturation. The palate opens with some sweetness and fills out with rich mid-palate flavour, indicating very ripe fruit. A little oak tannin firms up the finish. Nice wine, nice bottle too.

Henschke Chardonnay

Stephen and Prue Henschke are best known for their statuesque reds, but they are equally competent with whites.

CURRENT RELEASE 1994 The aroma has a fascinating scent of lemon, laced with grassy and honey accents. It is quite restrained in its youth, fresh and crisp with attractive delicacy, and we would expect it to put on richness with more time in the bottle. Try it with lemon chicken.

QUALITY ♛♛♛♛
VALUE ★★★½
GRAPES chardonnay
REGION Eden Valley, SA
CELLAR 🍷 5
ALC./VOL. 13.7%
RRP $23.80

Henschke Chenin Blanc

Australian chenin blanc invariably tastes nothing like the great chenins of the Loire Valley's Vouvray region, but they can be pleasant quaffing wines.

CURRENT RELEASE 1994 This surprising wine has a certain nettley, herby aroma common to several Henschke whites. There's stacks of flavour in the mouth, with a lingering finish. Happily it is not sweet like many chenins. Try it with salads.

QUALITY ♛♛♛
VALUE ★★★
GRAPES chenin blanc
REGION Eden Valley, SA
CELLAR 🍷 1
ALC./VOL. 13.0%
RRP $12.40

Henschke Croft Chardonnay

This is the super-duper Henschke chardonnay from their new Lenswood vineyard, next door to the Knappsteins and Weavers. Maker Stephen Henschke.

CURRENT RELEASE 1994 This is a heavily worked chardonnay with stacks of butterscotchy malolactic character that adds interest to the rich, ripe peach/nectarine fruit. The wine appears slightly blousy on the tongue but the acid holds it together. Intense, long and well balanced. Drink with chicken and pistachio galantine.

QUALITY ♛♛♛♛
VALUE ★★★★
GRAPES chardonnay
REGION Adelaide Hills, SA
CELLAR 🍷 3
ALC./VOL. 13.7%
RRP $22.50

Henschke Gewürztraminer

QUALITY 🍷🍷🍷🍷
VALUE ★★★½
GRAPES gewürztraminer
REGION Eden Valley, SA
CELLAR 🍾 2
ALC./VOL. 12.0%
RRP $12.60

Traminer is thought to have been named after the town of Tramin in Italy's northern Alto Adige region. Traminer is one of the most pungent-quality wine grapes.

CURRENT RELEASE 1994 This is quite obviously traminer but not as domineeringly pungent as some. The nose is straightforward and lychee-like, the palate smooth, trim and tight, showing no signs of coarseness or flabbiness. Try it with cheese soufflé.

Henschke Green's Hill Riesling

QUALITY 🍷🍷🍷🍷🍷
VALUE ★★★★★
GRAPES riesling
REGION Adelaide Hills, SA
CELLAR 🍾 7+
ALC./VOL. 12.5%
RRP $15.50

For a late-ripening grape variety, riesling does remarkably well in ultra-cool climates: witness the Rhine Valley – and Lenswood. This provides an interesting comparison with Henschke's Eden Valley riesling.

CURRENT RELEASE 1994 High-altitude finesse is apparent here. The colour is pale; there are aromas of green apple and pear with a lightly toasty aspect; the acid is high and the impression is of intense, vibrant fruit and a tangy finish. Superb riesling to have with oysters.

Henschke Julius Eden Valley Riesling

QUALITY 🍷🍷🍷🍷
VALUE ★★★★
GRAPES riesling
REGION Eden Valley, SA
CELLAR ⬤— 2–6+
ALC./VOL. 12.5%
RRP $15.50

A brand-name has been introduced this year: Julius Henschke was an artist and sculptor of an earlier generation.

Previous outstanding vintages: '79, '82, '87, '90, '93

CURRENT RELEASE 1994 This is a very dry, lean, tight-structured riesling which needs time. The nose has floral and herbal aromas with a nettley aspect, and there are no concessions to the drink-now market. This wine will age well. Cellar, then have with Alsace onion tart.

Henschke Semillon

This wine is matured in French oak, and the Henschkes have lately come in for a bit of flak for toning down the oak level. Some people like drinking overtly woody wines.

CURRENT RELEASE 1994 We applaud the reduced wood level: the nose has delicate lanolin-like semillon fruit and subtle nuttiness. It's a very pleasing style, with controlled fullness, good balance, and a dry finish lengthened by the oak. Try it with smoked chicken.

QUALITY ♛♛♛♛
VALUE ★★★½
GRAPES semillon
REGION Eden Valley, SA
CELLAR 🍾 2+
ALC./VOL. 13.9%
RRP $16.90

Henschke Tilly's Vineyard

This is named after winemaker Stephen Henschke's great aunt, Ottilie Mathilde Henschke. The naughty words 'white burgundy' have been dropped from the label.

CURRENT RELEASE 1994 Another wooded white where the oak is taking a more background role. Tilly's has become a very popular wine in trendy circles. The nose is lightly toasty and nutty, the palate is smooth with a little richness; well balanced and round with a dry finish. Try pasta with herbs and broadbeans.

QUALITY ♛♛♛♛
VALUE ★★★½
GRAPES various
REGION Eden Valley, SA
CELLAR 🍾 2
ALC./VOL. 12.8%
RRP $12.90

Hillstowe Chardonnay

McLaren Vale is home to full-blown chardonnays and this makes an interesting contrast to the same maker's Adelaide Hills wine.

CURRENT RELEASE 1993 This is typically forward, deep yellow-coloured McLaren Vale chardonnay, and seems to be ageing rather quickly. It has a big buttery nose with slightly rough-edged oak and finishes with some wood astringency. Not a wine of subtlety: try it with coq au vin blanc.

QUALITY ♛♛♛
VALUE ★★★
GRAPES chardonnay
REGION McLaren Vale, SA
CELLAR 🍾 1
ALC./VOL. 13.5%
RRP $15.80 ⓢ

Hillstowe Sauvignon Blanc

QUALITY ♥♥♥♥
VALUE ★★★★
GRAPES sauvignon blanc
REGION McLaren Vale, SA
CELLAR 🍾 2
ALC./VOL. 13.0%
RRP $13.50 ⓢ

Hillstowe's owner Chris Laurie recently took a creative step by opening a cellar-door sales outlet in Hahndorf. His son Hamish also works for Hillstowe.
CURRENT RELEASE 1994 Typical pale colour of this variety, attractive varietal fruit on the nose with tropical and gooseberry aromas. The palate is generous yet retains the essential crispness of the variety, with excellent flavour and length. Drink while young, with white fish and salad.

Hillstowe Udy's Mill Chardonnay

QUALITY ♥♥♥♥♥
VALUE ★★★★
GRAPES chardonnay
REGION Adelaide Hills, SA
CELLAR 🍾 5+
ALC./VOL. 13.5%
RRP $22.50

This wine is grown on Chris Laurie's high-altitude vineyard, which is on the site of an extinct sawmill. Hillstowe wines are made by Martin Shaw and Wirra Wirra.
Previous outstanding vintages: '92, '93
CURRENT RELEASE 1994 Subtlety is a strong point of the Adelaide Hills chardonnays: refined pear/peach, nutty fruit with underplayed oak and tight structure are the features of this excellent wine. It should also age well, although it's lovely now with prawns.

Hollick Botrytis Riesling

QUALITY ♥♥♥♥♥
VALUE ★★★★
GRAPES riesling
REGION Coonawarra, SA
CELLAR 🍾 5+
ALC./VOL. 11.5%
RRP $15.30 (375ml)

Coonawarra has suffered from the double-edged sword of botrytis for many years: those who encourage it in their late-picked whites also risk it damaging their reds.
CURRENT RELEASE 1994 This is a restrained style of botrytis wine, with relatively subtle 'noble rot' influence. The nose shows abundant fresh floral riesling character; the palate is compact, fine, reserved, with lots of citrus and sweetness balanced by lively acid and tight structure. Should age well. Try it with fruit salad and ice-cream.

Hollick Terra

This is a clever way to repackage riesling, which at Hollick was not exactly rocketing out the door. Makers Ian Hollick and Pat Tocaciu.

CURRENT RELEASE 1994 This wine hides its light under the proverbial bushel. It's a delicate, high-acid, austere style, and chablis-like, if you like, with a slight floral aroma and a shy personality. Useful with seafood.

QUALITY 🍷🍷🍷
VALUE ★★★
GRAPES riesling, sauvignon blanc
REGION Coonawarra, SA
CELLAR 🍾 1
ALC./VOL. 11.5%
RRP $12.90 Ⓢ

Horseshoe Classic Hunter Semillon

John Hordern, a descendant of Sydney retailer Anthony Hordern, has a vineyard in the Upper Hunter, near Denman.

CURRENT RELEASE 1993 True to its label, this is a traditional Hunter style, lean and narrow in structure with tart lemony flavours, a lanolin nose, and delicacy that will build in flavour with bottle-age. Cellar or drink with a lighter fish dish.

QUALITY 🍷🍷🍷🍷
VALUE ★★★
GRAPES semillon
REGION Hunter Valley, NSW
CELLAR 🍾 5+
ALC./VOL. 11.5%
RRP $15.70

Houghton Gold Reserve Chardonnay

Houghton has access to fruit from most regions in WA and the best chardonnay is barrel-fermented for this label. Maker Paul Lapsley.

CURRENT RELEASE 1994 Typical fruit-salady cool-area WA style, with slightly sweaty/estery, tropical fruit and herbaceous aromas which turn passionfruity in the mouth. The wine has delicacy and yet good length and maintains your interest. The oak is subtle and it would go well with milk-fed veal.

QUALITY 🍷🍷🍷🍷
VALUE ★★★½
GRAPES chardonnay
REGION Frankland, Margaret River, Manjimup, WA
CELLAR 🍾 4
ALC./VOL. 13.5%
RRP $17.40 Ⓢ

Houghton Gold Reserve Verdelho

QUALITY 🍷🍷🍷
VALUE ★★½
GRAPES verdelho
REGION various, WA
CELLAR 🍾 3+
ALC./VOL. 13.5%
RRP $17.40 ⓢ

The winemaker's notes suggest this could be cellared up to ten years, which might raise a few customers' eyebrows.

CURRENT RELEASE 1994 There is apparent sweetness in this wine and a trace of coarseness, but the nose offers attractive lemon and herbal aromas with a trademark Houghton sweaty overtone. The palate has plenty of weight, enough to handle lemon chicken.

Houghton Rhine Riesling

QUALITY 🍷🍷🍷🍷
VALUE ★★★★½
GRAPES riesling
REGION Frankland River, WA
CELLAR 🍾 3
ALC./VOL. 12.5%
RRP $11.60 ⓢ

This terrifically aromatic wine is a major contrast to the Clare or Eden Valley styles. We wonder how much of that's the fruit, and how much is the yeast used to ferment it. Maker Paul Lapsley.

CURRENT RELEASE 1994 A perfect pale yellow-green hue reflects the zingy freshness of this extravagant riesling. The nose is intense lime juice and lolly with more than a hint of herbaceousness. Quite a full, rich palate with some phenolic grip, some subliminal sweetness and again herbaceous/lime flavours. Try it with lemon sole.

Houghton Semillon Sauvignon Blanc

QUALITY 🍷🍷🍷🍷
VALUE ★★★½
GRAPES semillon, sauvignon blanc
REGION South-west WA
CELLAR 🍾 1
ALC./VOL. 12.5%
RRP $11.60 ⓢ

All Houghton (and Moondah Brook) white wines seem to come from the same lolly shop: they all have a pineapple/tropical herbaceous note which verges on sweaty. In some, such as this one, it can be very appealing. Perhaps it's the yeast they use. Maker Paul Lapsley.

CURRENT RELEASE 1994 The highly aromatic tropical fruit nose is echoed in the mouth, resulting in an unusually up-front white which is very appealing in its youth. It lacks a little acid cut and seems rather too soft on the tongue, but it's beaut to drink now with a smoked chicken and lychee salad.

Houghton Show Reserve White Burgundy

Supposedly the same wine you buy as a tender one-year-old under the famous blue stripe label, except time has been given a chance to work its spell.

Previous outstanding vintages: '82, '83, '86, '88

CURRENT RELEASE 1987 Typical example of this aged dry white, full yellow in hue and smelling of toast, honey and vanilla. It is quite complex, mellow, soft on the gums, and fully mature. Try it with chicken casserole.

QUALITY 🍷🍷🍷🍷🍷
VALUE ★★★★½
GRAPES mainly chenin blanc & muscadelle
REGION various, WA
CELLAR 🍾 1
ALC./VOL. 12.0%
RRP $18.00

Houghton White Burgundy

The time must be approaching when this changes its name. Will it become Houghton Supreme as it is in the UK?

CURRENT RELEASE 1994 This has an estery, herbal nose with the sorts of guava tropical notes that are a Houghton trademark these days. It's not bone dry but soft and fruity, with a faint whiff of oak adding extra interest and length. A crowd-pleaser. Drink with fish and chips.

QUALITY 🍷🍷🍷
VALUE ★★★½
GRAPES chenin blanc, muscadelle, verdelho, chardonnay, etc
REGION various, WA
CELLAR 🍾 4
ALC./VOL. 12.5%
RRP $11.60 ⓢ

Howard Park Chardonnay

John Wade has been making his Howard Park wines from other people's grapes since 1986, but this is only the second HP chardonnay. They were worth the wait.

Previous outstanding vintages: '93

CURRENT RELEASE 1994 Sheer class! The colour is full yellow, the bouquet a Pandora's box of all the desirable chardonnay aromas: peach, tropical fruits, butterscotch and toasted nuts galore. The palate is intense and lively, tightly structured, which suggests it will age well, and has no rough edges. It is mouthfilling, rich and powerful with great balance and length. A stunner. Try it with lobster.

QUALITY 🍷🍷🍷🍷🍷
VALUE ★★★★★
GRAPES chardonnay
REGION Lower Great Southern, WA
CELLAR 🍾 6+
ALC./VOL. 13.5%
RRP $27.40

Howard Park Riesling

QUALITY ★★★★★
VALUE ★★★★★
GRAPES riesling
REGION Mount Barker, WA
CELLAR 🍾 8
ALC./VOL. 12.0%
RRP $18.50

John Wade does marvellous things with riesling grapes, although occasionally the weather's intervened and given the grapes a dose of botrytis. Happily, not in 1994.

Previous outstanding vintages: '86, '88, '90, '91, '92

CURRENT RELEASE 1994 This is a great Australian riesling. It's like sinking into the leather in the back of a new Roller. The flavours are in marvellous harmony with nothing out of place. The nose is not so aromatic but doughy and youthful; the taste is intense, rich, powerful, with great clarity and definition. The big floral flavour and limey afterpalate is firmed up by just the right amount of grip. Perfect with fish.

Hugh Hamilton Unwooded Chardonnay

QUALITY ★★★
VALUE ★★★
GRAPES chardonnay
REGION McLaren Vale, SA
CELLAR 🍾 1
ALC./VOL. 12.5%
RRP $15.00

Hugh is a member of the eminent SA wine family. He used to work with brother Richard Hamilton but went his own way in 1990. He has 15 hectares of vines in McLaren Vale.

CURRENT RELEASE 1994 This fresh, uncomplicated chardonnay is an honest wine without much winemaking influence. The fruit holds centre stage, with herbaceous/tropical fruit aromas and a passionfruity, albeit somewhat superficial, palate. Drink while it's young, with salads.

Hunter Park Sauvignon Blanc

QUALITY ★★★½
VALUE ★★★★
GRAPES sauvignon blanc
REGION Hunter Valley, NSW
CELLAR 🍾 1
ALC./VOL. 11.5%
RRP $12.00

This is a new label, aimed mainly at the American market. The grapes come from the Kenmarie vineyard in the Upper Hunter and the maker is Simon Gilbert.

CURRENT RELEASE 1994 An appealing, fruit-driven style with fresh, green cut-grass aromas which follow through to the mouth. The taste is light yet intense, crisp and fresh, ending pleasantly dry. A good food wine: try it with salads and seafood.

Huntington Estate Semillon

Although Mudgee wines are usually quite different to the nearby Hunter Valley, this one could easily be mistaken for a Hunter. Makers Susie and Bob Roberts.

Previous outstanding vintages: '76, '80, '82, '84, '88, '90, '92

CURRENT RELEASE 1994 This is a spotless unwooded semillon, showing lovely aromatic creamy lanolin straw fruit on the nose and a delicate, lemony palate. Soft and balanced, although it could use a little more intensity. Drink with white-fleshed fish.

QUALITY ♥♥♥♥
VALUE ★★★★
GRAPES semillon
REGION Mudgee, NSW
CELLAR 🍾 8+
ALC./VOL. 11.0%
RRP $10.50 (cellar door)

Jamiesons Run Chardonnay

As night follows day so chardonnay follows a successful red. This is a white wine success story. Maker 'Gifted' Gavin Hogg

CURRENT RELEASE 1994 The full-on malolactic and barrel-ferment treatment with lots of lees characters. That's the technical explanation and in the glass the wine has a buttery, caramel nose. The palate is chewy with soft peach flavours married to some well-integrated oak on a smooth, dry finish. A little chill and try it with smoked cod.

QUALITY ♥♥♥♥
VALUE ★★★★
GRAPES chardonnay
REGION various
CELLAR 🍾 3
ALC./VOL. 12.0%
RRP $11.95 Ⓢ

Jamiesons Run Sauvignon Blanc

You can't keep a good Jamiesons down. This marque started as a single red wine and now it looks like becoming a complete portfolio.

CURRENT RELEASE 1994 This is a full-on sauvignon blanc style with a very grassy nose. There are tropical fruit aromas plus a hint of herbs. The palate has strong tropical fruit flavours balanced by crisp acid on a clean zesty finish. It tastes good when well chilled. Try it with white asparagus.

QUALITY ♥♥♥♥
VALUE ★★★★
GRAPES sauvignon blanc
REGION Coonawarra, SA
CELLAR 🍾 2
ALC./VOL. 12.5%
RRP $11.95 Ⓢ

Jasper Hill Georgia's Paddock Riesling

QUALITY ♥♥♥
VALUE ★★★
GRAPES riesling
REGION Heathcote, Vic.
CELLAR 🍾 4
ALC./VOL. 12.0%
RRP $15.00

This vineyard is best known for rich reds, and justifiably so. The soil seems right for shiraz, but less so for riesling.

CURRENT RELEASE 1994 Slightly brassy hue and quite a classic floral riesling nose, but the palate is big and clumsy, with a grip like a Schwarzenegger handshake. It could have done with a fining. Chill well, and serve with flavoursome food such as barbecued king prawns.

Jenke Chardonnay

QUALITY ♥♥♥
VALUE ★★★
GRAPES chardonnay
REGION Barossa Valley, SA
CELLAR 🍾 2
ALC./VOL. 14.5%
RRP $17.00

Jenke is a relatively new Barossa brand, established in 1989, but drawing fruit from old vineyards established in 1926. Maker Kym Jenke.

CURRENT RELEASE 1994 This is a real shrinking violet. The nose is shy but faultless and the palate has attractive melon and cashew flavours which are lively. It may lack power and length but the wine is of good quality. Try it with cabbage rolls.

Jim Barry Chardonnay

QUALITY ♥♥♥♥
VALUE ★★★★
GRAPES chardonnay
REGION Clare Valley, SA
CELLAR 🍾 2
ALC./VOL. 12.3%
RRP $10.40 ⓢ

Jim Barry was the first trained winemaker to work in the Clare Valley. His three sons, Peter, Mark and John, now run the show.

CURRENT RELEASE 1994 This little charmer is light on the oak but strong on fruit. The nose is all raw cashews and nectarines, the palate is light and honest with good depth of fruit. Well-made wine in a style to please many. Try it with pasta with peas.

Jim Barry Lavender Hill

'I found a thrill, on lavender hill . . . ' Seems like a nice name for a wine, and many interpretations can be attached to it. Maker Mark Barry.

CURRENT RELEASE *non-vintage* This is a slightly sweet, aromatic white, flavoured with muscat or traminer grapes, which give a – dare we say – lavender quality to the nose. A crowd-pleasing style which should sell up a storm.

QUALITY 🍷🍷🍷
VALUE ★★★½
GRAPES not stated
REGION Clare Valley, SA
CELLAR 🍾 1
ALC./VOL. 11.1%
RRP $10.40 Ⓢ

Jim Barry Personal Selection Chardonnay

The label tells us the vines were 'hand pruned to 7.5 bottles per vine', and that 'wine in moderation is good for you'.

CURRENT RELEASE 1993 A more complex style than the cheaper label, with an extra year's maturity and lots of winemakerly characters. There's toasty barrel-ferment, plenty of oak and buttery malolactic overtones in this multi-faceted chardonnay. Richness, strength and intensity galore. Try Indian butter chicken.

QUALITY 🍷🍷🍷🍷
VALUE ★★★★½
GRAPES chardonnay
REGION Clare Valley, SA
CELLAR 🍾 3+
ALC./VOL. 12.7%
RRP $13.70 Ⓢ

Jim Barry Watervale Riesling

The Barry clan shocked the industry by buying the renowned Florita vineyard, source of many great Leo Buring rieslings, in 1986. Lindemans had been ordered to sell it by their US owner, Phillip Morris. And what a coup it was for the Barrys.

CURRENT RELEASE 1994 A rich, flavoursome, dry style that's true to the region. The nose is shy but softly floral and genuine; the palate soft and full with smooth floral notes that linger long on the finish. A dry but not austere style to go with Port Parham crab.

QUALITY 🍷🍷🍷🍷
VALUE ★★★★½
GRAPES riesling
REGION Clare Valley, SA
CELLAR 🍾 5+
ALC./VOL. 12.0%
RRP $10.40 Ⓢ

Kara Kara Vineyards Fumé Blanc

QUALITY 🍷🍷🍷🍷
VALUE ★★★½
GRAPES sauvignon blanc 70%, semillon 30%
REGION St Arnaud, Vic.
CELLAR 🍾 1
ALC./VOL. 11.7%
RRP $14.00

It seems in this case fumé blanc is a blend of sauvignon blanc and semillon. When will this meaningless marketing term find its way to the scrap heap?
CURRENT RELEASE 1994 Where's the smoke (fumes), there ain't no smoke? The nose has pawpaw and melon aromas and the palate reveals a hint of sweetness as well as tropical fruit flavours. The finish is dry with crisp acid. Serve well chilled with yabbies.

Kara Kara Vineyards Sauvignon Blanc

QUALITY 🍷🍷🍷🍷
VALUE ★★★½
GRAPES sauvignon blanc
REGION St Arnaud, Vic.
CELLAR 🍾 1
ALC./VOL. 12.7%
RRP $14.00

This vineyard was planted in 1977 and has an annual production of 1300 cases. Maker Steve Zsigmond.
CURRENT RELEASE 1994 This is a faithful reproduction of varietal character. The nose is grassy with hints of herbs and the palate offers gooseberry and tropical fruit flavours backed up by crisp acid on a dry finish. Serve well chilled with char-grilled seafood kebabs.

Karl Seppelt Chardonnay

QUALITY 🍷🍷🍷🍷
VALUE ★★★½
GRAPES chardonnay
REGION Eden Valley, SA
CELLAR 🍾 3
ALC./VOL. 14.0%
RRP $11.50

As the name suggest this is made by a member of a famous wine dynasty who is now located in the Eden Valley.
CURRENT RELEASE 1994 A deceptive wine that has high acid and well-disguised high alcohol. The colour is pale straw and the nose has lime and other citrus characters. The palate is crisp with grapefruit and lime flavours followed by discreet wood on a tingling finish. It can be served well chilled with spaghetti marinara.

Karriview Chardonnay

Established in 1986, Karriview is a small vineyard located near Denmark. According to geologists, this corner of Australia was the first dry land on earth. Maker John Wade (consultant).

CURRENT RELEASE 1994 The nose shows peach and melon with a hint of wood. The palate struts its stuff with peach and melon flavours and a hint of citrus tied to a sprightly wood treatment on a forceful finish. It needs time in the cellar, but if you drink it now don't overchill. Try it with a kedgeree.

QUALITY ▼▼▼▼
VALUE ★★★
GRAPES chardonnay
REGION Great Southern, WA
CELLAR ▮ 5
ALC./VOL. 13.0%
RRP $23.50

Katnook Coonawarra Riesling

Only a few companies persist with the riesling variety in Coonawarra. There it can produce interesting if not classic wines.

CURRENT RELEASE 1989 This is a re-release that shows the benefit of bottle-age. The colour is a bright green-gold and the nose has a distinct kerosene aroma. The palate shows concentrated lime flavours plus a mouthfilling texture with plenty of crisp acid on the finish. It can be served well chilled with whiting in beer batter.

QUALITY ▼▼▼▼
VALUE ★★★★
GRAPES riesling
REGION Coonawarra, SA
CELLAR ▮ 2
ALC./VOL. 11.5%
RRP $20.00

Katnook Sauvignon Blanc

Established in 1979, this is a good example of the expanding vineyards in Coonawarra – up to 20,000 cases and still counting. New plantings are underway. Maker Wayne Stehbens.

CURRENT RELEASE 1994 A benchmark in the district for sauvignon blanc. The nose is a medley of passionfruit, peach and mango; ditto the palate, which is rich in tropical fruit character. There's crisp acid on a clean and protracted finish. Serve well chilled with white asparagus.

QUALITY ▼▼▼▼▼
VALUE ★★★
GRAPES sauvignon blanc
REGION Coonawarra, SA
CELLAR ▮ 2
ALC./VOL. 12.5%
RRP $20.00

Killerby April Classic White

QUALITY ♛♛♛♛
VALUE ★★★½
GRAPES gewürztraminer 85%, semillon 15%
REGION Capel, WA
CELLAR 🍾 1
ALC./VOL. 12.5%
RRP $13.50

What makes a classic in April? In this case freshness is the essence – the wine is bottled as soon as possible after making.

CURRENT RELEASE 1995 There are fresh traminer aromas on the nose and the palate offers lively tropical fruit flavours and fresh herbs. The finish shows zingy crisp acid. It can be served well chilled with a leafy green salad.

Kingston Estate Chardonnay

QUALITY ♛♛♛♛
VALUE ★★★½
GRAPES chardonnay
REGION Riverland, SA
CELLAR 🍾 3
ALC./VOL. 12.2%
RRP $12.00

Kingston on Murray sounds terribly English but it is very Australian when you get there. The estate is owned and operated by the Moularadellis family.

CURRENT RELEASE 1994 The nose is sappy with hints of vanilla. The palate has strong tropical fruit plus peach and apricot flavours followed by assertive oak that adds a bit of backbone. It would go well with a chicken pie.

Krondorf Chardonnay

QUALITY ♛♛♛♛
VALUE ★★★★
GRAPES chardonnay
REGION Eden Valley, McLaren Vale, SA
CELLAR 🍾 3
ALC./VOL. 12.5%
RRP $9.95

New livery for the 'crown village' wine from the Mildara Blass stable. The label has endured many name changes, including Glenview and Augustine. Maker Nick Walker.

Previous outstanding vintages: '90

CURRENT RELEASE 1994 This is a polished style that is well balanced. The nose has stone-fruit aromas plus some warm oak smells. The middleweight palate has peach, grapefruit and melon flavour matched by some rich smoky bacon oak on a lingering finish. It drinks well with a little chill. Try it with pan-fried veal.

Krondorf Rhine Riesling

This is another reliable commercial style that usually delivers the varietal and regional goods. Maker Nick Walker.

CURRENT RELEASE 1994 Very honest style with straightforward varietal characters. The nose is floral with some acute citrus accents. The palate has rich lemon flavours balanced by a crisp acid snappin' fresh finish. Big chill won't kill; try it with a fisherman's basket.

QUALITY ????
VALUE ★★★★½
GRAPES riesling
REGION Eden Valley, SA
CELLAR 2
ALC./VOL. 11.0%
RRP $9.95

Krondorf Show Chardonnay

A lot of work goes into this style. It is the pick of the harvest and gets the best available wood treatment.

Previous outstanding vintages: '90, '91, '92, '93

CURRENT RELEASE 1993 This is a lusty style of great richness. The nose shows obvious wood aromas. The palate is chewy with a peaches-and-cream texture and lots of fruit followed by well-integrated oak on a dry, almost dusty finish. It shouldn't be served too cold; try it with mushroom risotto.

QUALITY ?????
VALUE ★★★★
GRAPES chardonnay
REGION McLaren Vale, Eden Valley, Barossa Valley, SA
CELLAR 4
ALC./VOL. 13.0%
RRP $18.00

Krondorf Wood-Aged Semillon

Cinderella dressed in yellow – Clare Valley semillon is an unknown quantity but has some beguiling qualities.

CURRENT RELEASE 1992 This is quite different to semillon from other parts of the country. There is a strong lemon component to the perfumed nose. The palate has strong lime and other citrus flavours which are balanced by enthusiastic wood. It doesn't need to be well chilled; try it with flounder with a lemon sauce.

QUALITY ????
VALUE ★★★
GRAPES semillon
REGION Clare Valley, SA
CELLAR 5
ALC./VOL. 11.5%
RRP $16.00

Lakes Folly Chardonnay

QUALITY 🍷🍷🍷
VALUE ★★½
GRAPES chardonnay
REGION Hunter Valley, NSW
CELLAR 🍾 3
ALC./VOL. 12.5%
RRP $29.00

This small Hunter estate-grown wine still enjoys some of the cachet it built in the '70s and early '80s thanks to its founder, the ebullient Max Lake. Maker Stephen Lake.
Previous outstanding vintages: '81, '83, '84, '86, '89, '91, '92
CURRENT RELEASE 1993 When it's hot it's hot, but in '93 it's not. This is a decent drink but not a classic Folly chardonnay. Has some coarse phenolic characters and a slight lack of fruit and charm – especially considering '93 was a very good Hunter vintage. Drink with chicken.

QUALITY 🍷🍷🍷🍷
VALUE ★★★★
GRAPES chardonnay
REGION Hunter Valley, NSW
CELLAR 🍾 5+
ALC./VOL. 12.5%
RRP $29.00

CURRENT RELEASE 1994 A much more attractive wine than '93, with beguiling tropical fruitiness, grapefruit and cashew nuances. Elegant, stylish, smooth and pure. A fruit-driven chardonnay that calls for Niçoise salad.

Lark Hill Chardonnay

QUALITY 🍷🍷🍷
VALUE ★★★
GRAPES chardonnay
REGION Canberra district, NSW
CELLAR 🍾 3
ALC./VOL. 13.5%
RRP $17.00 (cellar door)

Lark Hill's chilly climate is marginal for red wines but often hits the heights with whites.
CURRENT RELEASE 1993 Evidence of barrel-fermentation and malolactic and other winemaking tricks here: a complex amalgam of toasted oak, vanilla, grilled nuts and butter greets the nose. The palate is fresh and lively, with crisp cool fruit and acid, and a lean, fine profile. Drink with baked snapper.

Lark Hill Riesling

This vineyard is perched at 860 metres at Bungendore, just outside Canberra, a cool spot where vintage is April to May. Maker Sue Carpenter.

CURRENT RELEASE 1994 A powerfully fragrant nose reveals fresh doughy esters and citrus/flowery varietal fruit. The palate is juicy, irresistible, with limey and slightly grassy cool-grown accents. A fluent, harmonious riesling. Try it with scallops.

QUALITY 🍷🍷🍷🍷🍷
VALUE ★★★★½
GRAPES riesling
REGION Canberra district, NSW
CELLAR 🍾 6+
ALC./VOL. 12.0%
RRP $13.00 (cellar door)

Leasingham Bin 42 Semillon Sauvignon Blanc

This is a new wine from Leasingham, made from grapes off their Rogers and Provis vineyards. Maker Richard Rowe was looking to make a wine between riesling and chardonnay in style.

CURRENT RELEASE 1994 Coconut oak aromas and a trace of grassy semillon greet the nose, but the wine is not especially sauvignon blanc-like. It's a soft, dry, light to mediumweight with decent length and some nutty oak on the finish. Seafood here.

QUALITY 🍷🍷🍷🍷
VALUE ★★★½
GRAPES semillon, sauvignon blanc
REGION Clare Valley, SA
CELLAR 🍾 2
ALC./VOL. 12.5%
RRP $14.50 $

Leconfield Riesling

Coonawarra did not build its reputation on riesling, but there are several worthy examples in the district. This label has improved out of sight since Ralph Fowler took over.

CURRENT RELEASE 1994 A very delicate riesling, with a very pale hue and a subdued but fragrant aroma with a slightly traminer-ish spiciness that betrays its cool-grown origins. The palate is crisp and lively, with sherbety acid. This could improve after another 12 months in the bottle. Try it with sushi.

QUALITY 🍷🍷🍷
VALUE ★★★
GRAPES riesling
REGION Coonawarra, SA
CELLAR 🍾 3+
ALC./VOL. 11.5%
RRP $12.50

Leeuwin Estate Art Series Chardonnay

QUALITY 🍷🍷🍷🍷?
VALUE ★★★½
GRAPES chardonnay
REGION Margaret River, WA
CELLAR 🍾 1–6+
ALC./VOL. 13.0%
RRP $45.00

This wine is remarkable in that every vintage, including the formative first years, has been a terrific wine. And most have aged superbly. Maker Bob Cartwright.

Previous outstanding vintages: '80, '81, '82, '83, '86, '87, '88, '89

CURRENT RELEASE 1991 This is a big lump of a wine for those who like strong flavours. Although four years old it's still ascending: the nose is slightly shy with toasty, cedary scents and the overall impression is of great power and concentration. It fills the senses and the finish is endless. Cellar a year or two, then drink with sweetbreads in a mustard sauce.

QUALITY 🍷🍷🍷🍷?
VALUE ★★★½
GRAPES chardonnay
REGION Margaret River, WA
CELLAR 🍾 5+
ALC./VOL. 13.5%
RRP $48.30

CURRENT RELEASE 1992 A typical Leeuwin chardonnay in that it doesn't show its age and the concentrated fruit is cleverly infused with a generous quota of oak. Lots of winemaking complexities, including a slight leesy whiff. The taste is big, powerful, spicy and long. A good but not outstanding Leeuwin. Chicken and pistachio gallantine goes well.

Leeuwin Estate Art Series Rhine Riesling

QUALITY 🍷🍷🍷
VALUE ★★½
GRAPES riesling
REGION Margaret River, WA
CELLAR 🍾 3
ALC./VOL. 12.2%
RRP $16.00

Margaret River is not noted for its riesling, and Leeuwin has virtually cornered the market. The label features John Olsen's superb frog painting. Maker Bob Cartwright.

CURRENT RELEASE 1994 A slightly horsey nose to begin with, breathing to reveal an unusual orange/citrus character. The palate is full, ripe, soft and broad with figgy flavours and some grip. A wine of substance, if not finesse. Try it with frog's legs.

Leeuwin Estate Art Series Sauvignon Blanc

Along with Mouton-Rothschild, Leeuwin's art series wines were pioneers of the trend to beautifying labels with original artworks, no doubt procured at considerable expense for the winery's restaurant walls.

CURRENT RELEASE 1994 A very raw, youthful sauvignon with pale colour and rather one-dimensional grassy nose. The palate has good intensity and depth, is fruit-driven with no apparent oak, and an agreeably arid finish that suits sipping with food. Try it with asparagus.

QUALITY ♷♷♷♴
VALUE ★★★
GRAPES sauvignon blanc
REGION Margaret River, WA
CELLAR 🍾 3
ALC./VOL. 12.5%
RRP $16.00

Leeuwin Prelude Chardonnay

The label reads just Leeuwin, not Leeuwin Estate. Does this mean some of the grapes are from other vineyards? Whatever, it's a good wine and very much in Leeuwin Estate style.

CURRENT RELEASE 1994 This is a pungent, powerful, heavily worked style. The nose is tropical fruit plus toasty oak and lees characters: quite complex. The fruit has good concentration and liveliness. A rather over-the-top style that has to be admired for its exuberance. Try marron in a rich sauce.

QUALITY ♷♷♷♷♴
VALUE ★★★★
GRAPES chardonnay
REGION Margaret River, WA
CELLAR 🍾 4+
ALC./VOL. 13.0%
RRP $21.00

Leland Neudorf Valley Sauvignon Blanc

This small vineyard was planted by ex-Yalumba winemaker Robb Cootes. The sauvignon blanc is as exciting as any in the Hills but it's hard to track down due to the size of the vineyard. Mailing list imperative: consult the winery directory in this book.

CURRENT RELEASE 1994 A lighter wine than some previous vintages, with restrained varietal character yet very good depth, structure and middle. The finish is smooth and agreeable and the wine would go well with caesar salad.

QUALITY ♷♷♷♷
VALUE ★★★½
GRAPES sauvignon blanc
REGION Adelaide Hills, SA
CELLAR 🍾 2+
ALC./VOL. 12.5%
RRP $20.00

Lenswood Chardonnay

QUALITY ?????
VALUE ★★★★
GRAPES chardonnay
REGION Adelaide Hills, SA
CELLAR 🍾 4+
ALC./VOL. 14.5%
RRP $26.25

Tim Knappstein, not happy with the style of chardonnay Clare produces, went up into the cooler Adelaide Hills to find the right site to grow the style he wanted. Unfortunately, output is small.

CURRENT RELEASE 1993 The vines have yet to mature and find their balance, as can be seen from the dusty/herbaceous overtone in this unequivocally cool-climate number. In its favour are impressive intensity, liveliness on the tongue, tight structure. High alcohol adds warmth and length. Expect even better things in future.

Leo Buring Eden Valley Rhine Riesling DW T18

QUALITY ?????
VALUE ★★★★★
GRAPES riesling
REGION Eden Valley, SA
CELLAR 🍾 10
ALC./VOL. 12.0%
RRP $10.50 $

The big challenge for Southcorp is to preserve the individual style of each of its brands, despite making many of them in the same winery. So far they're succeeding with Leo Buring.

Previous outstanding vintages: '71, '73, '79, '84, '86, '87, '90, '91, '92, '93

CURRENT RELEASE 1994 This is a delicious traditional Buring riesling: fresh, fragrant doughy/floral pure fruit aroma, turning appley in the mouth where it's very intense and sprightly, with impeccable balance. A great and cellarable riesling to have with grilled whiting.

Leo Buring Watervale Rhine Riesling DW 33

QUALITY ?????
VALUE ★★★★★
GRAPES riesling
REGION Clare Valley, SA
CELLAR 🍾 5
ALC./VOL. 12.5%
RRP $9.30 $

This is Buring's commercial quaffing style, a fuller flavoured, up-front wine. Unlike some of the other wines, the bin number stays the same each year. Maker Geoff Henriks.

CURRENT RELEASE 1994 This is astonishingly good for the price, which is usually discounted to around $8. Doughy, yeasty and floral aromas, and in the mouth it's very limey, full flavoured and finishes dry. A good match with mild fish curry.

Lillydale Vineyards Chardonnay

This Yarra Valley winery is now controlled by McWilliam's, and the prices seem to have fallen to very reasonable levels. Maker Alex White.
CURRENT RELEASE 1993 This opens with a slight animal/gamey note, but settles into a toasty, cashew nutty style with a trace of herbaceousness. The taste is fresh, lively, fruit-driven and the clarity of varietal flavour is good. A subtle, restrained structure. Try it with spatchcock.

QUALITY ♛♛♛♛
VALUE ★★★★
GRAPES chardonnay
REGION Yarra Valley, Vic.
CELLAR 🍾 3
ALC./VOL. 12.5%
RRP $13.70

Lillydale Vineyards Gewürztraminer

The Yarra Valley seems well suited to traminer if Lillydale's consistently fine effort is any guide. If more people wanted to drink it, the Yarra would be sure to produce more of it. Maker Alex White.
CURRENT RELEASE 1993 Very fine, delicate traminer spice on the nose; a subtle example of a variety that can so easily bludgeon with its over-enthusiasm. A stylish and well-balanced wine. Goes well with Thai fish curry.

QUALITY ♛♛♛♛
VALUE ★★★★
GRAPES gewürztraminer
REGION Yarra Valley, Vic.
CELLAR 🍾 3
ALC./VOL. 12.0%
RRP $13.70

Lindemans Bin 65 Chardonnay

This is always a big hit in the US, especially at the *Wine Spectator* magazine, which raves it up every year for its value for money. Maker Phillip John and team.
CURRENT RELEASE 1994 A light, straightforward wine in its youth, with little apparent oak but a pleasant, delicate melon/nectarine aroma. No doubt it will put on some weight after a year in the bottle. Good with focaccia at lunchtime.

QUALITY ♛♛♛♛
VALUE ★★★½
GRAPES chardonnay
REGION Padthaway and various other SA & Vic.
CELLAR 🍾 1
ALC./VOL. 13.0%
RRP $8.80 ⓢ

Lindemans Bin 95 Sauvignon Blanc

QUALITY 🍷🍷🍷
VALUE ★★★½
GRAPES sauvignon blanc
REGION not stated
CELLAR 🍾 1
ALC./VOL. 11.5%
RRP $8.80 ⓢ

This is a companion wine to Bin 65 Chardonnay and the other 'bin' wines. Maker Phillip John and team.

CURRENT RELEASE 1994 This has true herbaceous, confectionery, sauvignon-blanc characters, together with the merest suggestion of oak and a pleasant light-bodied flavour. It borders on wispy but will appeal to many. Drink with a caesar salad.

Lindemans Cawarra Traminer Riesling

QUALITY 🍷🍷🍷
VALUE ★★★½
GRAPES gewürztraminer 67%, riesling 33%
REGION Coonawarra & Padthaway, SA
CELLAR 🍾
ALC./VOL. 12.0%
RRP $6.90 ⓢ

Cowra, Cawarra, Coonawarra, Cowaramup ... no wonder we get confused! Cawarra was the name of Dr Lindeman's Hunter Valley property, but this wine has nothing to do with the Hunter at all.

CURRENT RELEASE 1993 This wine doesn't have a lot of finesse but there's flavour in large dollops. Slightly coarse traminer spice aroma coupled with a broad, ripe, fruity taste that lingers well on the tongue. Not just sugary water like many of its ilk. Try it with a piece of fresh fruit.

Lindemans Classic Dry White

QUALITY 🍷🍷🍷?
VALUE ★★★½
GRAPES semillon, sauvignon blanc, chardonnay
REGION Padthaway & Coonawarra, SA
CELLAR 🍾 2
ALC./VOL. 12.0%
RRP $12.00 ⓢ

Still available a year later: does this mean the smart packaging didn't work?

CURRENT RELEASE 1993 We still like it! If you can manage to lift the hefty bottle, you'll find a nicely restrained wine with fresh grassy aromas, plenty of fruit with subtlety and appealing lemony straw-like semillon-style flavour. A deft blend of grape varieties that's good with seafood.

Lindemans Coonawarra Chardonnay

The new range of Lindemans Coonawarra whites is an impressive development, arguing a strong case for Coonawarra as a white wine region. The price will dip as low as $14.

CURRENT RELEASE 1994 A very attractive fruit-driven chardonnay style that's probably best drunk young for its delicious freshness. The nose holds melon and grassy fruit with a dusty aspect, and the flavour is intense, lively yet soft, fruity but dry. The oak is well controlled, leaving a peachy finish. Try it with a vegetarian meal.

QUALITY ★★★★
VALUE ★★★★
GRAPES chardonnay
REGION Coonawarra, SA
CELLAR 3
ALC./VOL. 12.5%
RRP $17.50 $

Lindemans Coonawarra Riesling

It doesn't seem long ago Lindemans announced an end to its Coonawarra rieslings. Things change. It's hard to say Coonawarra is only good for reds when whites of this quality surface.

CURRENT RELEASE 1994 The delicate but attractive, authentic riesling floral aromas of this wine build in the glass with airing. A fine, subtle riesling with impeccable balance, bell-clear varietal fruit and real finesse. Try an Alsatian onion tart.

QUALITY ★★★★½
VALUE ★★★★
GRAPES riesling
REGION Coonawarra, SA
CELLAR 5+
ALC./VOL. 11.5%
RRP $17.50 $

Lindemans Coonawarra Sauvignon Blanc

Having let the Padthaway range of whites slip down the hierarchy, Lindemans has released a new range of whites from Coonawarra as its premium white wines. Maker Greg Clayfield.

CURRENT RELEASE 1994 This lovely fresh sauvignon is all about immediate palate. The nose is shy and retiring with some light herbal grassy aromas, without obvious oak. The juicy fruit flavour is excellent and there are hints of tropical fruits. No great length of palate but it's a delicious drinking style. Try it with fresh goat's cheese.

QUALITY ★★★★
VALUE ★★★★
GRAPES sauvignon blanc
REGION Coonawarra, SA
CELLAR 1
ALC./VOL. 12.0%
RRP $17.50 $

Lindemans Hunter River Chablis

QUALITY 🍷🍷🍷🍷
VALUE ★★★½
GRAPES chardonnay, semillon
REGION Hunter Valley & Young, NSW
CELLAR 🍾 4
ALC./VOL. 11.0%
RRP $12.60 Ⓢ

Chablis, schmablis. The days are numbered for this appellation. It's not only moved away from being straight semillon, but there's non-Hunter grapes here, too.
CURRENT RELEASE 1993 *Bin 8275* An appealing cashew-nut and dusty herbal aroma opens into a suitably delicate and crisp, dry palate which has plenty of fruit and straw lanolin characters. Plenty of lemony acid should help it to age well. A general purpose seafood style.

Lindemans Hunter River Chardonnay Classic Release

QUALITY 🍷🍷🍷🍷🍷
VALUE ★★★★
GRAPES chardonnay 85%, verdelho 15%
REGION Hunter Valley, NSW
CELLAR 🍾 2
ALC./VOL. 11.0%
RRP $32.00

Lindemans' Classic Release program has the motto 'wines of excellence from outstanding vintages cellared until they near optimum maturity'. Maker Patrick Auld.
CURRENT RELEASE 1981 *Reserve Bin 5881* This has a very complex, mellow old Hunter white wine nose. It's more a Hunter than a chardonnay, with a toasted, smoked character. In the mouth it's very big and rich, a drought-year style, with a lemony flavour and a long dry finish. A true classic. Serve with lemon chicken.

Lindemans Hunter River Semillon Classic Release

QUALITY 🍷🍷🍷🍷🍷
VALUE ★★★★½
GRAPES semillon
REGION Hunter Valley, NSW
CELLAR 🍾 6+
ALC./VOL. 11.8%
RRP $34.00

The 1986 vintage was a top year for Hunter semillon, witness the Tyrrell's, Brokenwood and McWilliam's besides this.
Previous outstanding vintages: '68, '70, '79, '80
CURRENT RELEASE 1986 *Reserve Bin 6855* Every inch a classic, this. Incredibly fresh for its nine years, it has a light colour and a shy, straw-like nose. It comes into its own in the mouth, with intense, concentrated lemony flavour, crisp acid cut and a big finish. Really dances on the tongue. Try lemon sole.

Lindemans Hunter River White Burgundy

We cannot help but sigh, recalling the Hunter semillons of yesteryear, when we note that chardonnay is now the grape and the wine is no longer a solo Hunter act. Maker Pat Auld.

CURRENT RELEASE 1993 *Bin 8270* Lots of toasty vanilla oak on the nose is a real departure in style for this venerable label. There are stalky aromas and the palate holds peachy chardonnay and oak flavours in a broad, soft, ready-drinking style. Try it with vegetable tempura.

QUALITY ♟♟♟♝
VALUE ★★★½
GRAPES chardonnay
REGION Hunter Valley, Cowra & Mudgee, NSW
CELLAR 🍾 3
ALC./VOL. 12.0%
RRP $12.60 ⓢ

Lindemans Padthaway Botrytis Rhine Riesling

Lindemans held this wine back to release with some age to prove that Padthaway botrytis rieslings could develop well, building complexity. Maker Phillip John and team.

CURRENT RELEASE 1991 Very deep gold-amber colour reflects age, and the bouquet has complex aged toasty, fig-jam, vanilla and marmalade aromas with a buttery aspect. The palate is rich and chunky, smooth and very sweet, seductive and powerful. A little bit goes a long way. Try it with crème brûlée.

QUALITY ♟♟♟♟
VALUE ★★★★★
GRAPES riesling
REGION Padthaway, SA
CELLAR 🍾 2
ALC./VOL. 10.5%
RRP $11.60 (375ml) ⓢ

Lindemans Padthaway Chardonnay

QUALITY ▼▼▼▽
VALUE ★★★
GRAPES chardonnay
REGION Padthaway, SA
CELLAR 🍾 2
ALC./VOL. 13.5%
RRP $13.00 ⓢ

At one time this was the flagship chardonnay in the Lindemans and then the Southcorp fleet, but it's been relegated to a $10–13 slot. It's always been one of the oakier styles around.

CURRENT RELEASE 1993 A fairly straightforward wine that tries hard to be more than it is. Smoky-bacon and some peach characters open the act, airing to have a somewhat disappointingly monotone vanilla character. A pleasant wine with smoothness and drinkability. Try it with calamari.

QUALITY ▼▼▼▼
VALUE ★★★★
GRAPES chardonnay
REGION Padthaway, SA
CELLAR 🍾 3
ALC./VOL. 13.0%
RRP $13.30 ⓢ

CURRENT RELEASE 1994 The nose is all high-char oak, albeit attractive with its buttery, toasty, cedary aromas. There's butterscotch and peach on the palate and the fruit is well concentrated with plenty of impact. The finish is dry with some oak and alcohol astringency. Try it with turkey.

Lindemans Padthaway Verdelhao

QUALITY ▼▼▼▽
VALUE ★★★½
GRAPES verdelho 88%, chardonnay 12%
REGION Padthaway, SA
CELLAR 🍾 2
ALC./VOL. 13.0%
RRP $13.30 ⓢ

Lindemans doggedly sticks to its old-fashioned way of spelling this variety. The '94 is a welcome change of pace, without the assertive oak of the '93.

CURRENT RELEASE 1994 This has a fine nose of tropical/pineappley fruit and subtle oak. After a sweetish entry the palate is light, simple and fruity with fruit-salad flavours that pull up fairly quickly. What's there is attractive. Try it with chicken cooked with orange.

McWilliam's King Charles Mount Pleasant Chardonnay

Charles King was the first person to plant vines in what is now McWilliam's Mount Pleasant Vineyards. Maker Phillip Ryan.

CURRENT RELEASE 1993 The nose displays toasty oak plus hints of melon. The palate is rich with melon and citrus flavours, matched by some discreet oak on a dry finish. Serve it lightly chilled with a chicken pie.

QUALITY ♙♙♙♙
VALUE ★★★½
GRAPES chardonnay
REGION Hunter Valley, NSW
CELLAR 🍾 3
ALC./VOL. 13.0%
RRP $12.00 ⓢ

McWilliam's Mount Pleasant Chardonnay

Yet another label from the Mount Pleasant vineyard. This is a rather subdued affair in a dour blue.

CURRENT RELEASE 1992 Rather trendy oak (Vosges) dominates this style. The colour is a bright yellow-gold and the nose has oak and peach aromas. The palate is rich with a mouthfilling quality; peach and citrus are the main flavours, supported by the oak which makes for a dry and long finish. It should not be served too cold. Try it with a chicken pie.

QUALITY ♙♙♙♙
VALUE ★★★★
GRAPES chardonnay
REGION Hunter Valley, NSW
CELLAR 🍾 3
ALC./VOL. 12.5%
RRP $12.00

McWilliam's Mount Pleasant Elizabeth

'A taste of honey – a taste much sweeter than wine.' This is a wonderful style that has endured for decades. Long may it do so! Maker Phillip Ryan.

Previous outstanding vintages: '79, '82, '83, '86, '87

CURRENT RELEASE 1989 Back in the groove and still some of the best value on the market. Wonderful green-gold in colour and the nose has that hint of honey associated with the style. The palate is rich with mouthfilling texture and the flavours are many, including peach, lime and gooseberry. The finish shows soft acid. A modest chill and a warm quail salad is quite a thrill.

QUALITY ♙♙♙♙♙
VALUE ★★★★★
GRAPES semillon
REGION Hunter Valley, NSW
CELLAR 🍾 3
ALC./VOL. 12.0%
RRP $12.00 ⓢ

McWilliam's Rhine Riesling

QUALITY 🍷🍷🍷
VALUE ★★★
GRAPES riesling
REGION Hanwood, NSW
CELLAR 🍾 1
ALC./VOL. 11.5%
RRP $7.00

This wine signals yet another tier in the McWilliam's portfolio. At this level it is all about value for money.

CURRENT RELEASE 1994 A fresh, straightforward style that's easy to drink. The nose has fresh lime aromas that distinguishes the main flavour on a middleweight palate. There's soft acid that adds crispness to a gentle finish. Serve well chilled with scallops in a cream sauce.

Maglieri Ingleburne Estate Semillon

QUALITY 🍷🍷🍷🍷
VALUE ★★★½
GRAPES semillon
REGION McLaren Vale, SA
CELLAR 🍾 3
ALC./VOL. 12.9%
RRP $12.00

Established in 1972, this company made fame and fortune manufacturing spumante. These days it has a quality table wine component in its portfolio. Maker John Loxton.

CURRENT RELEASE 1994 An unwooded style that has plenty of rich flavour. The nose has some lanolin and gooseberry aromas and the palate is rich with gooseberry flavour and some firm acid. It can be served well chilled.

Marienberg Chardonnay

The original vineyard was established in 1966 by the Pridham family. It was sold to the Hill group in late 1991.

CURRENT RELEASE 1994 A fresh varietal style that has full-flavoured oak. The nose is peachy with a hint of sap. The palate continues the peach theme and this is followed by some smoky oak on a dry finish. It should not be overchilled. Serve it with a chicken pie.

QUALITY 🍷🍷🍷🍷
VALUE ★★★½
GRAPES chardonnay
REGION McLaren Vale, SA
CELLAR 🍾 3
ALC./VOL. 13.1%
RRP $14.00 ⓢ

Matthew Lang Colombard

This used to be the fighting brand for Lindemans, which became part of the Southcorp group. Matthew was a Melbourne wine merchant.

CURRENT RELEASE 1994 An attractive bit of everyday drinking and the bottle contains 5.9 standard drinks. The nose has distinct passionfruit aromas and the palate has a hint of sweetness plus tropical flavours. The finish is crisp and clean. Serve well chilled with calamari.

QUALITY 🍷🍷🍷🍷
VALUE ★★★½
GRAPES colombard, verdelho
REGION Mildura, Vic. & Hunter River, NSW
CELLAR 🍾
ALC./VOL. 10.0%
RRP $6.00

Matthew Lang Riesling

Matthew Lang is made at the Karadoc winery near Mildura. The proportions of this winery make it more akin to a refinery.

CURRENT RELEASE 1994 A straightforward commercial style that drinks well. The nose is floral with smoky undertones and the middleweight palate has lemon flavours on a crisp finish. Serve well chilled.

QUALITY 🍷🍷🍷
VALUE ★★★
GRAPES riesling
REGION Mildura, Vic.
CELLAR 🍾
ALC./VOL. 10.0%
RRP $6.00

Maxwell Chardonnay

QUALITY ♛♛♛♛
VALUE ★★★★
GRAPES chardonnay
REGION McLaren Vale, SA
CELLAR 🍷 3
ALC./VOL. 13.5%
RRP $13.50

Don't be fooled – behind the rather cutesie label lies a dynamic wine company. Maxwell was established in 1979 and produces over 4000 cases. Maker Mark Maxwell.

CURRENT RELEASE 1994 The nose is dominated by smoky oak which seems to foreshadow the palate. Not so, peach-flavoured fruit rises out of the fire, filling the mouth with flavour. Oak gets the last word, however, on a dry finish. Serve only slightly chilled with squid ink pasta and a seafood sauce.

Maxwell Sauvignon Blanc

QUALITY ♛♛♛♛
VALUE ★★★½
GRAPES sauvignon blanc
REGION McLaren Vale, SA
CELLAR 🍷 1
ALC./VOL. 12.5%
RRP $11.50

Sauvignon blanc shows considerable promise when grown in this region. It can make light, refreshing wines.

CURRENT RELEASE 1994 A very floral style that makes the most of the tropical fruit possibilities of the grape. The nose has passionfruit and pineapple that are again encountered on the palate. Fresh acid makes for a crisp finish. Serve well chilled with a leafy salad and lots of rocket.

Maxwell Semillon

QUALITY ♛♛♛♛
VALUE ★★★★
GRAPES semillon
REGION McLaren Vale, SA
CELLAR 🍷 4
ALC./VOL. 13.5%
RRP $9.95

This is the fourth release under this label and it is apparent a deliberate cellar style is evolving.

CURRENT RELEASE 1994 The nose is grassy and herbal with underlying fruit aromas. The palate show gooseberry and herb flavours and the finish offers fresh acid. It should develop well but it drinks quite nicely now. Try it with warm chicken salad and don't overchill.

Milburn Park Reserve Chardonnay

This is yet another label in the Alambie Wine Company portfolio. Maker Bob Shields.

CURRENT RELEASE 1993 The colour is a bright lemon yellow and the nose has very strong peach aromas. As could be expected, solid peach is encountered on the palate which does worthy combat with assertive oak on a lingering finish. Don't overchill, and serve with smoked cod in white sauce.

QUALITY ★★★★
VALUE ★★★★
CELLAR chardonnay
REGION Mildura, Vic.
CELLAR 3
ALC./VOL. 13.0%
RRP $12.00

CURRENT RELEASE 1994 The nose has a big butterscotch component as well as a hint of lanolin. The palate offers ripe peach flavour and a touch of tropical fruit. The finish shows a discreet use of oak. Don't overchill. It goes well with scallops in a light ginger sauce.

QUALITY ★★★★
VALUE ★★★★
GRAPES chardonnay
REGION Mildura, Vic.
CELLAR 2
ALC./VOL. 13.0%
RRP $13.00

Milburn Park Sauvignon Blanc

This is the top draw from the Alambie Wine Company, which uses advanced viticulture to minimise the effects of a hot climate, producing grapes that render authentic varietal flavour.

CURRENT RELEASE 1994 The nose is grassy with strong herbal overtones. The palate yields tropical fruit flavours with passionfruit to the fore, matched by crisp acid on a cleansing finish. The wine can be served well chilled with mussels poached in white wine.

QUALITY ★★★★
VALUE ★★★★
GRAPES sauvignon blanc
REGION Mildura, Vic.
CELLAR 2
ALC./VOL. 12.5%
RRP $11.00

Miramar Chardonnay

QUALITY 🍷🍷🍷🍷
VALUE ★★★★
GRAPES chardonnay
REGION Mudgee, NSW
CELLAR 🍾 3
ALC./VOL. 12.5%
RRP $14.80

Ian MacRae has quietly been making some of Mudgee's best wine since the '70s. He has 24 hectares of vineyard.

CURRENT RELEASE 1993 A big, full, upfront style of chardonnay with liberal toasty oak and lots of peach and pineapple flavours. A generous style but not without elegance. Drink now, with char-grilled octopus.

Miranda Rovalley Ridge Chardonnay

QUALITY 🍷🍷🍷🍷
VALUE ★★★★
GRAPES chardonnay
REGION Barossa, SA
CELLAR 🍾 2
ALC./VOL. 13.0%
RRP $14.00

The labelling is new and it goes a long way to dispel the confusion created by previous attempts. Miranda is a large winery in Griffith that purchased Rovalley in the Barossa. Maker Shayne Cunningham.

CURRENT RELEASE 1993 A developed style that has a bright green-gold colour. The nose has a heavy pawpaw aroma and the palate comes down on the peach side. The finish bristles with assertive oak. Serve lightly chilled.

Miranda Rovalley Ridge Rhine Riesling

QUALITY 🍷🍷🍷🍷
VALUE ★★★½
GRAPES riesling
REGION Barossa Valley, SA
CELLAR 🍾 1
ALC./VOL. 12.0%
RRP $12.00

Is that geographically correct? Can you have a ridge in a valley?

CURRENT RELEASE 1994 A straightforward style that makes appealing drinking. The nose is floral with lime and violet aromas. The palate offers lime and other citrus flavours matched by crisp acid on a clean dry finish. Serve well chilled with stir-fried chicken.

Mitchelton III Marsanne Viognier Roussanne

Varietally exotic (by Australian standards) this is a new generic from Mitchelton. It was conceived under the old management and hopefully it will prosper under the new (Mitchelton is now part of the Petaluma group). Maker Don Lewis.

CURRENT RELEASE 1994 Talk about the dance of the seven veils – the more you drink the more you see. The nose is perfumed with jasmine and heather aromas and the chewy palate is full with a creamy texture, thanks to barrel fermentation. Underneath the nuttiness there are tropical fruit and gooseberry flavours, and the finish shows well-integrated oak. It's splendid when lightly chilled and served with an authentic kedgeree.

QUALITY 🍷🍷🍷🍷🍷
VALUE ★★★★★
GRAPES marsanne, viognier, roussanne
REGION Goulburn Valley, Vic.
CELLAR 🍾 4
ALC./VOL. 12.5%
RRP $16.85

Best White Blend

Mitchelton Reserve Marsanne

The reserve label means the wine has been held back for bottle-ageing.

Previous outstanding vintages: '80, '82, '84, '86, '88, '90, '91

CURRENT RELEASE 1992 This has settled down since last year but the wood still calls the tune. The chippy quality has been subdued and replaced by an aniseed character. There are honeyed overtones on the nose and the honey texture can also be found on the palate. Wood still dominates the finish and the wine looks rather mean when it's too cold. Try it with Singapore noodles.

QUALITY 🍷🍷🍷🍷
VALUE ★★★½
GRAPES marsanne
REGION Goulburn Valley, Vic.
CELLAR 🍾 4
ALC./VOL. 13.3%
RRP $17.00

Moondah Brook Chardonnay

QUALITY 🍷🍷🍷🍷
VALUE ★★★★
GRAPES chardonnay
REGION Gingin, WA
CELLAR 🍾 3
ALC./VOL. 13.0%
RRP $13.50

Moondah Brook is a real babbler, chock full of water cress. Fresh bread, cress and a bottle of wine on the banks of the Moondah are a real treat.

CURRENT RELEASE 1994 This wine won a gong in last year's guide. It remains a very fine example of value for money. The nose has melon and tropical fruit aromas plus a hint of talcum powder. The palate is nutty with some stewed peach flavours, and drying oak fills out the finish. It goes well with roast turkey.

Moondah Brook Chenin Blanc

QUALITY 🍷🍷🍷🍷
VALUE ★★★★
GRAPES chenin blanc
REGION Gingin, WA
CELLAR 🍾 2
ALC./VOL. 12.5%
RRP $12.00

Chenin blanc is an interesting variety that makes a flavoursome wine. Being out of fashion it usually means the price is right.

CURRENT RELEASE 1994 The nose is sappy with hints of tart green fruit aromas. The palate is full flavoured with fresh green herb characters and hints of apple. The finish shows some crisp acid. Serve well chilled with a seafood cocktail.

Moondah Brook Verdelho

QUALITY 🍷🍷🍷🍷
VALUE ★★★½
GRAPES verdelho
REGION Gingin, WA
CELLAR 🍾 3
ALC./VOL. 12.5%
RRP $12.00

This is a madeira grape that Australian winemakers have press-ganged into white wine service. Interestingly, in the Hunter Valley Lindemans spell it 'verdelhao'.

CURRENT RELEASE 1994 This is a bit like stiletto heels – the next minute it'll be out of fashion. Face it, there is nothing sexy about this variety but it is a 'nice' drink. The nose is sappy with a hint of herbs. The palate has tropical fruit flavours, including pineapple and passionfruit with crisp acid on the finish. Chill it and serve it with a chicken kiev.

Moorilla Estate Chardonnay

Big drama in the Moorilla camp. A major management upheaval has resulted in the overthrow of Julian Alcorso.
CURRENT RELEASE 1994 A delicious, fruit-driven cool-climate wine which makes you wonder why some winemakers persist in overwooding chardonnay. The fruit is of the melon, gooseberry, tropical persuasion with a light overtone of butter and bacon from malolactic fermentation. Very fresh and light, but also intense and long. It dances on the tongue. Take it to a vego restaurant.

QUALITY 🍷🍷🍷🍷🍷
VALUE ★★★★½
GRAPES chardonnay
REGION various, Tas.
CELLAR 🍾 7+
ALC./VOL. 13.0%
RRP $33.20

Moorilla Estate Riesling

Is this the dearest current-release Aussie riesling on the market? Quite possibly, but at least it delivers. Maker Julian Alcorso.
CURRENT RELEASE 1994 Riesling is Tasmania's most underrated wine, and this is a beauty in the fine, delicate, understated style the state does so well. Very aromatic, with apple, pear and flowery scents, it has a refined flavour with lively acid and great balance. Try it with buttery scallops.

QUALITY 🍷🍷🍷🍷
VALUE ★★★½
GRAPES riesling
REGION various, Tas.
CELLAR 🍾 7+
ALC./VOL. 12.0%
RRP $26.70

Mornington Vineyards Chardonnay

Founded in 1988 and not open to the public, this is a small vineyard that produces around 800 cases per annum. Maker Tod Dexter (consultant).
CURRENT RELEASE 1993 Big mutha! This is a full-frontal style with plenty of grunt. The nose has a mix of citrus, peach and smoky oak. The palate shows rich developed peach flavour matched by some assertive French oak which contributes a toasty character. The wine should be served near room temperature.

QUALITY 🍷🍷🍷🍷
VALUE ★★★★
GRAPES chardonnay
REGION Mornington Peninsula, Vic.
CELLAR 🍾 4
ALC./VOL. 14.0%
RRP $19.00

Mount Avoca Sauvignon Blanc

QUALITY ♥♥♥♥
VALUE ★★★★
GRAPES sauvignon blanc
REGION Pyrenees, Vic.
CELLAR 🍾 4
ALC./VOL. 12.5%
RRP $12.80

This winery was established in 1978 and is currently (in conjunction with CSIRO) experimenting with the use of irrigation – a necessary facility in this fairly dry area.

CURRENT RELEASE 1994 A solid wine that starts like a New Zealand model but ends like a Californian. The nose is pungent with tinned-pea, tomato-bush and herbal aromas. In contrast the palate is dominated by tropical fruit flavours with the accent on pineapple. The finish is crisp and almost tart. Serve well chilled with poached mussels.

Mount Bold Chardonnay

QUALITY ♥♥♥♥♥
VALUE ★★★★½
GRAPES chardonnay
REGION McLaren Vale, SA
CELLAR 🍾 4
ALC./VOL. 13.5%
RRP $15.75

This is the top of the line for Maxwells wines in McLaren Vale. Evidently Mount Bold is a vineyard site as well as a Christmas Tree farm – hence the label. The wines can be found in restaurants and at cellar door. Maker Mark Maxwell.

CURRENT RELEASE 1993 A very polished wine that pulls no punches but still retains finesse. The colour is a bright yellow-gold and the nose has peach and ripe tropical fruit aromas. The palate is rich with intense peach and mango flavour attended by a well-tuned finish that adds balance and mouth-cleansing properties. Don't overchill, then serve with a sushi of Atlantic salmon.

Mount Chalambar Four Sisters Chardonnay

Mount Chalambar is a small vineyard in western Victoria. Proprietor Trevor Mast is also the winemaker at Mount Langi Ghiran.

CURRENT RELEASE 1994 This is a fruit-driven style that shows plenty of varietal character. The nose has strong peach aromas and this is the main flavour on an ample palate. Crisp acid completes the finish. Serve well chilled with a spaghetti marinara.

QUALITY 🍷🍷🍷🍷
VALUE ★★★★
GRAPES chardonnay
REGION Ararat, Vic.
CELLAR 🍾 4
ALC./VOL. 13.0%
RRP $13.85

Mount Chalambar Four Sisters Riesling

Trevor and Sandy Mast have four daughters, hence this label (they should talk to the highly productive Barry family at Clare ...). Maker Trevor Mast.

CURRENT RELEASE 1994 An intense style with lots of varietal character. The nose has strong lime aromas and the palate is crisp with a hint of sweetness and lime. The finish is crisp, showing fresh acid. Serve well chilled with a seafood mousse.

QUALITY 🍷🍷🍷🍷
VALUE ★★★★
GRAPES riesling
REGION Ararat, Vic.
CELLAR 🍾 3
ALC./VOL. 13.0%
RRP $11.95

Mount Horrocks Cordon Cut

This is an interesting viticultural technique which has the vine arms (cordons) severed when the grapes are ripe. The fruit is left on the vines to dehydrate and concentrate the sugar.

CURRENT RELEASE 1994 A fresh, sweet style that manages to capture the essence of the variety. The nose shows aromatic lime; the lime theme is picked up on the sweet palate. Crisp acid evens out a fresh finish. The freshness permits a good chill; serve with smoked salmon.

QUALITY 🍷🍷🍷🍷
VALUE ★★★★
GRAPES riesling
REGION Clare Valley, SA
CELLAR 🍾 4
ALC./VOL. 11.0%
RRP $11.00

Mount Horrocks Riesling

QUALITY ????
VALUE ★★★★
GRAPES riesling
REGION Clare Valley, SA
CELLAR 🍾 4
ALC./VOL. 12.5%
RRP $13.00

The vineyard was established in 1982 and these days the annual production is around 3500 cases. Maker Jeffrey Grosset (contract).

CURRENT RELEASE 1994 Good ol' Watervale riesling. It's aromatic and limey on the nose. The palate is keen with a zesty lime and associated citrus flavours, plus a hint of biscuit. The finish shows zingy acid. It should be served well chilled with oysters and caviar.

Mount Horrocks Wood-Aged Semillon

QUALITY ????
VALUE ★★★½
GRAPES semillon
REGION Clare Valley, SA
CELLAR ➞ 2–6
ALC./VOL. 12.5%
RRP $14.00

This variety is not fully recognised in the Clare district but it can produce some spectacular results. A good cellar bet.

CURRENT RELEASE 1994 The nose offers a mix of lime, citrus and straw aromas. The palate is mouthfilling with gooseberry fruit and hints of lemon. The oak makes the finish dry and toasty. A youthful style that should be served near room temperature with smoked chicken.

Mount Hurtle Chardonnay

QUALITY ????
VALUE ★★★½
GRAPES chardonnay
REGION McLaren Vale 45%, Coonawarra 22%, SA & Goulburn Valley 8%, Mildura 25%, Vic.
CELLAR 🍾 4
ALC./VOL. 13.0%
RRP $11.50

Mount Hurtle is a great restoration success story. It is now located in suburban Adelaide but in the '40s it was a rural winery with a considerable production. These days it is the HQ for Geoffrey Lewis Merrill. Maker Goe De Fabio.

CURRENT RELEASE 1994 A toasty oak-driven style that gives the impression it needs more time in the cellar. The nose is woody and the palate has some grapefruit and peach flavours. Wood fills out the finish. The label says it should be served at 14°C, which seems spot on. Serve it with lightly curried Tommy Ruffs.

Mount Hurtle Sauvignon Blanc

The winery was originally built in 1897 and was rebuilt in 1987. It is a charming site much loved as a wedding venue for besotted wine dots.

CURRENT RELEASE 1994 A grassy and elegant nose reveals the variety. You'll find gooseberry and tropical fruit (particularly passionfruit) on the palate, all of which are supported by crisp acid on a clean dry finish. Serve well chilled with oysters in a light ginger sauce.

QUALITY ♛♛♛♛
VALUE ★★★★
GRAPES sauvignon blanc
REGION McLaren Vale 44%, SA & Goulburn Valley 25%, Mildura 31% Vic.
CELLAR 🍾 2
ALC./VOL. 12.0%
RRP $11.50

Mount Langi Ghiran Riesling

This vineyard was established in 1969 by the Fratin Brothers. Since then it has changed hands and taken an organic bent. Maker Trevor Mast.

CURRENT RELEASE 1994 The nose is spicy with hints of lime, the palate continues the intensity with keen lime flavours followed by snappin' fresh acid that adds a tingling sensation. It drinks well now and should be served well chilled. Try it with salty prawns.

QUALITY ♛♛♛♛
VALUE ★★★★
GRAPES riesling
REGION Grampians, Vic.
CELLAR 🍾 4
ALC./VOL. 12.5%
RRP $11.00

Mount Prior Chardonnay

This winery was originally founded in 1860 and was re-established in 1989. The annual production is in the order of 9000 cases.

CURRENT RELEASE 1990 The colour is a bright yellow-gold and the nose has a strong banana and tropical fruit aroma. The palate offers tropical fruit and developed peach flavours on an integrated finish. Serve medium chilled with smoked chicken.

QUALITY ♛♛♛♛
VALUE ★★★½
GRAPES chardonnay
REGION Rutherglen, Vic.
CELLAR 🍾 2
ALC./VOL. 13.4%
RRP $12.50

Mount Prior Dry White Wine

QUALITY ♟♟♟
VALUE ★★★
GRAPES chenin blanc
REGION Rutherglen, Vic.
CELLAR 🍾 1
ALC./VOL. 11.0%
RRP $ 9.90

An honest label description: 'Dry White Wine', which is also an indication of the marketing cachet of the variety involved. Maker Garry Wall.
CURRENT RELEASE 1994 The colour is pale straw and the nose has a strong geranium aroma. The palate has apple and herb flavours with a crisp, dry finish. Serve well chilled with a warm salad of chicken.

Murrindindi Chardonnay

QUALITY ♟♟♟♟♟
VALUE ★★★★★
GRAPES chardonnay
REGION Murrindindi, Vic.
CELLAR 🍾 6
ALC./VOL. 13.0%
RRP $20.00

Greatly encouraged by the sale of their wines and grapes, the Cuthbertson family are expanding the vineyard into the major league. At this stage the plan is to sell the grapes rather than drastically increase the production. Made on contract at Tarrawarra winery.
Previous outstanding vintages: '92, '93
CURRENT RELEASE 1994 Very stylish and enjoyable right to the last drop; this is a high-tensile style with great complexity. The nose has citrus and peach aromas and the palate offers many flavours: peach, citrus, aniseed and cashew interwoven with wood that provides a stylish and long finish. Don't serve too cold. Try it with chicken cacciatore.

Ninth Island Chardonnay

QUALITY ♟♟♟
VALUE ★★½
GRAPES chardonnay
REGION Pipers Brook, Tas.
CELLAR 🍾 2
ALC./VOL. 13.0%
RRP $17.70

You know you're on a winner when your second-string chardonnay pulls $17.70 a bottle ... Maker Andrew Pirie.
CURRENT RELEASE 1994 This unwooded style has a light, herbaceous peachy melony flavour and quite searing acidity. The finish chops off quickly but the immediate palate is very pleasant, especially when you team that acid with food. Try it with white fish meunière.

Normans Chais Clarendon Chardonnay

Chais is a French word meaning winery or cellar. Chais Clarendon is the premium range of wines from Normans' Clarendon winery. This one is made from Adelaide Hills fruit. Maker Brian Light.

CURRENT RELEASE 1994 This is a restrained style for Normans, with a light yellow colour and shy, slightly green/herbaceous nose. It's crisp and bracing to drink; the acid enlivening the palate, which is crisp and somewhat sauvignon blanc-like. A nice wine if not a definitive chardonnay. A partner for cold chicken and salads.

QUALITY 🍷🍷🍷🍷
VALUE ★★★
GRAPES chardonnay
REGION Adelaide Hills, SA
CELLAR 🍾 3+
ALC./VOL. 13.0%
RRP $24.00

Oakland Semillon Chardonnay

This is the second label for Grant Burge and designed to give value for money. Maker Grant Burge.

CURRENT RELEASE 1994 The colour is a bright green-gold and there is evidence of wood on the nose. The palate is quite rich with peach and tropical flavours. The finish is dominated by savoury oak. Serve lightly chilled with a chicken pie.

QUALITY 🍷🍷🍷🍷
VALUE ★★★★
GRAPES semillon 70%, chardonnay 30%
REGION Barossa Valley, SA
CELLAR 🍾 1
ALC./VOL. 13.0%
RRP $10.00

Oakland Semillon Sauvignon Blanc

This blend is popular with winemakers and presumably with the public too. Quite frequently it results in a wine that is neither fish nor fowl.

CURRENT RELEASE 1994 This is a fresh style that is easy to drink. The nose is dominated by sauvignon blanc smells, the palate by attractive tropical fruit and gooseberry flavours. The finish offers plenty of crisp acid. Serve well chilled with an asparagus quiche.

QUALITY 🍷🍷🍷🍷
VALUE ★★★★
GRAPES sauvignon blanc 50%, semillon 50%
REGION Barossa Valley, SA
CELLAR 🍾 1
ALC./VOL. 12.5%
RRP $10.00

Oakridge Estate Chardonnay

QUALITY 🍷🍷🍷🍷
VALUE ★★★★
GRAPES chardonnay
REGION Yarra Valley, Vic.
CELLAR 🍾 4
ALC./VOL. 13.5%
RRP $16.00

Oakridge was established in 1982 by the Zitzlaff family. The annual production is 2000 cases. Maker Michael Zitzlaff.

CURRENT RELEASE 1994 A bold style with lots of brio. The nose has strong wood aromas plus peach and citrus smells. The palate has peach and grapefruit flavours mingled with bright new oak on a firm finish. It should not be served too cold; try it with Thai-style prawns.

Olsen Wines Chardonnay Semillon Personal Reserve

QUALITY 🍷🍷🍷
VALUE ★★★
GRAPES chardonnay, semillon
REGION King Valley, Vic.
CELLAR 🍾 2
ALC./VOL. 13.0%
RRP $12.00

Who ever wrote and designed the label shouldn't give up their day job. Olsen wines are based in Hawthorn, Victoria.

CURRENT RELEASE 1994 The nose has tinned-pea and wood aromas. The palate is quite rich with a hint of sweetness and plenty of wood. Wood drives the finish relentlessly. It should not be served too cold; try it with a seafood cocktail.

Orlando Jacob's Creek Chardonnay

QUALITY 🍷🍷🍷
VALUE ★★★
GRAPES chardonnay
REGION South-east Australia
CELLAR 🍾 1
ALC./VOL. 12.5%
RRP $7.90 ⓢ

Jacob was the man who surveyed the Barossa Valley. In this case, thanks to demand, the fruit is sourced from all over.

CURRENT RELEASE 1994 This is an honest style with obvious varietal character. There is a strong peach aroma on the nose, while the palate is straightforward with a dominant peach flavour followed by a toasty finish. Try it lightly chilled with risotto.

Palmers Chardonnay

The main label is a deep-etched vine leaf, which makes for an arresting, if slightly garish, package. CURRENT RELEASE 1994 This is a lesson in how high-toast oak can dominate a wine. The effect is not disagreeable as long as you like that flavour. It has a charry, burnt-toasty effect which seems to simplify the taste. Get those tweezers out . . .

QUALITY ♥♥♥
VALUE ★★½
GRAPES chardonnay
REGION Margaret River, WA
CELLAR 🍾 2
ALC./VOL. 13.0%
RRP $21.75

Paradise Enough Chardonnay

Are the small vineyards from Victoria the products of reformed hippies? If you go by the names, that's a reasonable assumption.
CURRENT RELEASE 1994 A very stylish wine with lots of complexity. The nose is a mix of nuts, almonds, grapefruit and peach. The palate is chewy and well structured. The main flavour is citrus attended by cashew, fig and melon. The finish shows plenty of style with well-defined oak and high acid. A bit of time in the bottle should pay dividends. Try it with scallops coated in almonds.

QUALITY ♥♥♥♥♥
VALUE ★★★★★
GRAPES chardonnay
REGION Gippsland, Vic.
CELLAR 🍾 6
ALC./VOL. 13.1%
RRP $19.95

Pattersons Chardonnay

A small vineyard run as a sideline by school teachers, Pattersons came right out of left field to win two trophies with its '91 chardonnay at the Mount Barker Wine Show in 1992.
CURRENT RELEASE 1992 Age has helped fill out this wine. It has a deep yellow colour and big honey, butterscotch, oak and burnt-toast bottle-aged bouquet. It fills the mouth with rich, complex flavour and there's plenty happening on the mid-palate. Try it with char-grilled lobster.

QUALITY ♥♥♥♥
VALUE ★★★½
GRAPES chardonnay
REGION Mount Barker, WA
CELLAR 🍾 2
ALC./VOL. 13.0%
RRP $22.00

Paul Conti Late Picked Frontignac

QUALITY 🍷🍷🍷🍷🍷
VALUE ★★★★
GRAPES white frontignac
REGION South-west coastal, WA
CELLAR 🍾
ALC./VOL. 11.3%
RRP $13.70

The Conti Fronti is something of a legend way out west. Makers Paul and Jason Conti.
CURRENT RELEASE 1994 Wonderful fragrance of hi-fi muscat almost knocks you over. Grapey tropical/lychee fruit is here in abundance, lustily matched by generous sweetness. It's slightly fizzy from bottling CO_2, but that's no problem. This is an exemplary fronti that will lay 'em in the aisles.

Paulett's Polish Hill River Riesling

QUALITY 🍷🍷🍷🍷🍷
VALUE ★★★★★
GRAPES riesling
REGION Clare Valley, SA
CELLAR 🍾 9
ALC./VOL. 11.5%
RRP $12.90

Neil Paulett is active in the local winemakers' association. His hilltop winery has one of the most spectacular views in the district.
CURRENT RELEASE 1994 An impressive, slow-ageing youngster. This has a light hue and a delicate, youthfully slatey, minerally riesling aroma. Intense and fresh in the mouth, it has tangy acid, a crisp limey finish and marvellous balance. A top '94. Try it with whiting.

QUALITY 🍷🍷🍷🍷🍷
VALUE ★★★★★
GRAPES riesling
REGION Clare Valley, SA
CELLAR 🍾 5
ALC./VOL. 11.5%
RRP $12.90

Best Riesling

CURRENT RELEASE 1995 Very young and sassy with a strong lime aroma on the nose. The quintessence of a Clare riesling; they don't come much better than this. The palate has lime and other citrus flavours tuned to crisp acid on a long, lingering finish. It can be served well chilled with Coffin Bay scallops and a light ginger sauce.

Paulett's Polish Hill River Sauvignon Blanc

If there was an award for the best cellar-door view, this place would win hands down. It is spectacular yet very soothing. Maker Neil Paulett.

CURRENT RELEASE 1995 Pungent and focused, this is all about varietal character. There are strong tropical fruit characters on the nose plus a hint of green pea. The palate has passionfruit, lime and pawpaw flavours which are graced by some crisp acid on a lingering finish. It can be served well chilled with crispy fried noodles and shredded pork.

QUALITY ♛♛♛♛
VALUE ★★★★
GRAPES sauvignon blanc
REGION Clare Valley, SA
CELLAR 🍷 2
ALC./VOL. 12.5%
RRP $13.50

Pendarves Sauvignon Blanc Semillon

Pendarves Estate is the 22-hectare vineyard of noted Sydney GP Phil Norrie. The wines are made at Tamburlaine by Greg Silkman.

CURRENT RELEASE 1994 A very delicate white wine, showing fresh doughy aromas but lacking a little varietal character. The taste is straightforward and light, with pleasant grassy, lemony flavours and a soft finish. Try it with caesar salad.

QUALITY ♛♛♛
VALUE ★★★
GRAPES sauvignon blanc, semillon
REGION Hunter Valley, NSW
CELLAR 🍷 1
ALC./VOL. 12.5%
RRP $15.00

Pendarves Verdelho

The varietal character of verdelho is pretty difficult to pin down. They all seem to taste different. As a youngster, this one tastes remarkably like riesling. Maker Greg Silkman.

CURRENT RELEASE 1994 A delicate powderpuff floral aroma greets the nostrils and the flavour is lively, well balanced and has a trace of sweetness. It is clean and well made but should probably be drunk young for best effect. Try it with white-fleshed fish.

QUALITY ♛♛♛♛
VALUE ★★★½
GRAPES verdelho
REGION Hunter Valley, NSW
CELLAR 🍷 1
ALC./VOL. 13.0%
RRP $15.00

Penfolds Barrel Fermented Semillon

QUALITY 🍷🍷🍷🍷🍷
VALUE ★★★★
GRAPES semillon
REGION Clare & Barossa Valleys, McLaren Vale, SA
CELLAR 🍷 4+
ALC./VOL. 13.5%
RRP $17.00 Ⓢ

Penfolds is very much a wood-orientated company, and winemaker John Duval gets to stretch out with this semillon which is, interestingly, the top-priced Penfold white.
Previous outstanding vintages: '93

CURRENT RELEASE 1994 Oak-driven it may be, but delicious it is too. Cedar, toast and vanilla reflect liberal use of smart French oak, while grassy semillon aromas hover just below the surface. A rich, properly dry white with length, concentration and balance. Despite being full-bodied it stays lively on its feet. Try buttery char-grilled lobster.

Penfolds Chardonnay

QUALITY 🍷🍷🍷🍷
VALUE ★★★½
GRAPES chardonnay
REGION Clare Valley Adelaide Hills & McLaren Vale, SA
CELLAR 🍷 2
ALC./VOL. 13.0%
RRP $12.50 Ⓢ

Penfolds are known as masters of oak maturation, but their white wines – and some of the reds – are often excessively oaky when young. Oddly enough, a lot of Australians seem to like their chardonnay planky.

CURRENT RELEASE 1993 This is a fairly straight-up-and-down wine which is dominated by bottle-age and toasty oak characters. The nose is broad and figgy and there's a herbal flavour throughout. There's plenty of flavour and length. A generous style to drink with roast chicken.

QUALITY 🍷🍷🍷🍷
VALUE ★★★½
GRAPES chardonnay
REGION Adelaide Hills; Clare, Eden & Barossa Valleys, McLaren Vale, SA
CELLAR 🍷 4
ALC./VOL. 13.0%
RRP $12.50 Ⓢ

CURRENT RELEASE 1994 A wood-driven style, as we've come to expect from this maker, with pleasing intensity and dimensions. The dominant aromas and flavours are toasty, cedary French oak-derived, and the afterpalate is dry and slightly austere. Try smoked salmon.

Penfolds Clare Estate Chardonnay

Penfolds has 150 hectares of vines planted on its Clare property, on fertile red-brown soils on the south-eastern side of the valley in the Polish Hill River sub-region.

CURRENT RELEASE 1994 The nose is shy to begin with, then unfolds slightly gamey high-toast oak aromas over herbal, nettley fruit. The palate is a little hollow and the flavour zooms in on the front of the palate. Try it with a seafood terrine.

QUALITY 🍷🍷🍷
VALUE ★★★
GRAPES chardonnay
REGION Clare Valley, SA
CELLAR 🍾 2
ALC./VOL. 13.0%
RRP $12.50 ⑤

Penfolds Koonunga Hill Chardonnay

Koonunga Hill is the name of a Penfolds vineyard in the far north of the Barossa, but very little of this wine is likely to come from there. The company blurb cites seven major SA wine regions.

CURRENT RELEASE 1994 This is a very pleasing white and excellent value for money. It's lightly wooded, allowing the cashew and melon fruit flavours full expression. It's not bone dry, but there is fine balance with the mouthfilling flavour. A general purpose everyday white wine.

QUALITY 🍷🍷🍷🍷
VALUE ★★★★½
GRAPES chardonnay
REGION 'dryland' regions of SA
CELLAR 🍾 1
ALC./VOL. 12.5%
RRP $10.40 ⑤

Penley Estate Chardonnay

Proprietor and winemaker Kym Tolley feels the tug of destiny strongly, if the spiel on the back label is any guide.

CURRENT RELEASE 1993 Starting to show distinct aged characters now, this chardonnay is full yellow in hue with developed cedary and bottle-age nose that recalls fig, pawpaw and pineapple. It has liberal oak and a slight mid-palate hardness, but it's ready to drink up now. Try pan-fried veal.

QUALITY 🍷🍷🍷
VALUE ★★★
GRAPES chardonnay
REGION 60% Coonawarra, 40% McLaren Vale, SA
CELLAR 🍾 1
ALC./VOL. 14.0%
RRP $17.80

Petaluma Chardonnay

QUALITY ♛♛♛♛
VALUE ★★★★
GRAPES chardonnay
REGION Adelaide Hills, SA
CELLAR 🍾 2–5+
ALC./VOL. 13.0%
RRP $31.40

Brian Croser crafts his chardonnays to last. The corollary is that they develop slowly and don't aim to immediately charm your socks off with up-front allure.

Previous outstanding vintages: '89, '90, '91, '92

CURRENT RELEASE 1993 This is just a babe in nappies and needs a year or two to reveal its true potential. The concentration of its pear-like fruit is there and its finesse is impressive, although the oak sits slightly apart and needs patience to fully integrate. It'll be good with seafood paëlla when it does.

Petaluma Riesling

QUALITY ♛♛♛♛♛
VALUE ★★★★½
GRAPES riesling
REGION Clare Valley, SA
CELLAR 🍾 5+
ALC./VOL. 12.5%
RRP $18.50

Grown on Petaluma's elevated Hanlin Hill vineyard, this is what Brian Croser calls the traditional Australian dry late-picked style. In other words, the grapes were ripe compared to places like Germany and Austria.

Previous outstanding vintages: '80, '84, '87, '90, '92, '93

CURRENT RELEASE 1994 This is slightly shy in the aroma department but makes up for it in the mouth. Lovely big, full, flowery riesling flavour – clean, dry and as polished as a Clapton blues lick. The soft fruit fills the mouth and trails off in an extended finish, leaving the mouth fresh. Superb with flathead.

Peter Lehmann Barossa–Eden Valley Rhine Riesling

This is SA riesling as God meant it to be, without the steroids; ie. none of that oily enzyme-treated character.
Previous outstanding vintages: '93
CURRENT RELEASE 1994 A bone-dry, rock-solid style which should age like a charm. The nose is all fresh lifted limey, minerally aromatics, and there is very lively acid on the tongue. Crisp, tart and tangy, it's a refreshing hot-weather drink and goes well with any seafood.

QUALITY ♛♛♛♛
VALUE ★★★½
GRAPES riesling
REGION Eden Valley 60%, Barossa Valley 40%, SA
CELLAR 🍾 10+
ALC./VOL. 11.5%
RRP $10.45 ⓢ

Peter Lehmann Cellar Collection Chardonnay

Cellar Collection is a premium series of wines that have either been cellared by the winery or are recommended for further cellaring. This one, from the Stonewell sub-region, is fully mature now.
CURRENT RELEASE 1992 A forward developed chardonnay with deep buttercup-yellow colour and a broad, toasty bouquet. It's an old-fashioned style that's a bit of a dinosaur now, coming across with stacks of flavour but not a lot of finesse. A good match for chicken Maryland.

QUALITY ♛♛♛
VALUE ★★★
GRAPES chardonnay
REGION Barossa Valley, SA
CELLAR 🍾 1
ALC./VOL. 12.5%
RRP $19.00

Peter Lehmann Cellar Collection Rhine Riesling

Lehmann and his winemaker Andrew Wigan believe in making a bone-dry, traditional style of riesling from early-harvested grapes. They tend to age well.
Previous outstanding vintages: '91
CURRENT RELEASE 1990 This has a full yellow colour and a toasty, developed nose with a character known as 'kerosene'. There's honey and cloves too, and the taste is dry, minerally/flinty and verges on the austere, but it makes a superb food wine. Drink with grilled whiting and lemon.

QUALITY ♛♛♛♛
VALUE ★★★★
GRAPES riesling
REGION Eden Valley, SA
CELLAR 🍾 5+
ALC./VOL. 10.0%
RRP $15.50 ⓢ

Peter Lehmann Semillon

QUALITY ★★★★½
VALUE ★★★★★
GRAPES semillon
REGION Barossa Valley, SA
CELLAR 🍷 5+
ALC./VOL. 12.5%
RRP $10.45 Ⓢ

Thirty per cent of this has been barrel-fermented, but the wood doesn't show. Like all Lehmann dry whites, it's truly dry (and good with food), as opposed to the ubiquitous sugar-boosted styles. Previous outstanding vintages: '92, '93

CURRENT RELEASE 1994 This smells of lemons and lanolin, as opposed to the grassy style of some other regions. The taste is fruity yet dry, refined yet not without richness. It has stacks of flavour and is fresh and lively, with a lingering finish. Try it chilled with cold seafood salad.

Pierro Chardonnay

QUALITY ★★★★½
VALUE ★★★★
GRAPES chardonnay
REGION Margaret River, WA
CELLAR 🍷 1–5+
ALC./VOL. 14.0%
RRP $32.00

From this pocket-hankie sized vineyard comes one of Australia's best chardonnays. It's not always easy to track down, though. Trivia buffs will note that winemaker Mike Peterkin is married to Shelley, one of the daughters Cullen. Previous outstanding vintages: '90, '91, '92

CURRENT RELEASE 1993 A seriously rich, complex chardonnay which is fine now but will be better in a year. It's driven by toasty, nutty barrel-ferment/oak characters at present, with very good depth and length. The finish is pleasingly dry and savoury. Good with any spit-roasted poultry.

Pierro Semillon Sauvignon Blanc LTC

QUALITY ★★★½
VALUE ★★★
GRAPES semillon, sauvignon blanc, chardonnay
REGION Margaret River, WA
CELLAR 🍷 3+
ALC./VOL. 12.5%
RRP $17.00

Pierro wines run to just 4000 cases a year off Mike Peterkin's small ten-hectare vineyard on Caves Road, Willyabrup (Margaret River). Previous outstanding vintages: '91, '92, '93

CURRENT RELEASE 1994 The '94 seems less aromatic than recent vintages, with a candy-like fruit aspect and plenty of character. It is soft with a trace of sweetness filling out the palate, firming up on the finish. Good with cold meats and salads.

Pipers Brook Vineyards Chardonnay

Despite marked swings in style from year to year, this vineyard has crafted an enviable reputation for chardonnay, and the troops queue up to buy it. Maker Andrew Pirie.

Previous outstanding vintages: '84, '86, '90, '91, '92

CURRENT RELEASE 1993 This is developing in a curious direction, building attractive smoky and honey aspects to the peachy, slightly herbaceous fruit. There is some evidence of botrytis emerging with a slightly sweet-sour effect, but it has loads of character. Certainly more up-front than some recent issues. Experiment with antipasto here.

QUALITY ♛♛♛♛
VALUE ★★★½
GRAPES chardonnay
REGION Pipers Brook, Tas.
CELLAR 🍾 3+
ALC./VOL. 12.8%
RRP $28.00

CURRENT RELEASE 1994 A typically restrained cool dude from the wilds of Tassie. The nose has honey, herbaceous aromas and the taste is lively, with fruit sweetness and acid competing in a tangy structure which is proudly cool-grown. Despite all that alcohol it's a subtle wine with lightly handled oak. Should build complexity with age. Try it with scallops.

QUALITY ♛♛♛♛
VALUE ★★★★
GRAPES chardonnay
REGION Pipers Brook, Tas.
CELLAR 🍾 7
ALC./VOL. 13.9%
RRP $28.20

Pipers Brook Vineyards Riesling

Tasmania is an underrated place to grow riesling. It generally does much better than, say, cabernet – so why don't we see more of it?

Previous outstanding vintages: '82, '84, '85, '90, '91, '92, '93

CURRENT RELEASE 1994 Andrew Pirie points to the alcohol and says some of his strongest rieslings have aged best. Oddly, it still has that herbaceous aspect despite the obvious ripeness. Quite a full colour; developing toasty and herbal aromas; grassy flavour in a full, generous palate that ends firm and tart. This could handle chicken.

QUALITY ♛♛♛♛
VALUE ★★★
GRAPES riesling
REGION Pipers Brook, Tas.
CELLAR 🍾 8
ALC./VOL. 13.7%
RRP $18.00

Pirramimma Chardonnay

QUALITY ♛♛♛
VALUE ★★★
GRAPES chardonnay
REGION McLaren Vale, SA
CELLAR 🍷 1
ALC./VOL. 13.0%
RRP $14.50

Pirramimma is a very traditional winery which is undergoing a transformation, with major new vine plantings and a joint venture with Mildara Blass.

CURRENT RELEASE 1993 This is a robust, old-fashioned style of chardonnay, showing lashings of coconutty, rather unintegrated oak and a big, soft, broad palate. It's a straightforward but generous mouthful and the coconut flavour persists. Try it with mild Thai green fish curry in plenty of coconut milk.

Pirramimma Sauvignon Blanc Semillon

QUALITY ♛♛♛
VALUE ★★★½
GRAPES sauvignon blanc, semillon
REGION McLaren Vale, SA
CELLAR 🍷 2
ALC./VOL. 13.0%
RRP $9.70

This is subtitled 'chablis style' – yet another interpretation of a much-abused theme.

CURRENT RELEASE 1994 At least it's dry: but this is quite a big, rich, strong wine which has little to do with the French original. The bouquet is of straw and, although it's plain, the wine has plenty of flavour and grunt, finishing with a dry tannin grip. This could cope with chicken.

Pirramimma Stock's Hill Semillon Chardonnay

QUALITY ♛♛♛♛
VALUE ★★★★
GRAPES semillon, chardonnay
REGION McLaren Vale, SA
CELLAR 🍷 1
ALC./VOL. 13.0%
RRP $9.70

Avid readers of back labels will know that this is named after the Stock family, pioneers of McLaren Vale, and that the hill is the highest part of the property.

CURRENT RELEASE 1994 This is a little more subtle than the same maker's sauvignon/semillon, with typical semillon lemony/lanolin aromas. Again, it is pleasingly dry on the finish with good honest flavour. Try it with lemon sole.

Plantagenet Mount Barker Chardonnay

There are many stunning chardonnays coming out of the west and this marque is right up with the leaders. It's the more complex of Plantagenet's two chardonnays, with the full Burgundy treatment. Maker Gavin Berry.

CURRENT RELEASE 1993 Impressive depth and power of honey and tropical fruit flavour here, deftly interwoven with classy oak and a pungency that seduces immediately. There is enough subtlety and restraint to suggest it will improve further. Try it with marron.

QUALITY 🍷🍷🍷🍷🍷
VALUE ★★★★★
GRAPES chardonnay
REGION Mount Barker, WA
CELLAR 🍾 4+
ALC./VOL. 13.5%
RRP $21.00

Plantagenet Omrah Unoaked Chardonnay

This is one of the better unwooded chardonnays that seem to be gaining in popularity. The grapes come from the Omrah vineyard, which is owned by a unit trust. Maker Gavin Berry.

CURRENT RELEASE 1994 The nose offers tropical fruit and herbaceous accents typical of the Mount Barker area, coupled with cashew-nutty chardonnay character. It has a juicy flavour with crisp acidity and a hint of sweetness. Somewhat straightforward but very charming. Try it with asparagus.

QUALITY 🍷🍷🍷🍷
VALUE ★★★½
GRAPES chardonnay
REGION Mount Barker, WA
CELLAR 🍾 2
ALC./VOL. 13.5%
RRP $16.90

Plantagenet Riesling

This label's English-born founder Tony Smith can trace his lineage back to the Plantagenets, for what it's worth. Plantagenet was the first winery in the Great Southern and has been making wine since 1975. Maker Gavin Berry.

CURRENT RELEASE 1994 This is Mount Barker riesling at its best: a pure fragrance of floral riesling grapes, which builds intensity as the wine sits in the glass. It is soft and fruity in the mouth, well balanced towards a dry finish and drinks beautifully now with a bowl of Japanese noodles.

QUALITY 🍷🍷🍷🍷½
VALUE ★★★★
GRAPES riesling
REGION Great Southern, WA
CELLAR 🍾 5+
ALC./VOL. 12.0%
RRP $14.50

Plunkett Blackwood Ridge Sauvignon Blanc Semillon

QUALITY ♛♛♛
VALUE ★★½
GRAPES sauvignon blanc, semillon
REGION Strathbogie Ranges, Vic.
CELLAR 🍾
ALC./VOL. 12.4%
RRP $14.00

This wine from high in the Strathbogie Ranges features a novel, if somewhat kitsch, fragmented label.

CURRENT RELEASE 1994 The nose is a caricature of sauvignon blanc: dusty green herbaceousness which suggests shaded fruit. The sugar level is quite high, not quite covering the hard acid. For those who like their sauvignon blanc sweet.

Plunkett Chardonnay

QUALITY ♛♛♛♛
VALUE ★★★★
GRAPES chardonnay
REGION Strathbogie Ranges, Vic.
CELLAR 🍾 4+
ALC./VOL. 13.6%
RRP $17.70

The Strathbogie Ranges are in bushranger country near the Goulburn Valley. The Kelly gang would be surprised to see vineyards flourishing there today. Maker Sam Plunkett.

CURRENT RELEASE 1994 No problem getting the grapes ripe in '94 it seems: the wine is high in alcohol and rich in flavour. Big peach/fig fruit is liberally complemented by spicy oak. Slightly disjointed at present, but will come together with a few more months in the bottle. A promising drop to have with yabbies.

Pokolbin Creek Semillon Chardonnay

QUALITY ♛♛♛♛
VALUE ★★★
GRAPES semillon, chardonnay
REGION Hunter Valley, NSW
CELLAR 🍾 2
ALC./VOL. 12.5%
RRP $13.85

This is the second label of Briar Ridge, which is a small winery at Mount View in the southern end of the Hunter Valley. Winemakers Pip Treadwell and Karl Stockhausen.

CURRENT RELEASE 1994 A fresh, light-bodied white with bracing green herbal flavours. The semillon gives a dominant green-stick aroma. It's lively, fruity, light but intense in the mouth, with a slightly off-dry finish. Asparagus salad would work well.

Poole's Rock Chardonnay

This very small Hunter vineyard is owned by David Clarke, head of Macquarie Bank and chairman of more boards than we can count. Maker Iain Riggs.

CURRENT RELEASE 1994 A fairly straight-up-and-down wine, with some stone-fruit and oak characters and smokiness. Somewhat plain and lacking persistence. An acceptable wine but we liked the '93 better.

QUALITY ♛♛♛
VALUE ★★★
GRAPES chardonnay
REGION Hunter Valley, NSW
CELLAR 3
ALC./VOL. 12.0%
RRP $17.40

Primo Estate Botrytis Riesling

Joe Grilli at Primo was one of the first in this country to make a botrytis wine by inoculating fresh-picked grapes and letting them grow mould in a controlled environment. These days they're botrytised on the vine.

Previous outstanding vintages: '91, '93

CURRENT RELEASE 1994 In keeping with Grilli's direction, this has excellent clarity of varietal riesling fruit as well as complexing botrytis characters. Intense, citrusy flavour and lush sweetness, countered by zesty acid. It has great length and goes well with floating islands.

QUALITY ♛♛♛♛♛
VALUE ★★★★★
GRAPES riesling
REGION Eden Valley, Clare Valley, SA
CELLAR 6
ALC./VOL. 12.5%
RRP $17.70 (375ml)

Queen Adelaide Chardonnay

Ever lovin' Adelaide. MS incurred the wrath of a PR lady when he described the Queen on this label as a 'frumpy old bag'. These days she appears to be showing more cleavage. Maker, the Penfolds team.

CURRENT RELEASE 1994 Slightly disadvantaged by a pongy nose (which will only bother the purists). The peach palate redeems the situation and the finish is clean. Serve well chilled with KFC.

QUALITY ♛♛?
VALUE ★★★
GRAPES chardonnay
REGION not stated
CELLAR ♦
ALC./VOL. 12.0%
RRP $8.00 Ⓢ

Queen Adelaide Chenin Blanc

QUALITY ♀♀♀
VALUE ★★★
GRAPES chenin blanc
REGION not stated
CELLAR 🍷
ALC./VOL. 10.5%
RRP $8.00 Ⓢ

This winery was originally established in 1858 and it has changed hands several times. These days it is part of the Southcorp group.

CURRENT RELEASE 1994 The winemaker has stopped the fermentation to retain some sugar on the palate. The nose has soft apple smells and the palate is a sweet-and-sour affair which is followed by a clean finish. Serve well chilled with pork.

Queen Adelaide Riesling

QUALITY ♀♀♀♀
VALUE ★★★½
GRAPES riesling
REGION not stated
CELLAR 🍷 1
ALC./VOL. 12.0%
RRP $8.00 Ⓢ

This is a good example of a fighting brand. The company was established by Woodley. There is no cellar door.

CURRENT RELEASE 1994 A slightly sweet style that is none the worse for the sugar. The nose has citrus smells and the palate offers lime and the aforementioned sugar. The finish is crisp and clean. Serve well chilled with Singapore noodles.

Redbank Long Paddock Chardonnay

QUALITY ♀♀♀
VALUE ★★★
GRAPES chardonnay
REGION not stated
CELLAR 🍷 2
ALC./VOL. 13.5%
RRP $11.60

Long Paddock means the grapes can come from almost anywhere for Neill Robb's budget-priced range.

CURRENT RELEASE 1994 This is a fairly subdued wine with a vanillan aroma, but in the mouth it makes a strong statement about oak and alcohol. It's big and emphatic but lacks a little complexity. Try it with pork chops.

Renmano Chairman's Selection Chardonnay

For her first vintage as white winemaker at Renmano, Anne-Marie Wasley deliberately opted for less alcohol in this wine. There also seems to be less wood than prior vintages and both changes are for the better.

CURRENT RELEASE 1994 This wine needs some air to show its best. The nose has appealing baked-apple, vanilla and nutty oak aromas, and the palate has good intensity, more restraint than usual and well-balanced oak, although it could use a bit more verve. Barbecue some prawns.

QUALITY 🍷🍷🍷
VALUE ★★★
GRAPES chardonnay
REGION Riverland, SA
CELLAR 🍾 2
ALC./VOL. 13.0%
RRP $11.10 ⓢ

Richard Hamilton Chardonnay

Richard Hamilton's father Burton, a highly respected wineman in the Southern Vales, died last year. The son named a wine after the father in recognition of his life's work. It's called Burton's Vineyard.

Previous outstanding vintages: '93

CURRENT RELEASE 1994 This wine made the Sydney International Top 100 last year: it has an appealing tropical fruit aroma and it's lightly wooded. A highly commercial style, it is soft and fruity with a hint of sweetness: a real crowd-pleaser. Try it with a seafood cocktail.

QUALITY 🍷🍷🍷🍷
VALUE ★★★½
GRAPES chardonnay
REGION McLaren Vale, SA
CELLAR 🍾 2
ALC./VOL. 13.0%
RRP $13.75

Richard Hamilton Farm Block Semillon

The Hamiltons have been making wine in South Australia for as long as anyone – maybe longer than anyone. Richard is an Adelaide plastic surgeon. Maker Ralph Fowler.

Previous outstanding vintages: '93

CURRENT RELEASE 1994 Ralph Fowler has perfected this style of deliciously fruity, soft and just off-dry, drink-now white wine. It's fresh and nutty to sniff, with a slightly grassy aspect and marvellous drinkability. You could slosh it down very happily with a caesar salad.

QUALITY 🍷🍷🍷🍷
VALUE ★★★½
GRAPES semillon, sauvignon blanc
REGION McLaren Vale, SA
CELLAR 🍾 2
ALC./VOL. 11.0%
RRP $12.60

Richmond Grove Barossa Rhine Riesling

QUALITY 🍷🍷🍷🍷
VALUE ★★★★
GRAPES riesling
REGION Barossa Valley, SA
CELLAR 🍾 5
ALC./VOL. 12.5%
RRP $13.70 ⑤

John Vickery was poached from the Southcorp fold by arch rival Orlando, who installed him in the winery where he spent most of his life, the old Chateau Leonay, renamed Richmond Grove by its new owners.

CURRENT RELEASE 1994 This is a relatively big, rich, perhaps slightly unsubtle riesling with a light herbal, lemony nose and a somewhat phenolic, dry but soft finish. Heaps of flavour and a sure bet with asparagus and hollandaise.

Richmond Grove Traminer Riesling

QUALITY 🍷🍷🍷
VALUE ★★★
GRAPES gewürztraminer, riesling
REGION Eden Valley, SA
CELLAR 🍾 1
ALC./VOL. 11.0%
RRP $10.50 ⑤

Traditionally, traminer was blended with riesling to add its spicy aromatic nose to riesling's more structured, intense palate. Some are too sugary, but not this one.

CURRENT RELEASE 1994 The nose shows herbaceous as well as floral traminer muscat fragrance, and the palate is fruity with some well-judged sweetness. The acid also shows, giving a slight sweet-acid effect. Light and juicy. Try a chicken salad garnished with lychees.

Richmond Grove Watervale Rhine Riesling

QUALITY 🍷🍷🍷🍷
VALUE ★★★★
GRAPES riesling
REGION Clare Valley, SA
CELLAR 🍾 8+
ALC./VOL. 12.5%
RRP $13.70 ⑤

John Vickery made the name of Leo Buring and Watervale synonymous with great riesling, and while the Orlando style is very different to Buring's, he's being given his head at Richmond Grove's Barossa winery.

CURRENT RELEASE 1994 A more refined style than the Barossa, with a subtle peach/floral nose that has a hint of toastiness. On the tongue it's beautifully poised with crisp, pure riesling flavour, great harmony and a dry finish. Good with yabbies.

Riddoch Riesling

Riesling makers frustrated with sluggish sales are trying different bottle shapes to lure the customer. This one comes in a Burgundy bottle. Maker Wayne Stehbens.

CURRENT RELEASE 1994 Several '94 Coonawarra rieslings seem to have a more lifted, spicy aroma than usual, perhaps reflecting the cool summer. This is super-aromatic yet very delicate to sniff, and the flavour is light, with some phenolic coarseness on the finish that would disappear when paired with food. Try it with scampi.

QUALITY ♥♥♥
VALUE ★★★
GRAPES riesling
REGION Coonawarra, SA
CELLAR 🍷 3+
ALC./VOL. 13.0%
RRP $12.90

Riddoch Run (The) Chardonnay

At one time the Riddoch run covered much of south-eastern South Australia. John Riddoch's great grandson, Peter Rymill, produces this wine.

CURRENT RELEASE 1993 Not in the same class as the Rymill label, this is an unusual style that does offer stacks of flavour. The nose is butterscotch, spice and caramel, with an apricot note that grows in the glass. The punchy palate is strong on vanilla and caramel notes. Try it with roast chicken and caramellised pumpkin.

QUALITY ♥♥♥
VALUE ★★★
GRAPES chardonnay
REGION Coonawarra, SA
CELLAR 🍷 1
ALC./VOL. 13.8%
RRP $14.50

Riddoch Sauvignon Blanc

From the Katnook stable, where sauvignon blanc was first produced in 1980: a time when precious few others were available. Maker Wayne Stehbens.

CURRENT RELEASE 1994 This is a delicious wine and excellent value for money. The fruit is of the asparagus style with some tropical aromas thrown in for good measure. The taste is remarkably full, chockers with pure, stylish sauvignon flavour, perhaps a smidgin of wood, fine balance and length. Most impressive and goes well with whitebait fritters.

QUALITY ♥♥♥♥♥
VALUE ★★★★½
GRAPES sauvignon blanc
REGION Coonawarra, SA
CELLAR 🍷 2
ALC./VOL. 13.5%
RRP $12.90

Ridgeview Margaret River Sauvignon Blanc

QUALITY ♛♛♛♛
VALUE ★★★½
GRAPES sauvignon blanc
REGION Margaret River, WA
CELLAR 🍷 2
ALC./VOL. 12.5%
RRP $13.90

This is a new label in the Margaret River district and the wine is fine, but a new label design would not go astray.

CURRENT RELEASE 1994 A well-defined style that has good balance. There are soft herb and grass aromas. The palate has distinct tropical fruit characters plus some gooseberry flavours balanced by soft acid on a clean finish. Serve medium chilled with poached white asparagus.

Rockford Eden Valley Riesling

QUALITY ♛♛♛♛
VALUE ★★★½
GRAPES riesling
REGION Eden Valley, SA
CELLAR 🍷 3
ALC./VOL. 12.0%
RRP $9.70 (cellar door)

Robert O'Callaghan declares that he tries to make a traditional riesling style by letting the grapes get fully ripe, hand-harvesting, and maximising flavour with some skin contact.

CURRENT RELEASE 1994 The nose is a trifle timid, with yeasty and toasty hints, while the taste is full and soft without a lot of acid, which leaves you with a slight fruit-sweetness (as opposed to sugar). It is an honest wine without pungent aromatics, but generous flavour and a slight grip to the finish. Any white-fleshed fish will go.

Rockford Local Growers Semillon

QUALITY ♛♛♛♛
VALUE ★★★½
GRAPES semillon
REGION Barossa Valley, SA
CELLAR 🍷 2
ALC./VOL. 13.0%
RRP $11.00 (cellar door)

Robert O'Callaghan is very much his own man: he makes the styles he likes, and happily lots of others like 'em too.

CURRENT RELEASE 1993 The colour is deep yellow, suggesting early development. The wine is big and toasty with baked-apple and straw flavours: a very full-on style with oak and guts galore. A rich monster that you'll either love or hate. Needs big food such as char-grilled swordfish.

Rosemount Chardonnay

This is the wine that did it all for Rosemount back in 1983: 'Nifty' Neville Wran announced that half a bottle of it had facilitated his decision not to enter federal politics.

CURRENT RELEASE 1994 This has an odd, heavily spiced aroma and taste that reminds of German oak. The palate has an essency oak-driven aspect, dry and spicy without a lot of fruit poking through, but plenty of body and length. Try it with spicy Singapore crab.

QUALITY ♛♛♛
VALUE ★★★
GRAPES chardonnay
REGION mainly Hunter Valley, NSW
CELLAR 2
ALC./VOL. 13.0%
RRP $13.85 ⓢ

Rosemount Roxburgh Chardonnay

This is the cruiser in Rosemount's chardonnay fleet (which numbered about five at last count) and commonly held to be one of the pace-setters in this country. Renowned for its power and richness, if not its subtlety.

Previous outstanding vintages: '85, '86, '87, '89, '90, '91, '92

CURRENT RELEASE 1993 This is a powerhouse and epitomises the gentle swing away from the woody style of yesteryear, being deliciously fresh, fruit-driven and yet complex, with peachy, toasty, nutty flavours of great depth. Big, dry, structured and very long. Drink with roast pheasant.

QUALITY ♛♛♛♛♛
VALUE ★★★★½
GRAPES chardonnay
REGION Hunter Valley, NSW
CELLAR 6
ALC./VOL. 13.5%
RRP $42.00

CURRENT RELEASE 1994 (barrel sample) Lightish hue; exciting fresh grapefruity nose with lemon overtones and (at this stage) subtle oak. Mealy lees complexity; great underlying character, although undeveloped. Undoubtedly full-throttle, but balanced and lively in the mouth.

QUALITY ♛♛♛♛♛
VALUE ★★★★½
GRAPES chardonnay
REGION Hunter Valley, NSW
CELLAR 1–6
ALC./VOL. 13.5%
RRP $42.00

Rosemount Semillon Chardonnay

QUALITY 🍷🍷🍷🍷
VALUE ★★★½
GRAPES semillon, chardonnay
REGION Hunter Valley, NSW
CELLAR 🍶 2
ALC./VOL. 12.0%
RRP $11.90 ⓢ

In the early days of chardonnay (read the mid-'70s) winemakers used to make what little chardonnay they had go further by blending it with semillon. Sometimes it improved both.

CURRENT RELEASE 1994 A most acceptable wine at a very reasonable price. The nose has hints of toast and butter, it's light and fruity with a little sweetness that does not intrude. The finish reveals a hint of wood. Cleverly made and good with tempura.

Rosemount Semillon Sauvignon Blanc

QUALITY 🍷🍷🍷
VALUE ★★½
GRAPES semillon, sauvignon blanc
REGION not stated
CELLAR 🍶 2
ALC./VOL. 11.5%
RRP $11.90 ⓢ

This is one of the new split-label wines, where the different-coloured halves represent the shades suggested by the grape.

CURRENT RELEASE 1994 An unusual wine with a pepperminty aroma and a lean, slightly phenolic palate which could use a little more fruit. Try it with a Niçoise salad.

Rosemount Unoaked Semillon

QUALITY 🍷🍷🍷🍷
VALUE ★★★½
GRAPES semillon
REGION Hunter Valley, NSW
CELLAR 🍶 7+
ALC./VOL. 11.4%
RRP $12.00 ⓢ

Rosemount used to make a generous wood-smothered semillon. Now they're saving on the wood budget, and it's a better wine.

CURRENT RELEASE 1994 Typical Hunter lanolin, non-grassy nose, without any hint of oak, and in the mouth it's as big as ever – but what you're tasting is all fruit. Rich, ripe and powerful, it finishes dry and slightly phenolic. A boots-and-all semillon which teams well with swordfish.

Rosemount Yarrawa Vineyard Sauvignon Blanc

This vineyard, just across the Goulburn River from the Rosemount winery near Denman, has always yielded top sauvignon blanc and this wine is the first single-vineyard bottling.

CURRENT RELEASE 1994 This is a lean, herbaceous style which is well-made although not especially complex. The aromas are of crushed leaves and green-stick, and the palate is light and fruity with a slight grip to the finish. Try it with fresh goat's cheese.

QUALITY ♟♟♟♟
VALUE ★★★
GRAPES sauvignon blanc
REGION Hunter Valley, NSW
CELLAR 🍾 2+
ALC./VOL. 12.0%
RRP $20.00 ⓢ

Rothbury Estate Barrel Fermented Chardonnay

Most chardonnay is barrel-fermented these days, including two or three others at Rothbury, so it's a bit like saying it's made from grapes.

Previous outstanding vintages: '91, '92, '93

CURRENT RELEASE 1994 Continuing the more subtle wood treatment of the '93, this is a delicious fruit-driven style, smelling of cashewnut and creamy barrel-ferment aromas and stacks of fruit. In the mouth it's lively, crisp and subtle – yet mouthfilling – with tangy acid. It should build more complexity with a year or two. Try it with sushi.

QUALITY ♟♟♟♟
VALUE ★★★½
GRAPES chardonnay
REGION Hunter Valley, NSW
CELLAR 🍾 5+
ALC./VOL. 12.3%
RRP $19.30

Rothbury Estate Cowra Chardonnay

Rothbury was one of the first to realise the potential of the Cowra region. It's been making a Cowra chardonnay since 1981. The '95 will be very scarce due to Mother Nature's savage yield reduction.

Previous outstanding vintages: '81, '89, '90

CURRENT RELEASE 1994 Perhaps the best since 1981, this wine has a lovely cashew-nut and melon aroma, lots of fresh, clean, lively fruit and super balance. Don't cellar: it would be a pity to miss its delicious freshness. Try it with slow-braised tarragon calamari.

QUALITY ♟♟♟♟
VALUE ★★★★
GRAPES chardonnay
REGION Cowra, NSW
CELLAR 🍾 3+
ALC./VOL. 12.5%
RRP $13.30 ⓢ

Rothbury Estate Marlborough Chardonnay

QUALITY ★★★★★
VALUE ★★★★½
GRAPES chardonnay
REGION Marlborough, NZ
CELLAR 🍾 5
ALC./VOL. 13.2%
RRP $21.25

Although Hunter-based, Rothbury makes a sauvignon blanc, riesling and chardonnay from its New Zealand vineyard. This was 50-per cent barrel-fermented in new Vosges oak. Maker (Kiwi) Peter Hall.

CURRENT RELEASE 1994 A most arresting chardonnay, typically New Zealand with stacks of buttery malolactic character on the bouquet, and a lively, tangy acid finish that emphasises the long aftertaste and keeps you wanting more. A lovely wine: great with New Zealand scampi.

Rothbury Estate Semillon

QUALITY ★★★★
VALUE ★★★½
GRAPES semillon
REGION Hunter Valley, NSW
CELLAR 🍾 10+
ALC./VOL. 12.0%
RRP $13.30

This is the last of the Mohicans. Rothbury has a history of ageworthy semillons second to none in the Hunter, but the focus has swung onto chardonnay. There was a time when it released several semillons, but today, only one.

Previous outstanding vintages: '72, '73, '76, '79, '84, '89, '90, '91, '93

CURRENT RELEASE 1994 This little trimmer has the pale colour typical of young, unwooded semillon and a delicate nose of bread-dough, nuts and mint. It's fine and dry on the tongue with good fruit depth, and should age into a beauty. While it's young, drink with seafood.

Rothbury Estate Verdelho

QUALITY ★★★★
VALUE ★★★½
GRAPES verdelho
REGION not stated
CELLAR 🍾 3
ALC./VOL. 13.0%
RRP $13.30

The back label claims verdelho has the same flavour intensity as chardonnay, which is an innovative sales pitch! Maker Peter Hall.

CURRENT RELEASE 1994 This is a very juicy, fruit-driven wine which is drinking well right now. The nose offers a shy whiff of nut and spice; the palate has body and length coupled with individual character. Take it to a vegetarian restaurant.

Rouge Homme Chardonnay

At last count the Southcorp group had 25 chardonnays on the market, but only one or two of them ever scale the heights.

CURRENT RELEASE 1993 This is a forward developed wine with a deep yellow colour, big resiny wood/bottle-aged nose with some dried-apricot aspects, and a big, round, oily palate. It reminds of Mum's homemade fig jam. At least it's not short of flavour.

QUALITY ♛♛♛
VALUE ★★★
GRAPES chardonnay
REGION Coonawarra, SA
CELLAR 🍾 1
ALC./VOL. 13.0%
RRP $13.30 $

Rovalley Ridge Show Reserve Chardonnay

This is the old Rovalley winery at Rowland Flat, which has been reborn since Miranda took it over. Makers Mos Kaesler and Shayne Cunningham.

Previous outstanding vintages: '92

CURRENT RELEASE 1993 This is a rich, full-bodied dry white which owes a lot to high-toast new oak. It's a deftly made wine which is smooth and satisfying, lingering long on the finish. Try roast pork and apple sauce.

QUALITY ♛♛♛♛
VALUE ★★★★
GRAPES chardonnay
REGION Barossa Valley, SA
CELLAR 🍾 2
ALC./VOL. 13.0%
RRP $15.50

Rymill Chardonnay

Peter Rymill, descendant of John Riddoch, owns a lot of good vineyard land in the Coonawarra area. He's been producing his own wines since 1987. Maker John Innes.

CURRENT RELEASE 1994 A chardonnay of real finesse. The colour is light, and restraint is the keyword all round. The nose is shy and melony, and the palate has tightness and cool-grown subtlety, with a long finish. It should take age gracefully. Try it with prosciutto melone.

QUALITY ♛♛♛♛?
VALUE ★★★★½
GRAPES chardonnay
REGION Coonawarra, SA
CELLAR 🍾 5+
ALC./VOL. 13.5%
RRP $14.50

Rymill June Traminer

QUALITY ♛♛♛♛
VALUE ★★★★
GRAPES gewürztraminer
REGION Coonawarra, SA
CELLAR 🍾 2
ALC./VOL. 13.5%
RRP $10.50 (375ml)

The label proclaims the grapes for this wine were harvested in June, two months after most Coonawarra grapes are picked.

CURRENT RELEASE 1994 This is a very rich, sweet, dessert style traminer. The colour is deep golden, the nose typically spicy from the traminer fruit with candied citrus-peel notes. In the mouth it's syrupy, oily, sweet and lush, ending with nice balance. Try it with a rich fruit tart.

Salisbury Estate Chardonnay

QUALITY ♛♛♛?
VALUE ★★★★
GRAPES chardonnay
REGION Mildura, Vic.
CELLAR 🍾 2
ALC./VOL. 13.0%
RRP $9.00 ⓢ

This is the fighting brand for the Alambie Wine Company. It represents very good value for money. Maker Bob Shields (no relation to Mark Shield).

CURRENT RELEASE 1994 A young fresh wine that shows obvious oak. The colour is pale straw and the nose has melon and powdery oak aromas. The middleweight palate has citrus and grapefruit flavours and the finish shows toasty oak. Serve lightly chilled with pâté.

Salisbury Estate Show Reserve Chardonnay

QUALITY ♛♛♛♛
VALUE ★★★★
GRAPES chardonnay
REGION Mildura, Vic.
CELLAR 🍾 3
ALC./VOL. 12.0%
RRP $12.00

This is the top of the line for this label, which is part of the Alambie Wine Company at Mildura.

CURRENT RELEASE 1993 This is a very well-made wine with plenty of varietal character. It has a bright green-gold colour and a peachy nose. The mouthfilling palate has a strong peach flavour matched by savoury oak on a long finish. It drinks well near room temperature (18°C). Try it with Spanish mackerel.

Salitage Chardonnay

Early days for this painstaking venture that includes a state-of-the-art winery with a current production capacity of 15,000 cases. At this stage the capacity is not nearly realised. Makers John Wade (consultant) and Patrick Coutts.

CURRENT RELEASE 1994 Very classy wine with lots of potential. The nose shows the wine has been attending the best oak finishing school. The palate has stone-fruit and citrus flavours plus a creamy texture. There is firm oak as a follow-up on a lengthy finish. It should cellar well. Don't overchill, and try it with a warm salad of quail.

QUALITY 🍷🍷🍷🍷🍷
VALUE ★★★★
GRAPES chardonnay
REGION Great Southern, WA
CELLAR 🍾 6
ALC./VOL. 13.5%
RRP $26.00

Saltram Mamre Brook Chardonnay

The Mamre Brook red was once the top of the Saltram totem when the redoubtable Peter Leon Lehmann used to be at the helm. The white version followed after he left to found Masterson.

CURRENT RELEASE 1993 A little softening and more expression of fruit has taken place since the last review. The wine is big and cuddly with a strong ripe peach aroma on the nose plus an undertone of wet wood. Peach and fig are the main flavours on the mouthfilling palate, framed by earnest oak on a powerful finish. 'Strength through joy' stuff, so serve it with roast pork and apple sauce.

QUALITY 🍷🍷🍷🍷🍷
VALUE ★★★★½
GRAPES chardonnay
REGION Barossa & Eden Valleys, 85%, McLaren Vale, SA 15%
CELLAR 🍾 2
ALC./VOL. 13.5%
RRP $17.70

Saltram Pinnacle Chardonnay

QUALITY ★★★★★
VALUE ★★★★★
GRAPES chardonnay
REGION Eden Valley, SA
CELLAR 🍷 4
ALC./VOL. 13.5%
RRP $23.30

There has been some revisionist labelling and this wine continues to live up to its 'Pinnacle' appellation in terms of quality.

CURRENT RELEASE 1993 This has made some headway in complexity since last year's review. It remains an outstanding wine. The nose is complex with fig, melon and toasty oak aromas, the palate intense with strong peach flavours plus hints of cashew-nuts and figs, and the finish is well integrated showing a sophisticated oak treatment. Don't overchill, and serve with a scaloppine.

Saltram Pinnacle Rhine Riesling

QUALITY ★★★★½
VALUE ★★★★½
GRAPES riesling
REGION Eden Valley, SA
CELLAR 🍷 5
ALC./VOL. 11.8%
RRP $16.40 Ⓢ

Saltram is now part of the Rothbury group that has Len Evans as chairman. The annual production is almost 200,000 cases. Maker Nigel Dolan.

Previous outstanding vintages: '93

CURRENT RELEASE 1994 This is a classy wine that shows the best attributes of the variety. The nose is floral with citrus aromas, but the palate offers a big shock of lime balanced by crisp acid on a long clean finish. Try it well chilled with Asian food.

Sandalford 1840 Collection Chardonnay

QUALITY ★★★★
VALUE ★★★★
GRAPES chardonnay
REGION Mount Barker, WA
CELLAR 🍷 3
ALC./VOL. 12.5%
RRP $12.00

The 1840 refers to the establishment date of this winery. These days the production is 43,000 cases.

CURRENT RELEASE 1994 An oak-driven style that was barrel-fermented. The nose shows some smoky oak and the palate has intense peach flavours that mingle with caramel characters from the oak. The finish is dry and mouth-coating. Serve moderately cool with antipasto.

Sandalford 1840 Collection Classic Dry White

What is a 'classic dry white'? Quite often it is the name applied to the leftovers and United Nations blends. Maker Bill Crappsley.

CURRENT RELEASE 1994 The nose is pungent with strong grass and herb aromas, and the palate fruity with spice and green apple flavours. These are balanced by tart acid on a crisp, dry finish. Serve well chilled with roast chicken.

QUALITY ♛♛♛♛
VALUE ★★★½
GRAPES semillon, sauvignon blanc, chenin blanc
REGION Margaret River, Mount Barker, WA
CELLAR 🍾 1
ALC./VOL. 12.0%
RRP $11.00

Sandalford Verdelho

Verdelho is a Madeira grape variety that Australian winemakers have dragooned into making table wines. It is very difficult for wine writers to describe because it tends to mimic other varieties.

CURRENT RELEASE 1994 The nose is herbal with hints of citrus and the palate offers peach and tropical fruit flavours. The finish shows crisp acid and good length. Serve well chilled with scallops.

QUALITY ♛♛♛♛
VALUE ★★★★
GRAPES verdelho
REGION Margaret River, WA
CELLAR 🍾 1
ALC./VOL. 12.5%
RRP $12.00

Sandstone Semillon

Have bottles will travel – this is the label of qualified winemakers Mike and Jan Davies who also run a mobile bottling plant in Western Australia. Maker Mike Davies.

CURRENT RELEASE 1994 A full-frontal barrel-fermented style that begs no pardons. The nose has a creamy aroma of gooseberry, lemongrass and melon. The palate is mouthfilling with rich complexity. The main flavour is citrus but there are some straw characters. The finish is long and clean with discreet wood. Don't overchill, and serve with marron.

QUALITY ♛♛♛♛♛
VALUE ★★★★
GRAPES semillon
REGION Margaret River, WA
CELLAR 🍾 3
ALC./VOL. 13.5%
RRP $20.20

Schinus Chenin Blanc

QUALITY 🍷🍷🍷
VALUE ★★★
GRAPES chenin blanc
REGION King Valley, Lake Boga, Vic. & Barossa Valley, SA
CELLAR 🍷 1
ALC./VOL. 12.5%
RRP $13.00

This variety has been leaving glass slippers on ballroom steps across the land. It is a useful utility style. Makers G. Crittenden and S. Ireland.
CURRENT RELEASE 1994 A crisp, fresh style that is ready to drink now. The nose has a distinct biscuit quality and there are strong green apple flavours on the palate. The tartness on the finish is refreshing. It can be served well chilled with roast pork.

Schinus Riesling

QUALITY 🍷🍷🍷🍷
VALUE ★★★½
REGION Western District, Vic.
CELLAR 🍷 2
ALC./VOL. 12.5%
RRP $13.50

This is the second label for Dromana Estate on the Mornington Peninsula. The fruit from this label comes from premium growing districts around Australia. Maker Garry Crittenden.
CURRENT RELEASE 1994 A fresh, drinkable style. The nose has strong citrus aromas, and keen lime fills out the palate. There's a tingle of acid on a crisp finish. Serve well chilled with smoked salmon.

Schinus Sauvignon Blanc

QUALITY 🍷🍷🍷🍷
VALUE ★★★★
GRAPES sauvignon blanc
REGION Yarra Valley, King Valley, Vic. & McLaren Vale, SA
CELLAR 🍷 1
ALC./VOL. 12.5%
RRP $14.50

This is an advanced winery and a welcoming cellar door located on the Mornington Peninsula.
CURRENT RELEASE 1994 The nose is herbal with a hint of honey, and the palate has a touch of sweetness plus some attractive tropical fruit characters backed up by crisp acid on a refreshing finish. It can be served well chilled with steamed Chinese vegetables.

Seaview Chardonnay

Seaview is hardly small beer: they make over 500,000 cases and keep up a very impressive level of quality.

CURRENT RELEASE 1994 The nose has an interesting varietal signature of peach and citrus aromas underscored by nutty oak. The palate has a creamy texture with peach flavour dominating. Discreet oak marks a soft, balanced finish. Medium chill and a pork stir-fry are just the ticket.

QUALITY ♛♛♛♛
VALUE ★★★★
GRAPES chardonnay
REGION McLaren Vale, SA
CELLAR 🍾 1
ALC./VOL. 13.5%
RRP $8.00 ⓢ

Seaview Rhine Riesling

McLaren Vale is not known for riesling; at best it makes fair, average-quality wines.

CURRENT RELEASE 1994 The colour is a mid-green-gold and the nose is toasty with hints of lime. The palate is rich with a central core of sweetness. A crisp acid balance contributes to a dry finish. The wine can be served well chilled with oysters.

QUALITY ♛♛♛
VALUE ★★★
GRAPES riesling
REGION McLaren Vale, SA
CELLAR 🍾 1
ALC./VOL. 12.5%
RRP $8.00 ⓢ

Seaview White Burgundy

This label offers great value for money. The makers are going to have to rethink the generic labelling given the recent agreement on style names with the European Union.

CURRENT RELEASE 1994 Grassy sauvignon blanc dominates a powerful nose. There is a hint of sweetness on the gooseberry-flavoured palate followed by a soft finish. Served well chilled with a warm salad of chicken.

QUALITY ♛♛♛♛
VALUE ★★★★
GRAPES semillon, sauvignon blanc
REGION McLaren Vale, SA
CELLAR 🍾 1
ALC./VOL. 13%
RRP $8.00 ⓢ

Selak's Chardonnay

QUALITY 🍷🍷🍷🍷🍷
VALUE ★★★★
GRAPES chardonnay
REGION Marlborough, NZ
CELLAR 🍾 5
ALC./VOL. 13.5%
RRP $20.30

Selak's story is paralleled by many wineries which began in the Auckland district but moved their grape-sourcing to other areas better suited to grapegrowing. Selak's today has one of the biggest vineyards in the Marlborough area.

CURRENT RELEASE 1994 This is a seamless wine in which no single character dominates. There's nuttiness from barrel-fermentation, fine fruit and a whiff of malolactic, but it's all in impeccable harmony. The balance is almost Freudian. Try it with mussels mariniere.

Selak's Sauvignon Blanc

QUALITY 🍷🍷🍷🍷
VALUE ★★★½
GRAPES sauvignon blanc
REGION Marlborough, NZ
CELLAR 🍾 2
ALC./VOL. 12.5%
RRP $16.00

Selak's boss Ivan Selak is pleased that tin-lead capsules have been outlawed internationally, because the plastic ones cost him about three cents, compared to 14 for the lead. We can't see a lot of difference in eye-appeal and the package looks as good as ever.

CURRENT RELEASE 1994 Very aromatic racy, grassy/gooseberry Marlborough sauvignon aromas: classic New Zealand style and hugely appealing. There is a decent fullness on the mid-palate and the wine avoids the green skeletal style that one often sees. Try it with asparagus salad.

Selak's Sauvignon Blanc Semillon

QUALITY 🍷🍷🍷🍷🍷
VALUE ★★★★
GRAPES sauvignon blanc, semillon
REGION Marlborough, NZ
CELLAR 🍾 3
ALC./VOL. 12.5%
RRP $23.20

This is a richer style: the sauvignon is picked riper than the solo sauvignon blanc and it's blended with semillon to give a fuller middle palate. All barrel-fermented. Trophy runner-up in the Sydney International Top 100. Maker Ivan Selak.

CURRENT RELEASE 1994 A delicious wine bulging with refined fruit flavours subtly endorsed with stylish French oak characters. It has a softer middle palate than the straight sauvignon, with less acid and a fruit-sweet taste. Lovely wine: a treat with whitebait fritters.

Seppelt Great Western Rhine Riesling

This wine is an old favourite which usually ages gracefully and well. The grapes were actually grown at Great Western.

CURRENT RELEASE 1991 The colour shows there has been some bottle development, which is confirmed by the aromatic nose with a whiff of kero. The palate is soft with gentle lime flavours followed by soft acid on a clean finish. It can be served well chilled.

QUALITY ƳƳƳƳ
VALUE ★★★★
GRAPES riesling
REGION Great Western, Vic.
CELLAR 🍷 2
ALC./VOL. 11.0%
RRP $12.50

Seppelt Partalunga Chardonnay

This vineyard is located above 500 metres in the High Eden region. This is a cool-climate location that should produce complex goodies.

CURRENT RELEASE 1993 An intense style that is engaged in a wrestling match between wood and fruit. It starts with a nose of passionfruit, peach and lychee as well as some toasty oak. The palate is quite complex with peach and grapefruit flavours. The finish shows some toasty oak. It should be served moderately chilled with a rich chicken dish.

QUALITY ƳƳƳƳ
VALUE ★★★★
GRAPES chardonnay
REGION Eden Valley, SA
CELLAR 🍷 5
ALC./VOL. 13.0%
RRP $15.50

Seppelt Sheoak Spring Rhine Riesling

Here we go again – where is Sheoak Spring? Another pretty marketing name and not a district or vineyard. Maker Ian McKenzie (chief).

CURRENT RELEASE 1994 The nose shows soft lime and aromatic qualities. The palate is steely with a zest of lime matched by crisp acid on a firm finish. It should cellar well. Serve well chilled with oysters czarina.

QUALITY ƳƳƳƳ
VALUE ★★★★
GRAPES riesling
REGION Western District, Vic.
CELLAR 🍷 5
ALC./VOL. 12.0%
RRP $11.40 Ⓢ

Shantell Semillon

QUALITY 🍷🍷🍷
VALUE ★★★
GRAPES semillon
REGION Yarra Valley, Vic.
CELLAR 🍾 2
ALC./VOL. 11.0%
RRP $12.00

Semillon is not a common planting in the Yarra Valley, but it makes an interesting wine. Shantell was established in 1981 and produces 1400 cases.
CURRENT RELEASE 1992 A very aromatic style that shows an interesting facet to the variety. The nose has a strong geranium component. The palate is a mix of gooseberry and lychee flavours and the finish shows soft acid. Don't overchill, and try it with smoked cod.

Skillogalee Riesling

QUALITY 🍷🍷🍷🍷
VALUE ★★★★½
GRAPES riesling
REGION Clare Valley, SA
CELLAR 🍾 5 (bottle), 🍾 5–10 (magnum)
ALC./VOL. 12.5%
RRP $12.80 (bottle), $65.00 (magnum)

'Skilly' or Skillogalee was a poor man's gruel cooked up by the early settlers in Clare, South Australia. This winery has now released a limited number of riesling magnum flutes. The bottles were imported from Alsace. Maker Stephen John (contract).
CURRENT RELEASE 1994 A typical Clare style with strong aromatics on the nose. There are crisp lemon and lime flavours on the palate, backed up by very crisp acid on a long finish. It should cellar impressively, hence the magnums. Serve well chilled with yabbies.

Smithbrook Chardonnay

This is a new winery in Pemberton, Western Australia. They certainly have positive ideas about prices.

CURRENT RELEASE 1993 A youthful style with plenty of oak influence. The nose is toasty with hints of citrus. The palate is a middleweight with citrus flavour dominating. Oak quickly makes its presence felt, and the finish is dry and dusty. Don't overchill, and try it with a spaghetti marinara.

QUALITY ♛♛♛♛
VALUE ★★½
GRAPES chardonnay
REGION Pemberton, WA
CELLAR 🍷 3
ALC./VOL. 13.5%
RRP $28.50

CURRENT RELEASE 1994 Fresher and slightly bigger with more complexity. Oak still gives a good account of itself. The nose shows peach, melon and mango. The palate is complex with peach, melon and fig flavours plus a hint of cashew matched by well-integrated oak on a dry finish. Don't overchill, and serve it with a mushroom risotto.

QUALITY ♛♛♛♛
VALUE ★★★
GRAPES chardonnay
REGION Pemberton, WA
CELLAR 🍷 5
ALC./VOL. 13.5%
RRP $28.50

Sorrenberg Chardonnay

At a distance from the label you could be forgiven for thinking the wine comes from Burgundy, France. Obviously this is no accident.

CURRENT RELEASE 1994 A bold style with plenty of flavour. The nose is dominated by caramel and nutmeg oak flavours. There is an attractive mouthfilling quality, with lychee and peach flavours dominating. Strong oak gives the finish a zing. It needs time, but if you do pull the cork try it with smoked fish.

QUALITY ♛♛♛♛
VALUE ★★★★
GRAPES chardonnay
REGION Beechworth, Vic.
CELLAR ⇌ 2–5
ALC./VOL. 13.0%
RRP $18.00

Sorrenberg Sauvignon Blanc Semillon

QUALITY ▼▼▼▽
VALUE ★★★½
GRAPES sauvignon blanc, semillon
REGION Beechworth, Vic.
CELLAR 🍾 3
ALC./VOL. 13.0%
RRP $16.00

This vineyard was founded in 1986 and the production is in the order of 1000 cases.

CURRENT RELEASE 1994 An interesting style with a lot to appreciate. The nose is complex with nutmeg, cinnamon and spice aromas. The palate is chewy with gooseberry and tropical fruit flavours balanced by strong acid on a long dry finish. It can be served well chilled with an asparagus quiche.

St Hallett Chardonnay

QUALITY ▼▼▼▼
VALUE ★★★★
GRAPES chardonnay
REGION Barossa Valley, SA
CELLAR 🍾 4
ALC./VOL. 13.0%
RRP $15.00

This winery was established in 1944 and today the production is in the order of 15,000 cases. It also crushes grapes and makes wine for other companies. Maker Stuart Blackwell.

CURRENT RELEASE 1994 A fruit-driven style that strikes a nice balance with oak. The nose shows peach and smoky oak aromas. The palate has peach, nectarines and grapefruit followed by strong oak on a dry finish. It should be served lightly chilled with smoked chicken.

St Hallett Poacher's Blend

QUALITY ▼▼▼▽
VALUE ★★★½
GRAPES not stated
REGION Barossa Valley, SA
CELLAR 🍾 2
ALC./VOL. 11.5%
RRP $12.00

It's all a bit too cute. You can see the yarn on the back label going down a treat with Dover sole in a London club.

CURRENT RELEASE 1994 A herbal style with a hint of toast on the nose. There is a hint of sweetness on the palate, plus tropical and gooseberry fruit flavours. The finish is crisp and acid. It can be served well chilled with yabbies.

St Hallett Semillon Sauvignon Blanc

This label goes from strength to strength. It has strong export sales and a burgeoning home market.
CURRENT RELEASE 1994 A well-tuned style with balance and complexity. The nose is grassy with distinct herbal traits. The medium-bodied palate is quite complex with gooseberry and herb flavours framed by strong acid on a crisp, dry finish. It can be served well chilled with scallops in a light ginger sauce.

QUALITY ♛♛♛♛
VALUE ★★★★
GRAPES semillon, sauvignon blanc
REGION Barossa Valley, SA
CELLAR 🍾 2
ALC./VOL. 12.0%
RRP $13.00

Stanley Brothers Unwooded Semillon

There is a growing debate about non-wooded white styles. Some argue it makes for cheaper but no less interesting wines.
CURRENT RELEASE 1994 The nose has some gooseberry and talcum-powder aromas. The palate offers attractive gooseberry flavours balanced by clean acid on a crisp finish. It will be interesting to watch this one age. Serve lightly chilled with a seafood cocktail.

QUALITY ♛♛♛½
VALUE ★★★½
GRAPES semillon
REGION Clare Valley, SA
CELLAR 🍾 4
ALC./VOL. 12.0%
RRP $13.50

Sunnycliff Chardonnay

This is part of the Katnook empire. The grapes come from Victoria's Sunraysia district. Production is 38,000 cases. Maker Mark Zeppel.
CURRENT RELEASE 1993 The colour is a bright green-gold and the nose has melon and dusty oak aromas. The palate is rich with peach and melon flavours, plus hints of citrus and toasty oak and crisp acid. Serve lightly chilled with smoked cod.

QUALITY ♛♛♛½
VALUE ★★★½
GRAPES chardonnay
REGION Mildura, Vic.
CELLAR 🍾 2
ALC./VOL. 13.5%
RRP $9.00 Ⓢ

Sunnycliff Sauvignon Blanc

QUALITY ♛♛♛♝
VALUE ★★★½
GRAPES sauvignon blanc
REGION Mildura, Vic.
CELLAR 🍶 1
ALC./VOL. 10.5%
RRP $9.00 Ⓢ

This is the third label from Katnook (the other is Riddoch) and the grapes are usually grown in the Sunraysia district, but sometimes Coonawarra fruit finds its way into the label. Maker Mark Zeppel.

CURRENT RELEASE 1994 A young, vibrant style that was made to drink now. The nose identifies the variety with herb and cut-grass aromas. The palate is elegant with passionfruit and tropical fruit flavours followed by soft acid on a clean, gentle finish. It can be served well chilled with pipis and pasta.

Sutherland Smith (G.) Rhine Riesling

QUALITY ♛♛♛♝
VALUE ★★★½
GRAPES riesling
REGION Rutherglen, Vic.
CELLAR 🍶 1
ALC./VOL. 12.0%
RRP $12.00

This label marks the return of a famous wine name that was associated with All Saints before its financial collapse and sale to Brown Brothers.

CURRENT RELEASE 1994 The colour is a pale straw and the nose offers equal hints of citrus and kero. The palate has zesty lime flavours matched by clean, crisp acid. Serve well chilled with lightly curried scallops.

Tapestry Chardonnay

QUALITY ♛♛♛
VALUE ★★★
GRAPES chardonnay
REGION McLaren Vale, SA
CELLAR 🍶 2+
ALC./VOL. 13.0%
RRP $16.35

The old Merrivale winery has had a chequered career, with five owners and three different names since it was begun by the Starr family in 1969. Is this why Brian Light calls the new wines Tapestry?

CURRENT RELEASE 1993 This is a big, brassy chardonnay, typically McLaren Vale in style with a rich, full palate and lots of coconutty oak poking through the fruit. Soft, generous and ready to go with chicken.

Tapestry Rhine Riesling

Winemaker Brian Light likes to think of these wines as being woven together from strands of fruit from various vineyards, to create a sort of rich tapestry ...

CURRENT RELEASE 1994 This is a quite lovely, flowery perfumed riesling, the backward pale colour and restrained fruit betraying its cool-grown origins. Its flowery, slightly limey character hints at the traditional Eden Valley style, and the finish is delicate and dry-ish. Good with most white-fleshed fish.

QUALITY ♛♛♛♛
VALUE ★★★★
GRAPES riesling
REGION Adelaide Hills & Bakers Gully, SA
CELLAR 🍾 5
ALC./VOL. 12.0%
RRP $14.50

Tarrawarra Chardonnay

Owner, women's clothing purveyor Marc Besen, had an ambition to make an Australian Corton Charlemagne when he established this winery in 1983. He's getting close ...

Previous outstanding vintages: '88, '90, '91

CURRENT RELEASE 1992 This is a stunning chardonnay which benefits from three years' age before release. It is terrifically complex with rich sweet-peach, butter and tropical flavours, the cedary French oak in fine harmony with the subtle fruit. The finish is dry with a well-judged grip and lingers long. Try it with pheasant.

QUALITY ♛♛♛♛♛
VALUE ★★★★½
GRAPES chardonnay
REGION Yarra Valley, Vic.
CELLAR 🍾 4+
ALC./VOL. 13.7%
RRP $28.00

Tatachilla Chardonnay

This venerable winery is now being guided by ex-Kaiser Stuhl and ex-Wolf Blass marketer/manager Keith Smith.

CURRENT RELEASE 1994 Delicious young chardonnay without much wood, but bursting with tropical/passionfruit estery aromas and lots of stylish peachy flavour on the palate. A little more oak might have made for more complexity, but it's a lovely drink now.

QUALITY ♛♛♛♛
VALUE ★★★★
GRAPES chardonnay
REGION Adelaide Hills, McLaren Vale, SA
CELLAR 🍾 4
ALC./VOL. 13.5%
RRP $15.00

Tatachilla Growers

QUALITY 🍷🍷🍷🍷
VALUE ★★★★
GRAPES chenin blanc, semillon, sauvignon blanc
REGION McLaren Vale, SA
CELLAR 🍾 3
ALC./VOL. 12.6%
RRP $12.00

This is a multiple blend made to drink now and show off some of the characters of the region.
CURRENT RELEASE 1994 A very fragrant United Nations style that drinks well now. The nose is quite floral with sauvignon blanc herb-a-phonics dominating. The palate is loaded with tropical fruit flavours balanced by crisp acid on a clean, dry finish. It can be served well chilled with Vietnamese chicken soup.

Tatachilla Riesling

QUALITY 🍷🍷🍷🍷
VALUE ★★★½
GRAPES riesling
REGION Eden & Clare Valleys, SA
CELLAR 🍾 4
ALC./VOL. 11.4%
RRP $12.00

This label has had more starts than Phar Lap. It is a very historic name and if rumour can be believed, Buckingham Palace has a few 1959 Tatachilla burgundies under the floorboards. And they're supposed to be in fine fettle.
CURRENT RELEASE 1994 A very aromatic and limey nose, and lime dominates the palate too. The finish is crisp with firm acid. It is a chill-to-thrill style and the intensity of flavour is quite startling. Try it with a leafy salad or fried whitebait.

Thistle Hill Riesling

QUALITY 🍷🍷🍷
VALUE ★★★
GRAPES riesling
REGION Mudgee, NSW
CELLAR 🍾 3
ALC./VOL. 12.5%
RRP $9.95 (cellar door) ♥

This comes in a green claret bottle, which is a bit of a shock for riesling purists. It seems to be a '90s way of getting feeble-minded people interested in riesling. Maker Dave Robertson.
CURRENT RELEASE 1994 This is a sweeter style that lacks a bit of finesse, but has genuine floral and dry-grass young riesling aromas. The sweetness leaves the finish not so crisp, so chill well and serve with seafood bisque.

Tim Adams Botrytis Affected Semillon

Clare's dry, sunny autumns are not generally favourable to botrytis infection, but Tim Adams has pinpointed a vineyard which is better suited than most.

Previous outstanding vintages: '90, '91

CURRENT RELEASE 1994 This seems less heavily botrytised than usual, with grassy semillon fruit and little botrytis character on the nose. The palate is lean, firm, crisp in acid, with a relatively low sugar level. It is not luscious, but suits drinking with pâté.

QUALITY ♛♛♛
VALUE ★★★
GRAPES semillon
REGION Clare Valley, SA
CELLAR 🍷 3
ALC./VOL. 11.0%
RRP $12.60 (375ml)

Tim Adams Riesling

Adams has a commendable policy of crediting his grapegrowers on his back labels. This is very fair-minded, as growers are often unsung heroes while winemakers get star billing.

CURRENT RELEASE 1994 This is a well-crafted riesling but not what you might expect from a top year in Clare. The colour shows forward development, with a shy, burnt-toast aroma and there is lots of acid early on the rich, dry palate. It ends with some grip and is balanced, but lacks fruit definition and charm.

QUALITY ♛♛♛
VALUE ★★★
GRAPES riesling
REGION Clare Valley, SA
CELLAR 🍷 3
ALC./VOL. 12.0%
RRP $12.55

Tim Adams Semillon

QUALITY ♥♥♥♥♔
VALUE ★★★★
GRAPES semillon
REGION Clare Valley, SA
CELLAR 🍷 6
ALC./VOL. 13.0%
RRP $15.00

Tim Adams is generous about acknowledging the grapegrower on his back labels. This one's fruit arrived thanks to the Wards, the Crawleys and the Jackas. It was fermented in new oak, 75 per cent American and 25 per cent French.

Previous outstanding vintages: '88, '90, '91, '92, '93

CURRENT RELEASE 1994 This is an exercise in careful oak handling. The wood is there but doesn't overpower. The nose offers toasty and resiny notes together with lemon and lanolin. The varietal character will probably show better with a little age, but it's hard to resist that freshness now. Drink with gnocchi in a creamy sauce.

Tim Knappstein Chardonnay

QUALITY ♥♥♥♔
VALUE ★★★
GRAPES chardonnay
REGION Clare Valley 78%, Adelaide Hills 22%, SA
CELLAR 🍷 2
ALC./VOL. 13.5%
RRP $19.50

Knappstein now blends some of his Lenswood Adelaide Hills fruit with the Clare to give this chardonnay a lift. It works well.

CURRENT RELEASE 1993 This is a big, butch style with lots of toasty oak and deep fruit. The flavours are very generous and it's drinking at its peak now, although there is a trace of astringency. Pair it with quails.

Tim Knappstein Fumé Blanc

QUALITY ♥♥♥♔
VALUE ★★★
GRAPES sauvignon blanc 77%, semillon 23%
REGION Clare Valley & Adelaide Hills, SA
CELLAR 🍷 3
ALC./VOL. 12.8%
RRP $18.00

Knappstein claims to have been the first in this country to market a fumé blanc. Most makers give it a little semillon and oak, so it more resembles white Bordeaux than its Loire Valley model.

CURRENT RELEASE 1994 This has an interesting nose of green pea and cut grass from the hills fruit, plus pineapple from riper Clare material. The palate is delicate with straightforward lively flavour. A useful wine in a vegan restaurant.

Tim Knappstein Gewürztraminer

Few wineries bother to make a serious attempt at traminer these days, and even fewer make a good one.

CURRENT RELEASE 1994 This one announces itself from a fair distance: the pungent, spicy nose is unmistakably traminer. The palate contains full, spicy and herbal varietal flavours with a twist of lavender. The finish is dry and it goes well with Thai fish cakes.

QUALITY ★★★★
VALUE ★★★½
GRAPES gewürztraminer
REGION Clare Valley, SA
CELLAR 2
ALC./VOL. 12.8%
RRP $14.20

Tim Knappstein Riesling

Knappstein's riesling is a noted cellaring style that improves with age – it may appear somewhat reticent in its youth.

Previous outstanding vintages: '80, '85, '90, '92, '93

CURRENT RELEASE 1994 Very restrained now, this has a delicate aroma that hints at spices with a trace of yeastiness. The palate is lean and dry, and the wine is yet to open up. It demands cellaring, then drink it with white-fleshed fish.

QUALITY ★★★
VALUE ★★★
GRAPES riesling
REGION Clare Valley, SA
CELLAR 1–5+
ALC./VOL. 12.5%
RRP $14.20

Tisdall Chenin Blanc

Winemaker Toni Stockhausen looks after 2000 tonnes of fruit for the Mildara Blass group at this Echuca winery.

CURRENT RELEASE 1993 An unusual array of sweet, honeyed, fruit-conserve scents greet the nose and there is a power of ripe fruit flavour on the tongue, ending dry with nice soft mouthfeel. Take it to a Lebanese restaurant and try it with dips.

QUALITY ★★★
VALUE ★★★
GRAPES chenin blanc
REGION various, Vic.
CELLAR 1
ALC./VOL. 11.5%
RRP $9.00 Ⓢ

Tollana Botrytis Rhine Riesling

QUALITY ♛♛♛♕
VALUE ★★★½
GRAPES riesling
REGION Coonawarra & Eden Valley, SA
CELLAR 🍷 1
ALC./VOL. 11.0%
RRP $12.30 (375ml) ⓢ

Someone's calculator finger slipped here: the back label says 6.5 standard drinks, but they forgot to allow for the fact that it's only a half-bottle ...
CURRENT RELEASE 1993 The pungent honey-like scent will bring the bees from miles around. This has a lovely spicy, herbal, sweet nose and a rich, deep, unctuous palate to go well with citrus flans – it needs food as there's a slight sourness to the finish.

QUALITY ♛♛♛♛♛
VALUE ★★★★★
GRAPES riesling
REGION Coonawarra & Eden Valley, SA
CELLAR 🍷 3+
ALC./VOL. 11.2%
RRP $12.35 (375ml) ⓢ

CURRENT RELEASE 1994 Yum-oh! This has a deep golden colour and smells of tealeafy vanilla, honey and floral citrus riesling varietal character. In the mouth, citrus and marmalade are more pronounced, with luscious balance of fruit and sweetness. Fabulous stuff to have with lemony crème brûlée.

Tollana Eden Valley Chardonnay

QUALITY ♛♛♛♕
VALUE ★★★½
GRAPES chardonnay
REGION Eden Valley, SA
CELLAR 🍷 1
ALC./VOL. 13.5%
RRP $12.75 ⓢ

From a difficult year in the Eden Valley region, when yields were low but grape sugars high. Maker Neville Falkenberg.
CURRENT RELEASE 1993 An unusual chardonnay which shows a lot of early development: citrusy, resiny nose, and a big-flavoured palate which is losing its fruit quite quickly. Drink it up soon, with chicken satays.

QUALITY ♛♛♛♛♕
VALUE ★★★★★
GRAPES chardonnay
REGION Eden Valley, SA
CELLAR 🍷 4
ALC./VOL. 13.0%
RRP $12.75 ⓢ

CURRENT RELEASE 1994 Excellent value for money, this chardonnay has lots of winemakerly complexities: barrel fermentation and malolactic characters vie with peachy, honeyed fruit and the palate has intensity, life and focus. At its best now, with veal sweetbreads.

Tollana Eden Valley Riesling

Eden Valley is something of a misnomer, as most vineyards, like Tollana's, are in hilly country. The region is named after the town of Eden Valley. Maker Neville Falkenberg.

CURRENT RELEASE 1994 Forward development shows in a full yellow hue, and the bouquet is fragrant, floral and open. The flavour is big and generous, ending with dryness that allows some phenolics to show. But the finish is long and the wine has the strength to go with food such as Alsatian sauerkraut. Good value.

QUALITY ????
VALUE ★★★★
GRAPES riesling
REGION Eden Valley, SA
CELLAR 4
ALC./VOL. 12.5%
RRP $11.00 $

Tollana Semillon

Tollana winemaker Neville Falkenberg does a fine job of combining the seemingly incompatible flavours of high-toast oak and green-pea fruit in this entertaining dry white.

Previous outstanding vintages: '93

CURRENT RELEASE 1994 The nose is all about toasty oak, with green-pea semillon fruit lurking beneath. The palate reveals a sweet oak-fruit synergy: grassy, herbal, smoky and the dimensions are generous. Drink with a seafood cocktail.

QUALITY ????
VALUE ★★★★
GRAPES semillon
REGION Eden Valley, Adelaide Hills, SA
CELLAR 3
ALC./VOL. 13.5%
RRP $12.75 $

Tolley Cellar Reserve Chardonnay

The Tolley family is one of the oldest and most respected in South Australian winemaking, with a history dating back over 100 years.

CURRENT RELEASE 1994 This is somewhat plain and retiring on the nose, but has respectable depth of flavour for the price (which may be discounted). It has no frills but no faults either. There is some alcohol weight, a little grip and decent length. A basic wine at a price we may not see in chardonnay for much longer.

QUALITY ???
VALUE ★★★
GRAPES chardonnay
REGION various, SA
CELLAR 1
ALC./VOL. 13.5%
RRP $8.50 $

Tolley Hope Valley Cellars Padthaway Chardonnay

QUALITY ♥♥♥♪
VALUE ★★★
GRAPES chardonnay
REGION Padthaway, SA
CELLAR 🍾 2
ALC./VOL. 13.0%
RRP $18.00

In 1992, their centenary year, Tolleys resurrected a colourful, classy old export label from 1909. They put it on a special centenary red, then extended it to a premium chardonnay.

CURRENT RELEASE 1993 This is a complex wine with barrel-ferment character and a very deep yellow colour. It's quite forward in development, buttery, nutty and toasty, with a very dry finish and some oak astringency. Chill well and serve with pork and apple.

Tolley Pedare Chardonnay

QUALITY ♥♥♥♪
VALUE ★★★½
GRAPES chardonnay
REGION Padthaway 52%, Barossa Valley 48%, SA
CELLAR 🍾 1
ALC./VOL. 13.5%
RRP $13.85 ⑤

The Tolley family recently branched out and established vineyards in Padthaway, from which a fair share of this wine comes.

CURRENT RELEASE 1994 The 'in-your-face' fruit is very seductive in this exuberant, lightly wooded chardonnay. It reminds of ripe peach and fig, and the palate is rich, soft and full-bodied – albeit a little short. A good-value ready-drinking chardonnay. Try it with prosciutto and figs.

Tolley Pedare Gewürztraminer

QUALITY ♥♥♥♥♪
VALUE ★★★★
GRAPES gewürztraminer
REGION Barossa Valley, SA
CELLAR 🍾 2
ALC./VOL. 13.7%
RRP $13.80 ⑤

Year in, year out, this is one of the most reliable traminers on the market. Pedare is an acronym of Peter, David and Reg Tolley. Makers Chris Tolley and Di Heinrich.

CURRENT RELEASE 1994 What a wine! It's built along the lines of Alsace, where they get the grapes as ripe as possible. Powerful flavour, rose-petal and lychee-like perfume which carries onto the palate. Monumental depth and length. There's some tannin on the finish but the flavour carries it. As foie gras is pretty much out of the question in Oz, take it to your local Vietnamese and order noodles with shredded pork and mint.

Tolley Pedare Rhine Riesling

Pedare is Tolley's premium range of table wines. Reg Tolley runs the family company today, but tomorrow it will be part of Mildara Blass. Makers Chris Tolley and Di Heinrich.

CURRENT RELEASE 1994 This is a typical warm-area riesling, with a softly floral nose and a quite broad palate profile. It's slightly lean in the middle then winds up with fresh acid. Not a wine of finesse but very respectable. Try it with whitebait.

QUALITY 🍷🍷🍷
VALUE ★★★
GRAPES riesling
REGION Barossa Valley, SA
CELLAR 🍾 2
ALC./VOL. 10.5%
RRP $13.85 Ⓢ

Trentham Estate Colombard Chardonnay

Colombard, a traditional Cognac grape, is well suited to the hotter regions and blends admirably with chardonnay. Maker Anthony Murphy.

CURRENT RELEASE 1994 Great value here! This is a simple, fruity, soft white to be enjoyed while young and fresh. The nose has flowery and herbal scents; the taste is grassy/citrusy with a fresh lemony acid tang. It's a well-made wine to serve with vegetable terrines.

QUALITY 🍷🍷🍷
VALUE ★★★★
GRAPES colombard, chardonnay
REGION Murray River, NSW
CELLAR 🍾 1
ALC./VOL. 11.5%
RRP $8.85

Tunnel Hill Chardonnay

Tarrawarra's second label is also 100 per cent estate-grown. Winemaker since 1991 is Martin Williams, and chief winemaker since '95 is Michael Kluczko.

Previous outstanding vintages: '90, '91

CURRENT RELEASE 1993 This is a finely tuned food wine, dry but smooth. It has less obvious oak and complexity than the Tarrawarra, but is still full of character. The nose is subtle, fruit-driven and discreetly peachy; the taste buttery, gentle, fine yet up-front. Try it with whitebait fritters.

QUALITY 🍷🍷🍷🍷
VALUE ★★★½
GRAPES chardonnay
REGION Yarra Valley, Vic.
CELLAR 🍾 3
ALC./VOL. 13.0%
RRP $18.00

Tyrrell's Fordwich Verdelho

QUALITY ♛♛♛
VALUE ★★½
GRAPES verdelho
REGION Hunter Valley, NSW
CELLAR 🍷 1
ALC./VOL. 12.7%
RRP $16.00

This is a member of the new Tyrrell's individual vineyard line. Fordwich and Broke are a Hunter sub-region, off to the south of the main Pokolbin area.

CURRENT RELEASE 1994 This has a pleasant but essentially simple fruity nose, and in the mouth the weight and richness of the verdelho grape is apparent. Although there's a confectionery character typical of the variety, it finishes nice and dry. Try it with dim sum.

Tyrrell's Lost Block Semillon

QUALITY ♛♛♛
VALUE ★★½
GRAPES semillon
REGION Hunter Valley, NSW
CELLAR ⬌ 1–5+
ALC./VOL. 10.9%
RRP $16.00

The Lost Block is part of the HVD vineyard which Tyrrell's bought from the Penfold group. They decided to bottle it separately because it had an outstanding and individual style.

CURRENT RELEASE 1994 This has a pale hue and typical Tyrrell's semillon aroma: straw, lanolin and apples. It is lean, light and austere at this time. Needs a little age to soften. Until then, best drunk with food like whole trout with cashews.

Tyrrell's Shee-Oak Chardonnay

QUALITY ♛♛♛
VALUE ★★½
GRAPES chardonnay
REGION Hunter Valley, NSW
CELLAR 🍷 3
ALC./VOL. 13.0%
RRP $16.00 Ⓢ

Every time you turn around there's a new range of wines pouring out of one of the major wine companies. This is part of Tyrrell's new individual vineyard range.

CURRENT RELEASE 1994 The '93 was described as unwooded, but this seems to have a touch of barrel character. The lean palate begins with some sweetness and ends firm and dry but a little short. A slightly confusing wine that will probably be best with a few months more age. Try it with calamari.

Tyrrell's Vat 1 Semillon

Tyrrell's maintains its reputation as one of the leading makers of Hunter semillon, which it claims to have been producing for 130 years. It's an unwooded style that drinks well with seafood when fresh but mellows into a lovely full-bodied drink.

Previous outstanding vintages: '75, '76, '77, '84, '86, '87, '89, '90, '91, '92, '93

CURRENT RELEASE 1994 A typical shy young traditional Hunter, this has a pale yellow colour and subdued, slightly raw, undeveloped lemon and lanolin nose. In the mouth it is fruit-sweet and slightly minty, difficult to judge young but undoubtedly will live and improve for many years. Suits Balmain bugs or scampi.

QUALITY ♛♛♛♛♕
VALUE ★★★★
GRAPES semillon
REGION Hunter Valley, NSW
CELLAR 🍾 1–10+
ALC./VOL. 10.8%
RRP $23.30

Tyrrell's Vat 47 Pinot Chardonnay

This vintage of Vat 47 did well in the wine shows, winning two trophies at Sydney in '95 including the best white table wine of the show. Maker Andrew Spinaze.

Previous outstanding vintages: '73, '77, '79, '80, '84, '86, '89, '91, '93

CURRENT RELEASE 1994 Here's a very smart young chardonnay with the world at its feet. Still showing quite a deal of oak, it also has excellent fruit concentration and length, promising to turn into a stunner with time. This could cope with roast pheasant.

QUALITY ♛♛♛♛♕
VALUE ★★★★
GRAPES chardonnay
REGION Hunter Valley, NSW
CELLAR 🍾 1–5+
ALC./VOL. 12.5%
RRP $28.00

Vasse Felix Classic Dry White

QUALITY ▼▼▼▼⸳
VALUE ★★★★
GRAPES semillon, sauvignon blanc, chardonnay
REGION Margaret River, WA
CELLAR 🍾 2
ALC./VOL. 13.0%
RRP $17.30

Vasse Felix was one of the pioneering Margaret River vineyards, begun by Tom Cullity in 1967 and bought by the Holmes à Court family along with Mount Barker's Forest Hill. Output is 22,000 cases.

Previous outstanding vintages: '92

CURRENT RELEASE 1994 This is a model classic dry white and a style others would do well to emulate. It has definite weight and structure, and the cut-grass/green-stick aromas typical of the district are more attractive than most. There's a generous mid-palate of nectarine and cashew flavours and impressive persistence. Try it with seafood salad.

Virage Semillon Sauvignon Blanc Chardonnay

QUALITY ▼▼▼
VALUE ★★½
GRAPES semillon, sauvignon blanc, chardonnay
REGION Margaret River, WA
CELLAR 🍾 3
ALC./VOL. 12.4%
RRP $15.00

Virage is French for curve, but the wine seems pretty straight to us. Winemaker Bernard Abbott used to work for Vasse Felix.

CURRENT RELEASE 1994 This has a rather neutral nose but good flavour on the palate. Soft yet dry, it has good depth and structure, and a long finish, without any particular varietal thumbprint. Try it with barbecued octopus.

Voyager Estate Classic

This is the reborn Freycinet of Margaret River, no relation to the one in Tassie. The back label suggests cellaring for three to five years. Well, maybe – if you kept it in a very cold fridge ...
CURRENT RELEASE 1994 This is a typical middle-of-the-road Margaret River white, sporting a grassy sauvignon blanc-like nose and a light, somewhat short palate of tangy green/herbaceousness. It finishes with a little alcohol heat but happily avoids the sugar hit one often finds in these 'classics'.

QUALITY ♛♛♛
VALUE ★★½
GRAPES sauvignon blanc, semillon
REGION Margaret River, WA
CELLAR 🍷 1
ALC./VOL. 13.0%
RRP $16.70

Warrenmang Estate Chardonnay

If you are in the Pyrenees and looking for a feed and a bunk, this is the place. There is a spectacular resort and a great restaurant and you won't go short of a drink. Maker Roland Kaval.
CURRENT RELEASE 1994 An interesting nose with biscuit and sap aromas. The rich palate has a buttery texture and strong melon and pawpaw flavours. The finish has a creamy character with some well-integrated oak. Don't overchill, then serve with yabbies in a cream sauce.

QUALITY ♛♛♛♝
VALUE ★★★
GRAPES chardonnay
REGION Pyrenees, Vic.
CELLAR 🍷 3
ALC./VOL. 14.0%
RRP $18.50

Warrenmang LH Traminer

This late harvest gewürztraminer is one out of the box for the Pyrenees. On paper it looks like an off-the-wall style, but in reality why not!
CURRENT RELEASE *non-vintage* 'A taste of honey, a taste much sweeter than wine ...' There is abundant honey on the nose and the palate offers lychee and honey flavours. It is not as rich as the nose would suggest and there is plenty of acid on the finish. It should be served well chilled with a summer pudding.

QUALITY ♛♛♛♝
VALUE ★★★½
GRAPES gewürztraminer
REGION Pyrenees, Vic.
CELLAR 🍷 3
ALC./VOL. 11.5%
RRP $11.50

Water Wheel Chardonnay

QUALITY 🍷🍷🍷🍷⸮
VALUE ★★★★½
GRAPES chardonnay
REGION Bendigo, Vic.
CELLAR 🍾 4
ALC./VOL. 15.0%
RRP $12.00

This vineyard cum winery was established in 1972, but it wasn't until it came into the hands of the Cumming family that it found a purple patch. The annual production is 7500 cases. Maker Peter Cumming.

CURRENT RELEASE 1994 A very natty style that is fun to drink. You won't believe the alcohol and it doesn't show in the wine. The nose has plenty of peach and cashew aroma and the palate is full with ripe fruit flavour. Peach, melon, fig line up for inspection and the drill sergeant is some strapping oak on a firm finish. A wine big enough to chill well. Try it with fish pie.

Weatherall Rhine Riesling

QUALITY 🍷🍷🍷🍷
VALUE ★★★
GRAPES riesling
REGION Coonawarra, SA
CELLAR 🍾 3
ALC./VOL. 12.0%
RRP $14.00

This is a long-established grapegrowing name in the district, but the winery and the label are very new.

CURRENT RELEASE 1993 In spite of the bottle-age this wine retains freshness. The nose is aromatic with a hint of violets. The palate still displays zesty lime characters and the finish shows some fresh acid and attractive cool crispness. Serve well chilled with oysters natural.

Willow Creek Tulum Chardonnay

QUALITY 🍷🍷🍷🍷
VALUE ★★★★
GRAPES chardonnay
REGION Mornington Peninsula, Vic.
CELLAR 🍾 3
ALC./VOL. 13.0%
RRP $19.90

This one is in black tie – it is the maker's top of the line and gets a lavish wood treatment. Willow Creek was established in 1980.

CURRENT RELEASE 1993 This is a rich, full style with good complexity. The nose offers peach and apricot aromas plus a hint of wood. The full-flavoured palate has ripe peach and apricot flavours followed by drying oak on an impressive finish. It shouldn't be served too cold.

Willow Creek Unoaked Chardonnay

More nude wine. It seems there is an epidemic of skinny dipping breaking out on the Mornington Peninsula, where makers see fit not to dress their wines in wood.

CURRENT RELEASE 1994 This is an interesting adventure in flavour. The nose is sappy with hints of citrus, and the palate is full of grapefruit and melon characters followed by crisp acid and a hint of natural tannin. Medium chill and serve with smoked chicken.

QUALITY ♛♛♛♟
VALUE ★★★½
GRAPES chardonnay
REGION Mornington Peninsula, Vic.
CELLAR 🍾 1
ALC./VOL. 13.5%
RRP $15.00

Willows (The) Semillon

The Scholz family have been medicos in the Barossa for a long while; these days they minister with wine.

CURRENT RELEASE 1993 This is a wooded semillon but the oak is in harmony with big, rich fruit. A nutty, toasty full Barossa style, rich and fruit-sweet, mouthfilling, long and round. The lemon/lanolin flavours linger well. Try it with chicken.

QUALITY ♛♛♛♛
VALUE ★★★★
GRAPES semillon
REGION Barossa Valley, SA
CELLAR 🍾 2
ALC./VOL. 13.0%
RRP $13.50

Wilson Vineyard Chardonnay

Dr John Wilson founded a winery in Clare in 1974. He is an interesting character, and not afraid to express his views. He produces 2800 cases a year. Maker John Wilson.

CURRENT RELEASE 1994 A lightly wooded style that was made to drink now. There are gentle melon aromas on the nose and the palate has clean grapefruit flavours supported by discreet oak on a clean dry finish. It can be served with a medium chill with a warm salad of quail.

QUALITY ♛♛♛♟
VALUE ★★★½
GRAPES chardonnay
REGION Clare Valley, SA
CELLAR 🍾 2
ALC./VOL. 13.5%
RRP $13.00

Wilson Vineyard Gallery Series Riesling

QUALITY 🍷🍷🍷🍷
VALUE ★★★★
GRAPES riesling
REGION Clare Valley, SA
CELLAR 🍾 4
ALC./VOL. 12.0%
RRP $14.00

There are no points for guessing that any gallery series will feature paintings on the label. Wilson's are usually very stylish wines.

CURRENT RELEASE Clare Valley riesling right down to the last drop. The nose has emphatic citrus aromas and the palate delivers with striking lime flavour. The finish is crisp and acidic – a flinty style that should age well. Give it a chill and try it with seafood mousse.

Wilton Estate Marsanne

QUALITY 🍷🍷🍷🍷
VALUE ★★★½
GRAPES marsanne
REGION Riverina, NSW
CELLAR 🍾 1
ALC./VOL. 12.3%
RRP $11.00

This is a large winery (60,000 cases) at Yenda, NSW, and was established in 1977. It produces mainly table wines, and Hidden Valley is its second label. Maker Adrian Sheridan.

CURRENT RELEASE 1991 The colour is a mid-lemon yellow and the nose is very toasty with honeysuckle undertones. The palate has a creamy texture and honeyed fruit flavours followed by toasty oak on a dry finish. Serve lightly chilled with pipis.

Wirilda Creek Oak Matured Semillon

QUALITY 🍷🍷🍷🍷
VALUE ★★★½
GRAPES semillon
REGION McLaren Vale, SA
CELLAR 🍾 2
ALC./VOL. 12.5%
RRP $13.90

A new label from the Southern Vales district, and the grapes were grown on the original Church Block. It is produced by the McLaren Vale Wine Company.

CURRENT RELEASE 1994 The wood is quite obvious and the fruit seems to tag along for the ride. The nose has toasty oak, and the palate offers straw and gooseberry flavours quickly followed by smoky, toasty oak. It could be served lightly chilled with marron in a rich dressing.

Wolf Blass Chardonnay

Another fighting brand from the Blass stable. As usual the theme is full-on flavours with finesse taking a back seat.

CURRENT RELEASE 1994 This is a fulsome style with no frills. The nose is peachy and that's exactly what you get in the glass, full-on peach. The finish has obvious oak with drying aspects. Medium chill and try it with fried chicken.

QUALITY 🍷🍷🍷
VALUE ★★★
GRAPES chardonnay
REGION various
CELLAR 🍾 2
ALC./VOL. 12.0%
RRP $10.95

Wolf Blass Chardonnay (Barrel fermented)

There was a time when Herr Blass refused to have a chardonnay on the books. It seems Mildara Blass changed his mind. Maker Mike Press (chief).

CURRENT RELEASE 1994 The nose offers melon and peach with a hint of wood. The palate has a creamy texture thanks to barrel fermentation and the main flavour is grapefruit with well-integrated oak on a balanced finish. Serve lightly chilled with tripe in a white sauce.

QUALITY 🍷🍷🍷🍷
VALUE ★★★½
GRAPES chardonnay
REGION South-east Australia
CELLAR 🍾 3
ALC./VOL. 12.0%
RRP $12.00

Wolf Blass Classic Dry White

What constitutes a 'classic' dry white remains one of the great wine mysteries. Herr Blass was one of the first (maybe the first) to coin the term.

CURRENT RELEASE 1994 Well-crafted wine that makes much of the fruit. The nose has sweet tropical fruit aromas. The palate continues the tropical theme and there is a hint of sweetness. This is offset by some soft wood on a gentle finish. It can be served fairly well chilled with trippa Italian style.

QUALITY 🍷🍷🍷🍷
VALUE ★★★½
GRAPES chardonnay, semillon, colombard
REGION various SA
CELLAR 🍾 1
ALC./VOL. 11.5%
RRP $12.95

Wolf Blass Gold Label Riesling

QUALITY ▼▼▼▼
VALUE ★★★★
GRAPES riesling
REGION Clare & Eden Valleys, SA
CELLAR 🍷 5
ALC./VOL. 11.5%
RRP $12.95

This label is designed to take the cream of the riesling crop. It is usually a good cellar proposition.

CURRENT RELEASE 1994 Bright green-gold in colour with lots of star-bright qualities. The nose has strong citrus aromas and the palate shows lime and lemon flavours. Acid does a boot scoot on the finish. This is a lively fresh style, so chill well and oysters natural are swell.

Wolf Blass Show Chardonnay

QUALITY ▼▼▼▼
VALUE ★★★★
GRAPES chardonnay
REGION McLaren Vale, SA
CELLAR 🍷 4
ALC./VOL. 12.5%
RRP $19.85

The Blass conversion to this variety came rather late in life. He was a 'riesling man' but the sale to Mildara changed all that ... Maker Chris Hatcher.

CURRENT RELEASE 1994 This is a big no beg-pardons style that shows a load of woodwork. The colour is a bright green-gold and the nose has charred wood characters. The palate is full of peach and melon flavours balanced by firm wood on a brisk finish. Don't overchill, and try it with stir-fried noodles and chicken.

Wolf Blass Spätlese Rhine Riesling

QUALITY ▼▼▼▼
VALUE ★★★★
GRAPES riesling
REGION Coonawarra, Eden Valley, SA
CELLAR 🍷 4
ALC./VOL. 11.5%
RRP $13.00

Boy, is this old-fashioned label in trouble! With the new EEC deal there will have to be a lot of revamping.

CURRENT RELEASE 1994 A light sweet white with plenty of complexity. This is eloquent proof that botrytis styles don't have to arrive with all guns blazing. The colour is pale yellow and there are honeyed botrytis and tropical fruit aromas on the nose. The medium-bodied palate is like a fruit salad that's been sprinkled with limes, and there is fresh acid on the finish. Serve well chilled with soft cheese.

Wolf Blass Traminer Riesling

According to folklore this blend is a drink much loved in the sunshine of the tropics. Wolf Blass traminer riesling has long been a Queensland favourite.

CURRENT RELEASE 1994 The nose is full of rose-petals and spice. The palate is a tad sweet with gooseberry and tropical fruit flavours. Soft acid completes a gentle finish. Give it a good chill and serve with a prawn cocktail.

QUALITY ♥♥♥
VALUE ★★★
GRAPES gewürztraminer, riesling
REGION Eden Valley, SA
CELLAR 1
ALC./VOL. 12.0%
RRP $9.90

Wolf Blass White Label

Blass was always into colours, and white is just one in a Jacob's coat. Mildara Blass continues the spectrum.

CURRENT RELEASE 1994 This is quite a complex wine with a strong talcum-powder aroma on the nose. The palate is herbal with muted gooseberry flavours and some tropical undertones. The finish shows crisp acid. Serve well chilled with scampi.

QUALITY ♥♥♥♥
VALUE ★★★½
GRAPES semillon, sauvignon blanc
REGION Barossa & Clare Valleys, SA
CELLAR 2
ALC./VOL. 11.0%
RRP $10.95

Wolf Blass Yellow Label Rhine Riesling

MS is part of Australian wine lore because he was present when it was suggested that Wolf Blass should make a riesling. WB's immortal response was, 'What – I am a red *vinemaker*!' The rest is drinking history.

CURRENT RELEASE 1994 Very smart stuff, and to tag it as a commercial wine is a put-down. The nose has acute acid and the palate makes a clever but not obvious use of sugar. Lime is the prominent flavour on the palate which follows up with crisp acid on a lean and lengthy finish. It was made to drink now – give it a big chill and serve it with a warm salad of quail.

QUALITY ♥♥♥♥♥
VALUE ★★★★★
GRAPES riesling
REGION Eden & Clare Valleys, SA
CELLAR 1
ALC./VOL. 11.0%
RRP $9.95

Woodstock Botrytis Sweet White

QUALITY 🍷🍷🍷🍷?
VALUE ★★★★½
GRAPES chenin blanc, frontignac, riesling
REGION McLaren Vale, SA
CELLAR 🍾 4
ALC./VOL. 11.0%
RRP $10.00 (375 ml)

When it comes to derring-do, none can match winemaker Scott Collett. He is a character right out of a boy's own annual.
CURRENT RELEASE 1994 This unusual blend has the sweet goods. The nose shows marked botrytis characters plus dried-fruit aromas. The palate is intense with a mixture of apricot, honey and lemon flavours. The finish is dry and crisp. Serve well chilled with a summer pudding.

Woodstock Chardonnay

QUALITY 🍷🍷🍷?
VALUE ★★★½
GRAPES chardonnay
REGION McLaren Vale, SA
CELLAR 🍾 3
ALC./VOL. 12.0%
RRP $13.00

For all the brio, maker Scott Collett tends to make whites of lower alcohol and surprising restraint.
CURRENT RELEASE 1994 Wood to the fore. The nose is nutty with toasty characters and the palate shows restrained peach/fruit flavours followed by assertive oak on a dry finish. It needs more time. Try it with smoked cod.

Woodstock Sauvignon Blanc

QUALITY 🍷🍷🍷🍷
VALUE ★★★★
GRAPES sauvignon blanc
REGION McLaren Vale, SA
CELLAR 🍾 2
ALC./VOL. 13.5%
RRP $12.50

Woodstock was established by Doug Collett in 1974. His son Scott is now the winemaker and produces around 15,000 cases a year.
CURRENT RELEASE 1994 A big wine with plenty of grunt. The nose has tropical fruit aromas and a herbal backdrop. Intense tropical fruit flavour floods the palate and there are also gooseberries lurking in the background. Swashbuckling acid rules the finish. Chill it down and take it to your favourite curry joint.

Woodstock Semillon

After a few beers (well, several actually) Scott Collett will admit his heart is really in red winemaking, and a good white wine is a 'prelude to a red'.

CURRENT RELEASE 1994 An unwooded style that makes for attractive drinking. The nose shows typical grass and gooseberry aromas. The palate is rich with herbs and gooseberry flavour. These are supported by fresh acid on an assertive finish. It should cellar well. Try it with Cajun mullet.

QUALITY ♛♛♛♛
VALUE ★★★★
GRAPES semillon
REGION McLaren Vale, SA
CELLAR ❢ 8
ALC./VOL. 11.5%
RRP $12.00

Wyndham Estate Chardonnay Bin 222

A hangover from the McGuigan days is the triple bin numbers, which old-timers will probably associate with cork-tipped cigarettes of yore.

CURRENT RELEASE 1994 There are peach and melon aromas on the nose and the palate is soft with a hint of sweetness; melon and peach flavours meld to a gentle finish. Serve well chilled with a medium-flavoured fish dish.

QUALITY ♛♛♛♛
VALUE ★★★½
GRAPES chardonnay
REGION Hunter Valley, NSW
CELLAR ❢ 2
ALC./VOL. 12.5%
RRP $11.00 Ⓢ

Wyndham Estate Oak Cask Chardonnay

Wyndham Estate was first established in 1828 but experienced a rebirth with the McGuigan brothers as midwives. It is now part of the Orlando group, owned by Pernod Ricard of France.

CURRENT RELEASE 1994 The colour is a strong lemon yellow and the wine has admirable legs. Wood dominates the nose with a smoky character. The palate is peachy with some sweet fruit flavours buttressed by the aforementioned oak. Serve lightly chilled with smoked cod.

QUALITY ♛♛♛♛
VALUE ★★★½
GRAPES chardonnay
REGION Hunter Valley, NSW
CELLAR ❢ 3
ALC./VOL. 13.0%
RRP $12.00 Ⓢ

Wynns Coonawarra Chardonnay

QUALITY ♘♘♘♘
VALUE ★★★★
GRAPES chardonnay
REGION Coonawarra, SA
CELLAR 🍾 3
ALC./VOL. 13.5%
RRP $13.00 ⓢ

This wine is always the poor cousin to the reds. In recent years there has been a lot of work on the style. Maker Peter Douglas.

CURRENT RELEASE 1993 The colour is a bright lemon yellow and the nose has some intense melon and peach aromas. The same fruit flavours dominate the palate and there is also a hint of mango, pawpaw and other tropical characters. These are supported by discreet oak on the finish. Don't overchill, and try it with a seafood jambalaya.

Wynns Coonawarra Rhine Riesling

QUALITY ♘♘♘♘
VALUE ★★★★½
GRAPES riesling
REGION Coonawarra, SA
CELLAR 🍾 1
ALC./VOL. 12.0%
RRP $9.00 ⓢ

Wynns continue to make and believe in this variety from Coonawarra. Many competitors have grafted over to red varieties. Maker Peter Douglas.

CURRENT RELEASE 1994 This shows the muscat end of the riesling flavour spectrum. The nose has muscat and lime aromas and the palate lime and other citrus flavours. There's crisp acid on a clean dry finish.

Yarra Valley Hills Riesling

QUALITY ♘♘♘♘♘
VALUE ★★★★½
GRAPES riesling
REGION Yarra Valley, Vic.
CELLAR 🍾 3
ALC./VOL. 11.5%
RRP $13.00

This variety is not widely planted in the valley, but judging by this result it is hard to see why.

CURRENT RELEASE 1994 An intense style with a lot of flavour. The nose has a siren's song of citrus. The palate has plenty of fresh lime flavour with mega acid on the finish. A groovy wine when chilled, it needs tandoori chicken wings.

Yarra Valley Hills Sauvignon Blanc

Be it known there are 7.4 standard drinks in this bottle. That means two blokes can drink an equal share with safety. Heterosexual couples must discard 1.4 drinks and lesbian couples have to lose 3.4 drinks.

CURRENT RELEASE 1994 This wine misses the point in terms of varietal signature. It is well made with herbs and citrus on the nose, and the palate has tropical fruit and lemon flavours followed by crisp acid on a clean finish. Chill well and try it with a designer salad.

QUALITY ♛♛♛♚
VALUE ★★★½
GRAPES sauvignon blanc
REGION Yarra Valley, Vic.
CELLAR 🍾 1
ALC./VOL. 12.6%
RRP $14.50

Yering Station Botrytis Semillon

The grapes come from a very dedicated grower at Yenda who encouraged botrytis to attack his grapes. He has many customers for the result.

CURRENT RELEASE 1991 The colour is bright yellow and the nose has plenty of evidence of botrytis character as well as honey and marmalade. The palate is complex with rich sweet apricot, butterscotch and marmalade flavours balanced by high acid on a dry finish. Serve well chilled with a sticky date pudding.

QUALITY ♛♛♛♛♚
VALUE ★★★★½
GRAPES semillon
REGION Riverina, NSW
CELLAR 🍾 4
ALC./VOL. 11.0%
RRP $12.50 (375ml)

Yering Station Chardonnay

QUALITY 🍷🍷🍷🍷
VALUE ★★★★
GRAPES chardonnay
REGION Yarra Valley, Vic.
CELLAR 🍾 5
ALC./VOL. 13.8%
RRP $13.50

This vineyard was established in 1988, and is planted on the site of the Yarra Valley's first vineyard, circa 1840. Today the annual production is around 2000 cases.

CURRENT RELEASE 1993 Heavy metal chardonnay with all the fermentation stops full out. The nose is nutty and creamy with obvious biscuit barrel-ferment characters. The palate also shows the influence of wood plus some peach flavour. Nutty oak completes the picture on the finish. It should be lightly chilled and it goes well with rabbit pie.

Sparkling Wines

All Saints Méthode Traditionelle

Why this revitalised marque needs a fizzy is a moot point. There is a strong case for specialising in fortified wine at the historic castle-like winery. Maker Neil Jericho.

CURRENT RELEASE 1992 A straightforward style with rather coarse bubbles and simple flavours. There are apples and hints of honey on a slightly sweet palate followed by a soft, yeasty, clean finish. It should be served well chilled as a pre-dinner drink.

QUALITY ♛♛♛
VALUE ★★★
GRAPES not stated
REGION Rutherglen, Vic.
CELLAR 🍾 1
ALC./VOL. 12.5%
RRP $13.50

All Saints NV Cabernet Sauvignon

This is yet another sparkling burgundy style that uses cabernet sauvignon. It is a rich, ripe formulation.

CURRENT RELEASE *non-vintage* The colour is deep ruby and the nose has ripe fruit aromas plus hints of spice. The palate is a middleweight with ripe raspberry flavours and more than a touch of sweetness. The finish is clean and the bubbles enliven the palate. Serve well chilled with turkey.

QUALITY ♛♛♛♛
VALUE ★★★★
GRAPES cabernet sauvignon
REGION Rutherglen, Vic.
CELLAR 🍾 3
ALC./VOL. 13.5%
RRP $13.50

Andrew Garrett Chardonnay NV

QUALITY ♛♛♛♝
VALUE ★★★½
GRAPES chardonnay
REGION not stated
CELLAR 🍷 1
ALC./VOL. 12.5%
RRP $10.95

Informed observers have been known to ask what happened to Andrew G. Well, he's started the Garrett 'family' label in opposition to the Andrew Garrett label. When Mildara Blass purchased the latter they waved a cheque book around and reportedly finished the former. If it sounds like a riddle, you're not wrong!

CURRENT RELEASE *non-vintage* Very heavy chardonnay character with a biscuit/grapefruit nose. The palate is austere with strong citrus character and a mouth-cleansing quality. The finish is dry and flinty. Serve well chilled as a pre-dinner drink.

Andrew Garrett Pinot Noir NV

QUALITY ♛♛♛♛
VALUE ★★★★
GRAPES pinot noir
REGION not stated
CELLAR 🍷 1
ALC./VOL. 12.0%
RRP $10.95

This is a well-established style that uses the varietal character to promote generosity of flavour.

CURRENT RELEASE *non-vintage* The colour is a pale pink and the nose has bread and meat aromas. The palate is a middleweight with soft fruit and strawberry flavours backed by crisp acid on a lively finish. A good pre-dinner drink.

Ashton Hills Salmon Brut

QUALITY ♛♛♛♛
VALUE ★★★★
GRAPES chardonnay, pinot noir
REGION Adelaide Hills, SA
CELLAR 🍷 1
ALC./VOL. 12.7%
RRP $19.00

This is from a small winery in the Adelaide Hills near Mount Lofty. Production is strictly limited. Maker Steve George.

CURRENT RELEASE 1993 The colour is indeed salmon pink; the nose has strong strawberry aromas; the palate is quite rich with a hint of sweetness and strong strawberry flavours. The finish is balanced by crisp acid. A good afternoon-delight bedroom style.

Barossa Valley Estate E & E Sparkling Shiraz

Like the still dry red of the same name, this comes from the low-yielding old vineyards of Elmor Roehr and Elmore Schulz in the Barossa. They are both grower/members of the Valley Growers Co-operative which owns BVE. Maker Colin Glaetzer.

Previous outstanding vintages: '89, '90

CURRENT RELEASE 1991 An exciting colour here: very deep purple-red which matches the power of the wine. The nose is all coconutty/toasty American oak with some pine resin and herbal scents. It is a very big style: massive fruit, tannin and forests of oak come together in a Wagnerian chorus that lifts the roof. Try roast duck.

QUALITY ♥♥♥♥♥
VALUE ★★★★
GRAPES shiraz
REGION Barossa Valley, SA
CELLAR 🍾 5+
ALC./VOL. 12.5%
RRP $22.00

Blue Pyrenees Reserve Brut

The grapes are all grown at Chateau Remy, near the winery, and speed is vital to prevent oxidation and off-flavours. These winemakers boast they can get the grapes from the vine to the press in just 15 minutes. They made 5000 cases of this vintage.

CURRENT RELEASE 1990 A fairly austere, serious sparkler with a dry acid finish, this also has some bready and biscuity characters from extended age on lees. It is soft and smooth in the mouth and retains its delicacy even after five years. A good bet with smoked trout.

QUALITY ♥♥♥♥
VALUE ★★★
GRAPES chardonnay 55%, pinot noir 35%, pinot meunier 10%
REGION Pyrenees, Vic.
CELLAR 🍾 2
ALC./VOL. 12.5%
RRP $23.50 ⓢ

CURRENT RELEASE 1991 An interesting style with an unusual touch of oak and considerable appeal. It is quite tight and restrained, with a creamy, chardonnay-like nose and herbal, dry-grass aspects. Intense and lean in the mouth, it is subtle, harmonious and the very dry finish lingers well. Try oysters.

QUALITY ♥♥♥♥♥
VALUE ★★★★
GRAPES chardonnay 55%, pinot noir 35%, pinot meunier 10%
REGION Pyrenees, Vic.
CELLAR 🍾 2
ALC./VOL. 12.5%
RRP $23.50

Blue Pyrenees Reserve Brut NV

QUALITY ♙♙♙
VALUE ★★★
GRAPES chardonnay 61%, pinot noir 36%, pinot meunier 3%
REGION Pyrenees, Vic.
CELLAR 🍾 3
ALC./VOL. 12.5%
RRP $17.70 $

Winemaker Vincent Gere, a Frenchman, believes in using traditional Champagne methods, with all three grape varieties and 10 per cent reserve wines. He produced 9000 cases of this cuvée.
CURRENT RELEASE *non-vintage* This continues the dry, delicate style of the vintage brut, although it's a little on the neutral side. The nose is shy but shows some gamey pinot character. The flavour is straightforward with a dry, slightly firm finish that demands food. Try it with fresh oysters.

Brown Brothers Pinot Chardonnay Brut Vintage

QUALITY ♙♙♙♙
VALUE ★★★★
GRAPES pinot noir, chardonnay
REGION King Valley, Vic.
CELLAR 🍾 3+
ALC./VOL. 12.0%
RRP $28.00

Browns entered the premium bubbly stakes a little after the starter's gun, but it's caught up with this one, which took out a major fizz trophy in 1994. Maker Roland Wahlquist.
CURRENT RELEASE 1991 A reserved, delicate style which wears its four years of age lightly. The toasty nose has some developed complexity and there're some candy/lollyshop notes from the pinot noir. The palate is appley with quite tart acidity. Serve with oysters.

Brown Brothers Pinot Chardonnay NV

QUALITY ♙♙♙♙
VALUE ★★★½
GRAPES pinot noir 56%, chardonnay 40%, pinot meunier 4%
REGION King Valley, Vic.
CELLAR 🍾 1
ALC./VOL. 12.0%
RRP $14.50 $

This is the younger and lighter of Browns' two premium bubblies. A fair percentage of grapes from the ultra-cool Whitlands vineyard are used in both.
CURRENT RELEASE *non-vintage* A soft, light style which has good complexity in its subtle bouquet and palate. Lightly bready from yeast contact, it's lean, crisp and lively with lemony flavours and a dry finish. Don't overchill, and try it with cucumber sandwiches.

Cofield Wines Sparkling Shiraz

Established by Max Cofield in 1986, this small winery in north-east Victoria produces around 2400 cases per annum.

CURRENT RELEASE *non-vintage* This is a big wine by any standards and, beware, it is highly charged. The nose is porty with pepper and plum aromas, the rich palate full of ripe fruit followed by slabs of tannin on a grippy finish. It should be served very well chilled.

QUALITY ♥♥♥♥
VALUE ★★★★
CELLAR shiraz
REGION North-east Victoria
CELLAR 🍾 3
ALC./VOL. 14.2%
RRP $15.00

De Bortoli Emeri Superiore Pinot Noir Brut

It's not widely appreciated, but De Bortoli has rapidly grown to be among the ten biggest winemakers in Australia. This wine is named after matriarch Emeri De Bortoli, wife of Deen, and Darren's mum.

CURRENT RELEASE *non-vintage* A gutsy style that's full of flavour but a tad short on finesse. The colour is light yellow; the nose offers straw, burnt toast and melon. It is a straightforward bubbly with a slight grip to the dry finish. Smoked oysters here.

QUALITY ♥♥♥
VALUE ★★★
GRAPES pinot noir
REGION Riverina, NSW
CELLAR 🍾
ALC./VOL. 11.0%
RRP $9.00

De Bortoli Windy Peak Prestige Cuvée

This is the first sparkling wine released under the Windy Peak label and slots in at the top of the De Bortoli range of bubbles.

CURRENT RELEASE *non-vintage* This has a palish salmon-pink hue and the nose is definitely pinot: gamey, smoky and quite complex. The mousse is very fluffy in the mouth and there's abundant smoky/toasty flavour winding up with a very dry, appley acid finish. An attractive drink with canapés.

QUALITY ♥♥♥⟨
VALUE ★★★½
GRAPES pinot noir
REGION 100% Yarra Valley, Vic.
CELLAR 🍾 2
ALC./VOL. 11.5%
RRP $12.20

Domaine Chandon Blanc de Blancs

QUALITY ♖♖♖♖♖
VALUE ★★★★★
GRAPES chardonnay
REGION various
CELLAR 🍷 3+
ALC./VOL. 12.0%
RRP $30.00 ⓢ

This winery, the Yarra Valley-based offshoot of Champagne giant Moët & Chandon, has a full range of sparkling wines that seems to get better year by year. Makers Wayne Donaldson and team.

CURRENT RELEASE 1990 What a wine! This is a charmer if ever there was one: a winning bouquet of creamy, lightly toasty chardonnay, and a palate that combines depth with finesse, richness with complexity. The long finish is endowed with honey and candied fruit flavours, beautifully harmonised. Pass the caviar, please.

Domaine Chandon Blanc de Noirs

QUALITY ♖♖♖?
VALUE ★★★
GRAPES pinot noir
REGION various
CELLAR 🍷 1
ALC./VOL. 12.9%
RRP $30.00 ⓢ

This is a curiosity wine, for those who like gutsy sparklings without the finesse of chardonnay. It has a cuvée number, as opposed to the vintage-dating system now in place.

Previous outstanding vintages: '88

CURRENT RELEASE *non-vintage* 90–3 This is based on the 1990 harvest. A year older, and it doesn't look quite as good. Pale pink colour and a rubbery, meaty, smoky nose betray the pinot noir grape. There's some aldehyde too. The palate has candied fruit and slight astringency from the red grapes, the tannin chopping it off a tad short. Try smoked salmon.

Domaine Chandon Brut

Domaine Chandon is taking grapes from 42 growers in 11 districts across southern Australia, and blending from 60 different lots of wine: very much the Champagne approach.

Previous outstanding vintages: 90–5, 90–1, 91–1

CURRENT RELEASE 1992 Perhaps the best of this line to date. Rich smoky, bready and dried-fruit characters, a mousse as fluffy as a Persian cat, and superb balance and drinkability. Perfect with Sydney rock oysters.

QUALITY ★★★★★
VALUE ★★★★★
GRAPES chardonnay 48%, pinot noir 50%, pinot meunier 2%
REGION various
CELLAR 3
ALC./VOL. 12.7%
RRP $30.00 ⓢ

Domaine Chandon Brut LD

'LD' stands for 'late disgorged', in the same way that Bollinger RD means recently disgorged. It denotes a wine that's been aged longer than usual on its yeast lees. This is a nice wine, but the latest DCA efforts are better still.

CURRENT RELEASE 1988 A slightly brassy hue – showing red fruit – and the nose is somewhat plain straw/toasty/earthy, despite the extra age. The lean, dry palate has light candied-fruit flavour and finishes quite firm. Don't overchill, and serve with pre-dinner nibbles.

QUALITY ★★★★
VALUE ★★★
GRAPES chardonnay 53%, pinot noir 47%
REGION various
CELLAR 2+
ALC./VOL. 11.5%
RRP $30.00

Eyton on Yarra Pinot Chardonnay

Fine food and premium wine is the credo for this winery in the rapidly developing Yarra Valley.

CURRENT RELEASE 1993 A yeasty style that shows some of the best attributes of both grapes. The nose has yeast and meaty characters, while the palate is full of citrus flavours with strong acid on a long finish. A very fresh style that makes an attractive pre-dinner drink.

QUALITY ★★★★
VALUE ★★★½
GRAPES chardonnay 50%, pinot noir 50%
REGION Yarra Valley, Vic.
CELLAR 3
ALC./VOL. 12.0%
RRP $18.00

Garden Gully Sparkling Burgundy

QUALITY ♥♥♥♥♥
VALUE ★★★★★
GRAPES shiraz
REGION Great Western, Vic.
CELLAR 🍾 4
ALC./VOL. 13.0%
RRP $17.00

This winery was established by Messrs Randall and Fletcher when they made sparkling and white wine for Seppelt. Maker Brian Fletcher.

CURRENT RELEASE 1993 This wine breaks the tradition of the style and shuns residual sugar in the middle palate. The nose is packed with pepper qualities and the palate is complex with mulberry, plum and cherry flavours. Oak adds dryness to the finish and there is considerable grip. Serve well chilled with turkey.

Grand Cru Estate Brut Tradition

QUALITY ♥♥♥
VALUE ★★★
GRAPES not stated
REGION Eden Valley, SA
CELLAR 🍾 2
ALC./VOL. 12.5%
RRP $20.00

The boundary that separates Eden Valley from the Adelaide Hills runs close to this vineyard at Springton, and Grand Cru found itself on the wrong side of the fence, but we're not sure it makes any difference.

CURRENT RELEASE 1991 This is a slightly austere, delicate style showing dry straw chardonnay-like aromas and not a lot of yeast complexity. It finishes very dry and firm, and would go down better with food. Try smoked salmon blinis.

Grand Cru Estate Sparkling Shiraz

QUALITY ♥♥♥
VALUE ★★★
GRAPES shiraz
REGION Eden Valley, SA
CELLAR 🍾 1
ALC./VOL. 12.5%
RRP $20.00

Having guided the family company Seppelt through the '70s and early '80s, Karl Seppelt apparently has a soft spot for the 'sparkling burgundy' style Seppelt made famous.

CURRENT RELEASE 1991 This has a developed colour and a mellow leafy/berry, somewhat Ribena-like bouquet. It is a lighter style, lean, and starts off sweet then finishes with drying tannin. Try turkey with plenty of cranberry sauce.

Hanging Rock Macedon

This is John Ellis's third release, a blend of 1987–92 wines. It is an uncompromising style which polarises tasters, but you can't argue that it's a wine without character.

CURRENT RELEASE *non-vintage* (MARK III) Slightly brassy pinot-tinted hue, and the nose is a riot of complex bready, aldehyde and candied fruit characters that combine to give a slightly feral aspect. This wine is different! It is rich and full in the mouth with a soft dry finish and is more than a little Champagne-like. Sip with blinis and caviar.

QUALITY 🍷🍷🍷🍷🍷
VALUE ★★★★
GRAPES pinot noir, chardonnay
REGION Macedon, Vic.
CELLAR 2
ALC./VOL. 12.0%
RRP $35.40

Best Sparkling Wine

Hardys Grand Reserve Brut

Funny how cheap and basic wines have impressive names. This is nothing grand, nor is it a true reserve wine.

CURRENT RELEASE *non-vintage* This will offend no one but neither will it light many fires. Neutral herbal fruit greets the sniff, and the taste is again simple and fairly short, but it's technically well made and is good value at below seven bucks. Clean dry finish. Add orange juice for a Buck's Fizz.

QUALITY 🍷🍷🍷
VALUE ★★★½
GRAPES not stated
REGION not stated
CELLAR
ALC./VOL. 12.0%
RRP $7.70 $

Hardys Sir James Brut de Brut

Sir James Hardy is at least as famous for sailing as wine, and recently published his autobiography detailing same. He was chairman of the company until the Berri Renmano takeover and public float of BRL Hardy.

CURRENT RELEASE *non-vintage* This wine is certainly drier than the Cuvée Brut but reveals a basic lack of flavour. Very shy aroma, and bland but dry palate. Throw in some cassis for a Kir Royale.

QUALITY 🍷🍷🍷
VALUE ★★½
GRAPES 'significant' amount of pinot noir and chardonnay
REGION not stated
CELLAR
ALC./VOL. 12.5%
RRP $14.00 $

Hardys Sir James Cuvée Brut

QUALITY 🍷🍷🍷
VALUE ★★½
GRAPES 'a significant proportion of pinot noir and chardonnay'
REGION not stated
CELLAR 🍾
ALC./VOL. 12.5%
RRP $14.00 ⓢ

Despite the appallingly pretentious Frenchman in the TV ad who mistakes this wine for Champagne, the product is selling enormously well.

CURRENT RELEASE *non-vintage* The nose has faintly smoky aromas from a high percentage of pinot noir grapes, and there is a hint of yeast. Basically a fairly plain wine with noticeable sweetness, and a creamy mouthfeel. Take it to a loud party.

Hardys Sir James Sparkling Shiraz

QUALITY 🍷🍷🍷🍷
VALUE ★★★
GRAPES shiraz
REGION McLaren Vale, Padthaway, SA
CELLAR 🍾 3
ALC./VOL. 13.0%
RRP $19.00 ⓢ

This style, alias sparkling burgundy, seems to be enjoying a revival of interest.

CURRENT RELEASE *non-vintage* The colour is deep and vibrant, the bouquet shows rather a lot of toasty, coconutty oak coupled with plum and spice shiraz fruit. It's sweet on entry, then the medium-bodied fruit and wood flavours dry towards the nice clean finish. Serve with party pies.

Hardys Sir James Vintage Brut

QUALITY 🍷🍷🍷🍷
VALUE ★★★½
GRAPES chardonnay, pinot noir
REGION Yarra Valley, Vic.
CELLAR 🍾 2
ALC./VOL. 12.9%
RRP $19.00 ⓢ

This range is growing like Topsy. Will there be a rosé, a blanc de blancs and a blush in time for next year's guide?

CURRENT RELEASE 1992 A big step up from the non-vintages, this has a richer, more complex bouquet with strong smoky pinot, burnt-toast bottle-age and yeast aromas, and good depth of dry flavour that is creamy in the mouth. Peachy and long with appealing balance.

Hollick Cornel Brut

Cornel takes its name from winemaker Pat Tocaciu's dad. 'Tocca' is a man of many talents: he was in charge of distilling gin and vodka as well as winemaking in his previous employment at Tollana.

CURRENT RELEASE 1990 This wine has been around for well over a year, but we like it so much we're giving it another plug. It's remarkably fresh for a five-year-old, and shows ample bready yeast characters and complexity from a long time on its lees. It has a fine bead and abundant crisp acidity.

QUALITY 🍷🍷🍷🍷🍷
VALUE ★★★★
GRAPES pinot noir 80%, chardonnay 20%
REGION Coonawarra, SA
CELLAR 🍾 2
ALC./VOL. 11.5%
RRP $22.50

Jansz Cuvée

The Heemskerk–Champagne Louis Roederer joint venture has come to an end and Heemskerk's been sold – but it's the dawn of a new era as the buyer is a wealthy beef rancher, serious about making good wine profitably. Jansz appears to be in good hands.

CURRENT RELEASE 1992 Definitely the best Jansz to date, with more up-front, appealing, smoky/toasty, dried-fruit characters and better balance. The high acid is still there but it's not searing like some prior releases. The colour is pale and the nose has biscuity accents, a hallmark of Jansz. Drink with Tassie salmon carpaccio.

QUALITY 🍷🍷🍷🍷🍷
VALUE ★★★★
GRAPES chardonnay 59%, pinot noir 41%
REGION Pipers River, Tas.
CELLAR 🍾 4+
ALC./VOL. 12.8%
RRP $29.80

Jean Pierre Rosé Celebration Cuvée

However incongruous it may seem, the De Bortolis – descended from Italian stock – have registered a separate company called Jean Pierre & Co, but ze Frenchman n'existe pas.

CURRENT RELEASE *non-vintage* A fresh pink/purple colour leads into a youthful aroma of strawberry and raspberry. There's decent flavour on the sweetish mid-palate and it dries towards a firm finish. Prosciutto melone, anyone?

QUALITY 🍷🍷🍷
VALUE ★★★½
GRAPES not stated
REGION Riverina, NSW
CELLAR 🍾
ALC./VOL. 11.0%
RRP $5.00 Ⓢ

Jim Barry Sparkling Burgundy

QUALITY 🍷🍷🍷
VALUE ★★½
GRAPES shiraz
REGION Clare Valley, SA
CELLAR 🍾 3
ALC./VOL. 12.0%
RRP $22.25 ⓢ

This 'splurgundy' has spent six months in oak and eight months on lees, and is claimed to be a 'cousin' of the Armagh Shiraz.

CURRENT RELEASE 1991 While not in the same league as the Armagh, this is a decent, youthful style. It is somewhat light but has a pleasant plum/spice nose, active bubbles and pleasingly mild sweetness. Neither does it have a lot of tannin, being soft and easy to drink. Try it with roast turkey.

Killawarra Brut Champagne

QUALITY 🍷🍷🍷🍷
VALUE ★★★★
GRAPES semillon, colombard, chardonnay, riesling, pinot noir
REGION not stated
CELLAR 🍾 1
ALC./VOL. 11.0%
RRP $11.00 ⓢ

Many moons ago, Killawarra was a wholesale company in Melbourne that made its mark by inventing and selling hexagonal wine casks.

CURRENT RELEASE *non-vintage* A fuller style that has plenty of weight on the palate; the nose is yeasty and the palate has developed fruit characters. The bubbles give balance to the weight of fruit flavour and the finish is clean. Serve well chilled as a good food style.

Killawarra Premier Brut Champagne

QUALITY 🍷🍷🍷🍷
VALUE ★★★★
GRAPES pinot noir, chardonnay
REGION not stated
CELLAR 🍾 1
ALC./VOL. 11.0%
RRP $11.00 ⓢ

Seems quaint to see the word 'champagne' on an Australian label these days. At least this was made from the traditional varieties.

CURRENT RELEASE 1993 A very good example of value for money. The nose has a yeasty, brewery smell, the palate is full-bodied with ample citrus character, and the bubbles add a fluffy texture. The finish shows fresh clean acid. Serve well chilled with canapés.

Milburn Park Brut

This is another label from the Alambie Wine Company in Mildura. The range includes Castle Crossing and Salisbury Estate. Maker Bob Shields.

CURRENT RELEASE *non-vintage* The bubbles are enthusiastic and there are hints of fresh bread on the nose. The palate is subtle with gentle grape flavours and the finish is dry and clean. The bubbles work well in the mouth. Serve well chilled as a pre-dinner drink.

QUALITY ▧▧▧▧
VALUE ★★★½
GRAPES pinot noir, chardonnay
REGION Mildura, Vic.
CELLAR 🍾
ALC./VOL. 11.5%
RRP $13.00

Moorilla Estate Vintage Brut

Moorilla Estate impresses most with white and sparkling wines, which is pretty much in parallel with the state of Tasmania. Maker Julian Alcorso.

CURRENT RELEASE 1992 The colour is slightly brassy from pinot noir grapes, and the flavour reflects that with strawberry pinot and smoky/toasty overtones. There's some breadiness from pinot/yeast interaction. In the mouth it's smooth, dry, balanced and long. A stylish bubbly to have with smoked Tassie salmon.

QUALITY ▧▧▧▧▧
VALUE ★★★½
GRAPES pinot noir
REGION various, Tas.
CELLAR 🍾 3
ALC./VOL. 12.0%
RRP $37.00

Mount Pleasant Brut Champagne

When it comes to sparkling wines, McWilliam's have a toe in tepid water.

CURRENT RELEASE *non-vintage* There are cooked bread and biscuit aromas on the nose and the palate has some meaty characters and fresh fruit flavours. The finish is dry and crisp. It needs to be served well chilled.

QUALITY ▧▧▧▧
VALUE ★★★★
GRAPES pinot noir, chardonnay
REGION not stated
CELLAR 🍾 1
ALC./VOL. 11.5%
RRP $12.00

Mount Prior Brut Champagne

QUALITY 🍷🍷🍷🍷
VALUE ★★★½
GRAPES not stated
REGION North-east Victoria
CELLAR 🍾
ALC./VOL. 13.0%
RRP $12.00

Mount Prior is an historic property established in 1860. Today it produces around 9000 cases and sells fruit to other wineries. Maker Garry Wall.

CURRENT RELEASE *non-vintage* A straightforward style with more alcohol than most. The nose has soft citrus aromas, the palate offers lemon and apple flavours followed by crisp acid on a dry finish. Serve well chilled.

Mount William Winery Louise Clare

QUALITY 🍷🍷🍷🍷
VALUE ★★★★
GRAPES pinot noir, cabernet sauvignon, cabernet franc
REGION Macedon, Vic.
CELLAR 🍾 4
ALC./VOL. 12.5%
RRP $14.00

This is a small winery established in the Mount Macedon district of Victoria, circa 1987. It produces 200 cases of this sparkling red blend annually.

CURRENT RELEASE *non-vintage* The nose has ripe berry characters and hints of spice. Strawberry and raspberry flavours are encountered on the palate, which has an attractive level of sweetness. This is followed by discreet tannin on a clean finish. Serve well chilled with rhubarb tart.

Normans Conquest

QUALITY 🍷🍷🍷
VALUE ★★★
GRAPES mainly pinot noir
REGION not stated
CELLAR 🍾 1
ALC./VOL. 11.5%
RRP $10.50 Ⓢ

Someone's got a sense of humour: the port is called King William, and wasn't there a 1066 at one stage? We could think of worse titles for a bubbly. Maker Brian Light.

CURRENT RELEASE *non-vintage* A very creditworthy, inexpensive rosé style. The colour is fresh light pink; the nose raspberry-ish, reflecting red grapes. There is plenty of fluffy mousse and the flavour is definite if uncomplicated. A trace of liqueur is balanced by fresh acid. Good value at the price.

Passing Clouds Ondine Sparkling Shiraz Cabernet

The back label says this was made from a 1988 still wine which had been in bottle till '94. It was refermented with five per cent 1992 shiraz and liqueured with 1991 vintage port. A novel way to cobble together a splurgundy!

CURRENT RELEASE 1988 A lovely minty, ripe, sweet berry bouquet leaps from the glass. This is a wine with loads of character and regional minty/earthy flavours. Sweet berry and plum fruit, well-judged balance of fruit, sweetness and tannin, and it lingers long. Try it with duck.

QUALITY 🍷🍷🍷🍷?
VALUE ★★★★
GRAPES shiraz, cabernet sauvignon
REGION Bendigo, Vic.
CELLAR 🍾 5
ALC./VOL. 13.5%
RRP $29.00

Paulett's Trillians Méthode Champenoise

Paulett's winery and vineyard are situated in the Polish Hill River sub-region of the Clare Valley. Maker Neil Paulett.

CURRENT RELEASE *non-vintage* Bottle-age is the feature of this characterful sparkler. It has a full yellow colour, a big rich developed nose and stacks of flavour. What it lacks in subtlety it makes up in generosity. Chill well and serve with whitebait fritters.

QUALITY 🍷🍷🍷?
VALUE ★★★
GRAPES not stated
REGION Clare Valley, SA
CELLAR 🍾
ALC./VOL. 11.5%
RRP $14.50

Pelorus

Takes its name from a dolphin which used to guide ships through the waters of Marlborough Sound. Cloudy Bay is majority owned by Veuve Clicquot but this bubbly owes nothing to them. Maker Kevin Judd.

Previous outstanding vintages: '87, '88, '89

CURRENT RELEASE 1990 A marvellous wine, the best of this line so far and one of the leading Antipodean bubblies today. Complex butterscotch, biscuity, coconutty and very bready: lots happening in this wine. It has superb proportions: intense, full, and very, very long. Drink with caviar.

QUALITY 🍷🍷🍷🍷🍷
VALUE ★★★★★
GRAPES pinot noir, chardonnay
REGION Marlborough, NZ
CELLAR 🍾 3
ALC./VOL. 12.5%
RRP $32.00

Redbank Emily Non-Vintage Brut

QUALITY ♛♛♛♛
VALUE ★★★½
GRAPES not stated
REGION Pyrenees, Vic.
CELLAR 🍷 2
ALC./VOL. 11.5%
RRP $11.60

Neill Robb's father John was the first winemaker at Chateau Remy, and Neill himself has always dabbled in fizz. The label says 'chardonnay-inspired cuvée' which probably means it's not all chardonnay.

CURRENT RELEASE *non-vintage* Subtitled Cuvée 93/1, this has a clean, creamy chardonnay-like nose with some bready development. The palate is soft, light, fairly straightforward with herby chardonnay flavours and good balance. The mousse is frothy and the finish is pleasingly arid. Serve with oysters.

Rymill Méthode Champenoise

QUALITY ♛♛♛♛
VALUE ★★½
GRAPES pinot noir, chardonnay
REGION Coonawarra, SA
CELLAR 🍷 2
ALC./VOL. 12.0%
RRP $19.30

There's not a lot of competition for this wine, sparkling Coonawarras being thin on the ground, although Coonawarra grapes find their way into many blends. Maker John Innes.

CURRENT RELEASE 1991 This is a rather delicate, slightly stripped wine with an attractive herbal, smoky pinot noir-influenced bouquet. The palate is lean and tight, the finish tart and dry and slightly meagre. Add cassis and make a kir.

Seaview Brut Champagne

QUALITY ♛♛♛
VALUE ★★★
GRAPES not stated
REGION not stated
CELLAR 🍷
ALC./VOL. 11.5%
RRP $7.00 $

You're not meant to take this stuff seriously, just glug it and get down and let the good times roll.
CURRENT RELEASE *non-vintage* The nose has a hint of yeast and grape aromas. The palate shows slight fruit character, a hint of sweetness (a bit more than would be expected from a brut), followed by a clean acid finish. Serve well chilled or mix with orange juice.

Seaview Edwards and Chaffey Pinot Noir Chardonnay

This is a new line to commemorate two of the pioneers from the McLaren Vale district. It uses the classic French varieties.

CURRENT RELEASE 1991 A complex wine with extended lees age. The nose has biscuit and yeast aromas. The palate has some strawberry pinot characters and there are also meaty aspects. The finish is clean and satisfying. It would go well with cold chicken when served well chilled.

QUALITY ????½
VALUE ★★★★½
GRAPES pinot noir, chardonnay
REGION McLaren Vale, SA
CELLAR 4
ALC./VOL. 11.5%
RRP $19.00

Seaview Grande Cuvée Champagne

Still the term 'champagne' persists on Australian labels, but not for much longer.

CURRENT RELEASE *non-vintage* A reasonable economy style with a trace of yeast on the nose. The palate is quite grapey with just a hint of sugar and the finish is clean. Serve it well chilled at a party.

QUALITY ???
VALUE ★★★
GRAPES not stated
REGION not stated
CELLAR
ALC./VOL. 11.5%
RRP $7.00 ⓢ

Seaview Pinot Noir Chardonnay Brut

This is the great sleeper in the sparkling wine arena. What used to be a cheap and cheery brand is now putting on the Ritz!

CURRENT RELEASE 1992 A fine style with balance and poise. The bubbles are lively and the nose shows cracked yeast characters with pinot meatiness. The palate has marked citrus flavours balanced by some fluffy bubbles and exquisite acid on a very clean finish. A great pre-dinner drink.

QUALITY ????½
VALUE ★★★★½
GRAPES pinot noir, chardonnay
REGION not stated
CELLAR 2
ALC./VOL. 11.5%
RRP $18.00

Seppelt Great Western Brut Rosé

QUALITY 🍷🍷🍷
VALUE ★★★
GRAPES not stated
REGION not stated
CELLAR 🍾
ALC./VOL. 10.5%
RRP $6.90 (S)

There have been some interesting personnel changes at Great Western. The sparkling winemaker, Mike Kluczko, has left to become manager/winemaker at Tarrawarra in the Yarra Valley.

CURRENT RELEASE *non-vintage* The colour is an attractive pink-rose colour and the nose is almost neutral. There is a hint of sweetness on the palate and the bubbles are quite lively. The finish is clean and undemanding. Serve very well chilled.

Seppelt Great Western Imperial Reserve

QUALITY 🍷🍷🍷½
VALUE ★★★½
GRAPES not stated
REGION not stated
CELLAR 🍾
ALC./VOL. 12.0%
RRP $6.90 (S)

Melba took a bath in this stuff and some wag said that when it was rebottled they had one extra bottle. Maker Pamela Geddes.

CURRENT RELEASE *non-vintage* A faithful fluffy style that has a hint of sugar. The nose is neutral and the palate has sweet fruit flavours plus a creamy texture. The finish is soft and clean. It needs to be served well chilled.

Seppelt Show Sparkling Burgundy

QUALITY 🍷🍷🍷🍷🍷
VALUE ★★★★
GRAPES shiraz
REGION Great Western, Vic.
CELLAR 🍾 10
ALC./VOL. 12.5%
RRP $40.00

MS can recall tasting this wine as a base (pre-bubbles) in 1986. It was an outstanding table wine with loads of black pepper qualities. Maker Warren Randall.

CURRENT RELEASE 1984 A very fine style that is perhaps a little drier than usual. There are pepper, plum and wood aromas on the nose and the palate is medium-bodied. There is a complex mix of flavours including spice, cracked pepper and sweet berries balanced by clean acid on a softly tannic finish. Serve well chilled with turkey.

Tatachilla Sparkling Malbec

The Tatachilla name has been revived after an absence from the shelves. It is the former Southern Vales Co-operative winery.

CURRENT RELEASE *non-vintage* This was made from 1994 fruit and, boy, is it a bawling infant! The neon purple colour will blacken your teeth. It's a fresh wine which relies on brash primary fruit for its appeal. A vibrant plummy, stalky malbec, it is unsubtle and needs food. Try turkey and cranberry sauce.

QUALITY ♙♙♙♝
VALUE ★★★½
GRAPES malbec
REGION Padthaway, SA
CELLAR 🍷 5+
ALC./VOL. 14.2%
RRP $15.00

Tulloch Hunter Cuvée Brut

Is it just our imagination, or has this wine taken a major shift in style as well as quality, with the addition of some chardonnay into what used to be a straight semillon? Maker Patrick Auld.

CURRENT RELEASE 1991 The colour is quite deep and the style full-blown, more in a Seppelt than a Tulloch style (perhaps it is, since all the Southcorp fizz gets its bubbles at Great Western these days). Soft, up-front peach/nectarine fruit with a Seppelt-like herbal aspect. Very fruity, and superbly balanced. Best sipped by itself at a party.

QUALITY ♙♙♙♙
VALUE ★★★★½
GRAPES semillon, chardonnay
REGION mainly Hunter Valley, NSW
CELLAR 🍷 1
ALC./VOL. 11.5%
RRP $13.30 $

Best Bargain Sparkling

Tyrrell's Pinot Noir Brut

QUALITY ♛♛♛♛
VALUE ★★★
GRAPES pinot noir
REGION Hunter Valley, NSW
CELLAR 🍾 2
ALC./VOL. 12.5%
RRP $29.00

This is the torch-bearer for the Tyrrell range of bubblies, a gutsy style that's as Aussie as the day is long. It's picked riper than most, and some of it sees oak and also malolactic fermentation. Maker Andrew Spinaze.

Previous outstanding vintages: '91

CURRENT RELEASE 1992 A fullish yellow-pink hue warns of a full-bodied style. The nose has rich, fruity strawberry/cherry varietal character and the taste is full but tight and elegant thanks to acid and a slight grip. There is also some fruit sweetness. A ballsy blanc de noirs style. Try it with prosciutto and melon.

Tyrrell's Pinot Noir Chardonnay NV Brut

QUALITY ♛♛♛♛
VALUE ★★★½
GRAPES pinot noir, chardonnay
REGION Hunter Valley, NSW
CELLAR 🍾 1
ALC./VOL. 10.6%
RRP $17.70 Ⓢ

Tyrrell's bubbly style is fuller and richer, perhaps, than the more trend-setting Aussie bubblies, thanks to the Hunter climate. This has spent two years on lees.

CURRENT RELEASE *non-vintage* A very agreeable drink, smelling of ripe peaches and toasty bottle-development. The mousse is thick and fluffy; the palate soft and full. Not terrifically complex but well balanced and very drinkable. A good style to take to a party.

Wilson Vineyard Hippocrene

QUALITY ♛♛♛♛
VALUE ★★★★
GRAPES not stated
REGION Clare Valley, SA
CELLAR 🍾 3
ALC./VOL. 12.5%
RRP $18.00

The name is a reference to Keats. Maker John Wilson.

CURRENT RELEASE 1990 The colour is a dense ruby and the nose has ripe berry aromas, while the palate is positively bursting with ripe fruit flavours over plenty of mouthfilling sweetness. The bubbles add a bit of fluffy texture. Serve well chilled and try with black pudding.

Wolf Blass Brut

The first Wolf Blass sparkling wine was labelled 'Renepogel' (spell it backwards . . .). These days, Blass sparklings are much more respectable.

CURRENT RELEASE *non-vintage* This is a bright, yeasty style that has plenty of positive features: biscuit and yeast aromas on the nose and some gooseberry semillon flavours on the palate. The finish is dry and crisp. Serve well chilled with an antipasto platter.

QUALITY ŶŶŶȲ
VALUE ★★★★
GRAPES semillon, chardonnay
REGION not stated
CELLAR 🍶 1
ALC./VOL. 11.2%
RRP $9.95

Wood Ridge Sovereign Brut

Another label of the prolific Griffith-based De Bortoli company. The wine is the same as the Jean Pierre Classique Cuvée.

CURRENT RELEASE *non-vintage* Slightly meaty pungency on the nose, but who's sniffing it? The palate is basic and fairly short, but there's plenty of flavour and it finishes pleasingly dry with some floral fruit. More than adequate at the price. Good party punch base.

QUALITY ŶŶŶ
VALUE ★★★½
GRAPES not stated
REGION Riverina, NSW
CELLAR 🍶
ALC./VOL. 11.0%
RRP $4.85 ⓢ

Yellowglen Crémant NV

Crémant means creamy, which in this case is achieved by a lower gas pressure. Crémant has been aptly described as a great 'wedding style'.

CURRENT RELEASE *non-vintage* The main thing about the style here is the mouthfeel. The nose is yeasty and the palate has a lovely softness. There are citrus flavours and docile bubbles that cleanse and caress the tongue. The finish is mild but not lacking in support. Serve well chilled.

QUALITY ŶŶŶŶ
VALUE ★★★★
GRAPES pinot noir, chardonnay
REGION not stated
CELLAR 🍶 1
ALC./VOL. 11.5%
RRP $11.95

Yellowglen Cuvée Victoria

QUALITY ▟▟▟▟▘
VALUE ★★★★
GRAPES pinot noir, pinot meunier, chardonnay
REGION Ballarat, Bellarine Peninsula, Vic. & Coonawarra, SA
CELLAR 🍷 5
ALC./VOL. 12.0%
RRP $23.00

This is the top of the Mildara Blass sparkling wine tree. It used to be made exclusively from Victorian fruit but not any more. Maker Jeffrey Wilkinson.

CURRENT RELEASE 1991 A big, confident style with a very fluffy texture. The nose has meaty yeast aromas and the palate is quite rich. There are citrus and strawberry characters and a long dry finish that shows forceful acid. It will cellar well. Serve well chilled as a pre-dinner drink.

Yellowglen Pinot Chardonnay Brut NV

QUALITY ▟▟▟▟
VALUE ★★★★
GRAPES pinot noir, chardonnay
REGION not stated
CELLAR 🍷 1
ALC./VOL. 11.5%
RRP $11.95

This is the fighting label from a fighting brand that started in Ballarat but spread around the world.

CURRENT RELEASE *non-vintage* Tough stuff – an astringent style with high acid and lots of fresh characters. The nose has a soda-water quality with citrus and yeast. The palate is lean but not too austere and the finish shows zesty acid. A good pre-dinner drink that should be served well chilled.

Yellowglen Vintage Brut

QUALITY ▟▟▟▟
VALUE ★★★★
GRAPES pinot noir, pinot meunier, chardonnay
REGION Eden Valley SA, Yarra Valley, Vic.
CELLAR 🍷 4
ALC./VOL. 11.0%
RRP $18.00

This is the classic born-to-age style that you can drink now. It will be interesting to see this with some bottle-age.

CURRENT RELEASE 1992 A very lively, crisp style, and it could be argued that it's ready to drink now. The nose has some attractive yeast qualities. The palate is reserved yet crisp with a nutty character, and there is long high acid on the finish. Bubbles drive the style – a great pre-dinner drink.

Fortified Wines

All Saints Classic Release Vintage Port

Not many examples of vintage port are being made these days. It is good to see that the style persists.

CURRENT RELEASE 1992 A young style that has a deep ruby colour and a ripe blackberry nose. The palate is dominated by berry fruit, with blackberry and blackcurrant flavours that are graced by warming spirit of a heads-and-tails quality. It needs time in the bottle. Try it with stilton.

QUALITY 🍷🍷🍷🍷
VALUE ★★★★
GRAPES shiraz
REGION Rutherglen, Vic.
CELLAR ➔ 3–10
ALC./VOL. 18.5%
RRP $18.00

All Saints Classic Tawny Port

The 'classic' range is a commercial stream made at an affordable price. The material tends to be younger than the Show Reserve range.

CURRENT RELEASE *non-vintage* The colour is a deep amber and the nose has a milky character and direct raisin aromas. The palate is sweet with ripe dried-fruit flavours married to soft spirit on a clean, dry finish. The average age is seven years.

QUALITY 🍷🍷🍷🍷
VALUE ★★★½
GRAPES not stated
REGION Rutherglen, Vic.
CELLAR 🍾 1
ALC./VOL. 19.0%
RRP $13.00

All Saints Old Tawny

QUALITY ♀♀♀♀♁
VALUE ★★★★½
GRAPES not stated
REGION Rutherglen, Vic.
CELLAR 🍷 1
ALC./VOL. 17.0%
RRP $22.00

Rutherglen tawny holds a special part in every ageing boy/girl wonder's heart. It's the stuff of dreams and fable.

CURRENT RELEASE *non-vintage* The average age of this wine is over 20 years. It shows, particularly in the deep brown tawny colour. The nose is a fruitcake mix of raisins and other peel aromas. The palate is rich with concentrated rancio characters and dried fruit. The finish shows distinct acid and freshness. Aged, clean and well balanced, a great after-dinner spoil.

All Saints Show Reserve Amontillado

QUALITY ♀♀♀♀♁
VALUE ★★★★½
GRAPES not stated
REGION Rutherglen, Vic.
CELLAR 🍷 1
ALC./VOL. 19.0%
RRP $16.00

It's great to see companies persevering with sherry styles. Although it is probably pushing the proverbial up hill with a tooth pick, may they be rewarded.

CURRENT RELEASE *non-vintage* This is on the pale side for an amontillado but the nose displays the richness that careful ageing can bestow. There is also a lactic quality that seems to be a cellar style. The palate is austere yet robust with clean, nutty qualities matched by fresh acid on a very positive finish. Served chilled it goes very well with a game consommé. The blend dates back to the 1940s.

All Saints Show Reserve Madeira

'Reserve madeira' is a quaint term when applied to Australian wine. In essence we are dealing with a drier fortified wine which has probably been made using white grapes.

CURRENT RELEASE *non-vintage* This blend is 15 years old and the colour shows up like a traffic light: mid to light amber. The nose has lactic and rancio characters and the palate is dry and nutty. There's great depth of flavour balanced by bracing acid on an astringent finish. Given the acid, it is not far removed from its namesake in the middle of the Atlantic. Serve chilled as an after-dinner drink.

QUALITY 🍷🍷🍷🍷
VALUE ★★★★
GRAPES not stated
REGION Rutherglen, Vic.
CELLAR 🍾 1
ALC./VOL. 18.0%
RRP $18.00

All Saints Show Reserve Muscat

This historic property, which cloned the castle of Mey, now belongum Brown Brothers and the plan is to make it the 'fortified' wine arm of the empire. Maker Neil Jericho.

CURRENT RELEASE *non-vintage* A mixture of the young and the old. The colour is an amber tawny and the nose has sweet raisin with a hint of lactic character. The palate is sweet with considerable rancio and dried fruit character. The finish shows high acid but is slightly troubled by some sharp wood characters. It still goes well as an after-dinner spoil with a handrolled Havana cigar.

QUALITY 🍷🍷🍷🍷
VALUE ★★★½
GRAPES red frontignac
REGION Rutherglen, Vic.
CELLAR 🍾 1
ALC./VOL. 18.5%
RRP $22.00

All Saints Show Reserve Tokay

QUALITY ★★★★★
VALUE ★★★★★
GRAPES muscadelle
REGION Rutherglen, Vic.
CELLAR 🍾
ALC./VOL. 17.0%
RRP $18.00

Tokay is a misnomer; this is actually sweet white fortified wine that gains its colour from a long spell in wood. It has nothing in common with the Hungarian wine produced on the hill of Tokay.

CURRENT RELEASE *non-vintage* A lovely wine that shows age and charm. The colour is a mid-amber and the nose has a distinct honey quality. The palate is rich with mouthfilling sweetness and assertive acid on a clean finish. Shock the purists and serve it well chilled with vanilla ice-cream.

Angoves Fino Dry Flor Sherry

QUALITY ★★★★
VALUE ★★★★
GRAPES not stated
REGION Renmark, SA
CELLAR 🍾
ALC./VOL. 18.0%
RRP $11.00

Angoves is one of the few companies that promotes this style. It is a very good commercial wine at a fair price.

CURRENT RELEASE *non-vintage* A pale dry style that is a great pre-dinner drink. The nose has some nutty yeast plus a lactic quality. The austere palate has slight fruit characters and yeasty nuttiness. Acid and spirit make for a cleansing finish. It could be served well chilled.

Baileys Winemakers Selection Old Muscat

QUALITY ★★★★★
VALUE ★★★★½
GRAPES red frontignac
REGION Glenrowan, Vic.
CELLAR 🍾
ALC./VOL. 18.0%
RRP $50.00

This selection was started by the late Harry Tinson, who named it HJT after himself. When he began his own wine venture he took the initials with him.

CURRENT RELEASE *non-vintage* A staggeringly rich, luscious, hedonistic drink, the colour green-edged and the nose all prunes, raisins and concentrated old muscat fruit. This is beautifully mellowed by long wood-ageing and the finish has impressive power and length. An amazing muscat to have with chocolates.

Baileys Winemakers Selection Old Tokay

Baileys is now part of the Rothbury group, which is on record as being disappointed at finding how much the old fortified stocks had been run down when they took over. Happily, the wines remain excellent.

CURRENT RELEASE *non-vintage* Rich, complex toffee, pruney tokay nose and a powerful, intense, palate flavour that lingers long and is dried on the finish by spirit and acid. Marvellous depth of flavour; a very stylish tokay. Tops with stilton cheese.

QUALITY ♛♛♛♛
VALUE ★★★★
GRAPES muscadelle
REGION Glenrowan, Vic.
CELLAR ◊
ALC./VOL. 18.0%
RRP $50.00

Bethany Old Quarry Port

The Bethany winery is located in a disused quarry on the hillside above the sleepy town of Bethany. It has a fabulous view across the Barossa.

CURRENT RELEASE *non-vintage* Not really in tawny style, this is a fairly young port which smells of vanilla and raisiny fruitcake. The palate is lean but intense, with some marmalade flavour, only mild sweetness and – unexpectedly – a firm, slightly astringent finish. Serve with fruitcake – and put some in the cake mix.

QUALITY ♛♛♛♛
VALUE ★★★½
GRAPES shiraz, grenache
REGION Barossa Valley, SA
CELLAR ◊
ALC./VOL. 19.0%
RRP $13.50

Bethany White Port

This style is a blast from the past. Even in Portugal it's not very common, although it does cope very well as the Portuguese equivalent of a sherry when served chilled before a meal.

CURRENT RELEASE *non-vintage* The colour is full amber and the nose has attractive marmalade, caramel and vanilla characters of wood-aged sweet white material. The palate has lots of citrus peel with an agreeable bitterness to the finish that counters some of the sweetness. Serve chilled as an aperitif.

QUALITY ♛♛♛
VALUE ★★★
GRAPES muscadelle, frontignac, riesling
REGION Barossa Valley, SA
CELLAR ◊
ALC./VOL. 17.5%
RRP $13.50

Brown Brothers Golden Cream Sherry

QUALITY ▼▼▼
VALUE ★★★½
GRAPES muscadelle
REGION Murray Valley, Vic.
CELLAR 🍾
ALC./VOL. 18.0%
RRP $8.25 ⓢ

This is the sort of thing your parents used to keep in a decanter on the sideboard. It has nothing to do with the Spanish original, but is more like a young liqueur tokay.

CURRENT RELEASE *non-vintage* This is one to serve when Auntie Agnes comes around. Medium-dark amber colour and smoky, tealeafy nose are very attractive for openers. In the mouth it's lean and medium-sweet with some hot spirit that helps dry the finish. Goes with afternoon tea and fruitcake.

Brown Brothers Liqueur Muscat

QUALITY ▼▼▼▼?
VALUE ★★★★
GRAPES red frontignac
REGION North-east Victoria
CELLAR 🍾
ALC./VOL. 18.5%
RRP $24.60

Muscat grapes are used for all kinds of wines, but nowhere else in the world do they produce a wine of this style and character. Maker Neil Jericho.

CURRENT RELEASE *non-vintage* This has great depth of developed muscat fruit and mellow aged rancio character. The luscious palate recalls molasses, and there's a multi-faceted complexity to the wine. It goes beautifully with blue cheeses.

Brown Brothers Reserve Muscat

QUALITY ▼▼▼▼
VALUE ★★★★
GRAPES red frontignac
REGION North-east Victoria
CELLAR 🍾
ALC./VOL. 18.5%
RRP $13.80 ⓢ

Muscat grapes were among the first vines planted by the founder, John Francis Brown, at Milawa in 1885. This is the younger of the Browns muscats.

CURRENT RELEASE *non-vintage* This is very good for the price, sweet to the point of being luscious, and quite complex with some wood playing second fiddle to lifted muscat fruit. The flavour lingers well and it's a handy partner for plum pudding and caramel sauce.

Brown Brothers Reserve Port

This is a who's who of port varieties, all brought together in a solero system at Milawa. Maker Neil Jericho.
CURRENT RELEASE *non-vintage* A fruity young wine with echoes of older, smoother blending material lurking in the shadows. There's spicy plummy young fruit, and nutty, vanilla aspects. It starts out sweet and dries towards the finish with spirit and tannin. For after dinner, with nuts and coffee.

QUALITY 🍷🍷🍷
VALUE ★★★
GRAPES shiraz, grenache, mataro, carignan, cabernet sauvignon
REGION Murray Valley, Vic.
CELLAR 🍾
ALC./VOL. 18.0%
RRP $10.75 ⓢ

Brown Brothers Very Old Port

This is a serious port for the connoisseur: the blend is based on vintages of the 1950s with selected parcels from the best years since. Maker Neil Jericho.
CURRENT RELEASE *non-vintage* A deep brick-red tawny hue and the bouquet has a developed earthy, undergrowth note to the rancio character. It comes alive in the mouth, with rich, chunky chocolatey, vanillan, oaky flavours of real complexity. Lovely texture and length. Serve with chocolates and coffee.

QUALITY 🍷🍷🍷🍷
VALUE ★★★★
GRAPES mainly shiraz
REGION mainly Milawa, Vic.
CELLAR 🍾
ALC./VOL. 18.5%
RRP $20.45

Brown Brothers Very Old Tokay

John C. Brown, the family's patriarch who turned 80 in 1995, is a big fan of tokay, and kept planting it when others were grubbing it out.
CURRENT RELEASE *non-vintage* Transcendental stuff! A magnificent wine, with deep tawny/amber colour, a tealeafy cedary nose made complex by rancio from extended wood age and even a hint of Vegemite. The palate has immense power and concentration, length, balance ... it has it all. Serve with caramels and coffee.

QUALITY 🍷🍷🍷🍷🍷
VALUE ★★★★★
GRAPES muscadelle
REGION North-east Victoria
CELLAR 🍾
ALC./VOL. 18.5%
RRP $24.60

Brown Brothers Vintage Port

QUALITY ?????
VALUE ★★★★
GRAPES shiraz
REGION Glenrowan & Milawa, Vic.
CELLAR 🍷 2–15+
ALC./VOL. 18.4%
RRP $16.75 Ⓢ

One of fortified winemaker Neil Jericho's pet projects at Brown's has been to rejuvenate the vintage port, and he's been to Portugal to deepen his knowledge of the style.

Previous outstanding vintages: '91

CURRENT RELEASE 1992 Spirit plays a big part in this, with a strong liquorice character on the nose while the palate is smooth with mild tannins, making it accessible already. It's not a style that needs cellaring for ages. The complex, sweet plummy, spicy flavours are very attractive. Serve with stilton cheese.

Buller Museum Release Rutherglen Muscat

QUALITY ????
VALUE ★★★½
GRAPES red frontignac
REGION Rutherglen, Vic.
CELLAR 🍷
ALC./VOL. 18.5%
RRP $48.30

This was voted best wine of the show at the 1994 Sydney International Wine Competition. Maybe the blend has changed, but it didn't rise to the same heights in '95.

CURRENT RELEASE *non-vintage* This has a textbook old muscat colour, tawny/amber with green edges, and a complex rancio and oak nose together with old muscat fruit. The taste is semi-luscious and slightly salty with an unusual aftertaste. A good and individual style. Try it with gorgonzola.

Buller Museum Release Rutherglen Tokay

QUALITY ?????
VALUE ★★★★
GRAPES muscadelle
REGION Rutherglen, Vic.
CELLAR 🍷
ALC./VOL. 18.5%
RRP $48.30

Virtually all the Rutherglen wineries now issue a small bottling of their very best and oldest muscats and tokays, at a premium price which reflects the high cost of ageing them.

CURRENT RELEASE *non-vintage* This is very old, with burnt, singed overtones to the mellow toffee aromas. The taste is very rich, deep, sweet and liqueury. The flavours are complex with plenty of rancio and good length. A quite voluptuous old tokay with a lot of sweetness. Try it with chocolate truffles.

Buller Vintage Port

Sadly, vintage port is now an esoteric drink that's slipped out of fashion with the chardonnay generation. In days of yore, entire reputations rested on VP in regions such as Rutherglen. Maker Andrew Buller.

CURRENT RELEASE 1987 Marvellous blackberry/plum fruit and liquorice spirit aromas are overlaid with tarry developed characters in this relatively dry, almost Portuguese style. There's a solid thump of tannin on the finish, which we would give still more time to soften. An intriguing style. Stilton here.

QUALITY ♛♛♛♛
VALUE ★★★½
GRAPES durif, touriga
REGION Rutherglen, Vic.
CELLAR ⬤ 3–10
ALC./VOL. 18.0%
RRP $16.25

Campbells Isabella Tokay

Isabella Campbell was a co-founder of what has become one of the great cellars of Rutherglen. This wine is a fitting tribute.

CURRENT RELEASE *non-vintage* The colour is a bright orange/amber and the nose has a linctus quality tinged by citrus and malt extract aromas. The palate is rich with sweet honey flavours plus citrus and malt. The viscosity is mouthcoating but not cloying. The concentration of flavour is formidable and fresh acid balances out the finish. This is honey from the Rutherglen fortified rock! After dinner with reverence.

QUALITY ♛♛♛♛♛
VALUE ★★★★★
GRAPES muscadelle
REGION Rutherglen, Vic.
CELLAR ↑
ALC./VOL. 18.5%
RRP $57.50

Best Fortified Wine

Campbells Liqueur Muscat

QUALITY ♙♙♙♙
VALUE ★★★★
GRAPES red frontignac
REGION Rutherglen, Vic.
CELLAR 🍶
ALC./VOL. 18.0%
RRP $15.00

This is the honest worker's muscat at an affordable price. It gives clues about what can be achieved with more age and blending.

CURRENT RELEASE *non-vintage* The nose has a cheeky freshness with a hint of malt. The palate is a middleweight with some sweet fruit flavours and a strong raisin sensation. The finish shows acid and warming spirit. It is simple and enjoyable, and could be used as a topping for ice cream.

Campbells Liqueur Tokay

QUALITY ♙♙♙♙
VALUE ★★★★
GRAPES muscadelle
REGION Rutherglen, Vic.
CELLAR 🍶
ALC./VOL. 18.0%
RRP $15.00

Rutherglen is the cradle of Australian tokay, though the original comes from Hungary and is made from the grape variety furmint.

CURRENT RELEASE *non-vintage* This is a good example of the style. The nose has caramel and malt extract aromas. The palate is sweet with honey and toffee flavours counterbalanced by warming spirit on an equitable finish. A great after-dinner drink. Try it with walnuts.

Campbells Merchant Prince

QUALITY ♙♙♙♙♙
VALUE ★★★★★
GRAPES red frontignac
REGION Rutherglen, Vic.
CELLAR 🍶
ALC./VOL. 18.5%
RRP $57.50

John Campbell came from the home of golf, St Andrews, Scotland, on board the *Merchant Prince*, arriving in Port Phillip Bay in 1858. He selected land at Rutherglen in 1870 and the rest is winemaking history. Full marks for a great label.

CURRENT RELEASE *non-vintage* A princely wine with lots of flavour and style. This is a superior Rutherglen muscat of fine quality. The nose is emphatic raisin and wrinkled berry aromas; the palate is thick and complex with rich, sweet dried-fruit flavours, hints of fruitcake and strong rancio characters. The finish is long, dry and tingling. Try it after dinner with the right company.

Campbells Old Rutherglen Muscat

This is the mid-range of the Campbells fortified line-up. From many other cellars it would be considered top of the range.

CURRENT RELEASE *non-vintage* An elegant iron fist in a velvet glove. The key is balance between fruit and acid and the old and the new. The colour is mid-amber and the strong nose is dominated by spirit and dried fruit. The palate is quite rich with sweet muscat flavours that give way to lively spirit on a high acid finish. It would go well with a sticky date pudding.

QUALITY ★★★★½
VALUE ★★★★½
GRAPES red frontignac
REGION Rutherglen, Vic.
CELLAR 🍷
ALC./VOL. 18.0%
RRP $28.50

Campbells Old Rutherglen Tokay

The canny Campbell winemakers Colin and Malcolm have assiduously stored away fortified material so it can be used in the next century. Expect this line to continue long after these authors have had their time.

CURRENT RELEASE *non-vintage* The colour is a deceptively light amber because intensity is encountered on both nose and palate. The nose has a honeyed syrup and malt extract aroma. The palate continues the honey theme with a touch of malt and toffee. Clean acid makes the finish tidy and fresh. A good after-dinner drink.

QUALITY ★★★★½
VALUE ★★★★½
GRAPES muscadelle
REGION Rutherglen, Vic.
CELLAR 🍷
ALC./VOL. 18.0%
RRP $28.50

Chambers Old Liqueur Muscat

QUALITY ★★★★★
VALUE ★★★★★
GRAPES red frontignac
REGION Rutherglen, Vic
CELLAR 🍾
ALC./VOL. 18.0%
RRP $85.00 (cellar door)

Boring, isn't it? Year after year we hand out five stars to this wine, but what else could be expected for such a unique product. Maker Bill Chambers.
CURRENT RELEASE *non-vintage* Almost daunting, this wine pushes the flavour envelope. It has a strong raisin nose and the colour is like greenish treacle. The palate is so mouthfilling that you think it needs dissolving rather than drinking. The flavour is complex with muscat, toffee, prunes and peel flavours matched by lifted acid on a concentrated finish. A special-occasion wine.

Chambers Old Liqueur Tokay

QUALITY ★★★★★
VALUE ★★★★★
GRAPES muscadelle
REGION Rutherglen, Vic.
CELLAR 🍾
ALC./VOL. 18.0%
RRP $85.00 (cellar door)

Although he is one of the most laidback characters in the wine industry, Bill Chambers is the long-standing Chairman of Judges at the Royal Agricultural Show in Melbourne.
CURRENT RELEASE *non-vintage* Absolutely fabulous! They don't come any better than this. The colour is a deep amber with green highlights, the nose a rich mixture of coffee, raisins, toffee, orange peel and nutty rancio; ditto the palate which has concentrated sweetness and profound rancio characters. The highpoint of the wine is the balance – it's impeccable. Serve sparingly to those who can understand the style.

Chateau Yaldara Lakewood Old Tawny Port

More labels than we've had ... (never mind), this is another contribution from a Barossa-based company that enters wines in every segment of the market.

CURRENT RELEASE *non-vintage* This wine won't break the bank but neither will the earth move. It is a straightforward style with crushed raisins on the nose. The palate is relatively simple with sweet dried-fruit flavours followed by warming spirit on a warming finish.

QUALITY ♛♛♛
VALUE ★★★
GRAPES shiraz, mataro
REGION Barossa Valley, SA
CELLAR 🍾
ALC./VOL. 18.0%
RRP $11.00

Chateau Yaldara Lakewood Show Liqueur Port

This was the best fortified in our 1993–94 edition and it still ranks as a world beater. Age and careful blending play their part to make a superior wine.

CURRENT RELEASE *non-vintage* The colour does the dance of the seven veils, the more you look the more you see – orange, amber, tawny brown. The palate is intense with rancio characters, orange peel, dried fruit and hints of caramel. The finish shows some refreshing acid and profound length. The average age of this wine is 24 years. A great after-dinner treat.

QUALITY ♛♛♛♛♛
VALUE ★★★★
GRAPES not stated
REGION Barossa Valley, SA
CELLAR 🍾
ALC./VOL. 19.0%
RRP $80.00

Craigmoor Rummy Port

Folklore has it that the winery ran out of barrels and got some old rum casks from the local pub.

CURRENT RELEASE *non-vintage* Can't taste the rum. This is a young tawny style that is easy to drink. The colour is a medium tawny brown and the nose is fruity with some brandied prune aromas. The medium-bodied palate is quite sweet and the finish is soft.

QUALITY ♛♛♛
VALUE ★★★
GRAPES not stated
REGION Mudgee, NSW
VALUE 🍾
ALC./VOL. 17.5%
RRP $10.00 Ⓢ

d'Arenberg Nostalgia Very Old Port

QUALITY ▼▼▼▽
VALUE ★★★½
GRAPES grenache, shiraz
REGION McLaren Vale, SA
CELLAR 🍷
ALC./VOL. 18.5%
RRP $15.45

D'Arry Osborn was famous for his ports, especially the vintages. His son Chester carries the flame today.

CURRENT RELEASE *non-vintage* This is a very sweet, rich, liqueur style with searing acidity which enlivens the palate. Our sample was a trace bottle-stale but the nose had vanilla, caramel, rancio and estery overtones and lots of raisin and prune flavour. The finish seems to resonate forever.

De Bortoli 8-Year-Old Tawny Port

QUALITY ▼▼▼▽
VALUE ★★★½
GRAPES shiraz, grenache
REGION Riverina, NSW
CELLAR 🍷
ALC./VOL. 19.0%
RRP $12.20

The habit of declaring average ages on ports is a fairly recent phenomenon, with a proliferation of ten-year-olds on the market.

CURRENT RELEASE *non-vintage* This has a good dollop of aged, rancio material in the blend, giving complexity to the dried fig and prune flavours. The finish is quite firm with some fire from the spirit. Sip with dried fruits and nuts.

De Bortoli 10-Year-Old Liqueur Muscat

QUALITY ▼▼▼▼▽
VALUE ★★★★★
GRAPES red frontignac
REGION mainly Riverina, NSW
CELLAR 🍷
ALC./VOL. 19.0%
RRP $12.20

Bottled in 1994. Our spies tell us this has been smartened up with an injection of Rutherglen material, which explains a lot. It has to be one of the best-value muscats around.

CURRENT RELEASE *non-vintage* A most impressive muscat, with excellent rancio aged character and heaps of dinky-di muscat fruit. Thick, luscious, rich and treacly, this is beautifully balanced and the aftertaste is endless. Drink with caramels and coffee.

De Bortoli Sacred Hill Old Tawny Port

This has an average age of five years. Is that enough to qualify for the epithet 'old'?

CURRENT RELEASE *non-vintage* This starts off well, with a medium tawny-red hue and fruity nose of caramel and raisins. The palate is moderately sweet and the fruit fades fast leaving an astringency that makes it austere. Take it bush for post-prandial sipping round the campfire.

QUALITY ♛♛♛
VALUE ★★★
GRAPES not stated
REGION Riverina, NSW
CELLAR 🍾
ALC./VOL. 18.0%
RRP $6.75 ⓢ

Gramp's Tawny Port

This is an affordable tawny that commemorates a famous Australian wine family.

CURRENT RELEASE *non-vintage* A young style that doesn't want for richness. The nose has rich raisin aromas and the palate is a sweet number with concentrated dried-fruit character. The finish is clean with warming spirit. A good after-dinner tipple.

QUALITY ♛♛♛♛
VALUE ★★★½
GRAPES not stated
REGION South-east Australia
CELLAR 🍾
ALC./VOL. 17.0%
RRP $12.00 ⓢ

Grand Cru Estate Flor Fino Sherry

Karl Seppelt's heyday in the wine business began in the fortified era, so it's no surprise that he's making several, although this is unusual for a boutique winery.

CURRENT RELEASE *non-vintage* This declares that it's bottled from the family barrel, so we have to forgive it a slightly hazy appearance. There is some flor character and aged bouquet reflecting developed rather than a fresh style. In the mouth it's soft, broad and slightly tangy from the flor yeast. Chill as an aperitif.

QUALITY ♛♛♛
VALUE ★★★
GRAPES not stated
REGION not stated
CELLAR 🍾
ALC./VOL. 18.5%
RRP $9.00 (cellar door)

Grand Cru Estate Vintage Port

QUALITY 🍷🍷🍷🍷
VALUE ★★★★
GRAPES not stated
REGION Eden Valley, SA
CELLAR 6+
ALC./VOL. 18.5%
RRP $9.00 (cellar door)

Karl Seppelt, a mover and shaker in the wine industry for many years, set up his own vineyard near Springton after retiring from Seppelt. The wines are made at Petaluma.

CURRENT RELEASE 1991 This is an exuberantly fruity port, perhaps lacking classic vintage port structure and leaning towards the 'blackberry nip' style, but a delicious drink. It has a deep red/black hue, a rich nose of cassis, black olive and liquorice, and a very soft, sweet, fruity taste. Ready to drink now with after-dinner mints.

Grant Burge Percy's Particular Fine Old Tawny

QUALITY 🍷🍷🍷🍷🍷
VALUE ★★★★
GRAPES grenache, shiraz, mataro, 'madeira'
REGION Barossa Valley, SA
CELLAR
ALC./VOL. 18.0%
RRP $50.00

Named after Percival Norman Burge who lived to the age of 96 and was grandfather to Grant Burge. According to Percy, his longevity was achieved by a nightly glass of port (an old Barossa custom!).

CURRENT RELEASE *non-vintage* This is a very elegant style with evidence of white grapes in the mix. It shows superb balance. The palate is sweet with a pronounced raisin character countered by nutty rancio characters and fresh acid and spirit on the finish. It wouldn't be bad as a nightcap, but much better after dinner.

Hardys Show Port

QUALITY 🍷🍷🍷🍷🍷
VALUE ★★★★½
GRAPES shiraz, grenache
REGION McLaren Vale, SA
CELLAR
ALC./VOL. 19.5%
RRP $34.80

This is the most classic of Hardy's tawny ports and the only one that isn't called a tawny.

CURRENT RELEASE *non-vintage* A serious port that's dry and almost austere on the palate. The bouquet has dried peel, nutty, malty and vanilla characters and there is plenty of rancio. It's big and powerful with excellent length. A top port for sipping after dinner.

Hardys Tall Ships Tawny Port

When the fleet of square-riggers entered Sydney Harbour on Australia Day 1988 for the bicentenary, the phrase 'tall ships' entered the language. It lingers on in that most seafaring of wine companies, Hardys.

CURRENT RELEASE *non-vintage* A very good tawny style and great value for money. This has textbook tawny-red hue, good port character with raisiny red fruit, a little rancio, and generous sweet rich depths on the palate. The prune and raisin flavours are very more-ish.

QUALITY ♛♛♛♛
VALUE ★★★★★
GRAPES not stated
REGION McLaren Vale, SA
CELLAR 🍷
ALC./VOL. 17.5%
RRP $9.40 ⓢ

Best Bargain Fortified

Hardys Vintage Port

Hardys' vintage ports are among the most highly regarded in this country. They're released with some age to save us the trouble of cellaring them ourselves.

Previous outstanding vintages: '69, '70, '71, '72, '75, '76, '78, '81

CURRENT RELEASE 1983 Deep red-black colour with a brick-red edge and a bouquet of black olive, leather and creosote show that this wine has entered its drinking phase. It is a very big, tough, rather extractive drought-year style that finishes with some bitterness. A forbidding wine of concentration and length. It needs stilton.

QUALITY ♛♛♛♛
VALUE ★★★
GRAPES shiraz
REGION McLaren Vale, SA
CELLAR 🍷 10
ALC./VOL. 19.0%
RRP $22.00 ⓢ 🍷

Hardys Whiskers Blake Tawny Port

QUALITY 🍷🍷🍷
VALUE ★★★
GRAPES not stated
REGION McLaren Vale, Riverland, Barossa Valley, SA
CELLAR 🍾
ALC./VOL. 18.0%
RRP $11.00 ⓢ

Whiskers Blake was an old codger who used a shotgun to scare the birds off the grapes at Hardys' McLaren Vale vineyards. He used to liberate the occasional dram of port as well, which is why this new one is named after him.

CURRENT RELEASE *non-vintage* The colour is medium-light tawny/amber and the light style follows throughout the wine. There's a fish-oil character of aged sweet white material and the palate is light and very sweet, with a slightly cloying finish. A very different style from other Hardy ports.

Jim Barry Old Walnut Tawny Port

QUALITY 🍷🍷🍷🍷
VALUE ★★★
GRAPES not stated
REGION Clare Valley, SA
CELLAR 🍾
ALC./VOL. 18.5%
RRP $55.50

The Barry winery is a family affair: Mark is winemaker, Peter is in marketing and John in the vineyards. Their dad Jim is semi-retired these days.

CURRENT RELEASE *non-vintage* This is very much the lighter, 'old sweet white' style and while it's not a great true tawny port, it's a superb old fortified. The colour is light tawny-amber; the nose has lots of nutty aged oloroso sherry character, and the sweet, mellow palate is shot through with vanilla and caramel nuances.

Jim Barry Sentimental Bloke Port

QUALITY 🍷🍷🍷?
VALUE ★★★
GRAPES not stated
REGION Clare Valley, SA
CELLAR 🍾
ALC./VOL. 18.5%
RRP $23.35

A curiously labelled wine, this has a verse from C.J. Dennis's 'The Singing Soldiers' on the back of the bottle.

CURRENT RELEASE *non-vintage* This is a heart-warming drop of port which combines genuine aged material with younger fruitier wine. The bouquet is complex, nutty, vanillan and shows some fruit, and the palate is sweet and fruity. Good general-purpose after-dinner sipper.

Kay Brothers Centenary Very Old Tawny Port

It's not every year you clock up a century in the winemaking score. This is a special release to mark that milestone. Maker Colin Kay.

CURRENT RELEASE *non-vintage* There is some old material in the blend but assertive oak seems to dominate. The colour is a mid-amber and there is plenty of rancio character on the nose. The palate has rich raisin flavours followed by grumpy oak on a firm finish. The oak seems slightly out of keeping with the blend.

QUALITY ♦♦♦♦
VALUE ★★★
GRAPES shiraz, grenache
REGION McLaren Vale, SA
CELLAR 🍾
ALC./VOL. 19.0%
RRP $22.00

Kay Brothers Liqueur Muscat

This district doesn't really have much of a track record for muscat, and while this is a drinkable wine it's not going to give the Rutherglen boys sleepless nights.

CURRENT RELEASE *non-vintage* The colour vacillates between pale yellow and light amber, and the nose has a broad raisin flavour. The palate is light with straightforward dried-fruit flavours followed by warming spirit. It is a clean and simple style that could be used as ice-cream topping.

QUALITY ♦♦♦
VALUE ★★★
GRAPES red frontignac
REGION McLaren Vale, SA
CELLAR 🍾
ALC./VOL. 18.0%
RRP $12.00

Kay Brothers Tawny Port

A simple economy style that is young and easy to drink. It represents good value for money.

CURRENT RELEASE *non-vintage* Straightforward in style and just on the brink of establishing rancio character. The colour is a pale tawny, the nose offers sweet fruit aromas and the middleweight palate keeps up the theme. Clean spirit graces the finish.

QUALITY ♦♦♦
VALUE ★★★
GRAPES probably shiraz, grenache
REGION McLaren Vale, SA
CELLAR 🍾 1
ALC./VOL. 18.0%
RRP $11.00

Lindemans Classic Release Vintage Port

QUALITY ★★★★★
VALUE ★★★
GRAPES gran noir 92%, shiraz 8%
REGION Corowa, NSW & Adelaide Hills, SA
CELLAR 5+
ALC./VOL. 19.8%
RRP $82.00 ⓢ

Lindemans claims its Classic Releases have been cellared at a constant 14–15 degrees Celsius. After being a biennial event for several years, they're now going annual.
CURRENT RELEASE 1978 *Bin 5532* Whatever grape gran noir is, we need more of it! This is a lovely drink, mellow and fully mature, cast in a drier, dare we say Portuguese, mould with complex spirit and fruit combining to give liquorice and black-olive characters. It's smooth and prune-like on the palate with some gentle tannin and a dry, almost austere, finish.

Lindemans Macquarie Port

QUALITY ★★★★
VALUE ★★★★
GRAPES grenache, shiraz
REGION mainly Barossa Valley, SA
CELLAR
ALC./VOL. 18.5%
RRP $11.40 ⓢ

Governor Lachlan Macquarie was an early governor of the infant colony of New South Wales. This port was first produced in the early 1950s when Lindemans had a winery at Corowa.
CURRENT RELEASE *non-vintage* This port is a true young tawny style and good value at its usual price of less than $10. It has a grapey nose reflecting younger blending wines, laced with vanilla from oak. It is a sweet, rich and quite oaky commercial port style with remarkably good depth and balance. Affordable after-dinner sipping.

McWilliam's Cream Sherry

QUALITY ★★★
VALUE ★★★
GRAPES not stated
REGION Murrumbidgee Irrigation Area, NSW
CELLAR
ALC./VOL. 17.5%
RRP $7.90 ⓢ

Still selling after all these years, the Jolly Friar (on the label) was the power behind McWilliam's throne for many years. And it's still a high-volume line.
CURRENT RELEASE *non-vintage* A pale sweet white with a light colour (hence the cream appellation) and the nose has overt muscat characters. The palate is sweet with concentrated grape flavours followed by simple spirit. This is a commercial 'feel good' drink.

McWilliam's Show Amontillado Sherry

It's show time! That's about the only time this wine gets to strut its stuff. There must be more to life than just winning gold medals.

CURRENT RELEASE *non-vintage* Beguiling stuff, no wonder it seduces the judges. The colour is a vibrant amber and the nose has nutty rancio and yeast notes. The palate is austere and it gives hints of aged material and a dusty dryness. The finish is robust and cleansing. Just the thing for a consommé.

QUALITY 🍷🍷🍷🍷🍷
VALUE ★★★★★
GRAPES palomino, pedro
REGION Riverina, NSW
CELLAR 🍾
ALC./VOL. 18.5%
RRP $26.00

Mildara Chestnut Teal Sherry

You actually see chestnut teals (the feathered variety) at the back of the Mildara winery. Unlike the birds, this wine is probably an endangered species.

CURRENT RELEASE *non-vintage* A sweet style that drinks like a young tokay. You'll find vanilla and malt aromas on the nose and the same on the sweet palate. The finish is clean and smooth. A fine wine for high tea.

QUALITY 🍷🍷🍷
VALUE ★★★
GRAPES palomino, pedro
REGION Riverland, SA
CELLAR 🍾
ALC./VOL. 17.5%
RRP $9.95 Ⓢ

Mildara George Sherry

George Caro was a director of Mildara in the 1950s and because he was a diabetic he requested a special sugarless drink be created.

CURRENT RELEASE *non-vintage* A good value wine with a nose that shows nutty flor yeast characters and whispers of oak. The palate is austere and dry with an impressive body length. The finish is cleansing with fine spirit. It could be served well chilled as a pre-dinner drink.

QUALITY 🍷🍷🍷🍷
VALUE ★★★★½
GRAPES palomino, pedro, doradillo
REGION various
CELLAR 🍾
ALC./VOL. 17.5%
RRP $10.00 Ⓢ

Miranda Fireside Port

QUALITY ♛♛♛
VALUE ★★★
GRAPES not stated
REGION Murrumbidgee Irrigation Area, NSW
CELLAR 🍷
ALC./VOL. 18.0%
RRP $6.90

Cheap and cheery doesn't always mean nasty – young styles can make for a satisfying yet economic tipple.

CURRENT RELEASE *non-vintage* The colour is a light tawny and there are raisin aromas on the nose. The palate is sweet and simple and the finish is clean. With respect, it is a good cooking style and the cook should feel free to have a glug in the process.

Morris Old Premium Liqueur Tokay

QUALITY ♛♛♛♛♛
VALUE ★★★★★
GRAPES muscadelle
REGION Rutherglen, Vic.
CELLAR 🍷
ALC./VOL. 19.0%
RRP $35.00

Last year we might have made this style sound like a drink of consolation. The stuff can also be used for seduction. It's a very sexy wine.

CURRENT RELEASE *non-vintage* There's a very fine taste of honey with plenty of complexity here. The nose has cold tea, toffee and time-engendered aromas. The palate is sweet and rich with toffee and caramel flavours plus loads of dried fruit and rancio character matched by refreshing acid on a protracted finish. It is a weapon for lounge lizards armed with tea cake.

Morris Very Old Liqueur Muscat

The party trick at the Morris Mia Mia winery is to pour a sample of pre-phylloxera muscat from an old cognac barrel with cane hoops. The stuff is indescribable and almost undrinkable but you can see similar traces in the very old product. Made by generations of the Morris family.

CURRENT RELEASE *non-vintage* A great example of the Rutherglen style. There is plenty of evidence of very old material which has been deftly freshened, with younger material. The result is extreme finesse. The nose is malty with rancio and dried-fruit aromas. The palate is layered with aged characters, raisin, malt extract and peel flavours, freshened by attractive acid on a well-balanced finish. It is a great after-dinner drink.

QUALITY ♜♜♜♜♜
VALUE ★★★★★
GRAPES red frontignac
REGION Rutherglen, Vic.
CELLAR 🍷
ALC./VOL. 18.5%
RRP $45.00

Mount Prior Muscat

Mount Prior is the Rutherglen equivalent of a chateau – a very grand homestead with a long wine heritage. It was established in 1860 and these days it produces around 9000 cases. Maker Garry Wall.

CURRENT RELEASE *non-vintage* A full-frontal crunch in the mouth with intense muscat flavour: rich to the max. The nose has spirit and overt ripe fruit aromas; the palate is sweet with intense muscat flavour balanced by clean spirit on a dry finish. A very satisfying style that goes well with homemade vanilla ice-cream.

QUALITY ♜♜♜♜
VALUE ★★★★
GRAPES red frontignac
REGION Rutherglen, Vic.
CELLAR 🍷
ALC./VOL. 18.0%
RRP $13.50

Normans King William Tawny Port

QUALITY ▼▼▼▼▼
VALUE ★★★★½
GRAPES shiraz, grenache
REGION McLaren Vale, SA
CELLAR 🍾
ALC./VOL. 17.5%
RRP $16.60 ⓢ

A 12-year-old tawny from the company which was floated in 1994 by the Horlin Smith family, who previously owned it outright. Blender Brian Light.

CURRENT RELEASE *non-vintage* Good-value tawny with a medium-light tawny-red colour and attractive wood-aged rancio and raisin bouquet. There are lingering chocolate and vanilla flavours on a well-balanced palate that doesn't cloy. Good with nuts and dried fruit after dinner.

Orlando Liqueur Port

QUALITY ▼▼▼▼
VALUE ★★★½
GRAPES not stated
REGION not stated
CELLAR 🍾
ALC./VOL. 17.5%
RRP $13.00

The death of the three-hour lunch and the birth of a bowl of pasta and a glass of white wine has made port a declining market. Sad times indeed – will a style like this ever find a home?

CURRENT RELEASE *non-vintage* The wine is a tasty, sweet fortified that must have pleased the business drunks of yore. It has a certain muscat component and there is evidence of rancio character. The finish is clean and neat. Try it with a blue-mould cheese.

Penfolds Grandfather Port

QUALITY ▼▼▼▼▼
VALUE ★★★★½
GRAPES shiraz, mataro
REGION Barossa Valley, SA
CELLAR 🍾
ALC./VOL. 19.0%
RRP $66.80

The first small batches of this wine were made in 1915, and the current blend has an average age of 20 years. Blender Dean Kraehenbuhl.

CURRENT RELEASE *non-vintage* This is an old liqueur style, quite deep in its tawny hue and showing complex rancio characters in the bouquet. The palate is immensely intense, powerfully concentrated, penetrating and long, with richness and viscosity. A great old port and perfect for after-dinner sipping with dried fruits and nuts.

Penfolds Ten Year Old Port

This port is matured in small oak hogsheads and has a minimum age of ten years.

CURRENT RELEASE *non-vintage* Not a lot of genuine wood-aged rancio here, but rather more of the caramel, vanilla, toffee characters of a wine which has been given plenty of warmth while maturing in the wood. There are developed prune and raisin fruit flavours and plenty of sweetness. A good everyday port.

QUALITY ▮▮▮▮
VALUE ★★★½
GRAPES shiraz, grenache, mataro
REGION various, SA
CELLAR ▮
ALC./VOL. 19.0%
RRP $18.75 ⓢ

Peter Lehmann Cellar Door Reserve Fino Sherry

At the insistence of Margaret Lehmann, Andrew Wigan and his winemaking team recently revived this dinosaur style. It's only available at the winery.

CURRENT RELEASE *non-vintage* Worth a trip to the Barossa. A model fino – light, fresh and dry as a bone. The colour's pale yellow; the nose crisp and pungent with nutty, fresh flor yeast character. In the mouth it's lively and dry, yet smooth and balanced with a harmonious tangy finish. Perfect winter aperitif, or chill in summer with tapas.

QUALITY ▮▮▮▮▮
VALUE ★★★★★
GRAPES palomino
REGION Barossa Valley, SA
CELLAR ▮
ALC./VOL. 17.5%
RRP $10.00 (cellar door only)

Renmano Cromwell Tawny Port

What Oliver Cromwell has to do with this wine is unclear, but we guess it's the imagery the marketers are trying to capture.

CURRENT RELEASE *non-vintage* The colour is classic tawny-red but the nose reveals muscat fruit, which is a little out of style although very attractive. The palate holds lashings of sweet, rich, raisiny flavour, some evidence of age and a nice long finish. Good with gorgonzola.

QUALITY ▮▮▮▮
VALUE ★★★★
GRAPES grenache, gordo, shiraz
REGION Riverland, SA
CELLAR ▮
ALC./VOL. 18.0%
RRP $7.25 ⓢ

Renmano Rumpole Tawny Port

QUALITY ♛♛♛
VALUE ★★★
GRAPES shiraz, grenache
REGION Riverland, SA
CELLAR 🍾
ALC./VOL. 18.0%
RRP $11.60 ⓢ

Rumpole of the Bailey used to love claret rather than port, but it's doubtful he'd refuse a glass of this.

CURRENT RELEASE *non-vintage* This has lightened off over the years. It's now a light tawny-amber colour and has more in common with sweet oloroso sherry than port. There's abundant grapey 'old sweet white' character in a straightforward palate with a lot of sweetness.

Rockford P.S. Marion Tawny

QUALITY ♛♛♛♛♛
VALUE ★★★★★
GRAPES shiraz
REGION Barossa Valley, SA
CELLAR 🍾
ALC./VOL. 19.0%
RRP $15.50 (cellar door)

This is a 15-year-old tawny port. A few cents from every bottle sold go into a fund to restore the P.S. *Marion* – a steam-driven Murray River paddleboat.

CURRENT RELEASE *non-vintage* A model Barossa tawny which really reverberates around the mouth – long after it's gone. The hue is correct medium tawny-red; the bouquet is full of nutty, vanilla, rancio complexities, and there's rich, chunky chocolate/vanilla flavour aplenty in the mouth. Very long finish with superb style and character. Rises to the most demanding occasion.

Rovalley Cobweb Port

QUALITY ♛♛♛♛
VALUE ★★★★
GRAPES not stated
REGION Barossa Valley, SA
CELLAR 🍾
ALC./VOL. 18.0%
RRP $11.60 ⓢ

Before the Miranda buy-out, Rovalley was a mainly fortified-wine company and this has always been a good-value drop.

CURRENT RELEASE *non-vintage* The colour is deep and there's a hint of muscat fruit about this wine, as well as a lot of sweetness. The nose is complex and raisined, and it's big, soft, rich and liqueury in the mouth. A good drink for those who like their port with a sweet finish.

Saltram Ludlow's Tawny 8-Year-Old

After 60 years before the mast you'd think they'd find a wine of equal age to mark your achievement. Fred Ludlow worked his passage from cellar-hand to winemaker in a career that saw many changes.

CURRENT RELEASE *non-vintage* The colour is a mid-tawny and the nose has dried-fruit and prune aromas. The palate is sweet and straightforward with mature fruit. The finish has warming spirit. It has youth and simplicity on its side. Sip after dinner.

QUALITY ♟♟♟
VALUE ★★★
GRAPES not stated
REGION Barossa Valley, SA
CELLAR 🍷
ALC./VOL. 17.0%
RRP $12.00 Ⓢ

Saltram Mr Pickwick's Particular Port

This style was started by Peter Lehmann when he worked at Saltram. It started life as a sweet white.
CURRENT RELEASE *non-vintage* An old sweet white style that has plenty of rancio character. It could be considered a sherry with wood-aged rancio characters dominating the nose. The palate is quite sweet with concentrated grape flavour. The elegant finish is followed by clean acid and mellow spirit. A very friendly after-dinner drink.

QUALITY ♟♟♟♟♟
VALUE ★★★★½
GRAPES not stated
REGION Barossa Valley, SA
CELLAR 🍷
ALC./VOL. 19.0%
RRP $47.00

Seppelt 100 Year Old Para Port

Benno Seppelt set aside a cask of his best port in 1878 (and one every year thereafter) so they could be aged for 100 years. The result is a wine that creates instant wine-writer's block because it is so mysterious and challenging.

CURRENT RELEASE 1892 Where to start? The colour is a dark olive with brown and orange tinges. The palate is so thick and concentrated it explodes on the tongue and spreads through the palate. Complicated rancio characters hold the high ground. The finish shows acid and alcohol. You can walk around a couple of city blocks and still taste the stuff.

QUALITY ♟♟♟♟♟
VALUE ★★★★★
GRAPES shiraz, grenache, mataro
REGION Barossa Valley, SA
CELLAR 🍷
ALC./VOL. 24.0%
RRP $POA (usually auctioned)

Seppeltsfield DP 90 Show Tawny

QUALITY ★★★★★
VALUE ★★★★★
GRAPES shiraz, grenache, cabernet sauvignon
REGION Barossa Valley, SA
CELLAR 🍾
ALC./VOL. $21.5%
RRP $45.00

The average age of the blend is over 21 years and the show medal tally would make a field marshall turn green with envy.

CURRENT RELEASE *non-vintage* The subtlety here shows that a wine doesn't have to be a powerhouse to attract attention. The colour is a bright tawny brown and the nose is nutty with obvious rancio character. The palate is complex with aged rancio dominating some raisin-like fruit. The finish has zesty acid that lingers to eternity.

Seppeltsfield DP 116 Show Amontillado

QUALITY ★★★★★
VALUE ★★★★★
GRAPES palomino
REGION Barossa Valley, SA
CELLAR 🍾
ALC./VOL. 18.5%
RRP $21.50

An old, wise wine that unfortunately has a small audience of old, wise heads. For those in the know the rewards are great. This wine was awarded the 'Best Fortified' award in last year's edition. The average age of the blend is 16 years.

CURRENT RELEASE *non-vintage* A profound wine that needs a fireside and Miles Davis playing the Concerto d'Aranjuez. This is wonderfully complex with vanilla, citrus-peel, nut and dried-fruit aromas. The palate has a smooth and mouthfilling quality with mellow aged fruity flavours supported by a lifted acid finish. It could be served as a pre-dinner drink or with a game consommé.

Seppeltsfield DP 117 Show Flor Fino

This is a fine range of fortifieds that stirs romance and passion – pity the DP is an abbreviation for Duty Paid.

CURRENT RELEASE *non-vintage* You can almost hear the castanets – this is a very Spanish style that has been carefully crafted. It has an exotic nose with nutty aromas and a hint of seaweed. The palate is austere with steely fruit flavours followed by a crisp acid finish. A cleansing style and, although the purists might cringe, it could be served well chilled.

QUALITY ★★★★½
VALUE ★★★★★
GRAPES palomino
REGION Barossa valley, SA
CELLAR 🍷
ALC./VOL. 18.5%
RRP $21.50

St Hallett Krueke Tawny Port

Named after William Krueke, a Barossa pioneer. St Hallett is a dynamic winery that has made much progress in shucking off the old Barossa image. Krueke remains as a link to the past.

CURRENT RELEASE *non-vintage* The colour is a burnt brick-red and the nose smells of a fruitcake mix soaked in brandy. The palate is complex and full-bodied with evidence of both young and old material. The finish is clean and warming. It is a good after-dinner style.

QUALITY ★★★★
VALUE ★★★★
GRAPES shiraz
REGION Barossa Valley, SA
CELLAR 🍷
ALC./VOL. 18.0%
RRP $20.00

Stanton & Killeen Liqueur Muscat

As a cellar style this marque stands out for being able to capture the freshness and essence of the muscat grape.

CURRENT RELEASE *non-vintage* The colour is a rusty brown and the nose is bursting with dried fruit and a hint of eucalypt. The palate is like crunching into a bunch of ripe berries that are full of sugar and warm mellow spirit. A very clean, well-balanced wine.

QUALITY ★★★★½
VALUE ★★★★½
GRAPES red frontignac
REGION Rutherglen, Vic.
CELLAR 🍷
ALC./VOL. 18.5%
RRP $15.00

Stanton & Killeen Liqueur Port

QUALITY ♛♛♛♛
VALUE ★★★½
GRAPES not stated
REGION Rutherglen, Vic.
CELLAR 🍾
ALC./VOL. 18.5%
RRP $14.00

A liqueur port is supposed to be stored in barrels near the tin roof of the winery. The heat causes evaporation, concentrating the flavour.

CURRENT RELEASE *non-vintage* A fairly simple style with a colour that straddles the definition between a ruby and a tawny port. The nose has ripe fruit flavours and spirit. The sweet-centred palate has strong berry character balanced by spirit on a gentle finish. An after-dinner style.

Stanton & Killeen Liqueur Tokay

QUALITY ♛♛♛♛
VALUE ★★★★
GRAPES muscadelle
REGION Rutherglen, Vic.
CELLAR 🍾
ALC./VOL. 18.5%
RRP $15.90

A style that is unique to the Rutherglen district where they turn white grapes into tawny wine thanks to the influence of careful oxidation in wooden casks.

CURRENT RELEASE *non-vintage* The colour is a sprightly amber and the nose has strong sherry and caramel aromas. The palate is full of toffee and dried-fruit flavours buttressed by spirit on a clean dry finish. Drink only after eating.

Stanton & Killeen Old Tawny

QUALITY ♛♛♛♛
VALUE ★★★★
GRAPES shiraz, touriga
REGION Rutherglen, Vic.
CELLAR 🍾
ALC./VOL. 18.5%
RRP $15.00

Stanton & Killeen is a much respected small winery founded by the respective partners. As much as he doesn't like to be reminded, Norm Killeen was a local Rutherglen heart-throb due to his ability to croon. His rendition of 'Danny Boy' was worth a forest of Kleenex. Maker Chris Killeen.

CURRENT RELEASE *non-vintage* A middleweight style typical of the district. The colour is a mid-tawny and the nose has rancio and lactic characters. The palate displays a sweet raisin character balanced by a nutty quality. Warming spirit fills out the finish, adding a dry note. It is a good coffee-and-cigar tipple.

Wirra Wirra Fine Old Tawny

This is a much respected marque in the McLaren Vale district. Proprietor Greg Trott is one of nature's gentlemen.

CURRENT RELEASE *non-vintage* The colour is a mid-amber and the nose offers spice, raisin and lifted spirit. The palate is nutty with strong rancio character and complex dried-fruit flavours that give way to fresh spirit on a clean finish. The average age of the blend is 15 years.

QUALITY ♛♛♛♛
VALUE ★★★★
GRAPES shiraz, touriga, grenache
REGION McLaren Vale, SA
CELLAR 🍾 1
ALC./VOL. 18.2%
RRP $20.00

Woodstock Tawny Port

The Collett family have long held faith in tawny port styles, and to that end they have invested in sheds filled with barrels of fortified wines. The dividends are now being bottled. Maker Scott Collett.

CURRENT RELEASE *non-vintage* The colour is a deep amber with a rich walnut background. The nose shows some aged brandy spirit and nutty aromas. The palate is rich with concentrated sweet raisin flavours followed by warming brandy on a clean finish.

QUALITY ♛♛♛♛♛
VALUE ★★★★
GRAPES shiraz, grenache
REGION McLaren Vale, SA
CELLAR 🍾 1
ALC./VOL. 18.0%
RRP $22.00

Yalumba Clock Tower Port

Visit the winery and it is impossible to ignore the omnipresent clock tower which has been the feature of wine labels for eons.

CURRENT RELEASE *non-vintage* Is it a tawny or is it a vintage? Whatever, it drinks well. A young style with sweet fruit and a hint of liquorice. The finish shows some fresh spirit on a clean finish. It is a good commercial style that is very easy to drink.

QUALITY ♛♛♛♛
VALUE ★★★★
GRAPES not stated
REGION not stated
CELLAR 🍾
ALC./VOL. 17.5%
RRP $9.00 Ⓢ

Yalumba Director's Special Tawny Port

QUALITY ♱♱♱♱
VALUE ★★★★
GRAPES shiraz
REGION Barossa Valley, SA
CELLAR 🍾
ALC./VOL. 17.5%
RRP $12.00 💲

Just who is the director now, after the Mildara Blass acquisition! Perhaps it is the CEO Ray King. As they say in US golf galleries, 'you de man!'

CURRENT RELEASE *non-vintage* A middleweight style that shows plenty of finesse. The colour is a mid-amber and there is a generous rancio quality on the nose. The palate has sweet dried-fruit and mellow wood qualities. The finish is clean and balanced. And you don't have to be on the board to enjoy this after-dinner drink.

Yalumba Four Crown Port

QUALITY ♱♱♱♰
VALUE ★★★★
GRAPES not stated
REGION not stated
CELLAR 🍾
ALC./VOL. 17.5%
RRP $6.00 ($13.45 flagon)

Will this label survive the management change? It still comes in flagons and has a venerable history – Mawson took it to the South Pole to ward off the cold.

CURRENT RELEASE *non-vintage* Fresh and light with all things right, this young style is easy to drink. The nose offers dried fruit and spirit. The palate is light with uncomplicated sweet fruit followed by discreet spirit on a clean finish. A good commercial style that obviously could be served on the rocks.

Yalumba Galway Pipe Port

If this were a financial guide rather than a drinking guide, this entry would be a chapter in itself. Mildara Blass acquired the fortified portfolio from Yalumba. Why? That would be another chapter in itself, but the wines, styles and labels remain under new management.

CURRENT RELEASE *non-vintage* This is a very fine blend that shows poise and style. The colour is a mid-amber and the nose has rancio and fine spirit smells. The palate shows beautiful balance with complex rancio and sweet fruit flavours balanced by nutty wood and clean spirit. A very fine Australian fortified.

QUALITY ♛♛♛♛♛
VALUE ★★★★★
GRAPES not stated
REGION Barossa Valley, SA
CELLAR 🍾
ALC./VOL. 18.0%
RRP $25.00

Wine Casks

Although their market share is declining, wine casks are still a significant component of the market. And this year the amazing happened: imported wine from places like France was used to blend with local wine to make up for the shortfall in the low-production vintage. Australia's bulk wine is still in high demand on the export market.

While the demand for Australian wine is high, it's clear that other countries can produce wine more cheaply. It will be interesting to watch the progress of this segment of the market. It is difficult to believe that wine casks have been on allocation to retailers.

FORTIFIED	QUANTITY	QUALITY
De Bortoli Tawny Port	4 litres	♟♟♟?
Penfolds Wood Aged Tawny — BEST CASK	2 litres	♟♟♟♟
Renmano Aged Tawny Port	2 litres	♟♟♟♟
Stanley Tawny Port	2 litres	♟♟♟?
RED WINE		
Berri Claret	5 litres	♟♟?
Brown Brothers Dry Red	10 litres	♟♟♟♟
d'Arenberg Claret	4 litres	♟♟♟♟
De Bortoli Premium Shiraz Cab.	4 litres	♟♟♟♟
Lindemans Claret	4 litres	♟♟
Morris Pressings	4 litres	♟♟♟♟
Renmano Hermitage	2 litres	♟♟♟?
Renmano Shiraz Cabernet	2 litres	♟♟♟?
Stanley Shiraz Cabernet	2 litres	♟♟♟

| Yalumba Cabernet Sauvignon | 2 litres | 🍷🍷🍷🍷 |

WHITE WINE

Berri Fruity Gordo	5 litres	🍷🍷🍷🍷
Berri Riesling	5 litres	🍷🍷🍷
Brown Brothers Dry White	10 litres	🍷🍷🍷🍷
De Bortoli Semillon Chardonnay	4 litres	🍷🍷🍷
Lindemans Semillon Chardonnay	2 litres	🍷🍷🍷🍷
Lindemans Verdelhao	2 litres	🍷🍷🍷🍷
McWilliam's Colombard Chardonnay	2 litres	🍷🍷🍷🍷
McWilliam's Traminer Riesling	2 litres	🍷🍷🍷🍷
Morris Colombard Chardonnay	4 litres	🍷🍷🍷
Orlando Coolabah Chablis	4 litres	🍷🍷
Orlando Coolabah Riesling	4 litres	🍷🍷
Renmano Chenin Blanc	2 litres	🍷🍷🍷🍷
Renmano Sauvignon Blanc	2 litres	🍷🍷🍷🍷
Stanley Fumé Blanc	2 litres	🍷🍷🍷
Stanley White Burgundy	4 litres	🍷🍷🍷
Yalumba Rhine Riesling 1994	2 litres	🍷🍷🍷🍷
Yalumba Semillon Chardonnay	2 litres	🍷🍷🍷🍷

Food/Wine Combinations – Reds

BEEF *(roast, pot roast, rolled roast, grilled, raw, steaks, standing rib, topside)*

All Saints Shiraz
Bailey's 1920s Block Shiraz
Balgownie Estate Cabernet Sauvignon
Best's Bin O Shiraz
Bethany Cabernet Merlot
Brokenwood Hermitage
Canobolas-Smith Alchemy
Cape Mentelle Shiraz
Charles Melton Cabernet Sauvignon
Chateau Xanadu Cabernet Sauvignon
Coriole Shiraz
Crawford River Cabernet Sauvignon
De Bortoli Windy Peak Cabernets Shiraz Merlot
De Bortoli Yarra Valley Shiraz
Elderton Cabernet Sauvignon
Gehrig Shiraz
Giesen Marlborough Pinot Noir
Haselgrove Grenache Shiraz
Henschke Cyril Henschke Cabernet Sauvignon
Holm Oak Cabernet Sauvignon
Jasper Hill Emily's Paddock Shiraz Cabernet Franc
Jim Barry Personal Selection Cabernet Sauvignon
Leo Bruing DR 150 Cabernet sauvignon
Hardys Eileen Hardy Shiraz
Leasingham Classic Clare Cabernet Sauvignon
Lindemans Limestone Ridge
Lindemans Pyrus
Maxwell Ellen Street Shiraz
Maxwell Lime Cave Cabernet Sauvignon

Mount Avoca Cabernet Sauvignon
Mount Hurtle cabernet merlot
Penfolds Bin 707
Penfolds Clare Estate
Penfolds St Henri Shiraz
Penley Estate Shiraz Cabernet
Petaluma Coonawarra
Peter Lehmann Cabernet Sauvignon
Redman Cabernet Merlot
Redman Coonawarra Cabernet Sauvignon
Richard Hamilton Old Vines Shiraz
Rotherhythe Cabernet Sauvignon
Ryecroft Traditional
Salisbury Estate Cabernet Sauvignon
St Hallett Cabernet Merlot
St Hallett Old Block Shiraz
Stanton and Killeen Moodemere Red Shiraz
Summerfield Cabernet Sauvignon
Tolley Hope Valley Cellars Barossa Shiraz
Turkey Flat Shiraz
Wolf Blass Grey Label
Woodstock The Stocks

CASSEROLES (beef, lamb, veal, kid, cassoulet)

Andrew Garrett Bold Style Shiraz
Arrowfield Cabernet Merlot
Arrowfield Shiraz Cabernet
Bethany Cabernet Merlot
Botobolar Shiraz
Bowen Cabernet Sauvignon Merlot Cabernet Franc
Burge Family Draycott Shiraz
Charles Melton Nine Popes
Eden Ridge Cabernet Sauvignon
Evans & Tate Margaret River Hermitage
Hillstowe Buxton Cabernet Merlot
Houghton Gold Reserve Cabernet Sauvignon
Hungerford Hill Shiraz
Krondorf Show Cabernet Sauvignon Shiraz
Leasingham Bin 56 Cabernet Malbec

Lindemans Bin 50
Marienberg Cabernet Sauvignon
Pikes Cabernet Sauvignon
Rosemount McLaren Vale Shiraz
Schinus Cabernet
Seppelt Harper's Range
Stonyfell Metala
Tim Grant Shiraz
Wolf Blass Black Label
Wolf Blass Red Label

CHEESE (cheddar, brie, camembert, stilton, washed rind, goat's, sheep's)

Barwang Shiraz
Brown Brothers Classic Vintage Release Cabernet Sauvignon
Hardys Eileen Hardy
Leeuwin Art Series Cabernet Sauvignon
Lindemans Hunter River Burgundy
Mount Langi Ghiran Shiaz
Penfolds Grange
Peter Lehmann Cabernet Sauvignon
Taltarni Cabernet Sauvignon
Tim Knappstein Cabernet Merlot

CURRY (mild)

Balgownie Estate Hermitage

DUCK (roast, Peking, warm salad, Westlake, confit)

Bowen Estate Shiraz
Garden Gully Shiraz
Haselgrove Reserve Coonawarra Cabernet Sauvignon
Petaluma Merlot
Salitage Pinot Noir
Smithbrook Pinot Noir

Stanton & Killeen Moodemere Dry Red
Tyrrell's Old Winery Pinot Noir
Tyrrell's Vat 9
Wild Duck Creek Shiraz
Wolf Blass Brown Label

FAST FOOD (Big Mac, KFC, pizza)

Houghton Cabernet Sauvignon

GAME (pheasant, quail, squab, venison, hare, rabbit, Guinea fowl)

Ashton Hills Cabernet Merlot
Ashton Hills Pinot Noir
Bannockburn Cabernet Sauvignon Merlot
Barwang Cabernet Sauvignon
Brokenwood Graveyard Vineyard
Brookland Valley Cabernet Sauvignon Merlot Cabernet Franc
Campbells The Barkley
Coldstream Hills Pinot Noir
Coriole Mary Kathleen
Craigow Pinot Noir
Diamond Valley Estate Pinot Noir
Freycinet Cabernet Sauvignon
Freycinet Pinot Noir
Galafrey Pinot Noir
Geoff Merrill Cabernet Sauvignon
Grosset Gaia
Henschke Mount Edelstone
Jim Barry The Armagh
Karriview Pinot Noir
Leconfield Shiraz
Normans Chais Clarendon Shiraz
Penfolds Bin 389
Penfolds Magill Estates
Peter Lehmann Cellar Collection Cabernet Malbec
Rothbury Estate Hunter Valley Shiraz

Rymill Shiraz
Taltarni Cabernet Sauvignon
Tyrrell's Stevens Shiraz

KANGAROO *(char-grilled, pan-fried, stewed, tail soup)*

Angoves Sarnia Farm Cabernet Sauvignon
Blackjack Shiraz
Brokenwood Rayner Vineyard Shiraz
Brown Brothers Shiraz
Dalwhinnie Shiraz
Doonkuna Estate Shiraz
Mitchelton III
Mount Bold Shiraz
Pikes Shiraz
Redbank Sally's Paddock
Seppelt Chalambar Shiraz
Sorrenberg Cabernet Sauvignon
Woodstock Cabernet Sauvignon
Wynns Coonawarra Hermitage
Yarra Edge Cabernets

LAMB *(rack of, sausages, kebabs, shanks, chops, straps, roast, BBQ, pumped, smoked)*

Andrew Garrett Cabernet Merlot
Bloodwood Cabernet Merlot
Bowen Estate Cabernet Sauvignon
Brands Laira Cabernet Sauvignon
Brindabella Hills Cabernets
Cape Mentelle Trinders
Casegrain Merlot
David Traeger Cabernet Sauvignon
De Bortoli Yarra Valley Pinot Noir
Dennis Cabernet Sauvignon
Devil's Lair Cabernet Merlot
Devil's Lair Cabernet Sauvignon
Doonkuna Estate Pinot Noir

Evans & Tate Barrique 61
Evans & Tate Margaret River Merlot
Eyton on Yarra Cabernet Merlot
Eyton on Yarra Merlot
Fire Gully Cabernets Merlot
Frankland Estate Olmo's Reward
Galafrey Shiraz
Grant Burge Meshach
Henschke Abbott's Prayer
Hollick Coonawarra
Hollick Ravenswood
Jamiesons Run
Jim Barry Cabernet Merlot
Killerby Shiraz
Kingston Estate Reserve Shiraz
Lakes Folly Cabernet
Leconfield Cabernet Sauvignon
Lindemans Padthaway Cabernet Merlot
Passing Clouds Shiraz Cabernet
Penfolds Bin 407
Richard Hamilton Hut Block Cabernet Sauvignon
Riddoch The Run Cabernet Sauvignon
Robertson's Well Cabernet Sauvignon
Seaview Edwards and Chaffey Cabernet Sauvignon
St Hallett Cabernet Merlot
Tatachilla Partners
Tim Adams The Fergus
Wyndham Estate Bin 444
Yanwirra Cabernet Sauvignon
Yarra Ridge Shiraz
Yarra Valley Hills Pinot Noir

OFFAL *(kidneys, tripe, liver, sweetbreads, oxtail)*

Bethany Shiraz
Charles Cimicky Signature Shiraz
Chateau Xanadu Cabernet Franc
Coriole Cabernet Sauvignon
Mitchell Pepper Tree Vineyard Shiraz
Mount Horrocks Cabernet Merlot

Peel Estate Shiraz
Penfolds Clare Estate
Wynns Coonawarra Cabernet Sauvignon

PASTA (meat, game, tomato sauce)

Brands Laira Shiraz
Buller Classic Red
Delamere Pinot Noir
Galah Wine
Henschke Abbott's Prayer
Lindemans Nyrang Hermitage
Oakland Cabernet Mataro Grenache
Riddoch Cabernet Shiraz
Seppelt Drumborg Cabernet Sauvignon
Shottesbrooke Merlot
Wynns Coonawarra Cabernet Hermitage Merlot

VEAL (pan-fried, roast, schnitzel, chops)

Basedows Oscar's Hermitage
Bethany Shiraz
Dennis Cabernet Sauvignon
Diamond Valley Blue Label Cabernet Sauvignon
Mount Hurtle Shiraz
Plunkett Cabernet Merlot
Preece Cabernet Sauvignon
Tapestry Cabernet Sauvignon
Temple Bruer Cornucopia Grenache

Food/Wine Combinations – Whites

ASPARAGUS (green, white, steamed, poached, quiche)

Alta Sauvignon Blanc
Bridgewater Mill Sauvignon Blanc
Brookland Valley sauvignon Blanc
Deen De Bortoli Vat 2 Sauvignon Blanc
Gloucester Ridge Sauvignon Blanc
Jamiesons Run Sauvignon Blanc
Katnook Sauvignon Blanc
Leeuwin Estate Art Series Sauvignon Blanc
Oakland Semillon Sauvignon Blanc
Plantagenet Omrah Unoaked Chardonnay
Richmond Grove Barossa Rhine Riesling
Ridgeview Margaret River Sauvignon Blanc
Selak's Sauvignon Blanc
Sorrenberg Sauvignon Blanc Semillon.

CAESAR SALAD

Hanging Rock Victoria Chardonnay
Leland Neudorf Valley Sauvignon Blanc
Lindemans Bin 95 Sauvignon Blanc
Pendarves Sauvignon Blanc Semillon

CALAMARI

Ashton Hills Chardonnay
Balgownie Premier Cuvée Chardonnay
De Bortoli Windy Peak Chardonnay
Lindemans Padthaway Chardonnay

Matthew Lang Colombard
Tyrrell's Shee-Oak Chardonnay

CHEESE *(camembert, brie, soft blue, smoked, goat's, sheep's, soufflé)*

Brown Brothers Late Harvest Orange Muscat & Flora
Henschke Gewürztraminer
Lindemans Coonawarra Sauvignon Blanc
Rosemount Yarrawa Vineyard Sauvignon Blanc
Wolf Blass Spätlese Rhine Riesling

CHICKEN

Allandale Chardonnay
Andrew Garrett Chardonnay
Angoves Colombard
Arrowfield Chardonnay
Basedow Chardonnay
Basedow White Burgundy
Bloodwood Chardonnay
Brokenwood Chardonnay
Brook Eden Chardonnay
Campbells Semillon Chardonnay
Campbells Silverburn
Coriole Semillon Sauvignon Blanc
De Bortoli Yarra Valley Chardonnay
Delatite Chardonnay
Doonkuna Chardonnay
Gloucester Ridge Chardonnay
Henschke Chardonnay
Henschke Croft Chardonnay
Henschke Semillon
Houghton Gold Reserve Verdelho
Houghton Semillon Sauvignon Blanc
Houghton Show Reserve White Burgundy
Jim Barry Personal Selection Chardonnay
Kingston Estate Chardonnay

Lakes Folly Chardonnay
Lindemans Padthaway Verdelhao
Marienberg Chardonnay
Maxwell Semillon
Miranda Rovalley Ridge Rhine Riesling
Moondah Brook Verdelho
Mount Horrocks Wood Aged Semillon
Mount Prior Chardonnay
Mount Prior Dry White
Normans Chais Clarendon Chardonnay
Oakland Semillon Chardonnay
Penfolds Chardonnay
Peter Lehmann Cellar Collection Chardonnay
Pipers Brook Vineyard Riesling
Pirramimma Sauvignon Blanc Semillon
Richmond Grove Traminer Riesling
Riddoch The Run Chardonnay
Sandalford Classic Dry White
Seaview White Burgundy
Seppelt Partalunga Chardonnay
St Hallett Chardonnay
Tapestry Chardonnay
Tollana Eden Valley Chardonnay
Willow Creek Unoaked Chardonnay
Willows Semillon
Wolf Blass Chardonnay
Wolf Blass Show Chardonnay
Yarra Valley Hills Riesling

CRAYFISH/MARRON

Bannockburn Chardonnay
Freycinet Chardonnay
Galafrey Rhine Riesling
Hardys Eileen Hardy Chardonnay
Leeuwin Prelude Chardonnay
Plantagenet Mount Barker Chardonnay

DUCK

Brown Brothers Gewürztraminer

FAST FOOD (Big Mac, KFC, pizza)

Angoves Butterfly Ridge Chablis
Galafrey Unwooded Chardonnay
Hardys Nottage Hill Rhine Riesling
Queen Adelaide Chardonnay

FISH (all varieties, including smoked salmon and whitebait)

Aquila Estate Reflections
Bethany Riesling
Bowen Estate Chardonnay
Cranswick Estate Autumn Gold Botrytis Semillon
David Wynn Riesling
Geoff Merrill Chardonnay
Giesen Marlborough Riesling
Hardys Siegersdorf Chardonnay
Hillstowe Sauvignon Blanc
Hillstowe Udy's Mill Chardonnay
Hollick Terra
Horseshoe Classic Hunter Semillon
Houghton Rhine Riesling
Houghton White Burgundy
Howard Park Riesling
Huntington Estate Semillon
Jamiesons Run Chardonnay
Kara Kara Vineyards Sauvignon Blanc
Karriview Chardonnay
Katnook Coonawarra Riesling
Krondorf Rhine Riesling
Lark Hill Chardonnay
Leasingham Bin 42
Leconfield Riesling

Leo Buring Eden valley Rhine Riesling DWY 18
Leo Buring Watervale Rhine Riesling DW 33
Lillydale Vineyards Gewürztraminer
Lindemans Classic Dry White
Lindemans Hunter River Chablis
Lindemans Hunter River Semillon Classic Release
Miramar Chardonnay
Mitchelton III
Moondah Brook Chenin Blanc
Mount Bold Chardonnay
Mount Chalambar Four Sisters Riesling
Mount Horrocks Cordon Cut
Mount Hurtle Chardonnay
Ninth Island Chardonnay
Olsen Wines Chardonnay Semillon
Paulett's Polish Hill River Riesling
Pendarves Verdelho
Penfolds Chardonnay
Penfolds Clare Estate Chardonnay
Petaluma Chardonnay
Petaluma Riesling
Peter Lehmann Barossa-Eden Valley Rhine Riesling
Peter Lehmann Cellar Collection Rhine Riesling
Pirramimma Stock's Hill Semillon Chardonnay
Richard Hamilton Chardonnay
Riddoch Riesling
Riddoch Sauvignon Blanc

MUSSELS

Giesen Marlbrough Sauvignon Blanc
Milburn Park Sauvignon Blanc
Mount Avoca Sauvignon Blanc
Selak's Chardonnay

ONION TART

Henschke Julius Eden Valley Riesling

OYSTERS

Angoves Rhine Riesling
Ashton Hills Riesling
Dromana Estate Chardonnay
Grant Burge Riesling
Henschke Green Hill Rielsing
Mount Horrocks Riesling
Mount Hurtle Sauvignon Blanc
Seaview Rhine Riesling
Seppelt Sheoak Spring Rhine Riesling
Weatherall Rhine Riesling
Wolf Blass Gold Label Riesling

PASTA *(marinara, chicken, pesto)*

Cassegrain Fromenteau Chardonnay
Fire Gully Margaret River Classic
Henschke Tilly's Vineyard
Jim Barry Chardonnay
Karl Seppelt Chardonnay
Maxwell Chardonnay
Mount Chalambar Four Sisters Chardonnay
Smithbrook Chardonnay
Sunnycliff Sauvignon Blanc

PORK *(grilled, fried, roast, casserole)*

All Saints Chenin Blanc
Brown Brothers Family Reserve Chardonnay
Coriole Chenin Blanc
Deen De Bortoli Vat 7 Chardonnay
Paulett's Polish Hill River Sauvignon Blanc
Queen Adelaide Chenin Blanc
Redbank Long Paddock Chardonnay
Rovalley Ridge Show Reserve Chardonnay
Saltram Mamre Brook Chardonnay
Schinus Chenin Blanc

Seaview Chardonnay
Tolley Hope Valley Cellars Padthaway Chardonnay
Tolley Pedare Gewürztraminer

SALADS

Henschke Chenin Blanc
Hillstowe Sauvignon Blanc
Hugh Hamilton Unwooded Chardonnay
Hunter Park Sauvignon Blanc
Killerby April Classic White
Lakes Folly Chardonnay
McWilliam's Mount Pleasant Elizabeth
Maxwell Sauvignon Blanc
Maxwell Semillon
Mount Prior Dry White
Normans Chais Clarendon Chardonnay
Peter Lehmann Semillon
Pierro Semillon Sauvignon Blanc
Richmond Grove Traminer Riesling
Vasse Felix Classic Dry White
Wilson Chardonnay
Wolf Blass Yellow Label Rhine Riesling
Yarra Valley Hills Sauvignon Blanc

SCALLOPS

Diamond Valley Blue Label Chardonnay
Grosset Piccadilly
Grosset Polish Hill
Heggies Riesling
Lark Hill Riesling
McWilliam's Rhine Riesling
Milburn Park Reserve Chardonnay
Moorilla Estate Riesling
Paradise Enough Chardonnay
Paulett's Polish Hill River Riesling
Pipers Brook Chardonnay
Sandalford Verdelho

St Hallett Semillon Sauvignon Blanc
Sutherland Smith Rhine Riesling

TURKEY

Lindemans Padthaway Chardonnay
Moondah Brook Chardonnay

VEAL

Augustine Chardonnay
Cassegrain Semillon
Galafrey Chardonnay
Houghton Gold Reserve Chardonnay
Krondorf Chardonnay
Tollana Eden Valley Chardonnay

YABBIES

Campbells Limited Release Semillon
Eldredge Watervale Riesling
Evans & Tate Western Australian Classic
Kara Kara Vineyards Fumé Blanc

Index of Common Names

(F) = Fortified; (R) = Reds; (S) = Sparkling; (W) = Whites

ABERFELDY (THE), *see* Tim Adams (R)
ABBOTT'S PRAYER, *see* Henschke (R)
ALAN'S, *see* Wild Duck Creek (R)
ALCHEMY, *see* Canobolas-Smith (R)
ALEXANDERS, *see* Mildara (R)
ARMAGH (THE), *see* Jim Barry (R)
BALMORAL, *see* Rosemount (R)
BARKLEY (THE), *see* Campbells (R)
BOBBIE BURNS, *see* Campbells (R&W)
BURTON'S VINEYARD, *see* Richard Hamilton (R)
CHESTNUT TEAL, *see* Mildara (F)
CHINAMAN'S BRIDGE, *see* Mitchelton (R)
CLOCK TOWER, *see* Yalumba (F)
COBWEB, *see* Rovalley (F)
CORNEL, *see* Hollick (S)
CORNUCOPIA, *see* Temple Bruer (R)
CRICKET PITCH, *see* Brokenwood (R)
CROMWELL, *see* Renmano (F)
DEAD MAN'S HILL, *see* Delatite (W)
DRAYCOTT, *see* Burge Family (R)
EDWARDS AND CHAFFEY, *see* Seaview (R&S)
ELLEN STREET, *see* Maxwell (R)
EMERI SUPERIORE, *see* De Bortoli (S)
EMILY'S PADDOCK, *see* Jasper Hill (R)
EMILY, *see* Redbank (S)
FERGUS (THE), *see* Tim Adams (R)
FIRESIDE, *see* Mildara (F)
FLAME TREE, *see* Ryecroft (R)
FOUR CROWN, *see* Yalumba (F)
FOUR SISTERS, *see* Mount Chalambar (W)

GAIA, *see* Grosset (R)
GALWAY PIPE, *see* Yalumba (F)
GEORGE, *see* Mildara (F)
GEORGIA'S PADDOCK, *see* Jasper Hill (R&W)
GRANGE, *see* Penfolds (R)
GRAVEYARD, *see* Brokenwood (R)
GREEN'S HILL, *see* Henschke (W)
HILL OF GRACE, *see* Henschke (R)
HIPPOCRENE, *see* Wilson Vineyard (S)
HUT BLOCK, *see* Richard Hamilton (R)
ISABELLA, *see* Campbells (F)
JACOB'S CREEK, *see* Orlando (W)
JUD'S HILL, *see* Brian Barry (W)
KEYSTONE, *see* Tatachilla (R)
KING WILLIAM, *see* Normans (F)
LAVENDER HILL, *see* Jim Barry (W)
LAWSON'S, *see* Orlando (R)
LIME CAVE (THE), *see* Maxwell (R)
LIMESTONE RIDGE, *see* Lindemans (R)
LOST BLOCK, *see* Tyrrell's (W)
LOUISE CLARE, *see* Mount William Winery (S)
LUDLOW'S, *see* Saltram (F)
MAMRE BROOK, *see* Saltram (W)
MERCHANT PRICE, *see* Campbells (F)
MESHACH, *see* Grant Burge (R)
METALA, *see* Stonyfell (R)
MOUNT PLEASANT, *see* McWilliam's (W)
MR PICKWICK'S, *see* Saltram (F)
NINE POPES, *see* Charles Melton (R)
NOSTALGIA, *see* d'Arenberg (F)
NOTTAGE HILL, *see* Hardys (W)

INDEX OF COMMON NAMES

OLD QUARRY, *see* Bethany (F)
OLD WALNUT, *see* Jim Barry (F)
OLMO'S REWARD, *see* Frankland Estate (R)
OMRAH, *see* Plantagenet (W)
OSCAR'S HERITAGE, *see* Basedow (R)
P.S. MARION, *see* Rockford (F)
PARTNERS, *see* Tatachilla (R)
PATRIARCH, *see* David Wynn (R)
PEDARE, *see* Tolley (W)
PINNACLE, *see* Saltram (W)
POACHER'S BLEND, *see* St Hallett (W)
POLISH HILL RIVER, *see* Paulett's (W)
PYRUS, *see* Lindemans (R)
RAYNER, *see* Brokenwood (R)
RED (THE), *see* Mountadam (R)
REDSTONE, *see* Coriole (R)
ROSE OF VIRGINIA, *see* Charles Melton (R)
RUMPOLE, *see* Renmano (F)
SACRED HILL, *see* De Bortoli (R)

SALLY'S PADDOCK, *see* Redbank (R)
SALMON, *see* Ashton Hills (S)
SARINA FARM, *see* Angoves (R&W)
SENTIMENTAL BLOKE, *see* Jim Barry (F)
SHEE-OAK, *see* Tyrrell's (W)
SHEOAK SPRING, *see* Seppelt (W)
SIEGERSDORF, *see* Hardys (W)
SIR JAMES, *see* Hardys (S)
SPRINGFLAT, *see* Wild Duck Creek (R)
ST GEORGE, *see* Lindemans (R)
STOCKS (THE), *see* Woodstock (R)
TALL SHIPS, *see* Hardys (F)
THOROUGHBRED, *see* Stanley Brothers (R)
TILLY'S VINEYARD, *see* Henschke (W)
TRILLIANS, *see* Paulett's (S)
TRINDERS, *see* Cape Mentelle (R)
UDY'S MILL, *see* Hillstowe (W)
WHISKERS BLAKE, *see* Hardys (F)
WINDY PEAK, *see* De Bortoli (S)

Wine Terms

The following are commonly used winemaking terms.

ACID There are many acids that occur naturally in grapes and it is in the winemaker's interest to retain the favourable ones because these promote freshness and longevity.

AGRAFE A metal clip used to secure champagne corks during secondary bottle fermentation.

ALCOHOL Ethyl alcohol (C_2H_5OH) is a by-product of fermentation of sugars. It is the stuff that makes people happy and it adds warmth and texture to wine.

ALCOHOL BY VOLUME (A/V) The measurement of the amount of alcohol in a wine. It is expressed as a percentage, eg. 13.0% A/V means there is 13.0% pure alcohol as a percentage of the total volume.

ALDEHYDE An unwanted and unpleasant organic compound formed between acid and alcohol by oxidation. It is removed by sulphur dioxide.

ALLIER A type of oak harvested in the French forest of the same name.

APERITIF A wine that stimulates the appetite.

AROMATIC A family of grape varieties that have a high terpene content. Riesling and gewürztraminer are examples, and terpenes produce their floral qualities.

AUTOLYSIS A Vegemite or fresh-baked bread taste and smell imparted by spent yeast cells in sparkling wines.

BACK BLEND To add unfermented grape juice to wine; or to add young wine to old wine in fortifieds.

BARREL FERMENTATION The process of fermenting a red or white wine in a small barrel, thereby adding a creamy texture and toasty or nutty characters, and better integrating the wood and fruit flavours.

BARRIQUE A 225-litre barrel.

BAUMÉ The measure of sugar in grape juice used to estimate potential alcohol content. It is usually expressed as a degree, eg. 12 degrees baumé juice will produce approximately 12.0% A/V if it is fermented to dryness. The alternative brix scale is approximately double baumé and must be divided by 1.8 to estimate potential alcohol.

BENTONITE A fine clay (drillers mud) used as a clarifying (fining) agent.

BLEND A combination of two or more grape varieties and/or vintages. *see* Cuveé

BOTRYTIS CINEREA A fungus that thrives on grape vines in humid conditions and sucks out the water of the grapes thereby concentrating the flavour. Good in white wine but not so good in red. (There is also a loss in quantity.)

BREATHING Uncorking a wine and allowing it to stand for a couple of hours before serving; this introduces oxygen and dissipates bottle odours. Decanting aids breathing.

BRIX *see* Baumé

BRUT The second lowest level of sweetness in sparkling wine; it does not mean there is no added sugar.

BUSH VINE Although pruned the vine is self-supporting in a low-to-the-ground bush; still common in the Barossa Valley.

CARBONIC MACERATION Fermentation in whole (uncrushed) bunches. This is a popular technique in Beaujolais. It produces bright colour and softer tannins.

CHARMAT PROCESS A process for making sparkling wine where the wine is fermented in a tank rather than a bottle.

CLONE (CLONAL) A recognisable sub-species of vine within a varietal family, eg. there are numerous clones of pinot noir and these all have subtle character differences.

COLD FERMENTATION (Also Controlled Temperature Fermentation) Usually applied to white wines where the ferment is kept at a low temperature (10-12 degrees Centigrade)

CORDON The arms of the trained grape vine that bear the fruit.

CORDON CUT A technique of cutting the fruit-bearing arms and allowing the berries to dehydrate to concentrate the flavour.

CRUSH Crushing the berries to liberate the free-run juice (qv). Also used as an expression of a wine company's output: 'This winery has a 1000-tonne crush.'

CUVÉE A Champagne term meaning a selected blend or batch.

DISGORGE The process of removing the yeast lees from a sparkling wine. It involves freezing the neck of the bottle and firing out a plug of ice and yeast. The bottle is then topped up and recorked.

DOWNY MILDEW A disease that attacks vine leaves and fruit. It is associated with humidity and lack of air circulation.

DRIP IRRIGATION An accurate way of watering a vineyard. Each vine has its own dripper and a controlled amount of water is applied.

DRYLAND VINEYARD A vineyard that has no irrigation.

ESTERS Volatile compounds that can occur during fermentation or maturation. They impart a distinctive chemical taste.

FERMENTATION The process by which yeast converts sugar to alcohol with a by-product of carbon dioxide.

FINING The process of removing solids from wine to make it clear. There are several methods used.

FORTIFY The addition of spirit to increase the amount of alcohol in a wine.

FREE-RUN JUICE The first juice to come out of the press or drainer (as opposed to pressings).

GENERIC Wines labelled after their district of origin rather than their grape variety. eg. Burgundy, Chablis, Champagne etc. These terms can no longer legally be used on Australian labels. (cf. *Varietal*.)

GRAFT Changing the nature/variety of a vine by grafting a different variety on to a root stock.

IMPERIAL A 6-litre bottle (ie. contains eight 750 ml bottles).

JEROBOAM A 4.5-litre champagne bottle.

LACCASE A milky condition on the surface of red wine caused by noble rot (see botrytis cinerea). The wine is usually pasteurised.

LACTIC ACID One of the acids found in grape juice; as the name suggests it is milky and soft.

LACTOBACILLUS A micro-organism that ferments carbohydrates (glucose) or malic acid to produce lactic acid.

LEES The sediment left after fermentation. It consists mainly of dead yeast cells.

MALIC ACID One of the acids found in grape juice. It has a hard/sharp taste like a Granny Smith apple.

MALOLACTIC FERMENTATION A secondary fermentation process that converts malic acid into lactic acid. It is encouraged in red wines when they are in barrel. If it occurs after bottling, the wine will be fizzy and cloudy.

MERCAPTAN   Ethyl mercaptan is a sulphur compound with a smell like garlic, burnt rubber or asparagus water.

MÉTHODE CHAMPENOISE   The French method for producing effervescence in the bottle; a secondary fermentation process where the carbon dioxide produced is dissolved into the wine.

METHOXYPYRAZINES   Substances that give sauvignon blanc and cabernet sauvignon that added herbaceousness when the grapes aren't fully ripe.

MOUSSE   The froth or head on sparkling wine.

MUST   *see* Free-run juice

NOBLE ROT   *see* Botrytis cinerea

NON-VINTAGE   A wine that is a blend of two or more years.

OAK   The least porous wood, genus *Quercus*, and used for wine storage containers

OENOLOGY   The science of winemaking.

ORGANIC VITICULTURE   Growing grapes without the use of pesticides, fungicides or chemical fertilizers. Certain chemicals (eg. copper sulphate) are permitted.

ORGANIC WINES   Wines made from organically grown fruit without the addition of chemicals.

OXIDATION   Browning caused by excessive exposure to air.

pH   The measure of the strength of acidity. The higher the pH the higher the alkalinity and the lower the acidity. Wines with high pH values should not be cellared.

PHENOLICS   A group of chemical compounds which includes the tannins and colour pigments of grapes. A white wine described as 'phenolic' has an excess of tannin, making it taste coarse.

PHYLLOXERA   A louse that attacks the roots of a vine, eventually killing the plant.

PIGEAGE   To foot-press the grapes.

PRESSINGS   The juice extracted by applying pressure to the skins after the free-run juice has been drained.

PUNCHEON   A 500-litre barrel.

PRICKED   A wine that is spoilt and smells of vinegar, due to excessive volatile acidity. (cf. Volatile.)

RACKING   Draining off wine from the lees or other sediment to clarify it.

SAIGNÉE   French for bleeding: the winemaker has run off part of the juice of a red fermentation to concentrate what's left.

SKIN CONTACT Allowing the free-run juice to remain in contact with the skins; in the case of white wines usually for a very short time.

SOLERO SYSTEM Usually a stack of barrels used for blending maturing wines. The oldest material is at the bottom and is topped up with younger material from the top barrels.

SOLIDS Minute particles suspended in a wine.

SULFUR DIOXIDE SO2 (Code 220) A chemical added to a wine as a preservative and a bactericide.

SUR LIE Wine that has been kept on lees and not racked or filtered before bottling.

TACHÉ A French term that means to stain, usually by the addition of a small amount of red wine to sparkling wine to turn it pink.

TANNIN A complex substance derived from skins, pips and stalks of grapes as well as the oak casks. It has a preservative function and imparts dryness and grip to the finish.

TERROIR Arcane French expression which describes the complete growing environment of the vine, including climate, aspect, soil, etc., and the direct effect this has on the character of its wine.

VARIETAL An industry-coined term used to refer to a wine by its grape variety, eg. 'a shiraz'. (cf. *Generic*.)

VÉRAISON The moment when the grapes change colour and gain sugar.

VERTICAL TASTING A tasting of consecutive vintages of one wine.

VIGNERON A grape-grower or vineyard worker.

VINEGAR Acetic acid produced from fruit.

VINIFY The process of turning grapes into wine.

VINTAGE The year of harvest, and the produce of a particular year.

VOLATILE Excessive volatile acids in a wine.

YEAST The micro-organism which converts sugar into alcohol.

Tasting Terms

The following terms refer to the sensory evaluation of wine.

AFTERTASTE The taste (sensation) after the wine has been swallowed. It is usually called the finish.
ASTRINGENT (ASTRINGENCY) Applies to the finish of a wine. Astringency is caused by tannins that produce a mouth-puckering sensation and coat the teeth with dryness.
BALANCE 'The state of . . .'; the harmony between components of a wine.
BILGY An unfortunate taste like the bilge of a ship. Usually caused by mouldy old oak.
BITTERNESS A sensation detected at the back of the tongue. It is not correct in wine but desirable in beer.
BOUQUET The aroma of a finished or mature wine.
BROAD A wine that lacks fruit definition; usually qualified as soft or coarse.
CASSIS A blackcurrant flavour common in cabernet sauvignon. It refers to a liqueur produced in France.
CHALKY A sensation on the finish; extremely dry.
CHEESY A dairy character sometimes found in wine, particularly sherries.
CIGAR BOX A smell of tobacco and wood found in cabernet sauvignon.
CLOUDY A fault in wine which is caused by suspended solids that make it look dull.
CORKED Spoiled wine that has reacted with a tainted cork, and smells like wet cardboard. (The taint is caused by trichloroanisole, a mould.)
CLOYING Excessive sweetness that clogs the palate.
CREAMY The feeling of cream in the mouth, a texture.
CRISP Clean acid on the finish of a white wine.
DEPTH The amount of fruit on the palate.

DULL Pertaining to colour; the wine is not bright or shining.
DUMB Lacking nose or flavour on the palate.
DUSTY Applies to a very dry tannic finish; a sensation.
DRY A wine that does not register sugar in the mouth.
EARTHY Not as bad as it sounds, this is a loamy/mineral character that can add interest to the palate.
FINESSE The state of a wine, refers to balance and style.
FINISH (*see* aftertaste)
FIRM Wine with strong, unyielding tannins.
FLABBY Wine with insufficient acid to balance ripe fruit flavours.
FLESHY Wines of substance with plenty of fruit
FLINTY A character on the finish that is akin to sucking dry creek pebbles.
GARLIC *see* Mercaptan (in Wine Terms)
GRASSY A cut-grass odour, usually found in semillon and sauvignon blancs.
GRIP The effect on the mouth of tannin on the finish; a puckering sensation.
HARD More tannin or acid than fruit flavour.
HERBACEOUS Herbal smells or flavour in wine.
HOLLOW A wine with a lack of flavour in the middle palate.
HOT Wines high in alcohol that give a feeling of warmth and a slippery texture.
IMPLICIT SWEETNESS A just detectable sweetness from the presence of glycerin (rather than residual sugar).
INKY Tannate of iron present in a wine which imparts a metallic taste.
INTEGRATED (WELL) The component parts of a wine fit together without gaps or disorders.
JAMMY Ripe fruit that takes on the character of stewed jam.
LEATHERY A smell like old leather, not necessarily bad if it is in balance.
LENGTH (LONG) The measure of the registration of flavour in the mouth (the longer the better).
LIFTED The wine is given a lift by the presence of either volatile acid or wood tannins; eg. vanillian oak lift.
LIMPID A colour term usually applied to star-bright white wine.
MADEIRISED Wine that has aged to the point where it tastes like a madeira.
MOULDY Smells like bathroom mould; dank.

MOUTHFEEL The sensation the wine causes in the mouth; a textural term.

MUSTY Stale, flat, out-of-condition wine.

PEPPER A component in either the nose or the palate that smells or tastes like cracked pepper.

PUNGENT Wine with a strong nose.

RANCIO A nutty character found in aged fortifieds that is imparted by time on wood.

RESIDUAL SUGAR The presence of unfermented grape sugar on the palate; common in sweet wines.

ROUGH Unpleasant, aggressive wine.

ROUND A full-bodied wine with plenty of mouthfeel (*qv*).

SAPPY A herbaceous character that resembles sap.

SHORT A wine lacking in taste and structure (*see also* Length).

SPICY A wine with a high aromatic content; spicy character can also be imparted by wood.

STALKY Exposure to stalks (eg. during fermentation) leaves a bitter character in the wine.

TART A lively wine with a lot of fresh acid.

TOASTY A smell of cooked bread.

VANILLAN The smell and taste of vanilla beans; usually imparted by oak ageing.

VARIETAL Refers to the distinguishing qualities of the grape variety used in the wine.

Directory of Wineries

AFFLECK VINEYARD
RMB 244
Gundaroo Rd
Bungendore NSW 2651
(06) 236 9276

ALAMBIE WINES
Campbell Ave
Irymple Vic 3498
(050) 24 6800
fax (050) 24 6605

ALKOOMI
Wingeballup Rd
Frankland WA 6396
(098) 55 2229
fax (098) 55 2284

ALL SAINTS
All Saints Rd
Wahgunyah Vic 3687
(060) 33 1922
fax (060) 33 3515

ALLANDALE
Lovedale Rd
Pokolbin NSW 2320
(049) 90 4526
fax (049) 90 1714

ALLANMERE
Lovedale Rd
Pokolbin NSW 2320
(049) 30 7387

AMBERLEY ESTATE
Wildwood & Thornton Rds
Yallingup WA 6282
(097) 55 2288
fax (097) 55 2171

ANDERSON WINERY
Lot 13 Chiltern Road
Rutherglen Vic 3685
(060) 32 8111
fax (060) 32 9028

ANDREAS PARK ESTATE
PO Box 504
Chatswood NSW 2067
(02) 415 1649

ANDREW GARRETT
Kangarilla Rd
McLaren Vale SA 5171
(08) 323 8853
fax (08) 323 8550

ANGELSEY
Heaslip Rd
Angle Vale SA 5117
(085) 24 3157

ANGOVES
1320 North-East Rd
Tea Tree Gully SA 5091
(085) 85 1311
fax (085) 85 1583

ANTCLIFFE'S CHASE
RMB 4510
Caveat
via Seymour Vic 3660
(057) 90 4333

ARROWFIELD
Denman Rd
Jerry's Plains NSW 2330
(065) 76 4041
fax (065) 76 4144

ASHTON HILLS
Tregarthen Rd
Ashton SA 5137
(08) 390 1243
fax (08) 390 1243

AUGUSTINE
(*see* Rothbury)

AVALON
RMB 9556
Whitfield Rd
Wangaratta Vic 3677
(057) 29 3629

BABICH WINES
Babich Rd
Henderson, NZ
(09) 833 8909

BAILEYS
Taminick Gap Rd
Glenrowan Vic 3675
(057) 66 2392
fax (057) 66 2596

416 DIRECTORY OF WINERIES

BALDIVIS ESTATE
Lot 165 River Rd
Baldivis WA 6171
(09) 525 2066
fax (09) 525 2411

BALGOWNIE
Hermitage Rd
Maiden Gully Vic 3551
(054) 49 6222
fax (054) 49 6506

BALNARRING VINEYARD
Bittern-Dromana Rd
Balnarring Vic 3926
(059) 83 5258

BANNOCKBURN
Midland Highway
Bannockburn Vic 3331
(052) 81 1363
fax (052) 81 1349

BAROSSA SETTLERS
Trial Hill Rd
Lyndoch SA 5351
(085) 24 4017

BAROSSA VALLEY ESTATE
Heaslip Rd
Angle Vale SA 5117
(08) 284 7000
fax (08) 284 7219

BARWANG
(see McWilliam's)

BASEDOW
165 Murray Valley Hwy
Tanunda SA 5352
(085) 63 2060
fax (085) 63 2060

BASS PHILLIP
Tosch's Rd
Leongatha South
Vic 3953
(056) 64 3341

BERRI ESTATES
Sturt Highway
Glossop SA 5344
(085) 82 0300
fax (085) 83 2224

BESTS GREAT WESTERN
Western Hwy
Great Western
Vic 3377
(053) 56 2250
fax (053) 56 2430

BETHANY
Bethany Rd
Bethany
via Tanunda
SA 5352
(085) 63 2086
fax (085) 63 2086

BIANCHET
187 Victoria Rd
Lilydale Vic 3140
(03) 9739 1779
fax (03) 9739 1277

BIRDWOOD ESTATE
PO Box 194
Birdwood SA 5234
(08) 263 0986

BLACK OPAL
(not open to the public)
(02) 719 8790
fax (02) 719 8790

BLACKJACK VINEYARD
Calder Hwy
Harcourt Vic 3452
(054) 74 2528
fax (054) 75 2102

BLEASDALE
Wellington Rd
Langhorne Creek
SA 5255
(085) 37 3001

BLEWITT SPRINGS
Recreational Rd
McLaren Vale
SA 5171
(08) 323 8689

BLUE PYRENEES ESTATE
(see Chateau Remy)

BLOODWOOD ESTATE
4 Griffin Rd
via Orange NSW 2800
(063) 62 5631

BOSTON BAY
Lincoln Hwy
Port Lincoln SA 5605
(086) 84 3600

BOTOBOLAR
Botobolar Lane
PO Box 212
Mudgee NSW 2850
(063) 73 3840
fax (063) 73 3789

BOWEN ESTATE
Penola-Naracoorte Rd
Coonawarra SA 5263
(087) 37 2229
fax (087) 37 2173

BOYNTONS OF BRIGHT
Ovens Valley Hwy
Porepunkah Vic 3740
(057) 56 2356

BRANDS LAIRA
Naracoorte Hwy
Coonawarra SA 5263
(087) 36 3260
fax (087) 36 3208

BREMERTON LODGE
Strathalbyn Rd
Langhorne Creek SA 5255
(085) 37 3093
fax (085) 37 3109

DIRECTORY OF WINERIES 417

BRIAGOLONG ESTATE
118 Boisdale Street
Maffra Vic 3860
(051) 47 2322
fax (051) 47 2400

BRIAR RIDGE
Mount View
Mt View NSW 2321
(049) 90 3670
fax (049) 98 7802

BRIDGEWATER MILL
Mount Barker Rd
Bridgewater SA 5155
(08) 339 3422
fax (08) 339 5253

BRINDABELLA HILLS
Woodgrove Close
Via Hall ACT 2618
(06) 230 2583

BROKENWOOD
McDonalds Rd
Pokolbin NSW 2321
(049) 98 7559
fax (049) 98 7893

BROOK EDEN
Adams Rd
Lebrina Tas 7254
(003) 95 6244

BROOKLAND VALLEY
Caves Rd
Willyabrup WA 6284
(097) 55 6250
fax (097) 55 6214

BROWN BROTHERS
Meadow Crk Rd (off the Snow Rd)
Milawa Vic 3678
(057) 20 5500
fax (057) 20 5511

BROWNS OF PADTHAWAY
PMB 196
Naracoorte SA 5271
(087) 65 6063
fax (087) 65 6083

BUCHANAN WINES
Glendale Rd
Loira
West Tamar Tas 7275
(003) 94 7488
fax (003) 94 7581

BULLER & SONS, R L
Calliope
Three Chain Rd
Rutherglen Vic 3685
(050) 37 6305

BULLER (RL) & SON
Murray Valley Highway
Beverford Vic 3590
(050) 37 6305
fax (050) 37 6803
fax (060) 32 8005

BURGE FAMILY WINEMAKERS
Barossa Hwy
Lyndoch SA 5351
(085) 24 4644
fax (085) 24 4444

BURNBRAE
Hargraves Rd
Erudgere
Mudgee NSW 2850
(063) 73 3504
fax (063) 73 3601

CALAIS ESTATE
Palmers Lane
Pokolbin NSW 2321
(049) 98 7654
fax (049) 98 7813

CALLATOOTA ESTATE
Wybong Rd
Wybong NSW 2333
(065) 47 8149

CAMPBELLS
Murray Valley Hwy
Rutherglen Vic 3685
(060) 32 9458
fax (060) 32 9870

CANOBOLAS-SMITH
Cargo Rd
Orange NSW 2800
(063) 65 6113

CAPE CLAIRAULT
via Caves Rd
or Bussell Hwy
CMB Carbunup River
WA 6280
(097) 55 6225
fax (097) 55 6229

CAPE MENTELLE
Wallcliffe Rd
Margaret River
WA 6285
(097) 57 3266
fax (097) 57 3233

CAPELVALE
Lot 5
Capel North West Rd
Capel WA 6271
(097) 27 2439
fax (097) 27 2164

CASSEGRAIN
Fern Bank Ck Rd
Port Macquarie
NSW 2444
(065) 83 7777
fax (065) 84 0353

418 DIRECTORY OF WINERIES

CASTLE ROCK ESTATE
Porongarup Rd
Porongarup WA 6324
(098) 53 1035
fax (098) 53 1010

CHAMBERS ROSEWOOD
Corowa-Rutherglen Rd
Rutherglen Vic 3685
(060) 32 8641
fax (060) 32 8101

CHAPEL HILL
Chapel Hill Rd
McLaren Vale SA 5171
(08) 323 8429
fax (08) 323 9245

CHARLES CIMICKY
Gomersal Rd
Lyndoch SA 5351
(085) 24 4025
fax (085) 24 4772

CHARLES MELTON
Krondorf Rd
Tanunda SA 5352
(085) 63 3606
fax (085) 63 3422

CHARLES STURT UNIVERSITY
Boorooma St
North Wagga Wagga
NSW 2650
(069) 22 2435
fax (069) 22 2107

CHATEAU REMY
Vinoca Rd
Avoca Vic 3467
(054) 65 3202
fax (054) 65 3529

CHATEAU REYNELLA
Reynella Rd
Reynella SA 5161
(08) 392 2222
fax (08) 392 2202

CHATEAU TAHBILK
Tabilk Vic 3607
via Nagambie
(057) 94 2555
fax (057) 94 2360

CHATEAU XANADU
Terry Rd, off Railway Tce
Margaret River
WA 6285
(097) 57 2581
fax (097) 57 3389

CHATEAU YALDARA
Gomersal Rd
Lyndoch SA 5351
(085) 24 4200
fax (085) 24 4678

CHATSFIELD
O'Neill Rd
Mount Barker WA 6324
(098) 51 1704
fax (098) 41 6811

CLARENDON HILLS
(not open to public)
(08) 364 1484

CLEVELAND
(by appointment only)
Shannons Rd
Lancefield Vic 3435
(054) 29 1449
fax (054) 29 2017

COBAW RIDGE
Perc Boyer's Lane
East Pastoria
Via Kyneton Vic 3444
(054) 23 5227

CLONAKILLA
Crisps La
Murrumbateman
NSW 2582
(06) 251 1938 (A.H.)

CLOUDY BAY
(*see* Cape Mentelle)

CLOVER HILL
(*see* Taltarni)

CLYDE PARK
(*see* Bannockburn)

COLDSTREAM HILLS
31 Maddens La
Coldstream Vic 3770
(059) 64 9388
fax (059) 64 9389

COOLANGATTA ESTATE
Coolangatta Resort,
via Berry NSW 2535
(044) 48 7131
fax (044) 48 7997

COOMBEND
Swansea Tas 7190
(002) 57 8256
fax (002) 57 8484

COOPERS CREEK WINERY
Highway 16
Haupai Auckland NZ
(09) 412 8560

COPE WILLIAMS WINERY
Glenfern Rd
Romsey Vic 3434
(054) 29 5428
fax (054) 29 2655

CORIOLE
Chaffeys Rd
McLaren Vale SA 5171
(08) 323 8305
fax (08) 323 9136

COWRA ESTATE
Boorowa Rd
Cowra NSW 2794
(063) 42 3650

DIRECTORY OF WINERIES 419

CRABTREE WATERVALE CELLARS
North Tce
Watervale SA 5452
(08) 8843 0069
fax (08) 8843 0144

CRAIG AVON
Craig Avon La
Merricks North Vic 3926
(059) 89 7465

CRAIGIE KNOWE
Cranbrook Tas 7190
(002) 23 5620

CRAIGLEE
Sunbury Rd
Sunbury Vic 3429
(03) 744 1160

CRAIGMOOR
Craigmoor Rd
Mudgee NSW 2850
(063) 72 2208

CRAIGOW
Richmond Rd
Cambridge Tas 7170
(002) 48 5482

CRANEFORD
Main St
Springton SA 5235
(085) 68 2220
fax (085) 68 2538

CRAWFORD RIVER
Condah Vic 3303
(055) 78 2267

CULLENS
Caves Rd
Willyabrup via
Cowaramup
WA 6284
(097) 55 5277

CURRENCY CREEK
Winery Rd
Currency Creek SA 5214
(085) 55 4069

DALFARRAS
(*see* Chateau Tahbilk)

DALRYMPLE
Pipers Brook Rd
Pipers Brook Tas 7254
(003) 82 7222

DALWHINNIE
Taltarni Rd
Moonambel Vic 3478
(054) 67 2388

d'ARENBERG
Osborn Rd
McLaren Vale SA 5171
(08) 323 8206

DARLING PARK
Lot 1 Browne Lane
Red Hill 3937
(059) 89 2732
fax (059) 89 2254

DAVID TRAEGER
399 High St
Nagambie Vic 3608
(057) 94 2514

DAVID WYNN
(*see* Mountadam)

De BORTOLI
De Bortoli Rd
Bibul NSW 2680
(069) 64 9444
fax (069) 64 9400

De BORTOLI
Pinnacle La
Dixons Creek Vic 3775
(059) 65 2271

DELAMERE
Bridport Rd
Pipers Brook Tas 7254
(003) 82 7190

DELATITE
Stoney's Rd
Mansfield Vic 3722
(057) 75 2922
fax (057) 75 2911

DENNIS'S OF McLAREN VALE
Kangarilla Rd
McLaren Vale SA 5171
(08) 323 8665
fax (08) 323 9121

DEVIL'S LAIR
Rocky Rd
Forrest WA 6285
(09) 386 2200
fax (09) 381 5423

DIAMOND VALLEY VINEYARDS
Kinglake Rd
St Andrews Vic 3761
(03) 710 1484
fax (03) 739 1110

DOMAINE A STONEY VINEYARD
Teatree Rd
Campania Tas 7026
(002) 62 4174
fax (002) 62 4390

DOMAINE CHANDON
Maroondah Hwy
Coldstream Vic 3770
(03) 739 1110
fax (03) 739 1095

DOONKUNA ESTATE
Barton Hwy
Murrumbateman NSW 2582
(06) 227 5885
fax (06) 227 5085

420 DIRECTORY OF WINERIES

DRAYTON'S BELLEVUE
Oakey Creek Rd
Pokolbin NSW 2320
(049) 98 7513
fax (049) 98 7743

DROMANA ESTATE
Bittern-Dromana Rd
Dromana Vic 3936
(059) 87 3275
fax (059) 81 0714

DUNCAN ESTATE
Spring Gully Rd
Clare SA 5453
(088) 43 4335

EAGLEHAWK
Main North Rd
Watervale SA 5452
(088) 43 0003

EDEN RIDGE
(*see* Mountadam)

ELAN VINEYARD
17 Turners Rd
Bittern Vic 3918
(059) 83 1858

ELDERTON
3 Tanunda Rd
Nuriootpa SA 5355
(085) 62 1058 or
(008) 88 8500
fax (085) 62 2844

ELGEE PARK
(no cellar door)
Junction Rd
Merricks Nth
PO Box 211
Red Hill South Vic 3926
(059) 89 7338
fax (059) 89 7553

EPPALOCK RIDGE
Metcalfe Pool Rd
Redesdale Vic 3444
(054) 25 3135

EVANS & TATE
Metricup Rd
Willyabrup WA 6284
(09) 296 4666
fax (09) 296 1148

EVANS FAMILY
Palmers La
Pokolbin NSW 2320
(049) 98 7333

EYTON ON YARRA
Cnr Maroondah Hwy
& Hill Rd
Coldstream Vic 3770
(059) 62 2119
fax (059) 62 5319

FERGUSSON'S
Wills Rd
Yarra Glen Vic 3775
(059) 65 2237

FERN HILL ESTATE
Ingoldby Rd
McLaren Flat SA 5171
(08) 383 0167
fax (08) 383 0107

FIDDLER'S CREEK
(*see* Chateau Remy)

FIRE GULLY
(*see* Pierro)

FRANKLAND ESTATE
RMB 705
Frankland WA 6396
(098) 55 1555
fax (098) 55 1583

FREYCINET VINEYARD
Tasman Hwy
Bicheno Tas 7215
(002) 57 8587

GALAFREY
114 York St
Albany WA 6330
(098) 41 6533

GALAH WINES
Box 231
Ashton SA 5137
(08) 390 1243

GARDEN GULLY
Western Highway
Great Western Vic 3377
(053) 56 2400

GEOFF MERRILL
(*see* Mount Hurtle)

GIACONDA
(not open to public)
(057) 27 0246

GILBERT'S
Albany Hwy
Kendenup WA 6323
(098) 51 4028
(098) 51 4021

GLEN OSMOND
(*see* Seppelt)

GLENARA
126 Range Rd Nth
Upper Hermitage
SA 5131
(08) 380 5056
fax (08) 380 5056

GOONA WARRA
Sunbury Rd
Sunbury Vic 3429
(03) 744 7211
fax (03) 744 7648

DIRECTORY OF WINERIES 421

GOUNDREY
Muir Hwy
Mount Barker WA 6324
(098) 51 1777
fax (098) 48 1018

GRAMP'S
(see Orlando)

GRAND CRU ESTATE
Ross Dewell's Rd
Springton SA 5235
(085) 68 2378

GRANT BURGE
Jacobs Creek
Barossa Valley Hwy
Tanunda SA 5352
(085) 63 3700
fax (085) 63 2807

GREEN POINT
(see Domaine Chandon)

GREENOCK CREEK
Radford Rd
Seppeltsfield SA 5360
(085) 62 8103
fax (085) 62 8259

GROSSET
King St
Auburn SA 5451
(088) 49 2175

HANGING ROCK
Jim Rd
Newham Vic 3442
(054) 27 0542
fax (054) 27 0310

HANSON WINES
'Oolorong'
49 Cleveland Ave
Lower Plenty Vic 3093
(03) 439 7425

HAPP'S
Commonage Rd
Dunsborough WA 6281
(097) 55 3300
fax (097) 55 3846

HARCOURT VALLEY
Calder Highway
Harcourt Vic 3453
(054) 74 2223

HARDYS
(see Chateau Reynella)

HASELGROVE WINES
Foggo Rd
McLaren Vale
SA 5171
(08) 323 8706
fax (08) 323 8049

HEATHCOTE WINERY
183 High St
Heathcote Vic 3523
(054) 33 2595
fax (054) 33 3081

HEEMSKERK
Pipers Brook Tas 7254
(003) 82 7133
fax (003) 82 7242

HEGGIES
(see Yalumba)

HELM'S
Yass River Rd
Murrumbateman
NSW 2582
(06) 227 5536 (A.H.)
(06) 227 5953

HENSCHKE
Moculta Rd
Keyneton SA 5353
(085) 64 8223
fax (085) 64 8294

HERITAGE WINES
Seppeltsfield Rd
Marananga
via Tununda SA 5352
(085) 62 2880

HICKINBOTHAM
(not open to public)
(03) 397 1872
fax (03) 397 2629

HIGHBANK
Main Naracoorte/Penola Rd
Coonawarra SA 5263
(087) 37 2020

HILL SMITH ESTATE
(see Yalumba)

HILLSTOWE WINES
104 Main Rd
Hahndorf SA 5245
(08) 388 1400
fax (08) 388 1411

HOLLICK
Racecourse Rd
Coonawarra SA 5263
(087) 37 2318
fax (087) 37 2952

HOUGHTON
Dale Rd
Middle Swan
WA 6056
(09) 274 5100

HOWARD PARK
Lot 11
Little River Rd
Denmark WA 6333
(098) 48 1261
fax (098) 48 2064

422 DIRECTORY OF WINERIES

HUGH HAMILTON WINES
PO Box 615
McLaren Vale SA 5171
(08) 323 8689
fax (08) 323 9488

HUGO
Elliott Rd
McLaren Flat SA 5171
(08) 383 0098
fax (08) 383 0446

HUNGERFORD HILL
(*see* Tulloch or Lindemans)

HUNTER'S WINES
Rapaura Rd
Blenheim, NZ
(03) 572 8489
fax (03) 572 8457

HUNTINGTON ESTATE
Cassilis Rd
Mudgee NSW 2850
(063) 73 3825
fax (063) 73 3730

IAN LEAMON
Calder Hwy
Bendigo Vic 3550
(054) 47 7995

IDYLL
Ballan Rd
Moorabool Vic 3221
(052) 76 1280
fax (052) 76 1537

INGOLDBY
Ingoldby Rd
McLaren Flat
SA 5171
(08) 383 0005

INNISFAIL
(not open to public)
(052) 76 1258

JASPER HILL
Drummonds La
Heathcote Vic 3523
(054) 33 2528

JEIR CREEK WINES
Gooda Creek Rd
Murrumbateman
NSW 2582
(06) 227 5999

JENKE VINEYARDS
Jenke Rd
Rowland Flat SA 5352
(085) 24 4154
fax (085) 24 4154

JIM BARRY
Main North Rd
Clare SA 5453
(088) 842 2261

JOHN GEHRIG
Oxley Vic 3678
(057) 27 3395

JOSEPH
(*see* Primo Estate)

KAISER STUHL
Tanunda Rd
Nuriootpa SA 5355
(085) 62 0389 &
(085) 62 0408
fax (085) 62 8028

KARINA VINEYARDS
Harrisons Rd
Dromana Vic 3936
(059) 81 0137

KARRIVALE
Woodlands Rd
Porongurup WA 6324
(098) 53 1009
fax (098) 53 1129

KARRIVIEW
RMB 913
Roberts Rd
Denmark WA 6333
(098) 40 9381

KATNOOK ESTATE
Narracoorte Rd
Coonawarra SA 5263
(087) 37 2394
fax (087) 37 2397

KAYS
Kays Rd
McLaren Vale
SA 5171
(08) 323 8211
fax (08) 323 9199

KIES ESTATE
Hoffnungsthal Rd
Lyndoch SA 5351
(085) 24 4511

KILLAWARRA
(*see* Kaiser Stuhl)

KILLERBY LESCHENAULT
Minnimup Rd
Gelorup WA 6230
(097) 95 7222
fax (097) 95 7835

KINGS CREEK
(not open to public)
(059) 83 2102

DIRECTORY OF WINERIES 423

KNIGHTS
Burke and Wills Track
Baynton
via Kyneton Vic 3444
(054) 23 7264
mobile 015 843 676
fax (054) 23 7288

KOPPAMURRA
(no cellar door)
PO Box 110
Blackwood SA 5051
(08) 271 4127
fax (08) 271 0726

KRONDORF
Krondorf Rd
Tanunda SA 5352
(085) 63 2145
fax (085) 62 3055

LAANECOORIE
(cellar door by arrangement)
RMB 1330
Dunolly Vic 3472
(054) 68 7260
018 518 887

LAKE'S FOLLY
Broke Rd
Pokolbin NSW 2320
(049) 98 7507
fax (049) 98 7322

LANCEFIELD WINERY
Woodend Rd
Lancefield Vic 3435
(054) 29 1217

LARK HILL
RMB 281 Gundaroo Rd
Bungendore NSW 2621
(062) 38 1393

LEASINGHAM
7 Dominic St
Clare SA 5453
(088) 42 2555
fax (088) 42 3293

LECONFIELD
Penola-Narracoorte Rd
Coonawarra SA 5263
(087) 37 2326
fax (087) 37 2285

LEEUWIN ESTATE
Stevens Rd
Margaret River WA 6285
(097) 57 6253
fax (097) 57 6364

LELAND ESTATE
PO Lenswood SA 5240
(08) 389 6928

LENSWOOD
(see Tim Knappstein)

LEO BURING
Stuart Hwy
Tanunda SA 5352
(085) 63 2184
fax (085) 63 2804

LILLYDALE VINEYARDS
Davross Crt
Seville Vic 3139
(059) 64 2016

LILLYPILLY ESTATE
Farm 16
Lilly Pilly Rd
Leeton NSW 2705
(069) 53 4069
fax (069) 53 4980

LINDEMANS
McDonalds Rd
Pokolbin NSW 2320
(049) 98 7501
fax (049) 98 7682

LONG GULLY
Long Gully Rd
Healesville Vic 3777
(059) 62 3663
fax (059) 807 2213

LONGLEAT
Old Weir Rd
Murchison Vic 3610
(058) 26 2294
fax (058) 26 2510

LOVEGROVE OF COTTLES BRIDGE
Heidelberg Kinglake Road
Cottlesbridge Vic 3099
(03) 718 1569
fax (03) 718 1028

McALISTER
(not open to public)
(051) 49 7229

McGUIGAN BROTHERS
Cnr Broke and McDonalds Rd
Pokolbin NSW 2320
(049) 98 7400
fax (049) 98 7401

McWILLIAM'S
Hanwood NSW 2680
(069) 63 0001
fax (069) 63 0002

MADEW WINES
Appletree Hill Vineyard
Queanbeyan NSW 2620
(06) 299 2303

MADFISH BAY
(see Howard Park)

MAGLIERI
Douglas Gully Rd
McLaren Flat SA 5171
(08) 383 0177

424 DIRECTORY OF WINERIES

MAIN RIDGE
Lot 48 Williams Rd
Red Hill Vic 3937
(059) 89 2686

MALCOLM CREEK
(not open to public)
(08) 264 2255

MARIENBERG
2 Chalk Hill Rd
McClaren Vale
SA 5171
(08) 323 9666
fax (08) 323 9600

MASSONI
Mornington-Flinders Rd
Red Hill Vic 3937
(059) 89 2060
fax (059) 89 2348

MASTERSON
(see Peter Lehmann)

MAXWELL
26 Kangarilla Rd
McLaren Vale SA 5171
(08) 323 8200

MEADOWBANK
Glenora Tas 7140
(002) 86 1234
fax (002) 86 1133

MERRICKS ESTATE
Cnr Thompsons Lane
& Frankston-Flinders Rd
Merricks Vic 3916
(059) 89 8300
fax (03) 629 4035

MIDDLETON ESTATE
Flagstaff Hill Rd
Middleton SA 5213
(085) 55 4136
fax (085) 55 4108

MILBURN PARK
(see Salisbury Estate)

MILDARA
(various locations)
(03) 690 9966
(head office)

MILDURA VINEYARDS
Campbell Ave
Irymple Vic 3498

MINTARO CELLARS
Leasingham Rd
Mintaro SA 5415
(088) 43 9046

MIRAMAR
Henry Lawson Dr
Mudgee NSW 2850
(063) 73 3874

MIRANDA WINES
57 Jordaryan Ave
Griffith NSW 2680
(069) 62 4033
fax (069) 62 6944

MIRROOL CREEK
(see Miranda)

MITCHELL
Hughes Park Rd
Skillogalee Valley
via Clare SA 5453
(088) 43 4258

MITCHELTON WINES
Mitcheltstown
Nagambie 3608
(057) 94 2710
fax (057) 94 2615

MONTANA
PO Box 18-293
Glen Innis Auckland NZ
(09) 570 5549

MONTARA
Chalambar Rd
Ararat Vic 3377
(053) 52 3868
fax (053) 52 4968

MONTROSE
Henry Lawson Dr
Mudgee NSW 2850
(063) 73 3853

MOONDAH BROOK
(see Houghton)

MOORILLA ESTATE
655 Main Rd
Berridale Tas 7011
(002) 49 2949

MOOROODUC ESTATE
Derril Rd
Moorooduc Vic 3933
(059) 78 858

MORNING CLOUD
(cellar door by appointment)
15 Ocean View Ave
Red Hill South Vic 3937
(059) 89 2762
fax (059) 89 2700

MORNINGTON VINEYARDS
(by appointment only)
Mooroobuc Rd
Mornington Vic 3931
(059) 74 2097
fax (03) 416 1084

MORRIS
off Murray Valley Hwy
Mia Mia Vineyards
Rutherglen Vic 3685
(060) 26 7303
fax (060) 26 7445

DIRECTORY OF WINERIES

MOSS BROTHERS
Caves Rd
Willyabrup WA 6280
(097) 55 6270

MOSS WOOD
Metricup Rd
Willyabrup WA 6280
(097) 55 6266
fax (097) 55 6303

MOUNT ARROW
(see Arrowfield)

MOUNT AVOCA
Moates La
Avoca Vic 3467
(054) 65 3282

MOUNT HORROCKS
Mintaro Rd
Watervale SA 5452
Tel & fax (08) 884 92243

MOUNT HURTLE
291 Pimpala Rd
Woodcroft SA 5162
(08) 381 6877
fax (08) 322 2244

MOUNT LANGI GHIRAN
Vine Rd
Buangor Vic 3375
(053) 54 3207
fax (053) 54 3277

MOUNT MARY
(not open to public)
(03) 739 1761
fax (03) 739 0137

MOUNT PRIOR VINEYARD
Cnr River Rd
& Popes La
Rutherglen Vic 3685
(060) 26 5591
fax (060) 26 7456

MOUNTADAM
High Eden Ridge
Eden Valley SA 5235
(085) 64 1101
fax (08) 362 8942

MT PLEASANT
Marrowbone Rd
Pokolbin NSW 2320
(049) 98 7505

MT WILLIAM WINERY
Mount William Rd
Tantaraboo Vic 3764
(054) 29 1998
fax (054) 29 1595

MURRINDINDI
(not open to public)
(057) 97 8217

NATTIER
(see Mitchelton)

NAUTILUS
(see Yalumba)

NGATARAWA
Ngatarawa Rd
Bridge Pa
Hastings NZ
(070) 79 7603

NICHOLSON RIVER
Liddells Rd
Nicholson Vic 3882
(051) 56 8241

NINTH ISLAND
Pipers Brook
Tas 7254
(003) 82 7197
fax (003) 82 7226

NORMANS
Grants Gully Rd
Clarendon SA 5157
(08) 383 6138

NUTFIELD
(see Hickinbotham)

OAKRIDGE ESTATE
Aitken Rd
Seville Vic 3139
(059) 64 3379
fax (059) 64 2061

OAKVALE WINERY
Broke Rd
Pokolbin NSW 2320
(049) 98 7520

OLD KENT RIVER
Turpin Rd
Rocky Gully Wa 6397
(098) 55 1589
fax (098) 55 1589

ORLANDO
Barossa Valley Way
Rowland Flat SA 5352
(085) 21 3111
fax (085) 21 3102

PANKHURST WINES
Woodgrove Rd
Hall ACT 2618
(06) 230 2592

PARINGA ESTATE
44 Paringa Rd
Red Hill South
Vic 3937
(059) 89 2669

PARKER COONAWARRA ESTATE
Penola Rd
Coonawarra SA 5263
(Contact Leconfield)
(087) 37 2946
fax (087) 37 2465

DIRECTORY OF WINERIES

PASSING CLOUDS
Powlett Rd
via Inglewood
Kingower Vic 3517
(054) 38 8257

PAULETT'S
Polish Hill River Rd
Sevenhill SA 5453
(08) 843 4328
fax (08) 843 4202

PEEL ESTATE
Fletcher Rd
Baldivis WA 6171
(095) 24 1221

PENDARVES ESTATE
Lot 12 Old North Road
Belford NSW 2335
(065) 74 7222

PENFOLDS
Stuart Hwy
Nuriootpa SA 5355
(085) 62 0389
fax (085) 62 1669

PENINSULA ESTATE
Red Hill Rd
Red Hill Vic 3937
(059) 89 2866

PENLEY ESTATE
McLean's Rd
Coonawarra 5263
(087) 36 3211
fax (087) 36 3211

PEPPERS CREEK
Broke Rd
Pokolbin NSW 2321
(049) 98 7532

PETALUMA
(not open to public)
(08) 339 4122
fax (08) 339 5253

PETER LEHMANN
Para Rd
Tanunda SA 5352
(085) 63 2500
fax (085) 63 3402

PETERSONS
Mount View Rd
Mount View
NSW 2325
(049) 90 1704

PFEIFFER
Distillery Rd
Wahgunyah Vic 3687
(060) 33 2805
fax (060) 33 3158

PIBBIN FARM
Greenhill Rd
Balhannah SA 5242
(08) 388 7375
fax (08) 388 7685

PICCADILLY FIELDS
(not open to public)
(08) 390 1997

PIERRO
Caves Rd
Willyabrup WA 6280
(097) 55 6220
fax (097) 55 6308

PIKES POLISH HILL ESTATE
Polish Hill River Rd
Seven Hill SA 5453
(08) 8843 4370

PIPERS BROOK
(by appointment only)
(003) 82 7197
fax (003) 82 7226

PIRRAMIMMA
Johnston Rd
McLaren Vale SA 5171
(08) 323 8205
fax (08) 323 9224

PLANTAGENET
Albany Highway
Mount Barker WA 6324
(098) 51 2150
fax (098) 51 1839

PLUNKETT'S WINEGATE
Hume Highway
Avenel, Vic 3664
(057) 96 2275
fax (057) 96 2147

POOLE'S ROCK
Wollombi Rd
Broke NSW 2330
(065) 69 1251

PORTREE VINEYARD
RMB 700
Lancefield Vic 3435
(054) 29 1422
fax (054) 29 2205

PREECE
(*see* Mitchelton)

PRIMO ESTATE
Cnr Old Port Wakefield
& Angle Vale Rds
Virginia SA 5120
(08) 380 9442

PRINCE ALBERT
Lemins Rd
Waurn Ponds Vic 3221
(052) 43 5091
fax (052) 41 8091

DIRECTORY OF WINERIES 427

QUEEN ADELAIDE
(*see* Seppelt)

REDBANK
Sunraysia Hwy
Redbank Vic 3467
(054) 67 7255

REDMAN
Penola-Narracoorte Rd
Coonawarra SA 5263
(087) 36 3331
fax (087) 37 3013

RENMANO
Renmark Ave
Renmark SA 5341
(085) 86 6771
fax (085) 83 2224

RIBBON VALE ESTATE
Lot 5 Caves Rd
via Cowaramup
Willyabrup WA 6284
(097) 55 6272

RICHARD HAMILTON
Willunga Vineyards
Main South Rd
Willunga SA 5172
(085) 56 2288
fax (085) 56 2868

RICHMOND GROVE
(no cellar door)
Hermitage Rd
Pokolbin NSW 2321
(049) 98 7792
fax (049) 98 7783

RIDDOCH
(*see* Katnook)

ROBERT HAMILTON & SON
Hamiltons Rd
Springton SA 5235
(085) 68 2264

ROBERT THUMM
(*see* Chateau Yaldara)

ROBINVALE WINES
Sealake Rd
Robinvale Vic 3549
(050) 26 3955
fax (050) 26 4399

ROCHFORD
Romsey Park
via Woodend Rd
Rochford Vic 3442
(054) 29 1428

ROCKFORD
Krondorf Rd
Tanunda SA 5352
(085) 63 2720

ROMSEY VINEYARDS
(*see* Cope Williams)

ROSEMOUNT
Rosemount Rd
Denman NSW 2328
(065) 47 2467
fax (065) 47 2742

ROTHBURY ESTATE
Broke Rd
Pokolbin NSW 2321
(049) 98 7555
fax (049) 98 7553

ROUGE HOMME
(*see* Lindemans)

ROWAN
(*see* St Huberts)

RYECROFT
Ingoldby Rd
McLaren Flat SA 5171
(08) 383 0001

RYMILL COONAWARRA WINES
The Riddoch Run Vineyards
off Main Rd
Coonawarra SA 5263
(087) 36 5001
fax (087) 36 5040

SADDLERS CREEK WINERY
Marrowbone Rd
Pokolbin NSW 2321
(049) 91 1770
fax (049) 91 1778

SALISBURY ESTATE
see Alambie

SALITAGE
Vasse Hwy
Pemberton WA 6260
(097) 76 1599
fax (097) 76 1504

SALTRAM
Angaston Rd
Angaston SA 5353
(085) 63 8200

SANDALFORD
West Swan Rd
Caversham WA 6055
(09) 274 5922
fax (09) 274 2154

SANDSTONE VINEYARD
(cellar door by appointment)
Caves & Johnson Rds
Willyabrup WA 6280
(097) 55 6271
fax (097) 55 6292

SAXONVALE
Fordwich Estate
Broke Rd
Pokolbin NSW 2330
(065) 79 1009

428 DIRECTORY OF WINERIES

SCARBOROUGH WINES
Gillards Rd
Pokolbin NSW 2321
(049) 98 7563

SCARPANTONI
Kangarilla Rd
McLaren Flat SA 5171
(08) 383 0186
fax (08) 383 0490

SCHINUS
(*see* Dromana Estate)

SCOTCHMAN'S HILL
Scotchmans Rd
Drysdale Vic 3222
(052) 51 3176
fax (052) 53 1743

SEAVIEW
Chaffeys Rd
McLaren Vale SA 5171
(08) 323 8250

SEPPELT
Seppeltsfield via Tanunda
SA 5352
(085) 62 8028
fax (085) 62 8333

SEVENHILL
College Rd
Sevenhill via Clare 5453
(088) 43 4222
fax (088) 43 4382

SEVILLE ESTATE
Linwood Rd
Seville Vic 3139
(059) 64 4556
fax (059) 43 4222

SHANTELL
Melba Hwy
Dixons Creek Vic 3775
(059) 65 2264
fax (03) 819 5311

SHAREFARMERS
(*see* Petaluma)

SHAW & SMITH
(not open to public)
(08) 370 9725

SHOTTESBROOKE
(*see* Ryecroft)

SIMON GILBERT
(*see* Arrowfield)

SIMON HACKET
(not open to public)
(08) 331 7348

SIMON WHITLAM
(*see* Arrowfield)

SKILLOGALEE
Skillogalee Rd
via Sevenhill 5453
(08) 8843 4311
fax (08) 8843 4343

SMITHBROOK
(not open to public)
(097) 72 3557
fax (097) 72 3579

ST FRANCIS
Bridge St
Old Reynella SA 5161
(08) 381 1925
fax (08) 322 0921

ST HALLETT'S
St Halletts Rd
Tanunda SA 5352
(085) 63 2319
fax (085) 63 2901

ST HUBERTS
Maroondah Hwy
Coldstream Vic 3770
(03) 739 1421
fax (03) 739 1070

ST LEONARDS
St Leonard Rd
Wahgunyah Vic 3687
(060) 33 1004
fax (060) 33 3636

ST MARY'S VINEYARD
V and A Lane
via Coonawarra SA 5263
(087) 36 6070
fax (087) 36 6045

STAFFORD RIDGE
Geoff Weaver
(not open to public)
(08) 272 2105

STANTON & KILLEEN
Murray Valley Highway
Rutherglen Vic 3685
(060) 32 9457

STEVENS CAMBRAI
Hamiltons Rd
McLaren Flat SA 5171
(08) 323 0251

STONELEIGH
Corbans Wines
Great Northern Rd
Henderson NZ
(09) 836 6189

STONIER'S WINERY
362 Frankston-Flinders Rd
Merricks Vic 3916
(059) 89 8300
fax (059) 89 8709

SUMMERFIELD
Main Rd
Moonambel Vic 3478
(054) 67 2264
fax (054) 67 2380

DIRECTORY OF WINERIES 429

SUNNYCLIFF WINES
(*see* Katnook)

SUTHERLAND
Deasey's Rd
Pokolbin NSW 2321
(049) 98 7650

TALAVERA WINE CO.
C/o Seabrooks Tucker
& Co.

TALTARNI VINEYARDS
off Moonambel–Stawell Rd
Moonambel Vic 3478
(054) 67 2218
fax (054) 67 2306

TAMBURLAINE WINES
McDonalds Rd
Pokolbin NSW 2321
(049) 98 7570

TANGLEWOOD DOWNS
Bulldog Creek Rd
Merricks North
(059) 74 3325

TAPESTRY
Merrivale Wines
Olivers Rd
McLaren Vale SA 5171
(08) 323 9196
fax (08) 323 9746

TARRAWARRA
Healesville Rd
Yarra Glen Vic 3775
(059) 62 3311
fax (059) 62 3311

TATACHILLA WINERY
151 Main Rd
McLaren Vale SA 5171
(08) 323 8656
fax (08) 323 9096

TAYLORS
Mintaro Rd
Auburn SA 5451
(088) 49 2008

TEMPLE BRUER
Angas River Delta
via Strathalbyn SA 5255
(085) 37 0203
fax (085) 37 0131

T'GALLANT
Red Hill Rd
Red Hill Vic. 3937
(059) 89 2203
fax (059) 89 2961

THALGARA ESTATE
De Beyers Rd
Pokolbin NSW 2321
(049) 98 7717

THOMAS FERNHILL ESTATE
Ingoldby Rd
McLaren Flat SA 5171
(08) 383 0167
fax (08) 383 0107

TIM ADAMS
Wendouree Rd
Clare SA 5453
(08) 8842 2429
fax (08) 8842 2429

TIM GRAMP
PO Box 810
Unley Sa 5061
(08) 379 3658
fax (08) 338 2160

TIM KNAPPSTEIN
2 Pioneer Ave
Clare SA 5453
(088) 42 2600
fax (088) 42 3831

TISDALL
Cornelia Creek Rd
Echuca Vic 3564
(054) 82 1911
fax (054) 82 2516

TOLLANA
(*see* Penfolds)

TOLLEYS PEDARE
30 Barracks Rd
Hope Valley SA 5090
(08) 264 2255
fax (08) 263 7485

TORRESAN ESTATE
Manning Rd
Flagstaff Hill SA 5159
(08) 270 2500

TRENTHAM ESTATE
Sturt Hwy
Trentham Cliffs
via Gol Gol NSW 2738
(050) 24 8888
fax (050) 24 8800

TULLOCH
De Beyers Rd
Pokolbin NSW 2321
(049) 98 7503
fax (049) 98 7682

TUNNEL HILL
(*see* Tarrawarra)

TURKEY FLAT
James Rd
Tanunda Sa 5352
(085) 63 2851
fax (085) 63 3610

TYRRELL'S
Broke Rd
Pokolbin NSW 2321
(049) 98 7509

430 DIRECTORY OF WINERIES

VASSE FELIX
Cnr Caves & Harmans Rds
Cowaramup WA 6284
(097) 55 5242
fax (097) 55 5425

VERITAS
94 Langmeil Rd
Tanunda SA 5352
(085) 63 2330

VIRGIN HILLS
(not open to public)
(054) 23 9169

VOYAGER ESTATE
Stevens Rd
Margaret River WA 6285
(097) 57 6358
fax (097) 57 6405

WANDIN VALLEY ESTATE
Wilderness Rd
Rothbury NSW 2321
(049) 30 7317
fax (049) 30 7814

WANINGA
Hughes Park Rd
Sevenhill via Clare
SA 5453
(088) 43 4395
fax (08) 232 0653

WANTIRNA ESTATE
(not open to public)
(03) 801 2367

WARDS GATEWAY CELLARS
Barossa Valley Hwy
Lyndoch SA 5351
(085) 24 4138

WARRAMATE
27 Maddens La
Gruyere Vic 3770
(059) 64 9219

WATERWHEEL VINEYARDS
Lyndhurst St
Bridgewater-on-Loddon
Bridgewater Vic 3516
(054) 37 3060
fax (054) 37 3082

WENDOUREE
Wendouree Rd
Clare SA 5453
(088) 842 2896

WESTFIELD
Memorial Ave
Baskerville WA 6056
(09) 296 4356

WIGNALLS KING RIVER
Chester Pass Rd
Albany WA 6330
(098) 41 2848

WILDWOOD
St Johns Lane via
Wildwood Vic 3428
(03) 307 1118

WILLESPIE
Harmans Mill Rd
Willyabrup WA 6280
(097) 55 6248
fax (097) 55 6210

WILLOWS VINEYARD, THE
Light Pass Rd
Barossa Valley SA 5355
(085) 62 1080

WILSON VINEYARD, THE
Polish Hill River
via Clare SA 5453
(088) 43 4310

WILTON ESTATE
Whitton Stock Route
Yenda NSW 2681
(069) 68 1303
fax (069) 68 1328

WINCHELSEA ESTATE
C/o Nicks Wine
Merchants
(03) 639 0696

WING FIELDS
(*see* Water Wheel)

WIRILDA CREEK
Lot 32
McMurtrie Rd
McLaren Vale SA 5171
(08) 323 9688

WIRRA WIRRA
McMurtrie Rd
McLaren Vale SA 5171
(08) 323 8414
fax (08) 323 8596

WOLF BLASS
Sturt Hwy
Nuriootpa SA 5355
(085) 62 1955
fax (085) 62 2156

WOODSTOCK
Douglas Gully Rd
McLaren Flat SA 5171
(08) 383 0156
fax (08) 383 0437

WOODY NOOK
Metricup Rd
Metricup WA 6280
(097) 55 7547
fax (097) 55 7547

DIRECTORY OF WINERIES 431

WYANGA PARK
Baades Road
Lakes Entrance Vic
(051) 55 1508
fax (051) 55 1443

WYANGAN ESTATE
(*see* Miranda)

WYNDHAM ESTATE
Dalwood Rd
Dalwood NSW 2321
(049) 38 3444
fax (049) 38 3422

WYNNS
Memorial Dr
Coonawarra SA 5263
(087) 36 3266

YALUMBA
Eden Valley Rd
Angaston SA 5353
(085) 61 3200
fax (085) 61 3392

YARRA BURN
Settlement Rd
Yarra Junction Vic 3797
(059) 67 1428
fax (059) 67 1146

YARRA RIDGE
Glenview Rd
Yarra Glen Vic 3775
(03) 730 1022
fax (03) 730 1131

YARRA VALLEY HILLS
Old Don Rd
Healesville Vic
(059) 62 4173
fax (057) 62 4059

YARRA YERING
Briarty Rd
Gruyere Vic 3770
(059) 64 9267

YELLOWGLEN
White's Rd
Smythesdale Vic 3351
(053) 42 8617

YERING STATION
Melba Hwy
Yering Vic 3775
(03) 730 1107
fax (03) 739 0135

YERINGBERG
(not open to public)
(03) 739 1453

ZEMA ESTATE
Penola–Narracoorte Rd
Coonawarra SA 5263
(087) 36 3219
fax (087) 36 3280